Barbara Ewing is a New Zealand born actress and author who lives and works in London.

Also by Barbara Ewing

Strangers
The Actresses

A DANGEROUS VINE

Barbara Ewing

A *Virago* Book

First published in Great Britain by Little, Brown and Company in 1999
This edition published by Virago Press in 2000

A CIP catalogue record for this book is
available from the British Library.

ISBN 1 86049 830 2

Typeset in Palatino by M Rules
Printed and bound in Great Britain by
Clays Ltd, St Ives plc

Virago
A Division of
Little, Brown and Company (UK)
Brettenham House
Lancaster Place
London WC2E 7EN

A DANGEROUS VINE

Acknowledgements

TOO LATE NOW Words and Music by Alan Jay Lerner and Burton Lane © 1950 Loews Inc. Warner/Chappell Music Ltd. London W6 8BS. Reproduced by kind permission of International Music Publications Ltd.

CRY ME A RIVER Words and Music by Arthur Hamilton © 1973 (renewed) Chappell & Co Inc. Warner/Chappell Music Ltd. London W6 8BS. Reproduced by kind permission of International Music Publications Ltd.

SENTIMENTAL JOURNEY Words and Music by Les Brown, Benjamin Horner & Bud Green © 1944 Morley Music Co. & Edwin H. Morris & Co. Inc. Warner/Chappell Music Ltd. London W6 8BS. Reproduced by kind permission of International Music Publications Ltd.

THE PARTY'S OVER Words and Music by Betty Comden, Adolph Green & Jule Styne © 1964 (renewed) Stratford Music Corp U.S.A, Warner/Chappell Music Ltd. London W6 8BS. Reproduced by kind permission of International Music Publications Ltd.

BLUEBERRY HILL Words and Music by Al Lewis, Vincent Rose & Larry Stock © 1940 Chappell & Co Inc. Reproduced by kind permission of Warner/Chappell Music Ltd. London W6 8BS & Redwood Music Ltd. London NW1 8BD

When Elizabeth and Margaret-Rose Bennett were at primary school in the city after the Second World War they were taught to carefully draw and print – in exercise books decorated with a kiwi, the flightless bird – the history of their country.

This is what they learnt.

'Now children,' said the teacher, 'these islands used to be joined to the rest of the world millions and millions of years ago. But upheavals in the sea meant that bits of land broke off and floated far, far away. And that is why these islands of ours are so distant from the rest of the world.

'Then, about a thousand years ago, a Polynesian explorer called Kupe left his homeland and sailed here by mistake because he was chasing a big octopus. After a while he went home and told everybody about his discovery. Many years later a whole fleet of Polynesian canoes set sail and finally landed on different beaches of our islands. This is called the Great Migration. In their canoes they brought their wives and their dogs and their sweet potato so that they wouldn't get too homesick for Hawaiki, their homeland.'

'Miss, Miss, where's it? Hawaiki?'

'We don't know. Nobody knows.'

Sometimes the children were given big sheets of paper and with coloured crayons they drew pictures of long canoes and laboriously, with the teacher's help, wrote names on them: **Kurahaupo**,

Mataatua. *Sometimes they drew the Maori tribes fighting: fierce men in flax skirts with tattooed faces hitting each other with clubs made of green stone. The child who drew the neatest drawing with its Maori canoes and warriors got gold stars and their picture was put up on the classroom wall with drawing pins.*

Margaret-Rose Bennett was fascinated by the term 'sweet potato'. She bent over her exercise book, drawing in crayon with immense concentration. The potato she drew was like a big lolly, wrapped in coloured paper twisted at both ends. She was enchanted with her work, it was the biggest lolly she had ever seen.

'Miss, Miss,' she cried, putting up her hand. 'Miss, look at my sweet potato, will I get a star?'

The teacher came to look.

'No, that's not quite right Margaret-Rose,' said the teacher.

The Maoris, having settled, had a lot of visitors.

In the seventeenth century, the children learned, Abel Tasman came, a Dutch explorer. He went home after some fighting with the Maoris and said don't go to the South Seas, it's populated by savages who eat each other. But the teacher, with one Maori boy in the class, never stressed the cannibalism, felt it was not in the best interests of the country.

Whalers from all over the world came to these islands almost by mistake, the teacher said. The whalers tracked the whales in the spring as they travelled north for the mating season from their feeding grounds in the Antarctic. Elizabeth Bennett drew two whales dancing gracefully together, all alone in the wide, blue sea; it was an extraordinarily beautiful drawing; the teacher gave her five gold stars and mentioned the drawing in the staffroom after school. That girl could grow up to be an artist, said the teacher.

The whalers followed the whales, and while they were following them they called in at these islands for food and water and entertainment; whistling the popular songs of the countries they came from, and dancing with the brown-skinned maidens.

And the children learned about the huge harpoons the men used for catching the whales, how they threw them into the sea when they saw water spouting. But the children, drawing brave whalers and harpoons flying through the air, did not understand to paint the sea red with blood. (Although that's how it was with the whalers, red blood staining the sea for miles and miles around.)

For hundreds of years the whistling whalers came.

In 1769 Captain Cook arrived wearing a naval hat. He claimed the islands for Great Britain. This was almost the last of the land discoveries in the world; there was nowhere left to discover. The boy sitting next to Margaret-Rose Bennett got three gold stars for his drawing of Captain Cook in his hat looking through a telescope.

And then the missionaries came, bringing the word of God to these natives who had their own, heathen, gods. The missionaries told the Maoris that the world was created **not** when Ranginui, the sky, and Papatuanuku, the Earth, were forced out of each other's arms. The truth was that the world was created in six days by a hard-working, just – and celibate – God who had a long white beard and would think of the Maoris as his children. The missionaries also admonished the Maoris to put on more clothes. This too the school pupils drew, Maoris in top hats or trousers. The boy sitting next to Margaret-Rose Bennett got the strap for putting a Maori chief in a frock.

And after the missionaries, and the occasional criminal escaping from Australia, the British came in earnest, travelling twelve thousand miles across the sea in crowded, uncomfortable ships, wanting to stay; wanting land. In the ships that took six months to make the journey they brought oak seedlings and sheep and horses and roses and their wives, trying to make it like home.

And the school children learnt the Maori word **Pakeha**.

'It means white person,' said the teacher. 'They call us **Pakehas**. They are **Maoris** and we are **Pakehas**. Oh, except for you John, you are a **Maori**.' John was the son of a tram conductor.

The school children learnt about the Treaty of Waitangi signed in 1840 by many of the Maori chiefs with Queen Victoria, in the person *of her representative, Captain Hobson. In signing, making their mark on the document, the Maori chiefs agreed to give sovereignty to Queen Victoria, the Queen of England, and not to the French, who were hanging around. And she agreed that the Maoris would have undisturbed possession of the land they didn't want to sell and if they did want to sell they would sell it to Queen Victoria (in the person of her representative). And the Maoris were given, unusually for the time, all the rights and privileges of British subjects. The children drew the Queen and the chiefs smiling at each other. Margaret-Rose Bennett gave Queen Victoria long, blonde hair like her own beautiful mother, and a crown and a wand like a good fairy, and a glass slipper like Cinderella. Queen Victoria's frock was short, to show the glass slipper.*

'No, that's not quite right Margaret-Rose,' said the teacher.

But then they drew something else which the teacher called **the Maori Wars**. These were wars about land between the natives and the settlers. The children drew more fierce pictures of barefoot, tattooed Maoris in flax skirts and shirts, fighting, often with muskets, white men in uniform.

'You see, children,' said the teacher, 'Maoris sometimes sold their land illegally, they didn't have the right to sell it, it was owned by lots of people not just one. And sometimes I'm afraid, the British took land that didn't belong to them. And so there were these Maori Wars.'

Sometimes, if they'd been to rugby matches with their fathers and seen the All Blacks, the children drew the Maoris stamping their feet in the war-dance, the **haka**, and Margaret-Rose Bennett put thunder and lightning in the sky.

'But,' said the teacher, 'all those Maori Wars were over long ago and now everyone in this country is very happy. We supply our Homeland, Britain, with:

> 74% of her mutton and lamb
> 63% of her cheese

42% of her butter
23% of her wool

and we know Britain could not survive without us.

'And here we all live peacefully together, over two million of us, in the Greatest Little Country in the World. Sometimes, because we know we are so lucky, we call it God's Own Country.'

ONE

In that city, at the end of their street, was the sea.

If you walked down the street, past the wooden houses with their red-and-green corrugated-iron roofs and their neat front gardens, the road just ended, turned into sand, and there was the Pacific Ocean.

Ships sailed right past the end of their street; the top half of stately liners sometimes appeared unexpectedly above the houses as they came into port, glided past the dairy chimney. Small, scruffy fishing boats, or boats full of butter, would materialise suddenly also, passing the houses and the lupin bushes before disappearing again behind the cliffs along the beach, making for the Heads and the open sea.

In summer, some days were so hot and sunny and radiant that the sea seemed to actually dance and sparkle, as if diamonds lay there. White sails drifted sometimes; the sun sparked and danced off the reds and greens of the corrugated-iron roofs; the air shimmered along the gleaming tram lines and the asphalt pavements. Yellow gorse and broom shone on distant, dark hills.

But the sea, people knew, could be treacherous. Not far out there were jagged rocks, just below the surface.

During the wild storms, gales shook wooden window frames and roared dully down chimneys and the thunderous sound of the sea crashing on to the sandhills reached up to houses that had been precariously built right into the cliffs, verandahs jutting aggressively out into space, like bad temper.

Sometimes, in summer, people came to the beach, clambered past the sandhills and along the bottom of the cliffs, past ice-plants and sea-battered rock formations, slipping and sliding in loose stones and shells. Above, gorse hung wildly and strange, bright flowers grew in crevices, bending and fluttering with the wind.

Old wood was sometimes thrown up on the shore by the sea, and the odd tin.

Sometimes the wind was so strong that even seagulls couldn't fly against it: they hung for a moment in the sky, poised against such force, then turned and swooped in the opposite direction, crying and diving with the wind.

When the fog came down in the night the mournful sound of the foghorn warning the ships drifted along the quiet and empty streets, past the tram terminus, past the wooden houses; sometimes an echo of that sound murmured uneasily in people's dreams, in that city.

The city was old: over a hundred years old; already the prosperous businessmen spoke of pulling down some of the Victorian wooden buildings, of putting up shining banks. From the wharves the valuable, refrigerated ships sounded their hooters.

And the city spread out to the suburbs: men went home from work on tram cars.

At night, in the centre of the city, empty tram cars stood shadowy in the sheds, shops and office buildings were in darkness, the docks were silent. The main streets seemed to be utterly deserted, only a stray cat, streaking out from behind the old Gala Picture Theatre then winding itself round a dark lamp-post, or a newspaper blowing along the dark, empty pavements.

People thought that, at night, the city was closed.

Many, many miles from the city a long, dusty, unpaved road wound through totara trees and kauri trees, past ferns and manuka trees, to the small settlement: a cluster of wooden houses painted in bright, now-fading colours that nestled in the gentle hill, often bathed in sunshine. A stream at the bottom of the hill brought fresh, clear water to all the houses; the older people (the ones who had stayed, who had not gone to the city) grew sweet potatoes and beans and cabbages. And shining, bright-coloured hibiscus flowers, as if in memory of another time and place.

Down the road from the houses there was a small wooden church and a bright yellow community hall. The settlement had once been on the other side of the hill, facing the open sea. Only during the wild storms could the people hear the sea now; but some of the very old people had refused to come to the new settlement nestling in the hill: they stayed still in old shacks, no water, no electricity; staring out to the open sea past the lonely, jagged cliffs as their ancestors once had done.

At the top of the hill, between the old settlement and the new, a decaying wooden building dreamed against the sky; listened like the very old people, to the wild crashing of the waves against the cliffs below. Once it had been a Maori meeting house proudly battling against the elements. But the young people had gone to the city long ago, and the elements had won. The roof had collapsed, rotting rafters fell inside, across the gaping windows. The once-beautiful wall panels, intricately woven patterns of dried reeds and threads of flax, were torn and broken; hung now precariously, drifted in the wind like old, brown lace.

Sometimes, still, the old men went fishing, looked back from the sea at the few shacks left standing along the coast. The old meeting house stood silhouetted against the sky; they looked back from the wild sea at the ruin of their past.

*

In the Pacific Ocean, miles from anywhere else in the world, this country, God's Own Country, lay. This is the story of an explosion there.

TWO

Of course the lucky children who lived in God's Own Country and drew their history in coloured crayons, came home from school to mothers who waited for them with glasses of fresh milk in the neat houses with the neat gardens; mothers who smiled and wore lipstick and short frocks.

But women, not so very long ago, stepping ashore on those islands, found they soon had chafed working hands that had had to learn to aim a musket or wield an axe or kill a pig or deliver a baby. Stunned, the women clung to the fashions of enlightenment (even though it was now twelve thousand miles away): they still wore long dresses in the mud; still wore tight corsets as they rode in carts with iron wheels which caught in the rutted roads of their new, sinister civilisation. In trepidation as they did up their button boots they heard of wild men who were looking for gold; saw savage natives out of the corner of their eye as they held their bonnetted children to them.

Sometimes it must have seemed that the land and the elements (the malign, ever-encroaching trees and bush; the storms and the droughts, the endless, surrounding sea) might never be overcome. But slowly the settlers won. Whole forests were completely destroyed, leaving stark, blank hillsides; land was reclaimed from the sea; houses and banks and schools and more churches were built with the wood from the forests; roads and railways snaked through the islands, connecting lonely settlements. The women with the chafed hands still dreamed of Home, the security and order and history they had left behind. Sometimes the scent of lilac haunted them as they scrubbed out pig buckets.

But now, in the 1950s, women used Ponds Beauty Cream and looked after their husbands and children in clean, wooden houses. Very few of them went to work once they were married: their husbands did not like them to go to work. They would have tea on the table when their husbands came home from *their* work; they would call the children in from where their voices trailed in the warm evenings as they played on the neat, tree-lined streets, and the family would sit together at the table. After tea the grown-ups would listen to the BBC World Service on the wireless.

The women dusted and polished and vacuumed every day and in the front room that they called 'the lounge' they had china cabinets where they kept their best china locked away. Sometimes the best cups and saucers came out and the women wheeled tea-trolleys round their lounges on infinite afternoons, serving each other cakes they had baked and small sandwiches they had made and talking politely to each other (though not always truthfully to each other) about their husbands and their children. And they would always smile. Decorum, so hard won, had – at all cost – to be maintained.

Sometimes the women caught the tram cars into town, wearing neat frocks and hats and gloves, and they bought some yards of material and a Simplicity dress pattern and maybe an English 'Women's Weekly' that had arrived in the shops from twelve thousand miles away, two or three months late. They would come back on the tram before the children got home from school. They put their hats and gloves carefully away, put on their aprons and put the meat in the oven.

And their daughters anxiously aspired to be like their mothers, to have their own husbands and children and neat houses and were considered on the shelf if they were not engaged soon after leaving school. At school, they had seen all the old-maid school mistresses (whose young men had been killed in the war): they were terrified of ending up like them, unmarried and lumpy and cross. Relieved girls all over the city wore little, shining, diamond engagement rings on their left hands and had a *trousseau* (usually a suitcase) under their beds where they kept towels and pillowcases and sheets, though it is hard to say what they thought would happen between those sheets, for, except in hushed, shocked tones if a girl Got Herself into Trouble and had to be sent away, no one ever spoke of sex.

And if – once – the land on which the neat houses were built and the tram lines laid and the schools erected had belonged to somebody else; had once been somebody else's home, contained old spirits perhaps, and dreams – well, these things were quite forgotten now for it was the 1950s.

*

Margaret-Rose Bennett considered it an extreme tribulation to have been christened, on a South Sea island during the Second World War, *Margaret-Rose*. She would much rather have been christened Shirley or Beverley like her school-friends. Her older sister had been christened Elizabeth: they were named after the British princesses and when they were very young, even before Margaret-Rose could properly walk, their mother dressed them in clothes copied from photographs of the princesses in the English 'Women's Weekly'. The real princesses were much older, teenagers who wore pearls, but Mrs Bennett adapted the patterns: little twinsets, and kilts, and knitted berets. But both sisters had inherited the hair of their grandmother, their father's mother: dark, curly, wild – and very un-royal. The grandmother had died of TB before they were born but it could be seen from fading sepia photographs that even all those years ago she had had difficulty making *her* hair neat: in photographers' studios, beside potted ferns, that same hair flew out from under Edwardian hats: unruly strands and curls, defying time and place. This inherited wild hair made it a rather difficult task to present the sisters as little princesses.

Nevertheless, for Christmas and birthday presents Elizabeth would be given books like 'Elizabeth: Future Queen'. Margaret-Rose was *still* sometimes given books like 'Margaret-Rose of Britain: The Life of the Second Princess'. But Elizabeth had died when Margaret-Rose was three, so she was left with her name, like half of a joke. Except that they had been christened in all seriousness, at the Church of England church beside the sea, where they went at Christmas and at Easter and for christenings. At school Margaret-Rose persuaded people to call her Maggie, having found the name in a Scottish song-book. Now only her mother persisted with the original.

Maggie wasn't sure if she remembered Elizabeth or not, though when she looked at old photographs she sometimes was almost sure she did. There was a small black and white photo of the two sisters as flower girls at a wedding, wearing identical little dresses, eating pieces of the wedding cake. The smaller girl with the wild, brown, curly hair that nobody could flatten looked up at the bigger girl with the same curly hair that nobody could flatten, as they both gleefully stuffed cake and icing into their mouths and sometimes Maggie seemed to remember the *feeling* of that moment. Or was it only looking at the photograph that made her think she remembered? She didn't remember the day of Elizabeth's death at all, and nobody ever talked about it. She supposed she must have been too young, only three.

And now she was seventeen.

Tonight she was in town with Susan, her best friend; they had been to the five o'clock pictures to see 'Father of the Bride' starring Elizabeth Taylor in a lovely white wedding dress and were having a last milkshake at the White Daisy milk bar before they turned into grown-ups.

'How could you do this to me?' Maggie said to Susan again.

'I know,' Susan sighed hugely. 'But Mum said it was the best idea.'

'I thought you wanted to go to university, I thought you wanted to work in a government department, it was all your idea to begin with.'

'Mum said this way I'll meet a doctor.'

'But you never wanted to be a nurse, you wanted to be a famous diplomat and stop wars, you faint when you see blood!'

'Mum says you get over it, after you've fainted a couple of times.'

'I suppose your mother envisages a handsome doctor catching you even though he's in the middle of cutting some-one's leg off, *O Susan, my darling let me help you, Matron, hold my scalpel and that limb while I pick up this maiden and clasp her to my manly, hairy chest,*' and they both giggled morosely, suck-ing up the strawberry milkshakes.

'What did you get?' asked Susan.

'What do you mean, get *what*? Poliomyelitis? Whooping cough?' Maggie made loud noises through her straw.

'What government department were you allocated to?' said Susan patiently.

'Oh. That place called the Bureau.'

'What, the Maori Department?'

'Mmmmm. My mother is angry. She wants my father to try and get me reallocated, like to the Education Department or something. She says nice girls don't work with Maoris, she says they're dirty.'

'Oh, well, there probably won't be any *actual* Maoris actually working there; don't be silly, they're not educated enough, you'll just have to look after their little problems, I expect, and help them along.'

'Mmmm. I'll never see you. You're my best friend. That hospital is miles away and no one ever lets us use our driving licence.'

'I'll write to you. I'll ring you up.'

'You better.' Maggie looked at her watch. 'Oh – I've got to go.' She stood up very quickly, anxiously; she knocked her ankle hard as she slid out from the table but she seemed not to notice.

They came out into the warm, dark, February streets, ran to the tram stop, saw the tram clanking towards them in the distance, its pole sparking along the wires.

Then they stood slightly apart, looking at nothing in particular, trying not to cry.

'Goodbye,' they each called, to their best friend. Maggie waved to Susan, who lived in another part of the city, until she couldn't see her any more.

The tram was almost empty as it rattled out towards the sea. Maggie sat on the inside of the tram – the outside part was for men who smoked, and women who dyed their hair.

She stared at the big hoarding near where the tram lines turned into the first tunnel: a housewife smiled from that hoarding, Maggie knew, although she couldn't be seen now in the dark. What the housewife was saying, whether she could be seen or not, was: DON'T LET MRS NEXT-DOOR SNIFF TWICE. USE AIRWICK.

She could feel a slight breeze on her face as the tram stopped at the terminus and, as always, when she got off the tram she could smell the sea.

TIP-TOP said the closed dairy as she walked past in her summer frock and her cardigan, TIP-TOP ICE-CREAM.

All her life the same dairy, the same couple owning it, Mr and Mrs Watson, and on Saturday evenings it opened specially for one hour. This enabled everybody to buy the Saturday night sports paper that arrived on a tram with rugby and racing results and the comic strip 'Dagwood and Blondie' and the problems page where people wrote about kissing and spots to 'Dear George'. But on all the other evenings of course, like now, the dairy was closed. Like everything else in the city.

She turned into her street of wooden houses and neat gardens and corrugated-iron roofs and walked along past the streetlights, towards the sea.

In the front garden of the house at the end of the street there was a daphne bush. The clusters of dark pink and light pink flowers gave off a strong scent, especially at night: heavy, beautiful and – if Margaret-Rose Bennett had known the meaning of the word – languorous.

All her life she had walked down this street. The sea and the sand and the rocks at the end of the road and the breeze coming in from the Pacific Ocean were part of her. At her own front gate the footsteps stopped for a moment. But she didn't go inside: she kept walking to the end of the street, and the sea. The tar-sealing ended abruptly and she just walked on to the sand. It was a warm night but the dark beach was deserted. Stars shone and the moon made a path of light across the water; the tide was almost full and there was the sound of the sea rolling gently in across the sand and then slipping out again. Her unruly hair blew across her face. *My life will change now. Next week I'll start work and I'll start*

*university. Things will be different. I'll be a grown-up and I'll
understand things better.*

Then she took off all her clothes.

She laid them on the sand, her suspender belt and her
nylons on top, and then catching up her hair with a rubber
band she ran into the sea, diving into the moonlit path, shattering the light into a thousand shadowy murmurs of water.
She swam in the dark for a few moments, feeling the cold on
her skin. And then she came slowly out, a thin white shape in
the night; dried herself with her cardigan and put on her
clothes; saw the path of moonlight form again across the
water. Then she walked up the beach. The sound of the sea
rolling in on the sand merged with the sound of her footsteps,
echoing down the empty street in the darkness.

Her mother was perhaps asleep, in her bedroom anyway
with the door tightly closed. For a moment Maggie paused
outside the bedroom door, her weight on one foot, as if she
was listening, or waiting. Then she walked quietly into the
lounge. Her father was lost to a rugby match on the wireless
from somewhere across the world with a different time-zone:
he waved briefly, automatically looked at his watch acknowl-
edging her arrival, but he did not notice her wet hair. He was
in his pyjamas and dressing-gown with brown bottles of beer
on the floor beside him in the room where the couch and the
armchairs were covered in flowered chintz and where the
locked china cabinet held the best cups and saucers. Maggie
had often woken in the night to the sound of raised men's
voices but it would only be the rugby commentator in
England or Wales or France or South Africa excitedly urging
the All Blacks on to another victory while her father, his large
body running to fat now, sat hunched over the old Bakelite
radio, holding the beer in his good hand.

Long ago, just before the war, before his wound, Richard
Bennett, a huge, strong young man, had been chosen for the

All Black rugby trials: there was no greater accolade, in this country.

Then the war came.

Margaret-Rose Bennett said goodnight to her father, smelling the familiar but not unpleasant smell of DB bitter. She stepped over the hook he had unscrewed from his arm and placed on the floor beside him, and went to bed in her small pink bedroom.

For a long time she lay awake. She listened to the sound she knew best in the world: the sound of the sea.

Behind the closed door of the main bedroom a beautiful woman lay, hearing the sea also. She had heard the footsteps of her second daughter as they hesitated outside the door, seeming to wait.

As the beautiful woman fell into her frozen sleep a small girl in a red bathing suit ran away from her, laughing.

*

In that city, in the part where the views were the most panoramic and the houses the most expensive, there was a huge, white, wooden colonial-style house that had once belonged to one of the country's first prime ministers. It had wide halls with rooms opening off towards the sea and the sunshine. Big windows looked out over the harbour, at the sea and the ships; fishing boats unloaded, nudging little pilot tugs guided huge liners into the wooden wharves. At night the lights of cargo boats and fishing boats and ferries twinkled and glittered as they moved out towards the Heads.

John Evans, who had been able to buy the huge and beautiful house because he had been a very successful sheep farmer, was now a very successful member of parliament and planned to be prime minister also. He was hardly ever there, in the beautiful house.

Mrs Evans stared out of the big windows for hours on end, beside the frangipani plant that flowered for several months every second year, flower after beautiful cream flower that filled the rooms with their fragrance. So that for Emily Evans, their daughter, the heavy scent of frangipani and the unnaturally still figure of her mother staring down at the city were somehow indefinably intertwined.

No one noticed when Emily Evans got home from whatever she was doing: she drove her very own Morris Minor into the large garages near the house and ran up the steps of the verandah, pushing at her short blonde hair with her red-painted fingernails, her brightly coloured jacket over her arm. If her face was flushed, if there was the smell of cigarettes and the smell of beer on her breath, nobody noticed.

Emily Evans had a gramophone in her bedroom and sometimes Mrs Evans heard 'Smoke Gets In Your Eyes' blaring out late into the night. She did not complain; only remembered that she had once known that song, and those times. And now it was her daughter's turn.

Emily Evans, who had been one of the cleverest girls her school had ever taught, now held down a job in a government department and studied three subjects at university at the same time, an almost unheard of endeavour even on those islands, where working and studying at the same time were considered to be a great leveller. She read philosophy in the bath and in her room; she completed pages of mathematical equations in the early mornings before work. Second-year English she considered simple: she could remember huge chunks of Shakespeare and Milton and Jane Austen effortlessly while Elvis Presley observed that you could do anything, but lay off of his blue suede shoes.

On one of the few occasions he was home her father remonstrated with her. 'How can you read Shakespeare with that trash blaring out?'

Emily gave him her brightest smile. 'They're both the popular culture of their time.'

'I want you to get a good degree,' he complained. 'I want you to *do* things; you're my daughter, I've got all sorts of plans for you.'

Emily was sprawled on her bed. 'I will get a good degree,' she answered, 'and I will *do* things, but they won't be your sort of things. I despise your politics and what your party stands for.'

Mr Evans made an exasperated sound, standing uneasily at her bedroom door. 'You never talked like this until you started that ridiculous job. I've told you, there is no difference between the two political parties in this country, not really. You are talking nonsense, you don't even begin to understand. Politics is the art of the possible and my party knows what is possible and what is pie in the sky. This is a wonderful country with opportunities for all, but you're just too young and too inexperienced and too spoilt to understand that.'

Emily did not answer. She took the red nail polish from beside her bed and began painting her toenails, bending over her feet intently. Her father, somehow embarrassed, walked to the window, stared at the dark, swaying ferns outside.

'Why, *why* did you have to take a job as well as study? I can give you all the money you want! And if you must work – if it somehow makes you feel more independent or equal or some other ridiculous thing that you've no doubt got from the unsuitable books that you read – it shouldn't be in the Bureau. There's no future in that place, it's a backwater.'

Emily blew loudly on her red toenails. 'I didn't choose it, it chose me,' she said.

Her father turned back from the window. 'All right, all right. I know the names of students who want to study part-time and work in government departments all go into a metaphorical hat and it wasn't your choice but at least I could have got you into External Affairs! I've got influence, Emily – I am going to be the next prime minister of this country! The Bureau isn't for clever girls like you. The Maoris have got the vote – why do they need a special government department? In fact, if you want to know my opinion, I think the Bureau should be closed down. It holds Maoris back – it babies them, builds them special, cheap houses, looks after all their little problems. And most of all it perpetuates this ridiculous fragmenting of the land. Communal ownership is just a load of native rubbish – they don't *use* their land, most of it, so for God's sake what are they holding on to it for? – they should be consolidating it and selling it and making a profit. There's plenty of people who would buy it from them, believe me.'

'Mum's been looking for you,' was all Emily said and she turned up the gramophone as he left her room: music blared out.

She despised her father. She avoided the bathroom after he'd been using it: there was a particular smell of shaving soap that she could not bear, now. The first time – she had been thirteen – she had seen her father with another woman, his hand intimately under her arm as they crossed the tram lines down by the wharves, her heart had jumped in disbelief, which had turned to horror and fear as her father bent his head and *kissed* his companion. On the tram going home she couldn't stop her legs shaking, feeling her whole secure world shattering. Everything was gone.

But her father came home as usual that evening and talked about the day in Parliament quite unconcernedly, and her mother fetched his usual gin and they did not notice that their daughter's heart had broken.

Now nothing surprised Emily, except the risks her father

took when there was a weekly scandal newspaper called *THE FACTS!* around. But she knew perfectly well that all the newspapers, even the scandal newspaper, were respectful to members of parliament.

A door banged and John Evans was gone again.

So there was nobody to care what time Emily Evans got home at night, smelling of beer and cigarettes, her face flushed, her dress carelessly buttoned, as she ran up the wooden steps of the verandah of the beautiful big house.

She was eighteen.

*

Prudence McKenzie opened her eyes quickly the way she had trained herself to when the nightmares came. Her body was covered in sweat. She breathed in and out as slowly as she could so that her heart slowed down at last. Then she got up. She took an orange and went and sat out on the old verandah in her nightdress. She could smell the honeysuckle everywhere in the darkness and she kept breathing carefully and quietly as she had been taught, taking the honeysuckle into her heart.

She was surrounded by darkness, there were no other houses here, under the hill, behind the city. Her tall shadow, restless at first, became still.

Below her the city was asleep. The streetlights had gone off, the trams were long ago in the terminus, just a light flickering here and there; very occasionally a car moved in the distance. Far away down by the wharves, where fishing boats and lighters and small cargo boats lay, she could see that a big ship had docked that must have come from overseas.

She turned the orange carefully around in her hands, feeling its skin.

The darkness of the night did not frighten her. Nothing

frightened her when she was awake because nothing more frightening could happen to her than had happened to her already.

Prudence turned her head carefully. She had taught herself to find where the Bureau was in the darkness, to think of the building carefully, to bring it into her mind, to fill her mind.

The Bureau stood near a small, sloping piece of green grass in the city, next door to the Red Rose Parlour. The Red Rose Parlour had a red rose painted on the door, rather faded now: girls worked there in shifts and men, often sailors from the docks, rang the bell night and day and disappeared inside. If there was an incongruity in the old Red Rose Parlour being next door to a government department, nobody mentioned it. The Bureau stood, a modern, square building, respectably next door, with a nice little piece of green grass just across the road.

Old, gnarled pohutukawa trees grew up around the edges of the piece of grass. They'd been there as long as anyone could remember. Their roots pushed up and cracked the asphalt road and government trucks were always disgorging men with tools to try and deal with the problem. They'd hack away for a while and then drive off and the old trees would settle back into the asphalt and continue to spread their roots under the city. At Christmas time the dark red pohutukawa flowers shone in the hot sun and when the flowers died a spiky red dust fell on to the grass and on to the road and on to the Bureau steps, like a carpet.

Prudence McKenzie conjured up an image of the Bureau standing beside the grass and the old pohutukawa trees, with the shadowy Red Rose Parlour huddled slightly behind. Her heart beat normally at last and the last of the sweat dried on her skin. In her mind she could now see the Bureau quite clearly: the plain, ordinary office building, where, in the bright morning that would come, she would see her love, and life would start again, and there would be another whole day, before nightfall.

She turned the orange round and round in her hands.

She was eighteen.

THREE

The Red Rose Parlour, set back slightly from the small green and the government department known as the Bureau, was only one of the Parlours in that city where so many ships came to call. *Parlours* they were known as, a Victorian inheritance. Massage *Parlours*.

The building that housed the Red Rose Parlour had once belonged to the Women's Christian Temperance Union. There was a moment in history when the Women's Christian Temperance Union had almost persuaded the country to vote itself dry; now drunken sailors rang the same bell on the same front door. There was also a back door, out of view of the Bureau windows, hidden partially by overhanging grass and gorse. Discreet visitors used this entrance. Unbeknownst to these circumspect guests, or to the less salubrious ones, there was a room off to one side of the building where the kettle was kept boiling and where comfortable chairs surrounded an old table and where sometimes, when unavoidable, children were parked by their mothers. The curtains were always drawn, for customers would perhaps have been surprised, and possibly uneasy, to know that children played with toy cars not far away, or were read to about Bambi the dear little deer by the caretaker, Auntie Paki. Auntie Paki wasn't anyone's auntie in particular, just Auntie Paki.

The dark room was cool now on this hot, summer morning and empty except for Auntie Paki and a fat Maori man in a black singlet who sat at the table drinking tea out of a thick, white mug that had somehow made its way to the Red Rose Parlour from the Railway Station Refreshment Rooms. The man's curly hair was completely grey: it was only if you looked closely that you noticed how young his face was, in comparison. He and Auntie Paki had both lived in the city almost all their lives, they knew the streets and the hills like the back of their hands; they knew, too, the underbelly of their city: that was where they lived.

They spoke now of cousins and distant relations and people they knew; in particular of Auntie Paki's cousin's daughter.

'She could be a nursing aid,' said Auntie Paki. 'She's a clever girl, she shouldn't be working here. Her sister's even a dental nurse. You talk to her, Sinatra, you know about these things, I don't.' Auntie Paki was knitting a child's jersey, she had a pile already knitted on a chair beside her: she gave them to the Church. Sometimes the Church sent clothes to the poor people of Africa; sometimes it distributed them much nearer to home, Auntie Paki had more than once seen one of her jersies walking down the street. Auntie Paki's needles clicked fast; the man in the black singlet who had been nicknamed Sinatra after his mother's favourite singer, listened, nodded, smoothed the old table with his brown hand, feeling the knots and the planes of the wood. Over and over he stroked the kauri wood as they talked, as if, in the table, he was trying to find the ancient tree.

'I'll get someone at the Bureau to talk to her,' said Sinatra. 'Someone there will be able to persuade her there's more future in nursing than in the Red Rose Parlour.'

'I hope,' said Auntie Paki.

She saw Sinatra's hands, the slow but restless smoothing of

the wood; she felt that no one should have suffered the pain
that he had. She knew why he walked the streets at night, not
wanting to go home to his room. She wished she could give
him some comfort for his heart, but knew better than to
mention it.

'You could come and work here, Sinny,' she said, still
watching his hands. 'Never mind your work down at the
wharves, we could hire you here and dress you in a frock,'
and Sinatra threw back his head and laughed; they both
laughed, sat back in their chairs and laughed behind the
closed door, away from the customers.

Just as Sinatra stood, due back at his work down on the
wharves for the afternoon shift, just as he opened the door
and turned back to say goodbye again to Auntie Paki, a
scream flew along the long corridor and was cut short. For a
fat man Sinatra moved surprisingly quickly: he grabbed a key
from a nail on the wall and almost at once he was at the end of
the corridor, opening doors, catching the surprised face of an
American sailor lying on a table in one room and the outraged face of a member of parliament in another.

'Bugger off, you bloody hori,' bellowed the member of parliament, although it was a muffled kind of bellow.

'Sorry,' said Sinatra briefly, 'someone's been hurt.'

In the third room a young Maori girl crouched in a corner,
her arms protecting her face. There was blood on her arms.

A Dutchman stood naked in the small room: just as Sinatra
unlocked the door, the Dutchman hit the girl again.

'You cheating bitch!' he shouted and Sinatra saw her head
almost ricochet from one part of the wall to another, heard the
breath forced from her body and the cry of pain.

Sinatra roared, grabbed the Dutchman's hair and hurled
him against the other wall; as the man bounced off the wall
from the force of the throw and fell across the massage table,
Sinatra punched him in the face and knocked him to the

ground. Sinatra, the Dutchman and the girl all heard quite clearly the crack of bone; blood ran down the Dutchman's face now also. He looked like a human dog as he ended up on all fours, naked on the floor.

Auntie Paki came into the room quickly and helped the young girl from the corner. '*Turituri e hine, kaua e tangi,*' she whispered in another language, *sssssssshh*. Half holding, half lifting her, she took the girl from the room and back along the corridor. A door closed.

The Dutchman stared up at the big, fat, brown man who had appeared from nowhere. His eyes flickered with fright. He was still on all fours, his white, undignified body shaking. Blood dripped from his nose and his breath came in little, winded gasps.

Not a sound came from anywhere else in the Red Rose Parlour. It could have been empty.

'Please, she cheated me.' The Dutchman whispered now, as if anxious not to disturb the silence and his accent was thick with fear. 'She promised me.' His penis hung limp. Something dripped from it.

Sinatra looked at the Dutchman with dark, totally expressionless eyes. And then, oddly, he turned towards the small window.

'See that?' he said.

Disoriented, scared, expecting to be hit again, the Dutchman flicked a glance to the window. It was raining. Out of a cloudless, summer sky, it was suddenly raining.

The Maori spoke so quietly that the Dutchman wasn't sure he had heard.

'Sometimes my ancestors weep at what they see,' the Maori said. 'It means they will be avenged. It means they have cursed you.' Then out of his mouth came that same language that Auntie Paki had used to the girl, poured out, surrounded the Dutchman, disoriented him for a moment, so that he stared up at the fat Maori in horror, felt suddenly very cold. Then his trousers were thrown down onto the floor.

'Get out,' said Sinatra. 'This is my city. Don't come back.'

The Dutchman literally leapt into his trousers, pulling wildly at them, stumbling about, blood dripping from his nose. He grabbed his jacket and shirt and shoes, scuttled out. Although the rain had stopped as suddenly as it had started he did not wait at the green nearby to finish dressing respectably but, plunging his arms into his jacket and his feet into his shoes, kept on running down to the docks; ran past the rather surprised city workers in their lunch-hour who rightly assumed that he must be a foreigner; running from the curse that for all he knew might make his hair fall out or his bollocks fall off. He kept running till he got to his ship where he relapsed into his own language and told his companions how he'd got away from a fat Maori. After a few glasses of Bols he began to laugh and swagger and talk about the girl at some massage place and about how native curses couldn't frighten him.

But as the day wore on he couldn't get out of his head the unknown language that had surrounded him, mesmerised him. He began to shiver as if he had a fever. He double-locked his cabin door. He looked for rain but the sky was blue and bright and cloudless.

*

That evening the teacher at the night class looked around the small, high room and gave an imperceptible sigh. She had just signed up this year's pupils. Fourteen, only two of them Maori, and the class would be halved probably by the end of the first term as people lost their summer enthusiasms. She sighed again, well this was how it was at adult education, and then she addressed her new class.

It is a fact, she said, *that this beautiful language is dying. Its demise is, I believe, unstoppable. There are very few native speakers left and it saddens me greatly to say that I believe that in the course of one more generation the Maori language will not be spoken. Still, you have come here, so let us study it, even if we are to be the last.*

*

Sinatra worked the afternoon shift and then the evening shift on the wharves. Strong men loaded ships with lamb and butter and wool and talked of rugby; sweated; unloaded whisky (dropped one of the boxes so that it fell off the back of the lorry but didn't break, men grinned and whistled). Sinatra signed his evening shift pay to another Maori wharfie who had been hurt in a fall. As he was walking back along the docks he saw that the asbestos shed where the managers worked was empty. He strolled inside, picked up an alarm clock from a table and came out again, slipping the alarm clock deep into his big jacket pocket. Then he began his night walk through the city: a big, lonely figure along the dark empty streets. A man who did not want to go home.

'G'day, Sinatra,' said the night policemen.

'**Kia ora**, Sinatra,' said the boat girls, giggling past along to the wharves in the darkness, dodging the policemen, meeting sailors.

He went to the pie cart at the railway station, leaned against the counter eating a mince pie and drinking a mug of tea. He and the pieman exchanged news, spoke of the night people: of the sad, giggling boat girls, mainly young Maori girls new to the city; of an old man they'd found lying in an alley and taken to hospital, the pieman had visited him in his ward this evening, taken him a pie in a brown paper bag, avoiding the matron.

As Sinatra walked on through the deserted streets, he

thought for a time about the Dutchman in the Red Rose Parlour that morning. And then the surprised and angry face of the member of parliament in the second room flashed again into his mind. *That was Mr John Evans who called me a bloody hori* he thought. *That's the MP who wants to be prime minister. Well well.*

Sinatra whistled an old Victorian ballad in the night as he walked.

As well as the main streets, he knew the back streets and the massage parlours, the docks and the police, the streets up behind the city. He had become a city boy very quickly: his mother, avoiding his violent father, had brought him to the city when he was eight and his name was Mata, and at first she had tried to keep the boy with her as she survived in the city. But by the time the War came and with it the American sailors with their gramophone records of Frank Sinatra singing, Mata was big and strong and eleven: his mother, partying with these new, handsome strangers, couldn't manage him; left him with the Salvation Army, telling them in a laughing, drunken moment that the boy's name was Sinatra, after Frank. Other members of his family had come and gone, taken him and left him, the big wild boy who could fight anyone and often did. And he had stayed in the city, a street Maori, the new breed. But close to his heart he'd kept his language, the one he'd first known. And because he'd been on the streets so long he knew many things and some people called him the King of the City. Sinatra knew how the city worked.

John Evans as prime minister eh? And he whistled in the night.

Finally he made his way towards his room up behind the city. He came to a cluster of old falling-down sheds and garages: a disused motor workshop. Rusty cars piled outside, tyres and bonnets and engines; shadowy trucks and bits of old buses loomed darkly. He listened carefully: somewhere a guitar strummed. Sinatra whistled in a particular way: a young Maori appeared out of the shadows and the broken vehicles.

'So, did you get the job?'

'Yeah Sinny, I got the job, thanks,' and they both grinned. 'I start tomorrow on the rubbish truck, I can work Saturdays too, if I want. I start at five o'clock, so I thought I better stay up all night so's not to miss.'

'*E hoa*, you're in the big city now,' said Sinatra, 'you gotta get organised. Here.' And he pulled the alarm clock out of his jacket. 'Now get some sleep for a couple of hours,' and Sinatra was gone, across the road and into an old building: years ago a respectable boarding house for clean-living, single gentlemen, where the wooden floors made from old kauri trees now tilted unevenly and the doors didn't properly close.

Sinatra's room was at the top. He didn't put on the electric light, just walked in and partially closed the door. Before he lay down on the bed with the sagging springs he crossed to the open window, listened to the sounds of his city: a gramophone being played somewhere; in the distance a drunken voice, arguing. He stood beside the brightly coloured curtains. The curtains were the reason he didn't want to come home at night, but he could not bring himself to get rid of them. They were all he had kept after – he formed it carefully in his mind – *after the accident*.

The curtains were covered in cars: red sports cars and a big Mercedes Benz, and in the middle a bright yellow tractor. A little boy's curtains. The curtains of his four-year-old son, who was dead. A small sigh of wind blew the curtains inwards, they brushed Sinatra's face gently. For a brief, brief moment he allowed his head to rest there.

Then he took off his jacket and his boots and got into bed.

FOUR

A loud, piercing scream echoed round the government offices that were painted green.

People jumped up from their desks, startled, opened doors hurriedly, hoping perhaps for a bit of assault and battery to brighten the day. But all they saw was the Head Clerk in the Land Records room, bending over the new girl, Margaret-Rose Bennett, who was saying, blushing, deeply apologetic: 'I'm sorry. I'm sorry – but it's so BORING. It just came out of my mouth – I didn't mean to scream.'

Doors closed, heads were shaken in disapproval, in disappointment in some cases: something at least a little more interesting had been hoped for. But then a brown head appeared tentatively round the door. Manu Taihape, who was in charge of the office files, looked genuinely scared.

'Hey, boy, who was that? My heart nearly fell out of my pants,' he said. 'I hate women screaming, I hate that sound, it reminds me of dying.' He carried, at high speed, government files around from floor to floor on something rather like the trollies that suburban ladies served tea in china cups from, in their lounges, on infinite afternoons. He looked once more at the new girl with the funny hair.

'Hey, boy, don't scream,' said Manu Taihape, 'ghosts might come.'

To Margaret-Rose Bennett the brown man pushing the trolley might have been speaking in a foreign language. 'I'm sorry?' she said politely. 'Pardon?'

'I might get a heart attack if you do it again,' said Manu, 'and the Bureau would fall to pieces without me and my trolley. I'm the one who runs the place really,' and his face broke into a big, sunny smile that went from his mouth to his eyes and seemed to fly out to his ears so that she smiled back involuntarily.

'Sorry,' she said, 'I didn't mean to scream,' and Manu, smiling still, whistled off again, spinning his trolley of files in front of him.

The incredulous face of the Head Clerk loomed again into her view. 'Is this – are these –' his mouth opened and closed in disbelief, '– are these toothmarks on this land register?' He thrust a huge, old leather-bound volume in front of her, put his face down to her level, she could see the bristles growing out of his chin. 'Did you bite this land register?'

Margaret-Rose Bennett again turned bright red.

Three weeks now she'd been employed at the Bureau, her first job, and she'd never been so bored in her life. All day long, all she was meant to do was copy information from court documents into the land registers, all of it in unknown, unpronounceable words. If a Maori died his land was automatically shared among his children. She had to record the new names. That was it: that was what she had turned into a grown-up for.

She had done her best to make it interesting: she'd written in joined-up writing, she had printed, she had used different pens; in her second week she'd written every second letter in different coloured ink. She'd slanted her writing to the left, she'd slanted her writing to the right; this week she'd even written backwards in mirror writing, and at some stage she must've simply bitten the book in frustration without realising. She quickly grabbed the register before he could discover anything else, she felt perspiration running down inside her summer frock, her legs stuck to her seat.

'Sorry,' she said, rubbing at the bite mark, 'sorry Mr O'Brien, I won't bite or scream again.'

'You better not, girlie,' said the Head Clerk ominously. 'And by the way, I've been watching you, you only need ten minutes to run up that hill so don't you let me catch you going off early in the afternoons when you've got four o'clock lectures.' He leaned right over her again, he had hairs on the back of his hand and smelt of sweat.

'I'll be watching you,' he said. 'Ten to four you can leave, no earlier than ten to four. And get here in the morning the minute your eight o'clock lectures finish; you've got to sign the attendance book like everyone else or heads will roll, you understand? Ten past nine, no later. Just because the government believes you scroungers should attend lectures *and* get paid, we don't take any nonsense from you university types, OK?'

'Yes, Mr O'Brien,' said Maggie meekly. She wondered what would happen if she bit his horrible hairy arm. She saw his horrible hairy legs as he stomped away.

The women wore summer frocks with short sleeves, and because it was summer the men were allowed to wear shorts to work, as long as they wore shirts and ties and long socks. Maggie wondered if they knew how funny they looked, showing their hairy legs and their knobbly knees and wearing ties at the same time. *They're oxymorons*, she thought to herself.

All the clerks sat at joined-together desks with the Head Clerk's desk in the front, facing them. *Like school* thought Maggie, except that almost everyone smoked which you most certainly could not do at her girls' school. The smoke from Craven 'A' and de Reszke and Capstan Cork Tipped lay heavy and stale on the air. Maggie had bought her very first packet of ten de Reszke Ivory Filter Tip and now smoked experimentally every day, coughing. In the dark, smoky room it felt as if the temperature was a hundred degrees.

Her desk was next to that of a thin pale boy called Harry Beans. Harry Beans, she had soon learned, pulled girls' arms and pinched them at will. When he had pinched her on her third day she had bitten him.

'Your screaming sounded like a screeching hen,' said Harry Beans now. 'I suppose you think you can screech about the place because you're at university but you're just part of a long line of clerks who have been filling in these very registers for more than eighty years. Since 1873, look, look,' and he pulled her arm to show her the entries in the old-fashioned writing in the front of his register.

'I don't *care*,' said Maggie, pulling away from him, almost grinding her teeth in exasperation, 'I can't stand it! I'll die of tedium! I'd rather work in Woolworth's.'

Harry Beans took no notice, as if he didn't listen to girls, only talked at them. 'And another thing, just look at this,' and he grabbed her arm again to pull her to her feet, wanting her to look out of the window.

'Look at them, *look* at them,' said Harry Beans. Maggie pulled sharply away from him again. But she stared down out of the window. A group of Maoris sat on the little green outside. The men wore brown and grey hats like the one Maggie's father wore to work every morning. Old ladies were dressed in black.

'Look, look, look at that old girl with the tattoo on her chin,' said Harry Beans. 'They're out of the dark ages.' Children in bright colours with pants too big for them, and braces, ran and fell and laughed on the grass in the sunshine. The sound of their laughter drifted upwards.

'Look at them,' said Harry Beans again. 'They come to the city for the day and get big fat cheques from us for renting their land to farmers. Maoris still own about four million acres in spite of the fact that they're hopeless.'

'How many acres is our country altogether?' asked Maggie, curious despite herself.

'About sixty-six million,' said Harry Beans, 'more or less. And then these horis go to the pub or the betting shop and then they go all the way home – miles away – in taxis. Good life they've got, these horis.'

'Why do you call them horis?'

Harry Beans looked surprised. 'I dunno, everyone calls Maoris horis.'

'What does hori mean?'

'Hori means George,' said a voice behind her.

Maggie turned. A young Maori man in the desk behind was grinning. His shirt was undone, she could see the brown skin of his chest. 'I'm Hori Smith, you met me on the first day.'

'Oh – oh, yes, of course,' said Maggie, embarrassedly sitting back down, twisting in her seat. 'Yes, hello Hori, of course I remember, I've seen you after work with your little children.'

'I think we're called horis,' said Hori Smith, 'because so many of us are called Hori meaning George. And the reason so many of us are called Hori meaning George is that we're all named after the British Royal Family because Maoris are such staunch monarchists! I'm George and I've got four cousins called George.'

'Oh, heavens, don't worry, Hori,' said Maggie, 'my name is Margaret-Rose, that's much worse, and I've got a cousin called Edward Albert.'

The brown man burst out laughing. 'You fellas are worse than us!' he crowed, and after a minute Maggie laughed a little bit too, but self-consciously, as if laughing was hard.

'We've had enough trouble from you for one day, girlie,' said Mr O'Brien.

The hot, screaming afternoon wore slowly on. Maggie was now too comatose to even experiment with another cigarette. A very pretty blonde girl with short hair and red fingernails came in carrying some files and the atmosphere in the room brightened considerably for a couple of minutes. She wore a gaily coloured jacket: red and green and yellow and blue, as if she had just arrived from some exotic place like Mexico or Timbuktu and she lit up the room. The boys called out, *Hey, Emily, hey Emily, see you tonight at Prudence's place*? and the blonde girl waved at them and called back *see you at twenty past six, don't be late*, ignoring the disapproving looks of the Head Clerk.

Maggie wondered what Prudence's Place was. It could be a milk bar but she hadn't heard of it.

Droopingly, but like a good girl, she printed names in the old land registers in blue-black ink (although still grinding her teeth): her boss occasionally looked over her shoulder and neater entries would have been hard to find.

Finally, as she looked at her watch for the sixty-seventh time, it was ten to four. The boss couldn't stop her. This was the agreement for university students who worked in government departments. She could go.

English ivy grew over the brick walls and round the tall library windows of the university up on the hill. At the entrance there was a statue of a British duke who was sitting on a horse as if to indicate that equestrian skills and education were inextricably conjoined. The horse snorted in a noble manner. You might have thought you were in England.

You might as well have been in England.

At the beginning of the term three boys, farmers' sons, had caused a great furore by actually walking out of a history lecture. At first there was jubilation among some of the students, believing that the boys had walked out in protest at not learning the history of their own country. However it turned out that the farmers' sons, free at last from sheep, and drunk on copious quantities of DB bitter, had stood up in a history lecture and complained that they were men's men and they hadn't come to university in the city to write essays about a poofter king who cooked cakes; had then swaggered off to a rugby match. The university authorities took the matter extremely seriously: letters were sent to their farming fathers and the vice-chancellor made a speech on the sanctity of learning.

At school Maggie had been taught about the Magna Carta and the Industrial Revolution and had sat tests on the Kings and Queens of the Realm; like most school children she knew bits of English poetry by heart. Now, in her English lectures, she was studying Coleridge and Shakespeare and Wordsworth and Keats.

And she was studying French as well.

Maggie sighed. *Horrible old French.* It felt completely alien to her. It was her ***bête noire***. But you had to take a language for a Bachelor of Arts degree and French was the only one she knew anything about. ***Bête noire*** she repeated to herself gloomily as she walked up the steps past the ivy.

She was still finding her way to the huge lecture rooms or the small seminar rooms, up winding staircases and along corridors. She walked past lounging, Brylcreemed youths who – she knew perfectly well – had only a few months ago worn grey short pants and caps to school and noisily larked at tram stops, hitting each other with schoolbags. A professor in a black gown wafted the musty smell of chalk and books and stale pipe tobacco as he passed her. A crippled boy was slowly climbing the stairs backwards and Maggie smiled at him, *poor thing*: his wooden crutches made an echoing sound down concrete corridors as other students ran past in suede shoes or swishing skirts with full petticoats and wide belts. Maggie walked along a corridor behind a group of young men loudly discussing Indigenous Poetry, and she heard one with a beard shout, OUR POETRY! OUR OWN POETRY! A group of nuns walked sedately, their rosaries clicking against their habits.

Bête noire, bête noire, Maggie repeated under her breath as she made her way to the French lecture room.

'Come to the pictures,' said a boy to Maggie just as she was getting out her textbooks.

She blushed, and then recognised him: her school had had embarrassing dancing classes with the nearest boys' school and she and this boy had sweatily waltzed while the old-maid sports mistress had thumped 'Some Day My Prince Will Come' angrily on the piano.

'What to see?'

'"From Here to Eternity", at the Gala.'

Maggie knew only forbidden films were shown at the Gala Picture Theatre. 'I've got this French lecture,' she said. 'Yes thanks, I think I'll come.'

Deborah Kerr and Burt Lancaster kissed each other passionately in the sand on a beach like hers. But on a beach like hers women in sensible bathing suits sat neatly on towels in the sandhills and called to their children. In the Gala some old men snored in the back row and a cat leapt up on to Maggie's knee at one point but everyone knew there were cats in the Gala and she hardly even jumped. She had never seen anything so romantic or so disturbing as "From Here to Eternity" in her whole life: *was this actual sex?* Whatever this thing was, it was new to her and unsettling and exciting. Her companion ran his arm experimentally along the back of her seat but Maggie was lost in the way they kissed on the sand and in the sound of the sea. When the lights came up she blinked in surprise to find herself in the Gala with a boy who used to wear short pants who – she suddenly noticed – had pimples on his neck. Unlike Burt Lancaster. The boy must have seen something in her face: he hastily removed his arm in embarrassment. They stood for 'God Save the Queen' and then went and had a doughnut at the White Daisy milk bar.

It was too late now to go back to the university.

She parted from the boy, walked desultorily along the city streets towards the tram station, past the dark, wooden-verandahed shop-fronts, across the tram lines, past the docks. From the last wharf she could see beams of light moving around. A man's voice shouted. Maggie, curious, wandered down the wooden planks of the wharf and heard seagulls screaming excitedly in the darkness. She could smell the tarry smell of sea and ships and ropes. A group of men huddled with big torches; as she came nearer she sudden gasped, actually turned to go back, but stopped, transfixed. Something was being hauled up out of the sea with a big hook; men pulled, murmured, shone their lights on the dripping bundle. She was half turned to run away, half turned towards the water and in that odd position she saw her first dead body; or, rather, the first dead body she remembered.

A policeman spoke to some foreign sailors; one of them in thick-accented English told him that the dead man had been terrified by a native curse.

The policeman's sensible laugh rang out in the flickering darkness. 'I'd say drunk, sonny,' he said. 'We don't have any of that sort of mumbo-jumbo in this city; you're not in Africa you know.'

Maggie tried to leave, stepped one step nearer. The body had been laid out on the wharf now, water fell from it through the gaps between the wooden planks. The policeman shone his huge torch right on the face: what Maggie saw was white, white, blanched skin round the eye sockets, as if the eyes had already faded away.

Her mother stood in the kitchen.

Maggie's heart jumped as she quietly opened the back door and saw her there, her beautiful mother. Quite automatically, without her being aware of it, she stood stock still, her weight poised on one foot.

'Hello, Mum,' she said. 'I've just seen –' but she stopped. Although death haunted this house it was never, ever talked about.

'I've been studying John Keats,' said Maggie. '"Ode on a Grecian Urn." It's about time passing, or not moving.'

But her beautiful mother turned and walked out of the kitchen. At the doorway she said: 'Those poets knew nothing about real life.' Maggie heard the bedroom door close. And the sound of her own heart, beating fast.

In her bedroom the pink candlewick bedspread lay neatly over her thin bed: it hung neatly because her mother insisted that it not touch the floor at any point, that it hang evenly and neatly round the bottom of the bed, edges matching; she would sometimes stand at the door of her daughter's bedroom, checking. An old doll, Rosebud, whose eyes opened and closed, still sat on the windowsill dressed in white; the bookcase was crammed with books beside a small, neat desk. In the wardrobe frocks with wide belts and full skirts hung; neatly at the bottom stood her flat ballerina slip-ons and her stiletto-heeled shoes.

In the mirror she saw wild hair and dark, anxious eyes.

Margaret-Rose Bennett had taught herself to control her dreams. She often dreamed of books, which were safe. The dank, dark shape on the wharf with the talk of native curses was pushed away. Into her mind carefully as she fell asleep she brought the old edition of Keats that she had bought from a second-hand bookshop, its feel and its smell and its poetry. Burt Lancaster smiled, in swimming togs.

FIVE

The summer early mornings were beautiful, in that city.

Emily Evans's red, confident fingernails ran through her short, blonde hair as she walked in the sun after her early-morning philosophy lecture. She was so clever, so arrogant in tutorials, so articulate, that any of the students passing her would have assumed she was deep in philosophical thought: in fact she was thinking, as she so often did, about her father.

She heard footsteps running behind her, turned, saw the new girl running, her stiletto heels clicking on the pavement, her wild hair flying outwards.

'It's all right,' she said as Maggie came near, 'they won't eat you, you know,' slowing Maggie down with her hand.

'Oh –', said Maggie breathing hard, 'Oh, oh, I don't want to be late, ten-past nine he said. The English lecture ran on a few minutes extra.'

'He's a bully,' said Emily, 'your boss is a bully, don't let him bully you.'

'It's just – it's just that – I screamed yesterday.'

'So I heard,' said Emily drily.

Maggie looked both apologetic and defiant, an odd combination. 'I was so bored – I didn't mean to scream at all, I didn't know I was going to, it just seemed to come out of my mouth all by itself.' She looked hot and flustered, reluctantly adopted

Emily's strolling pace. The reds and yellows of Emily's exotic jacket shone in the sunshine. Maggie took little sidelong glances at the blonde hair and the red fingernails and an air of – she tried to work out what it was – boldness, or confidence. As if she owned the world and nothing frightened her. A body on a wharf with disappearing eyes wouldn't frighten her.

'What subjects are you doing at university?' Emily asked Maggie.

'English and French, Stage One, what about you?'

'English Stage Two and Maths Stage Two and Philosophy One.'

'Good heavens,' said Maggie, actually stopping walking altogether in amazement, 'you must be the cleverest person in the whole country, what a *lot* when you're working too. I think just two different subjects is hard, in fact, I'm thinking of giving up French I hate it so much – I don't see why we have to learn *French* – what's it got to do with us on the other side of the world? It's such a *foreign* language and so nasal and so boring and I'll never go to France so what's the point, and the professor's got hair sticking out of his ears – I hated it at school too: *la plume de ma tante* – what's the point, I HATE it.'

Emily stared in surprise as Maggie stood on the pavement almost shouting, breathing heavily, hair wild, but her weight all on one foot, poised. *As if she might run away at any moment*, thought Emily. *How odd.*

'You could always read "Madame Bovary" in its original language,' she suggested.

Maggie looked startled. 'Oh – yes,' she said politely, still breathing hard but walking again, 'Yes, yes, I could do that, I suppose. Only at the moment I'm more worried about handing in my first English essay on time. I haven't written a university essay before, we're studying the Romantic poets.

We have to write about "Ode on a Grecian Urn" by John Keats – I thought of writing it under my desk at the Bureau, I'm sure I could fill in the land registers at the same time no trouble but that's not very practical with Mr O'Brien stomping up and down all the time like a policeman.'

'That's what he was.'

'A policeman?'

'An army policeman. You think the land files are boring. You wait till they all start talking about the *war*.'

'Oh dear, yes, that's pretty boring too, isn't it.'

'I sometimes comfort myself,' said Emily, 'with the proposition "I'm bored therefore I am". Use the Maori Land Court in the lunch-hour, or just hide in there during the day, pretend you've got your period, no one'll find you, it's hardly ever used.'

'What's the Maori Land Court?'

'Hasn't anyone even shown you around?'

'No.'

'Well, it's just a big empty room in the middle of the Bureau where an ancient white judge makes decisions about Maori land and it's almost always empty and quiet. Oh look, there's the policeman.'

And there at the doorway of the Bureau, next to the Red Rose Parlour, down where the bright sunlight already covered the grass and the pohutukawa trees, Maggie's boss stood, looking at his watch and waiting for them.

In the Land Records room the boys had taken advantage of their boss's absence. When Maggie got to her desk, Harry Beans was arguing loudly with Manu who was sitting on top of the records on his trolley, Hori who was named after English kings, and Rangi Cox who always had a cigarette hanging from the corner of his mouth like Humphrey Bogart.

'You know what really annoys me about you people?' said Harry Beans. 'You're always laughing at nothing.'

'Yeah! True!' said Manu and Rangi and Hori, and they all laughed.

'But what are you laughing *at?*'

'We're just laughing,' said Manu, laughing.

Maggie listened to this conversation very carefully. She too had noticed how Maoris laughed. She had noticed it because she found laughing hard, she realised she didn't quite know how to do it.

Harry Beans could not leave it alone. 'What's so funny all the time?' he said, getting angrier and angrier as the laughter still went on. 'You sound like madmen.'

'Nothing's funny,' said Rangi, lighting another cigarette, drooping it from his lip.

'We are madmen,' said Manu solemnly.

'We just laugh,' said Hori and then they began to laugh again and their laughter filled the office, bounced off the government walls, until their boss arrived at the door and told them to get on with their work at once and Manu sped off with his trolley of files to another part of the building.

Maggie looked at the cigarette drooping from Rangi's mouth. When the boss went out of the room again she leaned across her desk and said to Rangi rather shyly, 'Excuse me. Did you know you smoke like Humphrey Bogart?'

'I've seen "Casablanca" fourteen times,' said Rangi, the cigarette going up and down.

'*Pardon?*'

'It was on in our community hall and it was Christmas and the bus didn't come with the replacement so they kept showing "Casablanca". I learnt it off by heart: "Here's looking at you kid",' and he and Hori laughed merrily again, leaning over their desks.

When the morning tea trolley was brought round by a lady

in a blue overall Maggie slipped out of her desk and went to look for the Maori Land Court. She opened the door into a dark, unwindowed room with a judge's bench at one end and shadowy rows of empty wooden chairs. She turned on the light and jumped slightly as the door swung slowly closed behind her. Hundreds and hundreds of old land files and old registers lay piled on shelves all round the walls of the room, right up to the ceiling, and there was a strange, rustling silence, of old papers, and of dust. The harsh electric light threw odd shadows onto the empty chairs and just for a moment she felt a tingling feeling at the back of her neck as she stood there, as if the rustling silence enclosed memories, or dreams.

'Well, it's only an old room,' she said aloud, more loudly than she meant to, and there was a kind of echo in the emptiness. *I suppose I could work in here.* As she opened the door firmly and turned off the light to move out again into the corridor, she could've sworn she heard a guitar strumming, somewhere.

While the sun shone brightly that morning John Evans, who so confidently expected to be the next prime minister, met another man in a hotel at the end of the city down by the wharves, in the lounge bar, far away from where most businessmen drank. People in this small city knew too much about other people's affairs, it was almost inescapable; but this was the wharfies' hotel, no one important came here. John Evans did not expect to bump in to anyone who knew him here, especially not at ten-thirty in the morning, especially not in the summer when most MPs were away tending their farms. Parliament didn't meet properly till the farmers' work was over for the year, and John Evans would be organised by then. The wharfies drank beer in the public bar next door in their singlets. But these two men drank gin and sat in leather chairs. They both wore suits and their heads came close together as they spoke. The clock in the hotel was striking eleven when the other man handed some papers across the small table beside the gin glasses. Then the MP took a thick envelope from the inside pocket of his suit jacket and passed it across. The second man, too polite to count the contents then and there, felt at the envelope surreptitiously.

John Evans left the hotel almost at once. He didn't notice a fat, grey-haired Maori wharfie in a black singlet leaning lazily against the hotel verandah; if he had he would have been extremely disconcerted to know it was the same Maori who had interrupted his activities at the Red Rose Parlour. He would have been even more disconcerted if he had known that some people called this Maori the King of the City. Sinatra, who looked as if he was almost asleep in the warm sunshine was surprised to see John Evans again; he watched carefully out of half-closed eyes as the MP, rifling through the papers he had just received inside, walked quickly to a waiting car.

In the afternoon the Head Clerk grudgingly gave permission for John Evans's daughter to show Margaret-Rose Bennett around the whole Bureau.

'Fifteen minutes,' he said. 'That's plenty of time for university types like you two, and watch out for that bloody Catholic from Donegal.'

Emily explained as they left the Land Records room. 'Your boss and my boss are both Irish,' she said. 'Second generation. They were both born here, but they fight about Ireland all the time, you'll get used to it, I saw my boss throw a typewriter at your boss once. To get the point of this place you only have to understand one thing – it's *absolutely packed* with weirdos, it's more or less like a loony bin.'

'I see,' said Maggie.

The first office they went into had MAORI ADOPTIONS on the door. An elderly Maori woman, Mrs Tipene, bustled about. Maggie noticed that she addressed only her, ignoring Emily completely. Emily only smiled to herself and picked at her red nail polish.

'We do things differently from you people,' said Mrs Tipene, showing Maggie the special adoption forms. 'We don't like our people to be lonely. See this one – their only son was run over, so a sister has given them her latest baby. And this one – little Egypt Potae has been adopted by his granny because she's all by herself down south.'

'Won't poor little Egypt Potae be lonely?' asked Emily, 'living with an old lady, away from all his mates?'

'Don't be silly,' said Mrs Tipene sharply, 'and don't talk about things you don't understand.'

A red-headed, freckled young man had come through the door. He shook Maggie's hand gravely. 'I'm Paul,' he said. 'I'm Mrs Tipene's assistant.'

When they were out of earshot Emily said, 'Paul's an epileptic. Mrs Tipene keeps a grey blanket and a piece of wood under her desk for when he has a fit. He reads Russian novels all the time. One of the weirdos. We've even got an unfrocked Methodist minister, I'll show him to you.'

'Quite a lot of Maoris work here, don't they?' said Maggie. 'I didn't expect that. I thought we'd just be helping them, not working with them.'

'None of them are the *bosses* though,' said Emily drily. 'Oh – except one, but he's a maniac, so he doesn't really count.'

Maggie pondered an office like a loony bin, full of weirdos and maniacs and felt that screaming with boredom was perhaps a mild offence, after all.

On the ground floor a notice with an arrow pointed to HOUSING. 'Now here's my department,' said Emily, 'and here's my boss, Paddy O'Rourke.'

A very thin, middle-aged man in an obvious, ill-fitting wig shook Maggie's hand. 'Welcome to the Bureau,' he said. 'I hear you're a bit bored up there. Don't worry, they always send new recruits to that Protestant O'Brien and his land files; it's to test your stamina.'

'My stamina, Mr O'Rourke,' said Maggie politely, 'has been tested to its *utmost limit*,' and Paddy O'Rourke laughed as he went to answer the telephone.

'Well, what do you do here?' Maggie felt she should show appropriate interest.

'We build Maoris *boxes* to live in, actually,' said Emily. 'Two-bedroom, three-bedroom, or very occasionally even four-bedroom boxes, look at this,' and she showed Maggie a little Bureau booklet with pastel drawings of plain, square, almost identical houses. The pastel artist had drawn lots of flowing foliage around the houses: roses and pretty apple trees flowered next to smiling, neatly-dressed brown families.

'Still, Maoris soon learned to jazz up their square houses with bright purple doors or wild, red windowsills,' said Emily. 'You'll start recognising them around the city once you get your eye in. Look for the most colourful houses. *Vulgar*, our mothers would say. And this tall person with the fluffy brown hair is Prudence McDonald, who's a part-time student like us and has the best parties in town.' The tall girl with the fluffy brown hair, passing by carrying files, smiled a gentle, very warm smile.

'Come to my place any night,' said Prudence.

So that's what Prudence's Place means thought Maggie.

'What are you studying, Prudence?' she asked politely.

'Psychology.'

'Oh,' said Maggie, somehow surprised. 'That must be interesting. You must learn a lot about people. Oh – and well – about yourself I suppose.'

'Yes,' said the girl called Prudence, and she smiled again the gentle smile.

At a desk by the door a Maori man in dark glasses was writing. He was also coughing and drinking Baxter's Lung Preserver from a small bottle.

'That's not Baxter's Lung Preserver,' whispered Emily.

'What is it then?'

'Rum.'

'You mean he drinks in the office?' Maggie asked, shocked.

Emily shrugged. 'He does his work. All you have to do in a government department is do your work. You can be as weird as a fish. Look, there's the unfrocked minister, Mr Porter. What do you reckon he did?'

Mr Porter had a round kind face, and spectacles that magnified his eyes. He was on his knees, not praying but putting a piece of paper under Prudence's desk, to stop it wobbling.

On the top floor was the Legal Department. In there a group of white men in suits pored over papers and files.

'I suppose there's no such thing as a Maori lawyer?' said Maggie.

'There was one, Timoti Pou, he was gorgeous, the only Maori I ever saw with blue eyes. He was *gorgeous*. They say both his parents are Maoris so it's some throw-back to some marauding Scandinavian whaler, I expect. But he was one of those serious sort of young men, didn't seem like a bundle of fun to me when he worked here. He's gone to work for a law firm now. Timoti Pou is a bit famous because everyone expects Maoris to be tram drivers really, or work at the freezing works.'

Along the corridor they passed two more doors: one said ALIENATIONS, the next, CONSOLIDATIONS.

'Aren't they quaint names?' said Emily. 'This is where I reckon most of the hanky-panky goes on. Just think about this, it's very simple: in Alienations they take what they call "uneconomic" land from Maoris; in Consolidations they join the bits up and sell them. I bet there's a profit being made somewhere and I wonder who's making it,' she laughed.

Through the glass of the door marked ALIENATIONS a fat Maori man bent over a file and another, with one leg, shouted on the telephone in a foreign language.

'Is he speaking *Maori*?'

'Yeah, that's Hui Windsor shouting, lost his leg in the war. Look – look, there's his false one, propped up in the corner with a shoe on it, see? He takes it off a lot, it's not a very good fit. He gets very bad tempered when he's drunk because his leg hurts as if it's still there but he's a great guitar player. And that fat man next to him, Gallipoli Gordon, is a *fantastic* singer, much better than Mario Lanza. He could've been an opera singer, just wait till you hear him. They often come to Prudence's place.'

'But who speaks Maori? I didn't know anyone spoke Maori.'

'Oh – a few people still do. It's dying of course.'

Manu Taihape whizzed past with his trolley of files down the long corridor, grinned at them both, disappeared round a corner.

Emily grinned too, watching him disappear. 'Manu speaks Maori,' she said. 'You know, one night I was coming home from a party really late and I saw him riding down the hill to the docks, doing about thirty miles an hour *on that trolley*, carrying hundreds of packets of biscuits. He said it must've been one of his cousins when I asked him about it, but it was him, I knew perfectly well it was him, who else would ride a government records trolley down a hill in the middle of the night! God knows what he was up to, he's probably a smuggler or a burglar!' and she laughed. 'We won't go to Welfare,' she continued; 'I hate going there. It's down that long corridor sort of by itself. That's the office where the boss is a maniac Maori,

Bay Ropata. Bay is short for Bayonet because he's got a huge bayonet wound from the war right across his stomach.'

Maggie giggled slightly. 'Have you seen it?'

'No, but all the boys have. They love it. It's from a Turk apparently. Bayonet Ropata, the maniac. He was a captain or a major or something and they say he personally gave all his prisoners of war a big feed before he shot them, in Italy or somewhere. There's always mad people and murderers in Welfare, shouting and screaming, I try to avoid it, too depressing,' and she led Maggie instead down a side flight of stairs to a big room from which a loud clattering sound emerged.

'This is the last office, the Accounts Department. I call it the Women's Room and I don't like coming here either.' As she opened the door the noise got much louder: about a dozen women in summer frocks, some Maori, mostly Pakeha, sat beside piles of files, hunched over their Burroughs book-keeping machines and their electric adding machines. Several of them smiled up at Emily and Maggie but nobody stopped working.

Something disturbed in the room, disturbed Emily and Maggie somewhere inside them; not just the noise but some tension in the air with the cigarette smoke of the working women, something.

They're not young like Emily and me, thought Maggie.

'They keep records of all the Bureau's financial transactions. We call them machinists,' said Emily as she closed the door on the women and the machines. And the two girls giggled for no reason, relieved.

'One of them is a *divorcée* and the rest are old maids,' said Emily as they ran down the corridor and she made *divorcée* sound very French and wicked. Maggie had never met a *divorcée*.

'Well that's enough of the tour,' said Emily, 'or we'll have your boring boss after us. There's also a roomful of typists. One of them, Hope, is blind and works from a dictaphone and she's the best guitarist in the Bureau. And then of course there's the bosses who are all ex-army types. All good, upstanding white chaps of course – except that maniac Bay Ropata. And that's about it. See you.' And Emily darted off down the corridor.

What a strange girl thought Maggie; *she's not like the girls at school*.

But suddenly Emily stopped and came back. 'And of course there's Roimata the telephone operator. I suppose I ought to warn you about her. She listens in to all our phone calls. You'll meet her soon enough, she's the fattest person in the Bureau. Don't expect to be able to keep any secrets here unless you *really* work at it,' and Emily Evans smiled a little smile to herself. 'Watch out for Roimata, she's very fat and she's very jolly and she's very dangerous. OK, can you find your way back? See you.' And Emily was gone.

Maggie stood there for just a moment, quite still in the green corridor. For there was something else in that building. Everywhere, just out of sight, almost out of earshot, there seemed to be a kind of buzzing of music only just contained: snatches of hit-parade songs whistled down passageways, a baritone voice from the lavatories or the stairwell *I found my thrill on blueberry hill* and she could almost swear she could hear again a guitar strumming somewhere in the distance, as if someone had just closed a door. She knew she must be mistaken, of course: this was a government department.

After work a young Maori woman, who Maggie recognised as the wife of Hori Smith who was named after the kings of England, came into the Bureau with their small son and daughter so they could go down town for Friday late-night shopping to buy the kids some shoes. Hori picked up his children and cuddled them, Maggie saw, tied his daughter's hair

back with a green ribbon and wiped her nose with his handkerchief. Later, by chance, in the main street crowded with
late-night shoppers, Maggie saw Hori hit his daughter hard
because she was crying.

The little girl stopped crying and looked up at her father
with huge, dark, totally expressionless eyes.

Maggie stood in the crowded street, motionless, watching,
her heart beating fast.

But when she got home, when she quietly opened the back
door, her mother was in the kitchen. Doing something with
a tea-towel, or a cake tin, but not really: as if she had been
waiting.

'Hello, Mum,' said Maggie, suddenly standing very still.
'Just been late-night shopping.'

'You've been smoking,' Mrs Bennett said. Then she hit
Maggie across the face.

After the first, instinctive raising of her hand to her face,
Maggie stood absolutely still, as she always did.

'Don't think you can just come and go from here as if you
were living in a hotel, not taking your share of responsibility,'
Mrs Bennett said, in her voice that never rose. 'And we have
warned you not to smoke. Women who smoke are disgust-
ing.'

And she turned and walked out of the kitchen, her beautiful mother. Maggie heard the bedroom door close.

Their second daughter stood in the kitchen till everything
was still. Faintly she heard the sound of the wireless that her
father was listening to coming through the wall, and the
sound of laughter. 'Much Binding in the Marsh' perhaps or
'Take it from Here'.

She did not cry. She never did. When her mother had gone
she made just one faint sound, as if to let out pain. Then she,
too, walked into her bedroom and closed the door. In her

narrow bed with the pink candlewick bedspread she listened to the sea.

Tonight she did not dream of a child being hit but made herself think of books again. Books were safe. Dreaming her neat, censored re-dreams of her day she dreamed – though even in her dream she knew they weren't quite books exactly – of the leather-covered registers and the rustling, silent land files in the courtroom. But they were books of a kind. And she thought of course that they were safe, and free from violence.

Just before she woke, Manu Taihape came speeding and laughing down her street by the sea with a trolley full of chocolate fish.

SIX

When the old bus was ready to pull away from the corner of the dusty road where the manuka and the blackberry bushes grew, Timoti Pou, who had such unusual blue eyes and who was almost a qualified lawyer, waved goodbye with a kind of relief.

His old Uncle Heke stood slightly apart from the others. All weekend his uncle had addressed him in Maori, embarrassed him. He had always been unhappy about the way Timoti had been sent away to school when he was young. '*He Pakeha ia; he has become a Pakeha*,' he would say to the family, and sometimes he spat.

Timoti's parents waved, and some small children, a cousin's small children, ran round and round, hitting each other and laughing and falling over in the dust. Timoti's younger brother, named Tumatauenga after the God of War but always called Pumpkin, stood smoking. An eighteen-year-old fat boy who seemed to be bored. Timoti did not see the look of longing on Pumpkin's face as he sometimes stole a glance at his clever older brother.

The bus driver had left the motor running; he kicked the tyres and cuffed the children and climbed back on board. The doors wheezed together. They all waved till the bus disappeared from view, a crowd of Maoris waving and waving in the late afternoon sunshine before they got into their broken-down cars to drive back to their small village that wasn't on the bus route.

Timoti sat back in his bus seat, felt the broken spring. He hadn't been home for over a year. He felt disoriented again, as he always did; uneasy in a way he couldn't understand; fell asleep almost at once, his head resting on his arm, leaning against the window.

'Hey, Timoti!' He opened his eyes again and to his amazement saw it was dark and they were on the outskirts of the city. The lights of the harbour shone in the distance. He must've been asleep for over four hours.

'Hey, Timoti!' said the voice again and he realised it was the bus driver. 'Wake up Timoti, good weekend, mate?'

'Yeah.' He rubbed at his face, looked around. The bus was now almost empty. 'I can't have been asleep that long?'

'Yeah. You were out to it. Been to your sister's unveiling?'

The bus driver came from a village near Timoti's, they were related somehow, knew each other's families: more than a year ago Timoti's young sister had been killed by a drunk driver as she crossed the road in the nearest town.

'Yeah. Long time since I've been home.' Timoti stretched and yawned.

'*E hoa*, don't you miss your family?' The driver looked at Timoti in his mirror.

'I'm very busy,' said Timoti, 'there isn't time. I had to work over Christmas.'

'How's your Mum?'

'She's OK. There were lots of them there, at the unveiling, it was good for her.'

'*Ka pai*, that's good.' And the bus driver murmured a small prayer for the spirit of Timoti's sister, who had been pretty and bright and who had been going to be a school teacher and help her people.

After a while he asked: 'You still work at the Bureau?'

'No,' said Timoti, 'I'm working for a law firm now.'

The driver laughed in approval. '*Ka pai*!' he said again. 'Man, you must be the first Maori lawyer we've ever had!'

'After this year maybe,' said Timoti drily, 'and there's others as well as me, there's always been Maori lawyers, famous ones. You should know your history.'

'Well, I've never seen one in the newspaper,' said the driver firmly, as if that settled things. 'You get those white fellas, man, play them at their own game, get all our land back,' and they both laughed. 'Did you have crayfish?'

'Yeah, my brother went out, we had heaps for lunch,' and Timoti glanced up at the old suitcase in the sagging luggage rack where two more crayfish that Pumpkin had given him lay carefully wrapped in newspaper among the shirts his mother had washed and ironed.

As the bus turned into the main road to the railway station, slowing in the darkness, waiting for a few cars coming the other way, the driver said: 'Not many left now in Rangimarie, eh, Ti? Just the old folks. I haven't been there for a while but I heard they've all gone.'

'Yeah. It's like a ghost village. There's a few babies the girls have had in the city, they take them home, leave them with the grandparents. And a few families still live there. But – almost nobody.'

'Yeah. Pretty dry, eh? They've even closed the shop at the crossroads since last year, they tell you?'

'Yeah.'

'My wife, she wants me to get off this bus route, settle in the city, drive the trams.'

'Yeah?'

'Better for the kids, she says.'

'Yeah. She's probably right.'

'Yeah. There'll be no one left soon, in our villages.' And the bus pulled in next to other buses at the station under a hoarding where a blonde girl smiled with white, white teeth and said

MAKE A DATE
WITH COLGATE
AND YOUR DATE WILL DATE YOU AGAIN!

Timoti swung his battered case with the crayfish and the shirts from the rack. In the lights shining out from the terminus he could see that the old bus was covered in dust from the country roads. He opened the case and took out one of the crayfish in newspaper and gave it to the bus driver, whose face lit up with pleasure. Timoti waved goodbye.

Carrying the suitcase he walked through the dark, empty, Sunday-evening streets, pausing for a moment under a streetlight to light a cigarette. He kept walking till he came to the Maori Men's Hostel run by the Presbyterian church, in a side street down by the docks; a huge old wooden house that had seen much grander days. He rang the bell and an elderly, yawning warden came to the door.

'Hello, Koro. Sorry to wake you.'

'Ah, *haere mai*, come in, come in Timoti, *kia ora, kia ora*, how was the unveiling, how's your Mum?'

'Good,' said Timoti, 'she's good, it was good.' The warden wanted to talk, to have a cup of tea, to sit and talk of death and families, but Timoti moved on firmly. He walked to his room at the back of the building by the fire escape. In the hall a handwritten notice said, NO FEMALE VISITORS WITHOUT PERMISSION.

He sat on the bed. Going home threw him, disturbed him: Rangimarie so quiet as if nothing had changed, the tiny cluster of houses; all the old people, doing nothing, wasting away. He wanted nothing to do with that life.

But now his boss at the law firm wanted him to *learn* some Maori language, thought it might be useful for business. But the language was dying, what was the point? And he thought again about how his Uncle Heke had spoken only Maori to him, as if he was trying to stop the bleeding away of the words he knew. Timoti had understood almost nothing, felt exasperated by his uncle's childishness; but he felt disoriented also, as if something drummed at his heart. He opened the old suitcase and took out the second crayfish. Someone had said that Pumpkin had put out the traps with a torch in the middle of the night so that Timoti could have a feed of crayfish before he left. He stared at it, at the red shell, at the claws, remembering how his father had caught them so often when Timoti was a child, brought them home for their mother to cook, how they'd watched them turn red in the big pot, how the sun had shone. How alien it all felt now.

There in the small bedroom, sitting on the narrow bed, still wearing his raincoat, Timoti Pou ate the whole crayfish, cracking the legs, sucking the flesh, eating and eating quite fast till it was finished.

He was twenty-three years old.

And in the dark, empty, silent streets Sinatra, King of the City, walked.

SEVEN

In the high room the teacher of the night class said: **Whenua** *is the Maori word for land, one of the most important words in the language. The fact that it is also the word for afterbirth (which was traditionally buried on the land:* **te whenua ki te whenua***) implies an irrevocable bonding. For Maoris, their land was their life.*

In the French lecture room, as evening fell over the city, the hairs coming out of the professor's ears curled around his ear lobes. As he spoke and threw his gowned arms around in a dramatic, Gallic fashion the ear lobes wiggled. Maggie watched the ears with a kind of grim fascination as he droned on in French about Guy de Maupassant.

There was something in her that baulked at the language; it wasn't just the professor's ears. France was on the other side of the world; she wanted to be free to live her life without seeing the Eiffel Tower. It would take six weeks – *forty-two days* – to get to England and then she would have to cross the English Channel and then she would have to go up to a Frenchman and say, *excusez-moi monsieur, voulez-vous dites moi ou est le Tour d'Eiffel*, carrying her collection of de Maupassant short stories in her purse.

She would rather go to Hollywood and meet Burt Lancaster in his bathing togs.

She sighed with relief when the lecture at last droned to a

close; stood then, undecided, in the big entrance hall of the university; *shall I go to the library and write my essay on 'Ode on a Grecian Urn', shall I go to the cafeteria, shall I go home?* Students milled about her, rushed past with intent. The bearded poet who she'd heard shouting, 'OUR POETRY, OUR POETRY', kissed a girl dressed in black who had black make-up round her eyes. They stood at the entrance, kissing passionately, oblivious. Maggie stared, fascinated: observed the poet's tongue roving about. Finally she looked at her watch and sighed. *Oh, well. I suppose I could go and see Eddie Albert.*

Edward Albert Bennett, Maggie's cousin, was much older than her. He was twenty-four and in advertising which he said was the road to the future. He lived with his colleagues in a flat near the university, he had three sisters of his own who lived down south and he treated Maggie as if she was his fourth and about ten years old. He spent a great deal of his advertising salary betting on the horses, as if gambling was the road to the future also, and tonight, when she called to see him he instructed her to fry him and herself some eggs and steak while he checked the racing results. Maggie bent over his gas stove, turning the big red pieces of meat over and over while he sat at the kitchen table with his shoes off, reciting names of horses like a kind of religious litany. She could smell his socks, slightly.

Later, when his girlfriend Shirley arrived, and the other advertising colleagues he shared the flat with, he looked at his watch and insisted everyone sit down and listen to his latest jingle which was getting a run on the wireless. The group of them listened with varying degrees of politeness and interest.

Maggie broke the silence. 'You don't mean you wrote that?' she said incredulously, 'And that you're *admitting* it?

WEETABIX IS CRISP AND CRUNCHEEEEEE
IT'S ALSO VERY MUNCHEEEE

'You didn't write that Eddie did you?'

Eddie Albert ignored her, told them he was being moved to Cleansing Agents. 'I'm going to make up little songs and poems about Reckitts Blue and Rinso and Clever Mary,' he said. 'I'm going to start a fashion for musical and literary commercials.'

Everyone was very impressed except Maggie who groaned and threw herself onto the landlord's orange sofa in disgust, her wild hair spreading everywhere. 'Literary commercials,' she cried, 'it's an oxymoron!'

'What's an oxymoron?' asked Eddie's friend Peter.

'You are,' said Eddie. 'And you, young lady, watch yourself, or they'll take you away to the loony bin.'

Maggie sighed. He always said this. She'd better not tell him she worked in one now.

Later he went into the bedroom with his girlfriend and shut the door while Maggie was listening to the 'Lever Hit Parade' on his wireless. Elvis Presley sang

> Well it's one for the money
> Two for the show
> Three to get ready
> Now go man go

and Eddie's friend Peter lounged beside her on the orange sofa. Maggie knew he was very proud of writing one of the hoarding advertisements by the railway station:

MAKE A DATE
WITH COLGATE
AND YOUR DATE WILL DATE YOU AGAIN !

and that he'd got a special commendation for thinking of such clever words even if he didn't know what an oxymoron was.

The love song drifted. Quite unexpectedly Peter, who had been leaning casually, rather patronisingly, towards her with his arm along the back of the sofa talking about his girlfriend, grabbed at her and, before she even properly understood what was happening, with a quick bit of expert twisting of underclothes he pushed his finger up into her vagina, moving his finger, flicking it. Maggie was deeply shocked, outraged, and shaken by feelings she didn't understand. She bit Peter extremely hard, and went home on the tram without saying goodbye to Eddie Albert, her body shaking as if she was suddenly very cold.

The almost empty tram rattled out towards the sea and in the inside compartment Maggie shivered still and felt an uncomfortable feeling between her legs. 'From Here to Eternity' and slow kissing seemed a long, long way away, if this was sex.

Her mother's bedroom door was closed.

Her father sat in an armchair. The wireless was still on but he had fallen asleep, his hook on the floor beside him, as usual. Maggie huddled in the doorway of the lounge and saw how sad his face was in repose. She crept away into her own room.

She held herself in her arms and for a long time lay listening to the sea. She only knew the word *vagina* because she'd seen an explicit drawing inside the cubicle of a public toilet at the railway station. An arrow pointed, and VAGINA was written neatly in red, as if a rude biology teacher was filling in time. In her mind Maggie pushed away what had happened to her until it began to recede: smaller and smaller, almost disappearing.

EIGHT

The summer early mornings were beautiful, in that city.

Timoti Pou, the Maori with blue eyes, always walked to work in his three-piece suit to the law office where he was employed. Every morning, as he walked to his life in the Pakeha world he passed notices in the windows of the big old boarding houses in the city:

ROOMS TO LET BREAKFAST PROVIDED
£2/10/- PER WEEK
NO CHILDREN MAORIS OR DOGS.

The beautiful summer morning shone brightly, although the summer was almost over.

*

'Ode on a Grecian Urn' was becoming an urgent problem.

At lunchtime the boys lounged in the office talking about rugby and Manu Taihape was speeding around the room on his records trolley, scoring nifty tries. A group of Maoris was sitting on the green in the sun outside the Bureau, so Maggie – desperate to find a place to write her essay – went back to the Maori Land Court and opened the door, pushing it open with

her bottom, her arms full of books and a peanut butter sandwich.

The Court was sitting. Judge Peters, old and bald, sat at the
bench in a black gown, there was a white wig beside him on
the bench. Maggie dropped her books in surprise, blushed,
slid into one of the empty chairs at the back of the courtroom,
trying to move her books towards her with her foot.

She had heard about Judge Peters: her boss had warned her
what Judge Peters would do if he found bite marks on legal
records. Maggie made herself extremely small. An even older
man than Judge Peters, a Maori, stood before the bench; he
walked about and hit a carved stick on the wooden floor-
boards as he spoke in Maori, giving what seemed to Maggie
to be a very flowery, twirly oration. *It sounds beautiful.* The
strange words soared, echoed, yet there was a softness and a
gentleness. *Shame it's dying.* She let herself sink into the sound.
The man would stop every now and then and give a little
cough and another Maori man sitting by the judge would
translate into English. It was about an extra son and some
land and a woman called Te Ngaire. There was only one other
person in the courtroom, an old Maori woman sitting on one
of the wooden chairs.

And then to Maggie's astonishment, Judge Peters, an
elderly white man, leaned forward and asked the old man a
question *in Maori* to which the old man replied quite simply,
dropping his oratorial tone altogether. The unfamiliar, soft
language drifted leisurely about the room, as if it belonged
there. The two bald heads, one white one brown, leant
together and Maggie thought: *they're chatting in Maori! I didn't
know it was a chatting language.*

Suddenly the elderly Maori woman stood up and began to
sing in a strange, chanting voice. After a moment the old
Maori man joined in. Strange atonal sounds in the dark room
under the harsh electric lightbulb, beside the rustling files and

the empty chairs. Again Maggie felt, in this odd place, a strange, cold, prickling feeling at the back of her neck. Disoriented, she clumsily got up with her books and left. In the sunny corridor she shook herself: *don't be silly.*

She went down the street to buy a bottle of Coca-Cola. As she walked she ate the peanut butter sandwich she'd made for herself early that morning. Coming back to the office she saw the old man and woman who had been in the courtroom sitting on the grass with the other Maoris, eating fish and chips out of a newspaper. The carved stick lay beside them; children ran and laughed and fell. The darkness of the Bureau building seemed oppressive when she went inside again and she could hear at once the boys still playing rugby in the Land Files office. Unwillingly she entered the Land Court again.

In that strange, dark room, cut off from the sunshine and the hint of guitars, Maggie dutifully read John Keats, and composed her essay.

> Heard melodies are sweet, but those unheard
> Are sweeter; therefore ye soft pipes play on;
> Not to the sensual ear, but, more endear'd,
> Pipe to the spirit ditties of no tone:
> Fair youth beneath the trees, thou canst not leave
> Thy song, nor ever can those trees be bare . . .

'Ode on a Grecian Urn' is a poem about time, she began. *About catching a moment in time and holding it forever.*

All around her the silent rustling of the old land files, and the dust.

The afternoon shimmered with late-summer heat and with cigarette smoke as the clerks sat in the airless room: filling in records, copying, smoking, murmuring to each other. Ties were loosened, socks pushed down. The door opened: a handsome, stocky, grey-haired Maori filled the room at once with his presence, the boys put down their pens.

'*Kia ora, Bay. Tena koe, Bay.*'

As he walked in to talk to their boss Maggie realised this must be the one called Bayonet, the one Maori boss in the whole Bureau, the one with the bayonet wound from a Turk right across his stomach. *A maniac,* Emily had said. Maggie looked at him suspiciously from under her eyes. She saw how proudly the boys looked at him, how they caught his eye-lashes, exchanged some words, laughed with him. And when he'd gone, the boys drooped again.

The monotonous work became almost hypnotic in the heat, the Maori names in the registers mixing in Maggie's mind with the Maori voices from the grass outside floating up through the open window. She caught again the soft beauty of the sounds, and there was a lot of laughter outside and the sun slanted in across the office floor and she wrote: *Aroha Pomana: 12 acres 3 roods 20 perches.* She did not yet know that *aroha* was the Maori word for love.

A woman sang beneath the open window in a high, clear voice:

Pa mai to reo aroha.

Maggie put down her pen, stared at the ink on her fingers and listened to the singing. Others were singing too, out in the sunshine. Inside the Bureau Hori Smith, named after English kings, but who Maggie had seen hitting his daughter, kept on writing but quite unconsciously had started singing with them,

ki te pae o Aotearoa

and from the front of the room where he was sorting files

Rangi Cox, with his cigarette drooping, joined in, only in harmony. Even Harry Beans stopped writing and listened. So that the hot, boring afternoon in a government office became something quite else, something odd, different: unseen people in the sun and people in the stuffy room above singing in unison.

This is a really funny place to work, thought Maggie. *It must be the weirdest place in the country. I bet they don't sing in the Education Department. I wonder what they're singing about.*

When the song finished Hori got up and called out the window in Maori to the people on the grass outside; a lot more laughter.

They're chatting again, thought Maggie.

'Come on, Hori, get on with your work,' said the Head Clerk, but not unkindly. Hori and Rangi laughed and chucked a few Maori words around and gradually the afternoon became itself again: clerks filling in land registers and cigarette smoke curling upwards in the still, hot room.

Margaret-Rose Bennett looked down at her own writing: *Aroha Pomana: 12 acres 3 roods 20 perches.*

She picked up her pen to copy the rest of the names into the old leather-bound book.

And then obliquely, out of nowhere, the thought came.

I wonder what would happen if I learnt that language?

NINE

In the high room the teacher at the night class said to her pupils: *Pakeha is a Maori word meaning, literally, a white person, someone who is not a Maori. There are various theories about how this word evolved: **pakepakeha** means imaginary beings resembling men, with fair skins. It seems to have no pejorative meaning: simply a white person. But there is, perhaps, another meaning. It is said that the first white people to arrive in the far north, the whalers and the sailors, were of very poor quality. 'Bugger yer,' they said, swaying drunkenly along the seafront at the first, rum-soaked, white settlements, 'Bugger yer.'*

*There is no 'B' sound in Maori: the natives puzzling over this often-used expression repeated it as they heard it. These men, these first white visitors were the 'Bugger yer' men. The **Pakeha**.*

*

In the university library books reached up to the ceiling, row on row; Maggie stared upwards: she had never seen so many books in her life. She breathed in the indefinable smell of them. All this knowledge was accessible to her; now at last she would become *knowledgeable*. Just at the corner of her mind, a thought scrabbled, tried to get in: *is there something different about me? Why is it like this?* But she pushed it away, shut the crack at the corner of her mind tightly, in case the crack turned out to be a ravine. But if she became more knowledgeable something might hold her down, root her, so that she could dare to push open the door, and understand everything at last. *And then I could fly up into the sky and be really brainy.*

She found, on reading the university syllabus, that there were courses in French and German and Italian and Russian and Spanish and Latin and Ancient Greek. But not Maori.

So she would never learn the singing language, after all.

She took a book about the life of John Keats from one of the shelves, sat at one of the library tables. As the evening light faded through the tall windows she occasionally looked up, covertly watched other people whispering together. The crippled boy's crutches were placed against the wall, near his seat. A wind got up outside, rattled at an open window; chillier night air blew in, girls put on cardigans. Later Maggie drifted into the student cafeteria and ate a meat pie, smiling nervously at some students she knew slightly.

As she wandered disconnectedly round the entrance hall she saw two things:

On the English Department noticeboard a typed notice announced that there was to be a lecture on Indigenous Writers in the third term. In brackets was written: KATHERINE MANSFIELD. Underneath someone had written in ink in big letters, AND OUR OWN POETS PLEASE!

And on another noticeboard a hand-written piece of paper informed her that adult education classes in the Maori language were held at the university at 7 PM on Thursdays.

She tried to phone her friend Susan at her hospital when she got home, to see if she'd got a doctor yet; was informed she was on night duty.

*

On Thursday Maggie very nearly didn't go. Her hated French lecture finished at five to seven and her stomach was rumbling and the summer seemed suddenly to have disappeared and she was cold. She found an old chocolate fish in her bag and climbed tiredly up the stairs, biting off its head.

In a small room right at the very top of the building she heard someone talking *French*. She turned on her heel, deciding she'd made a mistake, deciding to go home. She bumped, literally, into a Maori man who was coming in. He gave her such a look of disdain that she stopped walking and stared at him in surprise. What a snooty man. Why wasn't he laughing? Maoris *always* laughed, she knew that much. That's what they *did*.

And then she heard from inside the room a woman say: 'Good evening to anybody who is new this week. My name is Isobel Arapeta and I am your Maori tutor for this series of evening classes.' In a strong Scots accent.

Maggie actually giggled slightly in surprise, then pulled herself together and found a seat at the back. It was only an hour, she hadn't paid yet, she needn't come again. In the class there were two tired-looking nuns, a Greek man, an Indian; and there was an actual French woman who wanted to learn Maori: she wore a black brassiere under a white blouse and her husband wore a beret like the one Maggie had been forced to squash her unruly hair under, when she was at school. She stared at him in amazement. *Fancy wearing one voluntarily.* There were also several women of Maggie's mother's age who looked nothing at all, she thought, like her mother, not nearly so beautiful. And there were two Maoris, the snooty, unsmiling one she'd collided with and a very good-looking one in a grey, three-piece suit and a raincoat, who had blue eyes.

'Nau mai, haere mai,' said the teacher who had been born in Edinburgh, smiling at Maggie. 'Welcome.'

And then the teacher in the high room said to her pupils:

Matauranga is the Maori word for knowledge, for understanding. *It is my hope that if you persevere with these classes* **matauranga** *is what you will acquire.*

'What do you mean, you're learning *Maori*?' said her mother, sitting in the lounge, her needle going in and out of the cloth, in and out, as usual. Maggie's mother embroidered cloths: table cloths, tea cloths, tray cloths, tea-trolley cloths, napkins to go in silver rings, towels for guests to dry their hands on; intricate but similar patterns of ladies in crinolines standing at a trellised gate that had roses growing round it, and in the garden beyond, hyacinths and lilacs and pansies. Margaret-Rose Bennett grew up with that picture embroidered on her soul.

'What for?' said her mother. 'Nobody learns Maori.' She was so beautiful that Maggie's heart leapt sometimes, looking at her.

'It's only an hour a week,' said Maggie, standing in the doorway, 'it's nothing, it will come in handy for my work, that's all.'

'You don't really need it,' her father said doubtfully, 'just because you work in the Bureau. It's a dying language, it's no use, and surely you need the time for your English and your French.'

Maggie felt her parents staring at her, felt their disapproval, but stood there with an odd stubbornness. The grandfather clock ticked in the hall.

'It's only an hour,' she said, 'it's nothing.'

She tried to phone Susan at her hospital again but they said she was asleep.

By the second Thursday she had bought a copy of the one textbook, which she'd found in a second-hand bookshop.

'It was an oral language,' said Isobel Arapeta, 'passed on as all Maori culture and learning were passed on, orally, from generation to generation. It was never written down, the written word was not part of the Maori culture. But there were, of course, very important learning establishments where all aspects of Maori culture were carefully preserved and passed on by, and to, specially chosen men.'

'Not women?' said Maggie shyly.

'Not women,' said Isobel, and she threw an oblique glance in Maggie's direction for just a moment.

'The early missionaries wanted to translate the Bible of course, so they learnt the language and needed to write it down. And government officials of the nineteenth century needed it to be written in documents. These British people wrote it down phonetically as best they could. Every vowel is pronounced in Maori, as in the Italian language – in fact its similarity in sound to the Italian language is quite remarkable.'

She picked up a piece of chalk and wrote on the blackboard:

take

'This word is not pronounced "take" as in English but *ta-ke*: it means *a cause* or *a reason*. All you have to remember is that every vowel is pronounced – that is one of the keys to speaking this beautiful language.'

Then she picked up a large, old book. 'And, luckily for us, one of the early missionaries put together the first edition of this Maori–English dictionary and printed it on one of the first printing presses, over a hundred years ago.'

And then, just to give them something they knew, in translation, Isobel Arapeta, who had come out from Scotland as a young schoolteacher years ago and married a Maori taxi driver, read the twenty-third psalm aloud:

Ko Ihowa taku hepara, e kore ahau e hapa . . .

I shall not want. **E kore ahau e hapa.** Maggie wriggled slightly with the pleasure of listening. Isobel read the psalm with her beautiful Maori accent; the rich, soft words all ending in a vowel floated around the small, chilly classroom. Maggie felt sorry that one of the tired nuns was asleep and missing this; saw also how his unusual blue eyes made the good-looking Maori so striking.

Outside the window, March now, it was dark and the wind blew and the city lay glittering below them. That night Maggie brought the big, old dictionary carefully into her dreams.

Next day in the office she said to the Head Clerk: 'Could I be excused for a little while to lie down, I've got a sore stomach.' She saw he was terrified that she would say the word *period* out loud: he waved her away quickly, permission to leave.

She went into the university library. She read the regulations and conditions very carefully. Then she knocked at the door of one of the administrators. 'Excuse me, do you think I could sit Maori for my Bachelor of Arts language paper instead of French?' She stood anxiously in the doorway, her weight on one foot, like a nervous horse. He frowned, motioned her to sit down; she held her hands together tightly, poised on the very edge of the chair.

He looked down at her records, then peered at her over his glasses. The students called him Winston behind his back: he rather cultivated the look and manner of Winston Churchill. He had obviously been taught to speak, or endeavoured to speak, like an Englishman but his own vowel sounds kept popping through, flatter and more nasal.

'Mmmmmmmmmm. Margaret-Rose Bennett, Tiny Bennett's daughter, eh? I knew your father, he was a great rugby player in his time I remember, shame about the war. Does he still work for the government?'

'Yes.'

'Why?'

'Pardon?'

'Why do you want to learn Maori?'

Maggie fidgeted, not knowing what to answer, and at that moment into her mind came a vision of Manu Taihape whizzing down streets with trolleys full of chocolate biscuits, whizzing along and laughing. She could not of course say it was something to do with *laughing*: the thing Maggie found so hard to do.

She blushed and looked down at her hands and said: 'I don't know. I just do.'

'Of course you must take a language for your BA but what's wrong with French?'

'I want to learn Maori.'

'We have no examination in that language at this university.'

'I thought I could do it extramurally. I read in the university rules that it was possible, that another university could set and mark the papers . . .' Her voice fell away.

'French will be much more useful.'

'I *hate* French,' said Maggie suddenly, angrily. 'I'm no good at it, you can see from my records already – look, look, I got seven out of twenty for my first test! I hate it, I can't connect with it. I want to learn Maori, it's beautiful.'

'What do you mean you *hate* French? You can't just dismiss a whole language on your own little personal prejudices and failures you know, you sound like a schoolgirl. Please try and remember you're at university now.'

Maggie looked down at her hands. 'Sorry,' she said. He smiled a very Churchillian smile, looking over his glasses again. She had a very strong desire to bite him, wondered what exactly would happen to her if she bit a university administrator.

'My dear, you must understand, there isn't any *literature*. Learning a language is a way into another past, another culture, and most of all into another literature. What is there to find by studying a language, if there is not literature?'

'There's the Bible.'

He smiled more broadly. 'That's *our* literature, *our* culture, not theirs, that's something we enabled them to have, something we wrote down for them.'

'It wasn't written down in English first, someone enabled us as well.' She heard his fingers tapping impatiently on his desk. There was ink on her fingers and she thought about the singing. 'There's the songs.'

This time he laughed. 'Do you know where most of the melodies you hear come from? Even those are ours. They are not Maori tunes,' – the word *tunes* had a particularly un-British intonation to it, a rising inflection – 'but rather songs brought over here by Europeans. Cheap Victorian ballads most of them, whistled by the whalers.' He sat back, triumphant.

She sat very still, she had read the rules carefully. She thought of the strange chant she'd heard the old woman singing in the Maori Land Court. Not a Victorian ballad.

'I really very much want to do it extramurally for my degree. I'm working in the Bureau.'

'Well I'm sure *that* won't be a permanent career,' and it sounded something like a sneer.

But she tried again. 'The term is only a few weeks old, I've already enrolled in Maori adult education classes.'

'Isobel Arapeta?'

'Yes.'

'Ah.' Something stirred in the room, a feeling about ladies from Edinburgh marrying Maori taxi drivers drifted uneasily along the bookshelves. Finally he said, tapping his fingers again: 'Well, it's odd you should ask. I've had a request from two Maori gentlemen to do the same thing. If other universities don't mind marking our students' papers who, after all, am I to complain?' He stopped tapping and pulled at his shirt cuffs from under his jacket. 'Have you discussed this with your parents?'

'No.'

'Ah. Well I would if I were you, you would be embarking on something extremely difficult and I would like to feel you had your parents' permission to do something so –' he paused delicately, 'eccentric.'

'Oh – they'll understand completely,' said Margaret-Rose Bennett quickly. 'You can be sure of that. They'll want me to do it. They'll love it.'

He frowned. 'It is odd, your request. At least the other two are Maoris, clinging on to their past. I can't see that such a decision will be of much use to you in the future. I don't imagine there's much you can actually *do* with it once you've learnt it. And it will be very hard work to do it on your own, you obviously don't realise.'

The impulse to bite him was almost overpowering. But she smiled instead. A very Princess Margaret-Rose kind of smile, regal. NO MORE FRENCH.

'I will work very hard,' she said. 'Thank you.'

And down her street that evening where you could smell the sea, the wind blew and her hair danced and she danced herself, just a little bit. She passed her house and walked on to the sand: the tide was going out, she could see the dark shapes of the hidden rocks appearing, and the wind had whipped up the waves. She stood right near the water and tore pages out of her French textbooks and flung them as far as she could. Then she threw the remains of the books after them.

She watched them for a moment and then, although there was a real chill in the air now, she took off her clothes, laid them neatly on the sand under a stone to stop them blowing away, tied up her hair with a rubber band and ran into the cold, dark water, away from where she knew the rocks were. She reached the white, torn pages and the dark covers of the French books, grabbed them from the choppy waves, threw them further. She swam and then threw pages further out, swam and threw.

'Bugger off back to France!' she called loudly.

For a moment she watched, shivering, as the waves dragged all the paper further and further out to sea.

When she looked back at the dark water from the deserted beach, drying herself with her cardigan, she couldn't see any paper at all. Then she walked back up the road. In her bag the one Maori textbook lay.

At the front gate she smoothed down her hair and a shadow crossed her face briefly. Then she went inside.

On the beach only one torn piece of a French textbook remained. It blew along the beach, got caught in one of the sandhills; by morning it was buried under the sand.

TEN

In that city you couldn't see the sea, or smell the sea, or hear the sea, from Manu Taihape's street although it was named Brighton Street, in memory of Home.

Manu Taihape, the Bureau clerk who carried his files on a trolley, whose smile lit up his face like sunshine, lived in a Bureau house. There were two bedrooms. Manu slept in the sitting room with two of his younger brothers; their clothes were neatly folded on the floor in piles and Manu's jackets hung from a curtain rail. The four younger children still slept on an old mattress on a bedroom floor, their clothes folded neatly on the one chair and in the cardboard boxes in the room. The baby slept in a drawer in the parents' bedroom or sometimes in bed with them, though mostly the parents weren't there, they were out singing the old songs and drinking DB bitter. The younger children turned and nuzzled and fell against each other in the night; Manu stayed out late in his old maroon Chevrolet that he so treasured, making love to girls.

Manu's grandfather lived in Brighton Street too, a few doors along in a smaller house. He lived with two of his grandchildren from a daughter who had died of TB. One of the grandchildren was called a Mongol. She had funny eyes and was ten years old and leaned on the broken gate talking to passers-by. Some of Manu's aunties lived in Brighton Street too. Or in nearby streets, Hastings Street or Margate Street.

At 4.35 PM *sharp* every afternoon the fire bell was rung briefly and the Bureau emptied. The pens went down mid-sentence, the files were closed mid-entry, and the men were gone: down to the Prince of Wales Hotel in the city's main street for some urgent drinking before the pubs closed at six o'clock. But Manu Taihape always went straight home with loaves of bread and brown paper bags full of tomatoes or sweet corn or mutton chops or potatoes. Or sometimes fish and chips in newspapers.

In the summer time blowflies buzzed lazily at the open packet of sugar on the kitchen table of Manu's house and cats played around the meat-safe in the yard. When the wild storms came to that city, winds whipped round the rusty cars with no wheels that were parked at the front of the house on the overgrown lawn, and blew open the front door that didn't close properly, over the bare boards in the small hall and in under the torn lino in the kitchen. When it rained, the water leaked in over the windowsills of the house but Manu loved the sound of the rain falling and drumming on the corrugated-iron roof of his home.

'Listen,' he would say to the kids, 'listen to the rain on the roof, aren't we lucky to be cosy inside,' and all the kids would jostle and fall and laugh as the rain fell, and dance to music from the old wireless.

> I found my thrill,
> On Blueberry Hill

they would sing.

'Where's Blueberry Hill, Manu?'

'Oh – well, Blueberry Hill, yeah. It's a long, long way away. It's in town. Up on the hills. Blueberry Hill.'

'Can you get there on the tram?'

'Nah. Not really. You'd have to walk for days. Or go on the car.'

'Has it got blue berries?'

'Oh, yeah. Yeah, lots of blue berries. And honeysuckle. And just one house, where guitars play.'

'Can we go there and hear the guitars?'

'One day.'

'Will you take us on your car one day?'

'Yeah. 'Course.'

> I found my thrill,
> On the blue berry hill

sang the children.

Manu's grandfather had brought the family to the city years ago from his small village further north where there was no work. Manu had been nine years old. But Manu's father never got a job in the city either. He drank, was on social security and went to parties with his wife and sang old songs.

Manu! the children would cry seeing Manu come home from his work at the Bureau, *Manu!* And he would blow their noses on tea towels and butter bread every evening, before he put on the clothes he had carefully washed and ironed and went out in his old maroon Chevrolet to make love to girls, who were warmed by the sunshine in his smile.

He was eighteen.

The men almost ran at 4.35 PM: there was so little time. From all over the city men of all shapes and sizes in shorts and ties, hurrying.

Emily Evans, Prudence McKenzie and, this evening, their new colleague Margaret-Rose Bennett (Prudence holding the arm of Hope Green, the Maori typist who was blind) walked past the wide open window of the Prince of Wales and heard the roar of men drinking fast. They saw hoses attached to huge barrels of beer and hundreds of men jostling to get their glasses and jugs filled and emptied and filled again: the nightmare of the Women's Christian Temperance Union come true. Up and down the counter went the hoses and wet money slapped across. The noise and the smell of beer came cascading out of the window, the noise deafening as six o'clock approached.

Emily and Prudence and Margaret-Rose and Hope walked past the public bar in their stiletto heels. They knew they weren't allowed in: not only were they under twenty-one – a fact that might possibly be overlooked – but they were *women*. Women couldn't go in of course; it was against the law.

'Who'd want to go in that pig-swill place!' said Hope the blind Maori typist turning her nose away in distaste from the strong smell of the beer.

'Who'd want to go into that bedlam!' agreed Emily, glancing scornfully at the hoses and the wet pennies and the sweating men.

'Do they go every night?' asked Maggie, amazed at the noise and the crowds; there weren't any hotels out by the sea.

'Every single night of the week,' said Emily, 'they're terrified to write one more word on a file after 4.35 PM in case they miss some drinking time; they know they've only got till six, those hoses are pulled off the moment the clock strikes six, like Cinderella, that's it, finish, they'll turn into a row of pumpkins!' And she laughed. 'My father does it too, of course, but he drinks gins and things in the Parliament bar non-stop, they all do it, we're a nation of drunks.'

'Drunk *men*,' said Prudence mildly.

'Hmmmmm,' said Hope, who loved whisky.

'Hmmmm,' agreed Emily, who loved sherry, and she laughed again. 'But think of a nation of drunks being governed by a parliament of drunks, I suppose that's how we became the first welfare state in the world: *give them the money* they shouted pouring another gin, *give them free health care! give them free education!*'

'Someone said your Dad'll be the next prime minister,' said Hope, 'so tell him to give us our land back, eh?' and she laughed. As she walked, holding on to Prudence's arm, her head leaned sideways as if she was listening to the pavement.

'Don't trust him as far as you could kick him,' said Emily. 'Don't vote for him.'

'You've got to be twenty-one to vote,' said Hope.

As they passed the last wharf, Maggie suddenly turned her face away sharply, though of course no dead body lay on the wharf now, in the evening sunshine.

They were clicking along the city pavements and up to Prudence McKenzie's old place on the hill that was hidden almost in the wild honeysuckle bushes; because at twenty past six, they told Maggie, that's where the boys from the Bureau would be too, carrying crates of brown bottles of DB bitter from the bottle store of the Prince of Wales and bringing fish and chips.

Maggie had felt doubtful about going, she had her essays to write.

'Just come once,' said Emily, and there was a mocking tone to her voice as if she was teasing Maggie in some way. 'You only have to come once.'

'All right, just once,' said Maggie. 'But I haven't really got the time and I'll have to catch the nine o'clock tram. I'm not allowed out any later.'

Emily had given her a very old-fashioned look, but said nothing more.

The boys arrived in taxis, the older men in Bureau cars.

Rangi Cox at once picked up his guitar from behind the sofa where he'd left it the night before and began singing, his cigarette hanging out of the side of his mouth in his Humphrey Bogart fashion, *what do you want to make those eyes at me for*, and Prudence and Emily poured beer for everybody and laid out the fish and chips on the floor.

> Blue smoke
> Goes drifting by
> Into a deep blue sky

sang Hope Green the blind typist, staring up at the light bulb, and the men opened more bottles as the room filled up with people and cigarette smoke and music. Hope had a voice like Connie Francis, plaintive, that made all her songs sound like the blues. The more plaintively she sang, the more she stared up at the light bulb, as if a tiny prism of light might allow her to see something after all; to see the blue smoke, drifting.

> ***Pokarekare ana***
> ***Nga wai o Rotorua***

the waters of Lake Rotorua are troubled, sang Hui Windsor, lifting his wooden leg onto a chair and other, beautiful voices joined in from all around him, in harmony.

'Good heavens,' murmured Maggie, watching and listening and sipping at a glass of DB bitter. *I suppose that's a cheap Victorian ballad. But it's beautiful.*

And then Gallipoli Gordon sang.

> Just a song at twilight
> when the lights are low
> And the flickering shadows
> softly come and go

he sang, and Maggie thought her heart would stop. The beautiful, deep, resonant voice filled the room and everyone was quiet. Maggie remembered Emily pointing to him, a fat Maori man leaning over a file in Alienations, and Emily saying 'he could've been an opera singer.' When the song was finished everybody seemed to sigh, then Gallipoli turned away shyly and poured another beer.

'Hey Makareti,' said Manu Taihape, who always turned Pakehas' names into Maori, 'let's see if we can teach you to play the ukelele.' Maggie looked at him, surprised, because she had never seen without his trolley of files (even in her dreams). He handed Maggie the small instrument that she had seen George Formby holding in the comics she had read as a child.

'Now, look, first of all, it's only four strings, you just have to make sure they're tuned; you tune it by singing "*my dog has fleas*".'

'Pardon?' said Maggie, '*pardon?*' She always thought Manu Taihape spoke in riddles, never quite understood what he was talking about. But he showed her how to tune the ukelele and she noticed how brown his big hands were as he put them over her small white ones, showing her how to press the strings down and play a chord. She became fascinated, went into a corner and practised softly *just a song at CHANGE CHORD twilight*, holding down the strings, trying to strum. She was concentrating so hard that at first she didn't notice the room go quiet as people stopped to listen to her efforts.

When she became aware of them she stopped playing at once. 'Don't listen, don't listen,' she said almost angrily, 'I can't do it like you can.' The others laughed so she tried to laugh too. But the sound that came out of her was unexpected, uncontrollable, as if she didn't know how to laugh: a sort of loud neighing, like a horse.

'Boy, *listen* to that laugh!' said Rangi, laughing louder,

everyone in the room was laughing as Maggie, quite painfully, tried to stop.

'Don't make me laugh like this,' she hooted. 'I don't know how to laugh properly. Stop it!' And saw herself, for a moment outside herself, laughing *absolutely*. She was so surprised she stopped.

'I have to go now,' she said and ran for the tram.

Guitars strummed behind her, the sound fainter and fainter as she ran down the hill.

She lay awake in bed that night in her safe bedroom, staring at the ceiling.

It wasn't that they didn't laugh, hadn't laughed, in this house of her childhood. Of course they laughed, in a way, in the sunny garden where freesias grew neatly in lines. Her father with his bottles of DB bitter laughed beside the wireless at 'Much-Binding-in-the-Marsh' and 'Take it From Here', from England – she often heard him chuckling quietly and sometimes they laughed when they played Old Maid by the fire. But there was something constricted, something chilling. And she knew it was to do with Elizabeth, the death of Elizabeth that they never, ever talked about, the shadow over their lives. She could never remember laughing aloud with total abandon, no wonder her laughter was so odd, there was some anxiety just around the corner of the house where the hydrangeas and the cinnerarias grew, something in the air there, something in their house where the sun didn't shine by the back door; something.

So that when she laughed completely, as she had tonight, it was such a surprise, so unexpected, it was almost uncontrollable.

Is there something different about me? Why is it like this?

But she shut the crack at the corner of her mind tightly and the sea sighed quietly in the distance.

And up on the hill behind the city, when everybody had gone and the dark silence came, Prudence McKenzie had such a terrible nightmare that she bit her own hand till it bled, found blood on her sheets, drank tea on the verandah till it was morning.

At the Bureau, she phoned him. 'It's me,' and he heard the break in her voice.

'I'll be there,' he said.

The next night Maggie was back at Prudence's place, sitting rather stiffly with her glass of DB bitter as if to say: *well*, just *once* more. She watched Emily and Prudence, peering at them slightly suspiciously from a corner. They weren't anything like the girls she had known at school. Even the ones who had gone to university would be wondering by now when they would be engaged, who they would marry, how many children they would have. You were an old maid if you weren't engaged. But Emily and Prudence didn't seem to wonder about anything except having a good time. How freely they laughed, how easily they sang.

Hori was telling them all about an eel in a river that was really – so he said – a monster. *Heavens*, thought Maggie, *he's a grown man. He's got two children.*

'Boy, I *felt* it,' said Hori, waving his hands in the air, 'it was HUGE and slimy and it came sliding down the river past the dunnies and it had eyes like electric light bulbs, like a kind of dragon, but I fell on the stones and the water got in my pants.' And Maggie saw that although he was laughing he could see the monster yet, that he actually believed he'd seen it. How superstitious they were – it was an eel, obviously. She had been taught there were definitely no such things as monsters: in her family an overdeveloped imagination was considered a fault. Imagine Eddie Albert and his friends hearing all this – how they would laugh and mock. Maoris really were loonies:

Isobel said that they believed their spirit would fly off the northernmost part of the northernmost island when they died; that they believed people could have a *mate*, a sickness of the spirit that would actually kill them; that they had premonitions.

They spoke as if magic existed.

And yet, Maggie thought again, *they're grown men*.

Almost all the grown men in the room – who had been drinking since 4.35 when they hastened down the hill to the Prince of Wales – were drunk. Maggie had never seen people so drunk before. Paddy O'Rourke from Housing, Emily's boss, fell over completely. Manu helped Prudence put him on the sofa and make him a cup of tea.

'He lives by himself in a returned serviceman's house,' Emily whispered to Maggie, 'he was tortured by the Germans in the war and his hair fell out. That's why he wears a wig. He's usually the last to go and he always sings Irish songs as he's driving home, he says it helps him drive slowly.' Paddy's reddish-brown wig wasn't a very good fit but Maggie saw that nobody mentioned it, or laughed, even though it had moved slightly as he'd toppled over.

As they put him on the sofa Manu straightened the wig gently, 'There you go, *e hoa*,' he said, and Maggie already knew: *e hoa* was how they addressed their friends.

And then Hui Windsor from Alienations, the one with the wooden leg, got terribly angry and started shouting at every-body in Maori: 'It's his leg, he's drunk now,' said the others, 'when he starts shouting, it's time to go.'

Voices called back up the hill in the night. *Haere ra, e noho ra*, goodnight, *O Danny Boy the pipes the pipes are calling*.

Quite a few of the men had come in government cars and Maggie stared in amazement as the grey Ford Prefects or Austins belonging to the Bureau wobbled down the hill past the pohutukawa trees towards the sea, zig-zagging slowly along the empty main streets. For the city was already asleep: there was nothing but the White Daisy milk bar and the Wong Fu café open after seven o'clock, unless you knew what you were looking for, down the side streets.

Maggie waited at the tram stop for the nine o'clock tram, seeing its pole flash towards her along the overhead wires in the distance. In her mind she was composing an essay entitled 'The Uses of Gender in "As You Like It"' but she was also singing, *blue smoke goes drifting by into a deep blue sky* just quietly in the tram car.

And when they had all gone, and she had washed up the glasses and thrown away the cigarette ends and the newspapers, Prudence McKenzie came out on to her verandah, sat there in the dark on one of the wooden steps. In her mind's eye she conjured up the Bureau, next door to the Red Rose Parlour, down in the city. After a while a car could be heard; it stopped on the road below. Then the sound of his footsteps: he came up through the honeysuckle bushes.

'*Kia ora*,' he said softly, seeing her silhouetted above him and Prudence smiled her gentle smile in the darkness.

'Are you all right?'

'I'm all right, Bay,' she answered.

ELEVEN

Maggie saw Isobel Arapeta put her arms for a moment round the Maori with the blue eyes when he came into the small lecture room at the very top of the stairs.

'I've just heard about your sister's unveiling,' she said, 'how's your mum?' and, murmuring in Maori, she hugged her student, who looked slightly embarrassed. Maggie wanted to ask what an unveiling was, perhaps his sister was a Catholic nun, or a bride?

The French woman with the see-through blouse leant towards him as he came to sit down. 'You have such beautiful eyes, Timoti,' she said in her French-accented English. He smiled but he looked embarrassed, pulled at the collar of his shirt as if it was too tight for him. He was wearing a three-piece suit with a waistcoat, the sort of suit Maggie's father had stopped wearing years ago. There was a neat, white hand-kerchief in the jacket pocket. Maggie thought he looked a bit old-fashioned.

'Now have you made yourselves an English–Maori dictionary?' Isobel Arapeta asked her pupils briskly, 'seeing that no such thing exists in this imperfect world.'

'Indexed recipe books were really cheap after Mothers' Day,' said Maggie, holding up a book with a big pavlova cake on the cover: white meringue, red strawberries and yellow cream. In this book she had carefully written down the beautiful words under the appropriate letter, reminding herself that every vowel was pronounced. She tried to pronounce the word for funeral, it was also the word 'to weep'. Isobel, who was very strict on pronunciation, pounced at once.

'You've got a good ear, so use it; don't be lazy, feel the movement in the back of your throat: *ng* like in "singing": **tangi**.'

'**Ta–ngi**,' said Maggie.

'Yes, good,' said Isobel. And she repeated: 'You've got a good ear.'

'**Ta–ngi, tangi**,' said Maggie. '**Tangi**.'

Timoti Pou, his raincoat flapping in the wind, was some way behind Margaret-Rose Bennett that night as she walked by herself to the tram stop. He observed her jump and dance in an odd manner and pull her ear lobes.

'I've got a good ear,' he heard her sing, 'I've got a good ear,' on the road to the tram stop.

And he couldn't help smiling, walking behind the Pakeha girl with the wild hair as she danced so oddly in the darkness.

There seemed to be a party at Prudence's every night.

Maggie had never, never enjoyed herself so much in her life. She began to live for the evenings at Prudence's place. When she got an A-minus for her essay on 'Ode on a Grecian Urn' she said to her pleased parents, 'But I'll have to work later in the library every night after lectures, if I'm going to pass French.'

She stood with her weight on one foot in that way of hers, in the doorway of the lounge. Her parents were listening to an adaptation of 'The Thirty-nine Steps' on the wireless. Her mother's needle went in and out.

On that day years ago, in the summer sunshine (when the sea had danced and sparkled, as if diamonds lay there) Mrs Bennett had stopped, like a clock stopping – at a certain time, on a certain day, in a certain year. As long as she remained still: not too fast, not too loud, only her fingers moving over the embroidery, she could control the pain. She could control her life.

'Can't you work at home? How will you eat?' Her father turned the wireless down.

'There's a good cheap university cafeteria and my friend Prudence McKenzie lives near the university and we cook stews and talk to each other in French.' Maggie felt that her cheeks were very red. 'I won't pass French if I don't do extra work.'

'You'll get too tired,' said Richard Bennett.

'No, no I won't.'

'What time does the library close?'

'Nine o'clock. I could still catch the nine-thirty tram.'

Richard Bennett looked across at his wife, so still except for the needle, in and out, and so beautiful.

Mrs Bennett looked at her daughter carefully. 'I don't see why you should find French so difficult,' she said.

'I'm just not very good at it,' said Maggie humbly. 'I need to do extra work.'

'The half-past nine tram at the very latest,' said Mrs Bennett and she leaned across and turned up the radio. Neither of them saw the tiny flicker of relief in their daughter's eye. And something else, that had never been seen there before.

Glee.

The strumming of a guitar would start long before the girls had tidied away the last newspaper from the fish and chips (*as if they simply can't wait any longer for music*, Maggie thought). But no matter how many guitars played or how loudly they sang there were never complaints from the neighbours as there would have been down Maggie's street; there weren't any neighbours, not there, not up behind the centre of the city, under the hill, where the honeysuckle grew so wild. The previous occupant had been arrested, for murder it was rumoured, and sometimes the boys laughed oddly as they stumbled about the overgrown garden, as if there might be something hidden there.

'It's nice, isn't it,' said Maggie to Emily as they washed some glasses in Prudence's kitchen, 'that there's no age barrier at Prudence's parties. Your boss Paddy comes, and Hui Windsor even undoes his trousers and takes his leg off and nobody minds, and his friend that fat man, Gallipoli Gordon from Alienations, he's got such a beautiful voice, he's *much* better than Mario Lanza, I love hearing him sing and he must be about *fifty*.'

'Ah,' said Emily. 'But where are the older women? Where are the machinists?'

'Well – I suppose they have to go home and make the dinner for their families,' said Maggie.

Emily gave her a withering look. 'You didn't get it, did you?' she said, 'when I took you in there. Your mother doesn't work. My mother doesn't work. The machinists are the old maids, or the widows, and the *divorcée* I told you about. They haven't got men, so they have to work. But they don't come to the parties, even the gay *divorcée* doesn't come. Old women don't *fit*. So make the most of it, you won't be welcome when you're old.'

Rangi played the guitar usually, or Hope the blind typist.

> My tears have washed
> I Love You from
> the blackboard of my heart.

And the songs in Maori, the cheap Victorian ballads whistled by the whalers.

Up in the high, small room Isobel Arapeta said to her pupils:

In learning the Maori language it becomes impossible not to be aware that Maoris believe there is more to this world of ours than meets the eye. **Kehua** *is their word for ghost. Maoris believe there are ghosts, of a kind.* **Wairua** *is a Maori word meaning "spirit", the part of oneself that disappears when one dies. But it is not only human beings, Maoris believe, that possess this spirit. Trees and birds and the sea have a* **wairua**. *A house can have a* **wairua**. *There are* **wairua** *everywhere, and Maoris believe they can protect us.*

And Maggie thought to herself: *I know this, I have seen this, I have seen them, thinking like this.* And then she suddenly thought of the dead body on the wharf and the talk of curses: native curses.

She was the first one out of the high room, running down the hill from the university. She ran past the closed Prince of Wales: she had to step over an inert, drunk body outside the hotel, just part of the evening, lying there. She ran faster when she got to the wharves, twisting her head away. Some of the empty city streets grew darker and even emptier as she turned from the tram lines. At the top of one street she had to pass some old, falling-down sheds and garages, a disused motor workshop. She slowed for just a moment, could almost have sworn she could hear the strum of a guitar, wafting out from the darkness and the shadows of the old wrecks of cars and trucks. Was someone sitting there in among the wrecks, playing? But perhaps she was hearing things, hearing ghostly guitars again like she sometimes thought she did at the Bureau. She ran on, up the dark hill behind the city. She definitely heard a guitar strumming as she approached the old house, Prudence's place.

Hope was playing. She sat drinking whisky in her special corner of Prudence's flat and stared at the light bulb as she sang:

> *Tahi nei taru kino*
> *Mahi whaiaipo.*

'What's that mean, Hope?' asked Maggie. 'I haven't got to those words yet.'

Hope smiled her slightly knowing, blind smile and looked just past Maggie.

'It means *making love is like a dangerous vine,*' she said.

Emily grinned at the doorway, where Manu Taihape had just arrived.

'You smell of Sunlight soap,' she said to him and he laughed.

Later, the old maroon Chevrolet rattled rather a lot as it passed the tram stop and then screeched to a halt.

'I'll give you a ride home,' Manu said, and as Maggie got in doubtfully she glanced at the back seat, half expecting to see his files trolley.

Of course he didn't drive Maggie *home* exactly, not exactly stopping outside her house, coming in perhaps to say *good evening, how are you?* to her parents. He drove to the beach at the bottom of her street. He parked the old car on the sand and turned off the motor and then, as if it was the most natural thing in the world, he turned and took her into his big, warm arms, smoothing and petting her, kissing and stroking her, and somehow at the same time making her laugh. And she thought how much better this was than having a finger pushed up your vagina without any warning, and tentatively stroked him back as autumn arrived and the sea ran more wildly towards the sandhills, and the cutty grass swayed in the darkness.

Maggie's father said: 'You look as if you've got a temperature. Where are you eating at nights? I hope you're not going anywhere like the Wong Fu Café.'

'No, no, I eat at the varsity cafeteria, or I go to my friend Prudence McKenzie's house; she lives near the university, we cook stews and talk French like I told you.' Her heart beat fast.

Maggie's mother said: 'This place isn't a hotel, you know.'

'I'm always home at the weekends,' said Maggie. 'I'll do all the vacuuming then.'

Maggie's father said: 'We're not really happy with you trying to fit in one hour a week learning Maori. It's a waste of time and you'll get too tired – French and English, working during the day, studying at night. Surely that's quite enough without an adult education class in a dead language.'

Manu had called out gently as he drove away: '*Kia rangimarie to moe*', *sleep peacefully*.

'I'm fine,' said Maggie, 'that old Maori class doesn't take up hardly any time and it's handy for work to know a few words. That's all, I don't think about it really.'

Maggie's mother was brushing her long, fine, blonde hair that was turning grey, a hundred strokes night and morning. She was still so extraordinarily beautiful: tall, high cheekbones, deep dark eyes, the fading blonde hair pulled back tight. Maggie always thought her mother should have been a model: she'd worked for a women's magazine before her marriage.

'But couldn't you be a model, Mummy?' Maggie used to say when she was little, 'you could be in the "Women's Weekly", you're much prettier than those women,' and she would try to wind herself round her mother's arms, round the arms of the beautiful woman. But Mrs Bennett would move away.

'Before the war, women had to resign from their jobs when they got married,' she would answer. 'I told you.'

(In the linen cupboard, under the spare pillows, there was a framed wedding photo, a sort of sepia colour: the footballer in a suit and the beautiful woman with her fair hair in a veil and flowers. They smiled at the camera and their eyes seemed to dance still.)

'I can't think why you want to waste even an hour learning

Maori when you've so much else to do,' said Maggie's mother quietly, still brushing. 'It's a dead, primitive language, it's finished, everybody knows that. I think they're very irresponsible, putting a young girl like you in the Bureau. I don't like you working with Maoris, I know about Maoris. I've actually known one, we had a Maori cleaner where I worked before the war. He was a thief.'

'They're good chaps of course, fought well in the war,' said Maggie's father, 'but they're not really reliable, too happy-go-lucky, too lazy really. We've had one or two in the department but – they're not like us. The boss even asked a couple of them home, he actually asked them to where he lived – you know that corker house of theirs round the bay that they had specially designed by an architect from overseas – he asked them home and gave them a nice meal and everything, but you know, they weren't grateful. They never asked him back to their houses; he felt it keenly.'

'And those vulgar, vulgar carvings,' said Maggie's mother.

Maggie pushed down her hair where Manu's hands had been.

*

There was something sleek as a cat about John Evans now, as he sat across the desk from his lawyer. The lawyer's office, in the main street of the city, was long closed and a wind rattled at the dark windows.

'Right,' said John Evans. 'I've done it.' He pushed some papers across the desk; the lawyer's spectacles glinted in the light of the lamp on the desk as he leaned forward to take them. 'I want it sold on at least four times before I actually buy it, but surely you can do that in a couple of weeks. I'll pay you what it costs to do this, though I think you're a rogue – ,'and both men smiled very slightly, '– but there must be no way the sale can ever be traced back to me. Not that anybody'll ever ask. Everything from the Council is here, it's all arranged but I don't want the bulldozers moving in until after the election, just to be on the safe side.'

'There's nothing in writing about you?'

'It was a cash payment, I've still to pay the second half but I insisted on you seeing these documents first.'

'Who did you bribe? This is a lot of land.'

John Evans bristled slightly although he covered it with another smile. 'That's an emotive word,' he said. 'Nothing here is illegal. The Council will be following the letter of the law. I just found someone willing to do that.'

The lawyer scanned the documents in the lamplight. 'It'll still take a month or two.'

'Well, hurry it along,' said the MP impatiently, 'that's what I employ you for, I want to start building.' He stared for a moment down at the desk. 'It's beautiful,' he said softly, 'really beautiful. It's hard to believe there's land like that still left. Parts of it are wild. Parts of it are sheltered enough for a boat harbour. Fishing, beautiful sites looking out across the ocean for building. Completely unspoiled. Fantastic.' He seemed lost in a reverie and then pulled himself together. 'It's worth a bloody fortune used in the right way.' He pulled at his chin. 'I might even risk putting it in my daughter's name, I'll see. But I *want* it. I want it in my family.'

'It's a bit of a risk to do it too fast. The dates will give it away.'

'Oh come on, no one's going to bother to check back through four owners, nobody even understands the intricacies. And the papers will be among a million papers in the Council records and everyone knows the Bureau's land files are a mess.'

The lawyer pulled a bottle of gin and two glasses out of the bottom drawer of his desk.

'In fact,' continued John Evans, 'the law needs changing and then we won't have to go through these ridiculous sub-terfuges. I've looked into it, land is going to waste, not being utilised – valuable, commercial land. Ridiculous, outdated native customs are holding up progress in our little country. It should be unnecessary for me to go about my dealings in this way. The land could be sold, owners would benefit, for God's sake. The law should be changed.'

'Well, you'll soon be in a position to do that.'

John Evans stood and stretched. And then he smiled the sleek smile at his lawyer.

'Yes,' he said. 'I think so. I believe, if I play my cards right and get Benson on my side, I'll be prime minister of this country before the year is out.'

'Benson is the key?'

'Benson is the key. He owns the newspapers.'

Then the MP emptied his glass swiftly and was gone, down to the bottom of the building in the empty, ancient lift. The iron lift gates clanged behind him as he walked out into the street where a car was waiting. Timoti Pou, who often used the office at night to study for his law exams, passed him in the doorway of the building, took the old clanking lift upwards again. His boss, one of the cleverest lawyers in the city, was at his desk in the lamplight, as he was so often in the evenings.

'Is John Evans a client of ours?' asked Timoti, guessing where the MP might have been.

The lawyer leaned back in his chair, stretched, regarded the young, blue-eyed Maori. He had high hopes for him: he would make him a partner, shake up the city a little, surprise them all. But it wouldn't do for him to know about the business with John Evans. Not yet. There would be more of that kind of business, much more. But his protégé had to learn some of his own language, it would look better. A Maori lawyer, who spoke Maori, on the Pakeha side. That would solve a lot of problems. But not yet.

The lawyer tapped the side of his nose.

'Hear no evil, see no evil,' he said, and he smiled softly at Timoti Pou.

And in the dark, empty, silent streets Sinatra, King of the City, walked.

TWELVE

In the high room Isobel Arapeta said to her pupils: *According to Maori legend these islands we live on were fished up by Maui, one of their mythical, mischievous ancestors, with a magic fish-hook. This fisherman had other tricks too: he slowed down the sun's journey across the sky with his fishing net, so that the days would be longer.*

Perhaps these are fairy tales, you must make your own decisions. What is undisputed historically, and is surely a great nautical feat, is that, maybe a thousand years ago, the Maoris sailed here in their canoes from their homeland, the mystical Hawaiki, whose whereabouts remains a mystery to this day. After travelling for a long, long time with only the stars and the tides to guide them, what they finally saw, there in the distance, was a long white shape floating on the horizon, like a cloud. As they got nearer they saw that it was, at last, land. And so they named these islands **Aotearoa***: the land of the long, white cloud.*

Maggie's voice was unable to stop.

'We learnt about Maui tonight, fishing these islands up, making the days long, all those fairy tales; you are silly, you boys and your stories, the other boys don't *really* speak Maori, do they, not really, it's just words isn't it? They can't speak it like you can. I've noticed they use a few words but I've realised now, they don't know it really, only you, and then the older men, like Hui Windsor and Gallipoli Gordon. I love hearing Gallipoli sing, he's much better than Mario Lanza, don't you love Gallipoli's voice, all deep and echoing?'

Manu sat smoothing her skin by the sea in the old car while the cutty grass swayed and danced in the autumn wind in the night; she couldn't wait for the answer.

'Poor Paddy, isn't his wig awful, why doesn't someone tell him? There must be a better one than that, but he's a lovely man, he's always nice to people, not like our horrible boss, have you got brothers and sisters, Manu? How come you speak Maori?'

On and on her voice went, high and fast.

'Ssssh,' said Manu, smoothing his hand up her arm, pushing her cardigan away gently. 'Ssssssh.' And he rocked her gently. 'Sssssssssh.' And then he said, 'What's the matter?'

Maggie gave a kind of a gulp as she tried to slow down. 'My parents don't know I'm doing Maori for my degree,' she said, peering anxiously now at her watch. 'Or – mixing with Maoris or – or anything. They don't know I go to parties, I think they'll be – very angry with me when it all collapses, I keep lying. I don't know how to tell them.' She wanted to say: *last night my mother hit me again. I am seventeen years old and my mother hits me.*

'Won't they be proud if you pass a university exam in another language?'

Maggie gulped again. 'I don't think they think of Maori as a *language*, I think they think French and German and Italian are *languages*. Oh – sorry Manu,' – thinking she might have hurt his feelings – 'it's just that they are a bit funny.'

'You pass and make them proud,' said Manu. 'People like me aren't clever enough to go to university. They'll be proud because you're their daughter and you're clever.'

Maggie sighed.

'And you're only a *girl*!' said Manu.

She smiled wanly in the dark but she had stopped at last the incessant, nervous talking, relaxed now in his warm, warm arms. There was a bit of time before she had to go home.

'How come you speak Maori so well, Manu?' she asked again, but quieter now.

Manu smoothed the skin where her blouse was open. 'My grandfather brought me up for years up on the coast, till we came down here, and he made me speak it. He used to take me down to the old meeting house and he used to point at the carvings of my ancestors and say "*don't make them weep, hold on to their language*." We were strapped at my primary school if we spoke it in class. But when I got home I got bashed if I didn't speak Maori. Boy, sometimes I had a really sore head thinking what language to speak where and who was going to bash me next!' and he laughed in the night. 'He was a real pain that old fella, still is, strict and old and grumpy and I'm still scared of him. But I love him and I'm glad I can speak my own language, everyone should speak their own –'

'Did it hurt when your grandfather hit you?' she interrupted. 'Did he hurt you? Did he hit you really hard? How did he actually hit you, did he slap you? How many times? Does he still hit you?'

Manu laughed. '*E hoa*, don't make a fuss, I probably deserved it. And I can talk my language, can't I? Those other fellas, they know it too, in their hearts, they just don't know all the words.'

Maggie looked anxiously again at her watch, but she still had twenty minutes. She did not know what it was that she found so comforting sitting there, sitting talking in the car along the dark beach by the sandhills, Manu's warm, large hand on the back of her neck, stroking her gently over and over. It was a feeling she didn't know.

And then tonight, finally, he put his hand up underneath her blouse and in the moonlight shining through the car window she saw that his eyes were clouded with another, unfathomable emotion as with his other hand he undid the pins in her hair. And she recognised, even as she demurred, but unwillingly, *I'll have to go my parents will be waiting they get angry Manu* that the unfathomable look in Manu's eyes was the same look she had seen in that little Maori girl's eyes when her father, Hori, had hit her in the street. Something blanked out. *Is it me? Is he blanking out me?*

But still she turned her face up to his and his warm, large lips kissed her for a long time. No one had kissed her like that, ever.

'I'll have to go, Manu,' she said, breathing shakily. And she felt the strangest, oddest feeling, as he gently smoothed the whole of her breast and she suddenly, extraordinarily, threw her arms around him, held him to her.

Her mother was asleep when Maggie let herself in the back door. Or, at least, the bedroom door was closed.

She jumped into his old car after work. 'I want to come home with you and practise words. *Please* Manu,' she added, when he seemed reluctant, 'please, I've skipped an English lecture even, I need you to practise on,' and yet she knew too that what she really wanted was to feel again the warmth of his hand on her skin and for him to make her laugh again, the way he could.

They drove for some time away from the city centre and then turned off to a cluster of small box-like houses with orange and purple windowsills.

'Are these Bureau houses?' she asked curiously, sitting as near to him as she could, feeling the warmth of his arm against hers.

'Yeah, it's a special development because it's Maori land.

They don't usually let us live all together like this. They're scared we'll make too much noise. I've got my noisy aunties and my noisy grandfather living round here,' and he laughed and ruffled his hair. 'You want to sit in the car? I won't be long.'

'No,' said Maggie, surprised.

Manu shrugged.

They stepped over a rusting car with no wheels, and part of a truck, and then walked round the side of the shabby house to the back yard. A small, dirty girl and an older girl of about ten were playing in long grass with a kitten, teasing it with a piece of string, hitting it. They both wore long cardigans that were too big for them and they tripped over the cardigans as they played.

'These are my sisters,' said Manu. 'Say hello to Makareti, you two.' He picked up the little girl who stared with huge black eyes, unsmiling, at Maggie. Manu walked in the back door past a large pile of old coats and gumboots, washed the little girl's face at the kitchen sink. The older girl skipped in beside Maggie, smiling at her but saying nothing. In the kitchen a baby lay asleep in a drawer on the torn linoleum. Maggie saw there was snot running from its nose. Somewhere there was a low, rumbling noise.

'*Kia ore e Tame,*' said Manu to the drawer.

Maggie tried not to look shaken, smiled a lot, stepped gingerly past the drawer. There was no tablecloth on the table but there was a huge bottle of tomato sauce and a big open bag of sugar and some flies that rubbed their legs over crumbs on the table. She remembered suddenly her father saying: '*they never asked him back to their houses; they weren't grateful at all*'.

Manu put his head round the sitting-room door: several boys were roaring toy cars around the room, lying on the floor among Manu's clothes that were neatly folded in piles. Manu grinned at the boys then went back to the kitchen and filled a battered pot with water. He put it on the gas stove, lit a match, waited patiently till the gas finally flared and caught. Maggie heard the rumbling sound getting louder, didn't like to say anything, perhaps it was a hot water cylinder.

'I'll make us a cup of tea, eh?' Manu said and the older girl looked at him and looked at Maggie and then said shyly: 'Manu, where's our fish 'n' chips?'

Across the small hall from the kitchen Maggie suddenly saw, in another room, some very large brown legs protruding from a bed, then realised that the rumbling sound she was hearing was the sound of somebody snoring very loudly.

Manu fed the children. There were cold chops. Maggie reluctantly had a small piece of bread and jam. Even more children arrived, there was a lot of noise, and still the snoring sound. Manu sat the children in front of the wireless to listen to the "Lever Hit Parade", the littlest girl used Manu's jersies as a cushion. Maggie sang shyly with them:

> I found my thrill
> On a blue berry hill

'Do you know the blue berry hill?' they asked her. 'Manu says it's in town and it's got a house all by itself with no other houses and a honeysuckle and a guitar and lotsa blue berries.'

'Oh,' said Maggie. 'Yes, yes I know it.' But she felt very uncomfortable, looked anxiously back to where the snoring was coming from. The children offered to dance for her.

> Japanese Rhumba ay ay ay
> Japanese Rhumba ay ay ay

they sang, all dancing around the bare room, tripping some-times on Manu's clothes.

Manu came back smelling of soap in a neatly ironed, clean

shirt. The children waved as they drove away.

Manu stopped, parked the car somewhere, nowhere, and kissed Maggie. She felt so warm. She smelt the soap and she didn't want him to stop. Then he drove her to the hill up by Prudence's place but didn't get out of the car.

'Aren't you coming in?' she said, disappointed and she reached out and smoothed the brown skin of his arm.

'No,' he said, 'not tonight. I've got to see my cousin, but see you tomorrow,' and he smiled his enormous smile.

The guitars strummed as the Chevrolet rattled off down the hill and Maggie turned away, to the honeysuckle and the music.

As she walked into the crowded room full of laughter and music she saw to her surprise the Maori with the blue eyes, Timoti Pou. He was sitting at Prudence's table with a bottle of beer, talking to Hui Windsor, who had unscrewed his leg.

'Hello,' she said to Timoti Pou, stepping over the leg.

'Hello,' he answered, and smiled. Hui was talking very loudly, something about land: *they're always going on about land* she thought *only they don't have to fill in the boring land registers, LAND LAND LAND! I wish I never had to hear that word again.*

She sat down on the floor beside Hope, and Rangi passed her a bottle of beer that he had opened. Hope was drinking whisky, and tonight Paul the epileptic from Adoptions was sitting beside her, *hope he doesn't have a fit*, thought Maggie. Hope played the guitar and stared at the light. Maggie saw that Timoti Pou still wore his tie, unlike the others who always threw them off; did not sing like the others, didn't quite fit. But everyone was aware of him, sitting there.

A wind came up unexpectedly and tore at the corrugated iron of the roof; it banged there, punctuating the singing and the laughter. Gallipoli Gordon, the fat Maori man from Alienations sang, because they asked him to:

Just a song at twilight
when the lights are low
And the flickering shadows
softly come and go

and again the room was quiet as his beautiful deep voice poured out, just the banging of the iron on the roof outside sometimes and Hope's guitar strumming and Maggie looked around the room at the brown and white faces: all listening and smiling and dreaming. And she thought *we are the only shadows flickering, no other houses anywhere near, just us, it's sort of enchanted this old house and the honeysuckle and my new friends. I feel happy here and Manu makes me feel so* – she didn't know what word to use – *warm.* And she smiled across at Prudence who was holding a beer glass stolen from the pub and leaning against the windowsill. And Maggie saw something else: saw that Rangi with his Humphrey Bogart cigarette stared at Emily longingly, listening to the song: he looked at her as if he loved her but Emily did not notice.

Ka pai . . . ka pai . . . lovely murmured the voices round the room as the last notes of the song faded. And then the talking and the laughing rose again and Hope and Rangi began strumming the old songs again.

'Maggie, how do you know Timoti Pou?' Emily had taken to rolling her own cigarettes; her red nails twisted the paper expertly as she stared at the two men sitting at the table, talking together again; at least, Hui was talking and Timoti was listening, not saying much.

'He's in my Maori class.'

'Is he? How odd, a Maori learning Maori!'

'Is he the one you told me about? With the blue eyes, who's going to be a lawyer?'

'Yeah, he's the one who used to work at the Bureau.' Emily looked across at Timoti speculatively. 'He's so good looking, isn't he?' she said. 'But he doesn't laugh much.' And then, looking at the door, Emily said, 'I wonder where Manu is tonight.'

For some reason Maggie said nothing.

Tahi nei taru kino
Mahi whaiaipo

making love is like a dangerous vine, sang Hope, and Maggie saw again that she was smiling slightly, as if she had a secret, as she stared at the light.

When she left for the 9.30 tram Timoti came with her, his white raincoat flapping in the strong wind. Maggie's hair blew about her face as they walked down the hill; the sound of the iron banging on the roof of the old house echoed after them.

'Are you sitting the university Maori paper, Timoti?' asked Maggie shyly.

'Are *you*?' he asked in surprise.

'Yes, um – yes. I'm no good at French.'

'Why didn't you do German or Italian or something?'

'I like Maori. I kept hearing it around me at the Bureau, just snatches of it. I think it's beautiful.'

The wind blew. And he smiled at her as they walked. He had a very beautiful smile.

'There's another Maori in that class doing the exam too.'

'Oh,' said Maggie. 'I suppose it must be that snooty man.'

'It's just his way,' said Timoti.

'Why are you sitting it?' she asked shyly, remembering Emily's words: *a Maori learning Maori, how odd.*

For a moment he said nothing and she thought she saw him give a kind of grimace in the darkness. Finally he said slowly, 'I've spent most of my life getting a good Pakeha education. I left home when I was young, I don't know any Maori. But now my boss at my law firm thinks it might be – useful.' He shrugged.

'Doesn't your boss know it's dying?'

He shrugged again. 'I want to get on with the law, not Maori things,' he said. 'I'll qualify this year.'

They walked in silence for a while, the wind blew about them.

'Well, it's beautiful anyway,' said Maggie but he did not answer. For just a split second Maggie wondered if Manu, who spoke his own language so fluently, was luckier than Timoti, in some way. But then she thought of the flies and all the dirty children at Manu's house and knew, of course, that could not be true.

'Um – have you got a sister who's a nun?' she asked but the wind caught her words and she had to repeat them, louder: 'Have you got a sister who's a nun?'

Timoti was so surprised that he stopped walking, his coat flapped wildly. '*What*?' he said.

'I thought you might have a sister who was a nun,' she repeated again. 'You know, the unveiling, the Maori teacher was talking to you the other night about the unveiling.'

He stared at her for a moment and then walked on without saying anything. She hurried after him. When she drew level he said: 'My sister was run over. She was seventeen. We don't unveil the memorial stone on the grave for at least a year after a person dies.'

'Seventeen?' Maggie felt her cheeks burning, someone her own age dying. She didn't know how to talk about death: because of Elizabeth she never talked about death. 'Oh.' And she didn't know what else to say. She wondered if she could tell him she'd seen a dead man on the wharf.

The sparks of the 9.30 tram car flashed along the overhead wires in the dark. 'Oh, here's my tram. See you in Maori class on Thursday.' And then, floundering, wanting to say some-thing, she shyly put her hand on the sleeve of his raincoat. 'I'm very sorry about your sister. My sister died once too. Only that was a long time ago. I don't remember it.'

She waved hesitantly from the tram. Timoti Pou seemed to be looking at her but did not wave back.

The Maori tram conductor refused to understand when she pronounced Potautau Junction properly and gave him her ticket to clip. Everyone called it Potato, and he waited for her to do the same.

That night her dream was completely unexpected and not what she had planned. She dreamed of nuns in neat rows with transparent white veils over their heads ready for unveil-ing, hundreds of nuns. They all sat at a table where blowflies buzzed at an open packet of sugar and there, sitting beside the table too, was Manu. He was laughing. But Timoti Pou sat there also, unsmiling with blue, blue eyes.

Next day, Anzac Day, the Bureau was closed.

The war was over long ago. The young ones in the Bureau, especially the girls, were so bored with the war. They sighed, rolled their eyes every time the men began *overseas when we . . . when the Ities . . . when the Wogs*. The boys of course liked the battle stories; discussed among themselves often the stories about Bay Ropata, the boss of Welfare who some people called a maniac, about him giving prisoners of war a big feed before he shot them dead: the boys always laughed, not sure if they really believed it (though they'd all seen the exciting bayonet gash right across Bay's stomach when he did the *haka*). But even the boys got sick of the never-ending *overseas when we . . . when the Ities . . . when the Wogs*. The endless reminiscing of the men who came back again.

But Emily's boss, Paddy, never mentioned it because he

had been a prisoner of war and had been tortured by the Germans and his hair fell out.

So always, just before Anzac Day, shy and inarticulate, but somehow wanting Paddy to know they respected his experience too, the young ones in the Bureau would say, just casually, *we'll be waving you on at the parade, Paddy.*

Because Paddy never talked about the war.

So Maggie too dragged herself to the dawn service by the cenotaph with Prudence and Emily; they wore coats and gloves in the chill morning, yawning and listening to the band.

Maggie looked again at Paddy's wig and his thin body as he marched past. His clothes always looked too big, hung on him like on a broken coathanger rather than on a person and, watching him, she realised suddenly that her father sometimes had that same, bleak look of unkemptness about him even though his clothes fitted perfectly. Maggie remembered her father laboriously teaching himself to write all over again with his left hand at the kitchen table in the evenings when she was a little girl; and sometimes, the new hook in place of a right hand, he had looked – untidy – even though his clothes of course were washed and ironed to perfection.

The old soldiers marched past in the half light: serious, medalled. Everyone sang the National Anthem.

> God of Nations,
> At thy feet,
> In the bonds of love we meet.
> Hear our voices we entreat
> God defend our free land.

'That's an indigenous poem!' said Emily. 'Thomas Bracken, 1864.'

'Have you seen those boys with beards who go round shouting OUR POETRY?' said Maggie, huddling in her coat.

'They're not boys, they're poets. They've got a printing press. They print their own.'

'Oh.' said Maggie. 'Oh. Good.'

Maggie's boss marched proudly too, all the bosses from the Bureau did. And horses. And some Maoris.

'There's that maniac, Bay Ropata,' murmured Emily to Maggie as the stocky, grey-haired, handsome man marched past, 'I told you about him.' She and Maggie were busy scanning the crowd and yawning, did not see that Prudence stared at the man they called the maniac from hooded, loving eyes.

'Oh and look!' said Emily, 'there's my father of course, he wouldn't miss the publicity. But I'm not here for *him*,' she finished suddenly.

'Which one is he?'

Emily pointed to a tall man, his dark hair flecked with grey, who was part of the official party.

'Gosh, he's very good looking, for an oldish man,' said Maggie but Emily turned away at once.

'Not to me,' she muttered.

'Well he's more handsome than my father,' said Maggie disloyally. Her father never came to anything to do with the war (although Maggie had once seen him, standing very, very still, beside this cenotaph, all by himself). *Something about . . . something about . . .* Maggie thought it was to do with Elizabeth, the death of Elizabeth, that he never came.

First light drifted across the city as a minister intoned through a loudspeaker:

Age shall not weary, nor the years condemn,

and a lone bugle played and Maggie felt something hurting at the back of her eyes, because she loved her father and his hand had been shattered, and lost, at El Alamein and because he did not come and march with the other soldiers.

Straight after the Anzac Day parade Emily's father walked up the hill to a small room inside Parliament Buildings. There he met with three other members of his party and the most important businessman in the country. A bottle was put on the table, glasses were passed around, the five men leaned forward together.

'It's time to stop mucking around, waiting for the right moment,' said John Evans. 'I want us to be ready the moment the House reconvenes.'

The businessman cleared his throat and the four MPs turned towards him. He smiled at John Evans. 'You know I'm behind you,' he said. 'And the newspapers. As soon as the bugger goes to London to see the Queen.'

They spoke very quietly, although the big, grey offices were closed as a mark of respect to the fallen and there was nobody else there at all, only Sinatra in the distance, walking past the old Edwardian building by himself, after the parade.

THIRTEEN

Maggie signed a form that went round the Bureau, and paid two and sixpence to go on the Annual Office Fishing Trip.

Down at the docks the first rays of the autumn sun appeared. Beer crates were being enthusiastically lifted by the boys from the Bureau on to a fishing boat called the *Napoli*. When Maggie saw Manu her heart jumped: he was so elusive she never knew if he would be around or not. She stared, trying not to, at his large brown hands, thinking of them on her breast and the feeling. Prudence and Emily and Harry Beans and a Maori with spectacles and Sarah, one of the Pakeha typists, all stood on the wharf holding their coats and jackets around them in the chill morning.

The Maori with spectacles, who was carrying a sack of shellfish for bait, came up to Maggie. 'Hello,' he said, 'I'm Tane Thompson, I see you running along the corridors up at Varsity. We haven't really met, I'm in CONSOLIDATION,' and he heaved the sack of shellfish up onto his shoulder.

'What are you studying?' asked Maggie.

'He's a swot,' called Hori, hoisting a beer crate, 'look at his glasses.'

'Geology,' said Tane. 'I want to be a geologist.'

'What does a geologist *do* actually?' asked Maggie politely, and was aware that Sarah the Pakeha typist was staring at her.

'A geologist geologises,' said Tane and when Maggie smiled he said, 'no, really, it's fantastic. There are hundreds of earthquakes here each year, still changing the shape of these islands, did you know that? Did you know that the northern island and the southern island are just the mountaintops of a huge submerged mountain range? We're just sitting on the top of a mountain range that is changing it's shape all the time. If I can find out more about the land and its age we might learn more about ourselves, Maoris I mean. I might make all sorts of discoveries.' And he looked so keen and so serious that Maggie smiled again and Sarah the typist turned away into her jacket.

A fat, grey-haired Maori in a black singlet and a duffle coat drove past on one of the wharf loaders. He tooted his horn at the group and waved.

'*Kia ora*, Sinatra,' they all called. Everybody waved so Maggie gave a little wave also.

'Who's that?' she asked.

'That's Sinatra,' said Rangi. 'He's the King of the City.'

Manu pulled the girls on board; Maggie smiled at him as he grasped her, held her steady; a secret smile. *I'm beginning to learn about sex.* At school she had giggled and whispered round corners about boys, but that was really about who had looked at who, smiled at who, danced with who; from Beverley or Shirley or biology she had learnt nothing that conjured the word *sex*. Nobody had ever touched her breast before, unlocking something, something trembling that she had never heard of, that she had no idea how to put into words. So she smiled a secret smile at Manu.

And she looked at Prudence and Emily, her new friends. She wondered if they would be disapproving if they knew Manu had kissed her, because he was a Maori. They had all that fun at the parties but she wasn't sure if they actually kissed Maoris.

Mrs Tipene from Adoptions bustled up in the misty early morning with hard boiled eggs and loaves of bread in a flax basket. Rangi and Hori loaded even more beer. Hui from Alienations drove up in a Bureau car, parked it on the dock edge. He pushed his wooden leg out of the car till it touched the ground, grimacing and smiling.

'Mr Porter said he'll do the switchboard,' called Roimata, the very fat telephone operator, arriving in another Bureau car with Gallipoli Gordon. 'He said he'd done it in the army, good fella.' And she heaved her large body out of the car, smiling and sighing.

Mrs McMillan, who'd been born in Yorkshire and worked in Welfare, arrived in a taxi with Hope and with Paul the epileptic; Maggie hoped he wouldn't have an epileptic fit and sink the boat. Joking about dropping Hope in, the boys carefully led the blind girl on board. She was carrying her guitar.

'Gunna be an autumn scorcher maybe,' said Paddy looking at the brightening sky, 'let's go, Franco, the fish won't bite when it's too hot,' and the Italian boat-owner started the engine and after the fourth try the fishing boat moved carefully out through the other boats at the docks, past the *Ruahine*, loading for England.

It was 7.30 AM when Paddy and Gallipoli opened the first brown bottle. Rangi picked up the guitar, parked his cigarette between the frets, began singing. Harry Beans and Tane Thompson got out all the fishing lines, opened the bag of shellfish. The boat chugged out into the Heads; way in the distance Maggie saw her street. The first rays of the sun caught the sandhills and the cutty grass where Manu parked his Chevrolet in the dark: she quickly looked across at Manu but he was laughing with Mrs Tipene and Prudence, unravelling fishing lines.

They turned up the coast, felt the wind suddenly. Franco the Italian was discussing the war with Hui: once soldiers on opposite sides they now sat companionably together with their bottles in their hands. Hui's wooden leg rested on the side of the boat, wood to wood. Maggie and Emily sat at one end of the boat beside a huge coiled rope that had seaweed clinging to it and declaimed poetry together, rolling the words around on their tongues.

> In Xanadu did Khubla Khan,
> A stately pleasure dome decree:
> Where Alph, the sacred river, ran
> Through caverns measureless to man
> Down to a sunless sea.

'Coleridge knew about us, you know,' said Maggie.

'What?' Emily shaded her eyes, looked at her.

'The Ancient Mariner's boat goes through the South Pacific, right past here, probably just up there on the left.'

Emily laughed.

'*And* Shakespeare,' said Maggie. 'Rosalind says, "*One inch more is a South-sea of discovery*," that's about sex. Shakespeare knew about us, even though he died in 1616.'

'He knew a great deal more about sex than he did about the South Seas,' said Emily dryly. 'Why should you care? Our literature comes from Europe, not from here, that's why we study Coleridge. Can you see my roots?'

'Where?' said Maggie, 'where?' And she stared down and down through the deep, green water for some clue to their beginnings.

'No my *roots*, my hair,' said Emily crossly.

'Oh.' Maggie looked at Emily, surprised. 'Do you colour your hair? Do you put things on it?'

'Do you think I'm a real blonde?'

'Well – you seem to be.'

Emily lowered the top of her head down to Maggie's eye-level. 'Look,' she commanded.

'Oh, yes, you've got brown hair, yes, you can hardly see it though.'

'I do it myself from this bottle of stuff I've discovered, it's called –' and Emily giggled, '"Secret Sin." I just dab it on with cotton wool. I got braver and braver and now I'm *secret-sinned* all over!'

Maggie stared at Emily in fascination. 'Do you mean – all over?' she asked hesitantly.

'Maybe,' said Emily and she smiled with her own secret.

Too late now to forget your smile

sang Rangi, looking at Emily who didn't notice, strumming the guitar in the special Maori way.

'When I first did my whole head my father passed me in the street!' said Emily, 'he was really surprised when I chased him down the road calling out "Dad! Dad!" He was cross too, didn't think it was quite seemly – but he soon got over it; I persuaded him it was good for his image to have a blonde daughter, made him more sophisticated.' She laughed at the sea in a brittle, sharp way. 'He's always thinking about his *image*, how he can get people to vote for him. It seems to me if he chased a few less women he might improve things. He's lucky he doesn't get splashed all over *THE FACTS!*' and she splashed at the water angrily, for emphasis. 'He's lucky they wouldn't dream of writing the truth about Sex and Public Figures – murders in the bushes are more their **metier** and even my father would draw the line at that.' And she stared, as Maggie had, down and down through the water. 'Well – he would *probably* draw the line at that.'

Maggie digested all this and then said: 'What – um – what

does your mother say? About him chasing women?'

Emily's chirpy face changed, and at first she said nothing. 'I think it's horrible for her,' she said finally, seriously. 'But she doesn't *say* anything. She's been ground down somehow. Do you know, she was actually much taller when she was young. It's as if he's *flattened* her.' Then she shrugged. 'I just can't believe he'll go on and on, getting away with it. Sometimes I even find myself wishing he would get exposed in some way but what do I mean? Everyone in this country is so tight-lipped about sex, divorce is a terrible sin, who would "expose" him? Certainly not *THE FACTS!*' And again she splashed at the water angrily. 'I'd better do my roots tonight. The papers come and make us pose you know, as A Happy Family. And tomorrow night our Happy Little Family has to entertain the most important businessman in the country and his Happy Little Family, because my father wants to be King of the City. And Mum and I go along with it, wouldn't dream of not,' and she laughed again in the sharp, brittle way, pushed at her hair with her hands, her red nails bright against the blonde. 'Hypocrites, aren't we?'

Rangi strummed on, looking at Emily.

'Are you going to be an MP?' asked Maggie.

'You're *joking*,' said Emily. 'What a horrible, horrible life. Everyone in the country allowed to have your phone number and ring you up about their drains. And they don't want *women* there while they sit plotting to stab each other in that horrible, dark old building. It looks like a dignified, posh place on the outside but it's got lots of little murky corners, and they never have all the lights on. I think it's spooky. No, I'm going to be an economic philosopher and quarrel with government strategies, that'll blow his mind. At least –' and she suddenly smiled slyly down at her hands, '– that's what I'll *probably* be. But I just might end up as a housewife and sur-prise everybody.' She ran her fingers through her short hair again, in that way she had, and then she looked at Maggie and said, 'Things change when you fall in love. Have you ever been in love?'

Just at that moment they turned out towards the open sea and the wind caught the side of the boat as it rose on a peak of a wave; everyone was suddenly thrown to one side of the *Napoli* as it plunged down again and hit the water and everybody yelled and shouted.

'S'orright, s'orright!' cried Franco still holding his beer in one hand as he steered the boat. 'Just caught a gusto, s'orright!' and, in the way the weather can change so quickly on those islands, it began suddenly to rain.

'Good!' called Paddy, pushing slightly at his wig, 'this is what we want, now everybody take a line – here, bait your hooks, you girls,' and Emily and Maggie screeched as he threw some open mussel shells at them. Maggie saw Sarah the typist, who had long brown hair in a ponytail, smile up at Tane the geologist as he knelt beside her, helping to put a mussel on her hook, pushing his spectacles up on to his nose over and over again as he leaned forward. Roimata, the telephone operator, was baiting her hook expertly; Paul was standing beside her, copying her. Then Manu came from the other end of the boat and showed Maggie and Emily how to do it, smiling his big wide smile at them both and Maggie hugged her secret. Franco turned off the engine and the boat bobbed and knocked against the sea and rain fell gently.

Maggie threw her line overboard, just missing Sarah's, bumping into Harry Beans with her elbow, who pinched her.

'DON'T!' she said angrily.

'Well, look where you're going then,' said Harry Beans. 'And don't you dare bite me!'

'I'll bite you if you pinch me!' sparked Maggie.

Soon there were lines over both sides of the boat.

Mrs Tipene from Adoptions caught the first fish, a large kingfish. They all cheered as she pulled it aboard; it wriggled and slapped its tail on the wooden deck. Mrs Tipene expertly hit it on the head with a stone, took the hook out, baited up again. Maggie stared, half admiring, half shocked. The big fish hit its tail disconsolately once more on the wet deck, and died.

'I've caught his cousin!' called Paul, pulling in another big kingfish, and he grinned at them all.

Maggie's first fish was a snapper. She felt it jerk on the line, pulled up more in surprise than knowledge and then fell back slightly as she hauled her line in wildly. 'Look at it, look at it, it's *huge*!' she whooped. The fish flapped violently against her legs, knocking her off-balance, she slipped on the wet deck, fell, struggled up.

'Now what do I do?' she cried and the others looked at her.

'Come on, *e hoa*, don't be a girl,' said Manu. 'Look at *Emihi*.' And sure enough, there was Emily taking a hook out nonchalantly, throwing a large fish on the pile, smiling at Manu.

Maggie's snapper jumped and fought her and Maggie started screaming in alarm.

'Take out the hook,' called Paddy, hauling in his own big fish. She pulled at the hook which went harder into the fish and cold blood ran from its mouth down her skirt.

'I *can't*. Help! look at the poor thing, someone *help*!'

Tane cheerfully, but in some disdain, took out the hook. He held his spectacles on his nose with one hand and banged the fish hard on the deck with the other, then placed the bleeding, cold, scaly thing back on to Maggie's lap.

'You eat fish and chips,' he said reasonably. 'This is how they catch the fish,' and the others laughed at Maggie's face. She threw the fish on the deck and it stared coldly at her.

What do you want to make those eyes at me for

Rangi sang and everybody laughed again.

The rain cleared and the sun shone and finally the fish stopped biting; not that they needed any more fish. Everybody took off their coats and their jackets and their swannies. Franco turned the boat inshore to get out of the wind, then stopped the engine again and got his stove going. Mrs Tipene and Manu and Hori scaled and cut the fish, cooked them in butter. They all ate fish sandwiches and drank DB bitter and sighed and grunted in satisfaction. Shiny scales glittered on the bottom of the boat.

They threw the brown bottles into the water and watched them float slowly away.

> Got my seat and got my reservation
> Why did I decide to roam
> Gonna make a sentimental journey
> Sentimental journey home.

Hope's plaintive voice drifted out over the sea. People sat back in the sunshine, feeling it warm their faces and their arms.

Manu and Tane and Hori talked about rugby and the coming South African tour; Rangi pulled a jersey over his eyes and his cigarette and lay there singing quietly in harmony with Hope. Mrs Tipene snored gently beside Paul, who was reading 'War and Peace'. Maggie rinsed the bottom of her skirt in the sea, she hadn't known fish had all that *blood*. She lit a Senior Service cigarette and leaned back against the side of the boat, watching the small green waves. Sometimes she stared across at Manu. Once he smiled at her, his big, sunshine smile. She thought how happy she was, and it was a new feeling.

She had been learning Maori proverbs off by heart: she recited them to herself in the warm sun: *he whenua, he wahine, ka ngaro te tangata*; *For land and for women, men are lost.* Land again. It seemed to come into everything. And she thought of how they all sat there at their desks day after day filling in the huge land files with more and more names as the land got more and more fragmented. And as for women: the Maori poems and legends were weighed down with great love affairs, doomed love affairs; young people from different tribes not being able to marry each other, like Romeo and Juliet, doomed.

'Doomed! doomed!' she intoned to herself, giggling. 'For land and for women, men die!'

Gallipoli Gordon heard her talking to herself.

'With my people it wasn't the land,' he said to her in his deep voice, his eyes closed in the sunshine. 'With my people it was measles.'

'Measles? What?'

'Measles. Most of the tribes lost their young men fighting you fellas for our land. But where I was born in *Te Wai Pounamu*, the South Island, near the mountains, you fellas brought the measles.' Gallipoli had such a deep voice that she could feel the wood of the boat vibrating between them as he spoke. 'Almost all my people died.'

'Well, you don't *die* of measles,' said Maggie. 'I've had measles and all I got was a few red spots.'

'We died of measles,' said Gallipoli, his eyes still closed in the sunshine. 'Decimated. *Te Tatau o te Po.*'

Maggie repeated it after him curiously: '*Te Tatau o te Po.*'

'The door of the night,' said Gallipoli, as the wood of the boat vibrated between them and she understood that he meant death and for some reason, staring at his closed eyes, she shivered in the sunshine, felt the hair crawl on the back of her neck.

'Gallipoli?' she said uneasily after a moment.

But Gallipoli was asleep.

And the sea? she wondered later as the boat rocked gently and everybody slept in the sun, *who owns the sea, what are the proverbs about the sea? No one says 'for the sea men die'. Yet if I was away from the sea I don't think I could bear it.*

She saw that Manu slept against the ropes at the end of the boat, his face smooth and serious for once as his breath went in and out. She did not know how long she stared at his brown skin. She stood up finally, stiff; stretched; climbed over the dozing bodies to sit next to Prudence who handed her a cigarette from her packet.

'What a lovely day to remember,' said Prudence. 'How peaceful we all are. Even Harry Beans looks calm while he's asleep!' She lit their cigarettes, smiled her sweet smile. Smoke drifted above them.

'Emily seems to have a lot of trouble from her father, doesn't she?' said Maggie. 'What does your father do, Pru?'

Prudence said: 'My father is dead.'

'Oh – I'm – I'm sorry, sorry Pru,' said Maggie, embarrassed. She wished she hadn't asked the question, patted Prudence's arm awkwardly and they sat gently rocking in the sunshine, smoking in silence.

'Have you ever considered,' said Prudence after a while, the thought seeming to come from nowhere, 'whether there are Only Adults? Like there are Only Children?'

Maggie pondered what she might mean. 'Like – um – widows?'

'No,' said Prudence.

'Well – like old maids?'

'Maybe,' said Prudence.

'It's a funny question,' said Maggie.

'Oh, well.' Prudence gave a little shrug and smiled her

smile. 'You know I'm studying psychology at university – I just like to see what other people think about things, and it's just an expression I came across, "an only adult". They've got their heads buried in textbooks and theories up there, I like to try things out on real people.'

'Hey, look at the time!' called Paddy, 'we'll have to be getting back,' and Franco stood and stretched and at last turned the little boat back down the coast. In the distance the city shone in the sunshine, the corrugated-iron roofs glittered. Far away they saw the *Ruahine* sailing away to the other end of the world, twelve thousand miles.

'Just think,' said Roimata, 'it'll take them six weeks and it'll be winter when they get there, poor fellas,' and she stretched in the sunshine, large and content.

'No,' said Mrs McMillan from Welfare who had been born in Yorkshire. She looked in a little mirror and put on more lipstick. 'No, winter will be well over, it'll be spring when they arrive. They'll see daffodils in all the parks and blossom everywhere and those long, slow twilights.'

'Do you miss it? England?' Prudence was trailing her hand in the water, looking at Mrs McMillan. The angle of the sun caught Prudence's hair, Maggie thought she looked beautiful, wondered again what she'd meant: *an Only Adult*. Perhaps she'd said it because she lived alone, which was strange for a girl. Strange for anybody to live alone really, Maggie couldn't imagine it.

Mrs McMillan was quiet for a while, putting away her make-up, and then she said sensibly, 'Only sometimes. People always miss their home sometimes because that's where their memories are. But I came out here with my husband when I was twenty and my kids were born here and my parents are dead now. So this is where my life is, really.' But she looked sombre for a moment, stared at the *Ruahine* as it sailed away.

Tane, who was eighteen, pushed at his spectacles and put

his arm around her. "Course it is,' he said, "course your life's here. This is God's Own Country.'

She patted his arm but she looked at him curiously. 'I can't understand why you lot aren't more bitter,' she said.

'What d'you mean?'

'Well, remember I work in Welfare,' said Mrs McMillan. But then she shrugged and smiled. 'Never mind. It's a lovely day. Sing us a song, Hope,' and Hope sang:

> *Pokarekare ana*
> *Nga wai o Rotorua*

the troubled waters of Rotorua would grow calm if only you crossed them, my darling.

As the *Napoli* chugged back to the city Franco the boat-owner sang the loudest. The young people looked at him in surprise.

'I learnta thissa song in Italia,' he cried, steering the boat with one hand, waving his other in the air. 'The Maoris sang to us ina the camps ina the war, donna you know that? We all sounded the same, Italians, Maoris – our languages are almost the same. We taughta them *"O Solo Mio"* and they taughta us *"Pokarekare Ana*!" And as he sang on about the troubled waters of Rotorua and of love he suddenly surprised them all by kissing Hui on both cheeks, who laughed in great embarrassment and pushed Franco away with his wooden leg which he was holding on his lap.

When the singing boat docked, they shared out and wrapped up the rest of the fish and then the men, looking most anxiously at their watches, staggered quickly up to the Prince of Wales, as usual.

That night the singing at Prudence's house was more boisterous: a kind of wild energy took hold of all of them who had been drinking and singing all day; Hope and Rangi strummed and sang louder than ever so that the waters of Lake Rotorua grew even wilder and rougher, and even Maggie played on the little ukelele as Manu had taught her, and she sang loudly as she drank another bottle of beer and smiled at Manu who was straightening Paddy's wig. There was a lot of shouting and laughing: Emily had been dared by Hori and Rangi to stick a big, bright transfer of Elvis Presley on to her calf and leave it there for forty-eight hours including when the important businessman came to dinner.

'We'll bet you a flagon of sherry!'

'Easy!' said Emily, as Elvis appeared above her ankle and all the boys laughed, and looked, wistfully perhaps, at her beautiful legs.

'Oh, heavens,' said Maggie, grabbing her swannie and her fish, suddenly seeing the time, 'I must run.' She looked around then for Manu but he had somehow disappeared. She was surprised by the strength of her disappointment, but she could not wait. Waving and running she called goodbye to the others and disappeared down the hill to the tram stop.

She just caught the 9.30 tram, staggered to a seat with her fish, feeling her face red from the sun or the beer or the running or her own sudden anxiety.

'Hello Maggie,' said a voice from the seat opposite her. Ruth Page, she was Ruth Peterson now, had been several classes above her at secondary school. She had long hair and high cheekbones; at school she had told everybody loftily that she would become a writer and be a Bohemian and write about life. However she had married her boyfriend as soon as she turned eighteen and had had her picture in the paper on the Brides' page, white and flowing and smiling up at her husband, which didn't seem very Bohemian to Maggie.

'Been to a party?' Ruth enquired, raising her eyebrows at Maggie's appearance, or smelling the beer perhaps.

'Yes and fishing,' said Maggie, still breathless, 'I caught lots of snapper, look, do you want some?' and she thrust the pile of fish at Ruth, who pulled away hastily.

'No thanks,' she said, but she smiled politely. 'Nice to see you. Have you heard Denis and I are leaving for England as soon as we finish our degrees this year? We've already booked our passage, we'll pack all our belongings in tea chests and get away from here as fast as our little legs will carry us.'

Maggie remembered that in the embarrassing school dancing classes, dancing with Denis Peterson while the old-maid sports mistress thumped out *'Some Day My Prince Will Come'*, was even worse than dancing with a chair when there weren't enough boys.

'That'll be nice,' she said politely.

'And we'll also go to Egypt and Spain and France and Greece. I can't wait! I long to stand on old stones in old streets that go back to the beginning of time.'

'You could stand on old stones here,' suggested Maggie, 'there's plenty down the end of our street.' She hiccupped.

Ruth looked at her witheringly. 'I want to *feel history*,' she said, 'we don't get that feeling here, we haven't *got* any history. Did you know you can go to the Greek island of Kos and stand under the tree where medicine started? We haven't got anything like that here because this place hasn't *got* any history – we've only existed a hundred years!' And Ruth's eyes shone brighter than Maggie's beer-and-sunshine eyes as the tram clanked along the streets.

'What are you doing these days, Maggie, apart from going fishing and going to parties? I see you running along the corridors up at Varsity, you always seem to be running; you're only studying part-time, aren't you?'

Maggie explained about working at the Bureau and about learning Maori. Ruth looked mystified.

'Whatever for? Oh here's my stop.' She stood up and rang the bell. 'Whatever for?' she repeated.

Maggie said, 'Well it's there, in my work.'

'But it's a dying language,' said Ruth, puzzled, holding on to the leather strap, swaying with the swaying tram car.

'Yes, I know.'

Ruth shrugged. 'Can't see the point myself,' she said and she smiled goodbye as the tram lurched noisily to a standstill and she jumped down the metal steps. Her eyes shone back as she waved to Maggie from the tram stop, her search for her history mapped out and waiting.

The wind blew Maggie and her fish down her street and she wondered suddenly who it was that Emily was in love with.

FOURTEEN

The two men stood with their whisky glasses, in their dinner suits, beside the big windows. They looked down on the city: their suits and their cigar smoke seemed to say: *we own this place*. The lights of the cargo boats and the fishing boats and the ferries glittered back.

Dinner was over (two hired waiters had served discreetly); the two wives and the two daughters sat at the other end of the big room looking decorative in evening dress, even Emily had done her roots and dressed in pretty pink. Only if you had looked very carefully would you have noticed Elvis Presley appearing now and then, beneath the tulle.

John Evans had come home from Parliament early, had impressed upon his wife and daughter the importance of this dinner. 'This is an incredibly important evening,' he'd boomed, irritable with nerves. 'Benson can make or break people. I need him.' He had walked up and down anxiously. 'Talk to the women. Make a good impression, eat little chocolates after dinner or whatever.'

So now, while the men talked power and politics and business, Emily and her mother sat and talked in their best social manner; Emily sat demurely with her Elvis leg tucked away.

The businessman's daughter was called Angelique and she was telling them about rehearsing to be a debutante. She was an extremely pretty girl, her fair curls fell forward as she spoke and her wired, pointy bra, all the rage, pointed her breasts at her listeners like arrows.

'We are rehearsing a deep curtsey,' said Angelique. 'We meet on Tuesdays with a nun who knows about these things. One knee must be firmly placed behind the other, for balance. Then we must take four steps backwards before we turn.'

Once John Evans had suggested to Emily she be a debutante: she had laughed in his face: *Everyone knows it's just a meat market for suitable rich husbands*, she had said.

Now she said sweetly, 'And what is the curtsey *for*?'

'For the Vice-Regal chair, of course,' said Angelique's mother and Mrs Evans nodded knowingly.

'Is someone going to be *sitting* in the chair?' asked Emily. Her mother flicked her a warning glance but Emily was smiling demurely at Angelique.

'The Governor-General of course,' said Angelique's mother in reverent tones.

'Of course,' said Emily.

'Of course,' said her mother.

'Tell them about your frock, darling,' said Angelique's mother.

Angelique's eyes shone. 'It's layers and layers of white net and white satin and white tulle and white organza petticoats and it's all floaty and darling and gorgeous.'

'She looks like a princess,' said her mother. 'Her father would spare no expense, of course.'

The men came across, bending over their women, helping them to their feet.

'Time for you girls to come home,' said the businessman jovially. He assisted his wife, but he looked at his only daughter with adoring eyes.

Just as Angelique was slipping on her wrap in the hall she whispered to Emily, 'It's strapless. We're keeping it a secret.'

'What?'

'My debutante's dress. This kind of bra holds it up. It's strapless.' And she pointed her breasts at Emily in triumph.

Emily flicked the pink tulle so that her leg was suddenly clearly visible.

'That'll be exciting,' she said. 'Have a nice time.'

Angelique looked puzzled. 'I think you'll be there, won't you?' she said, staring uneasily at the sudden appearance of Elvis Presley.

As soon as they had gone the row erupted.

'I am not going to a bloody debutantes' ball!' shouted Emily. 'You can't make me!'

'It's absolutely crucial!' her father shouted back. 'Benson insists we join his party that night. These are the things I have to do if I'm going to be prime minister, I have to have him on my side.' He forced himself to be calmer, pulled another cigar from his pocket. 'I need you, Emmy,' he said. 'There's a ball afterwards. There'll be all sorts of important young men there for you and what's her name – Angelique – to dance with.'

'I have my own young men.' There was a dangerous glitter about Emily's eyes which he saw; he also thought he might have caught sight of something peculiar on her leg: he urgently looked away. He lit the cigar busily, pulled on it; the manly smoke spiralled upwards.

'When I become Prime Minister,' he said, 'you can have anything you want. Until I become Prime Minister, I must insist that you don't let me down.' And he stalked from the room leaving the thick, acrid smoke of the cigar as a reminder to his wife to deal with his recalcitrant daughter.

'You know this man owns newspapers,' said Mrs Evans gently. 'John needs the newspapers.'

Emily flung herself into an armchair, pink tulle everywhere. If Mrs Evans saw Elvis she did not mention it.

'Why do we do it, Mum?'

'So that we can be a –' and her mother's voice caught and she turned away, busied herself at the table, 'a – happy family.'

Emily thought of the photographs of her mother as a young girl, confident and laughing. She ran her hands through her hair, the red nails shone. She got up again, put her arms round her mother for a moment, poured herself a last sherry from the decanter.

'OK,' she said. 'But it's for you, not for him. No doubt it'll be a laugh.' She drained the glass quickly. 'I pity any poor man dancing with Angelique, he'll get stabbed. Those pointy bras are lethal weapons.'

'She's a very pretty girl,' said Mrs Evans.

'She told me her debutante frock is strapless.'

Mrs Evans looked quite shocked. 'Girls who go strapless are *fast*,' she said.

In the huge, gilded reception room at Government House where the young Queen of England stared down at her subjects, the floating, white girls curtseyed deeply to the Governor-General, took four steps backwards before turning from his presence. Only one girl tripped badly, fled screeching in mortification.

And Angelique Benson floated more, shone more, breast-pointed more. Her bare, white shoulders, her shining eyes, her flushed cheeks all added to the picture of a beautiful, young, untouched girl, coming out, just waiting to be plucked by Mr Right.

John Evans stared discreetly, transfixed by the vision of loveliness.

FIFTEEN

Emily Evans executed deep curtseys in the Housing Department.

People in the Bureau had heard of Angelique Benson: she was so pretty, somebody had suggested in the paper that she could win any Miss World contest: her father (the proprietor of the paper), proud but firm, said his only daughter would not be parading in a bathing suit in front of men.

When Maggie came in to find Emily after work, passing all the men running to the Prince of Wales, Emily showed Maggie how to curtsey too. They pointed their breasts at the Housing Statistics chart on the green wall, took four steps backwards as they put files away in the Housing-Cases Pending. Maggie fell over.

Prudence walked in and watched them, laughing, and then announced that as Paddy their Housing boss, and Gallipoli Gordon, who sang like Mario Lanza, were both, unimaginably, fifty this month, the Head Boss had somehow been persuaded to agree that on Friday night the Bureau could have an office party.

'Fifty? Gosh, imagine being *fifty*!' They giggled at the unimaginable and put on lipstick. The rain fell outside. The three girls made sure they left the office tidy before they put on their raincoats.

'An office party,' they sang as they ran out into the grey, raining evening and put up umbrellas.

As they laughed up the hill Emily said suddenly: 'I saw my father watching Angelique Benson. But I don't think even he would be quite so foolhardy.'

'And anyway,' said Maggie, 'he'd be stabbed by her pointy breasts.'

It was arranged that Prudence would make two birthday cakes and ice PADDY and GALLIPOLI on them; Emily would make pikelets; Hope would make sausage rolls ('*Blind sausage rolls!*' Harry Beans had said when he heard this, rolling his eyes up into his head). The men, of course, would provide the beer with a bit of a contribution from the Bureau Social Fund.

Maggie asked her mother if she would help her make some pavlovas.

'All right,' said Maggie's mother.

It was still raining. They had seen the evening paper's headlines and listened to the news on the wireless and had heard that the Leader of the Opposition, at present on a visit to London where he was to be graciously received by Queen Elizabeth, might have to step down from his position because of ill-health. A second paragraph in the paper suggested that should this sad resignation come to pass, Mr John Evans, ex-sheep farmer, was easily the man most fitted to step into his leader's shoes and take over – rejuvenate even – his party. A line mentioned his very bright daughter Emily Evans; Maggie's parents were astonished to hear that the politician's daughter worked at the Bureau also.

'I'm surprised he allows it,' said Mrs Bennett.

Now her father sat by the fire listening to 'Much Binding in the Marsh' and in the kitchen Maggie and her mother beat the egg whites, taking turns with the hand beater, slowly adding the sugar. Maggie listened to the sounds of her home: funny voices and occasional gales of laughter coming through the wall from the wireless, the grandfather clock in the hall chiming on the quarter, the rain drumming on the unlined corrugated iron of the wash-house roof. She felt a sudden shiver at time passing; felt it happen in the kitchen, imperceptibly winding her childhood away from her without her ever having understood it.

'Mum. Do you think of Elizabeth?'

Nobody mentioned Elizabeth, ever. Her mother had been spooning the stiff white mixture onto the oven trays covered with grease-proof paper and for a moment she stood motionless. The rain fell. Finally she said. 'Every day. Every day of my life,' and Maggie knew this was an accusation of some kind, for her.

*

Up in the high room Isobel Arapeta told her pupils: *Waiata is a Maori word meaning song. It also means to sing. There are many kinds of songs. The old pre-European Maori songs, kind of atonal chants about love and war and death and land, were not written down but passed through memory from generation to generation; they were ambiguous, cryptic and, like their proverbs, full of many meanings. From the time of the coming of the Pakeha the Victorian ballads and the German drinking songs and the Scandinavian lullabies were appropriated by the Maoris as their own; given new sounds and often new rhythms, a kind of bluesy country and western sound strummed on guitars, echoing in small towns and big cities, at bus stops and in dance halls; the same songs all over the country.*

*

At 4.35 PM sharp on Friday afternoon the pens went down, the files were closed, the men were gone to the pub.

'Now then,' said Mrs Tipene.

The men had placed the chairs around the walls of the Land Court in the lunch-hour, and put up big wooden trestle tables. Mrs Tipene and Hoana, one of the machinists, had brought in big, white, starched tablecloths and now they laid them across, carefully not to get their cigarette ash on the whiteness. They put jamjars full of daisies from Mrs Tipene's garden on all the tables, bustled in and out. Sarah the typist and Mrs McMillan from Welfare piled pies and pavlovas, sausage rolls and sandwiches, cheese scones and date scones, sponges, Anzac biscuits, pikelets, mussels, fruit, forks, glasses onto the tables. Maggie sliced and buttered loaves and loaves of bread with Roimata the telephone operator, both balancing their cigarettes on the butter dish.

'How many are coming?' asked Maggie, half joking, half serious, 'someone's army?' but Roimata just laughed and said they didn't want to be caught short, easing her large bulk against one of the tables as she worked.

Prudence and Emily had cut out HAPPY BIRTHDAY PADDY AND GALLIPOLI in pink crêpe paper and were sticking it along one wall of the courtroom with drawing pins, Emily balancing dangerously on a shelf of files in her white stiletto shoes and her pretty yellow dress that matched her hair. Mrs Tipene reappeared, staggering under the weight of four large legs of cold mutton on a huge tray. The two iced birthday cakes were put on the judge's bench.

'What extraordinarily revolting green icing, Pru!' said Emily, staring at the two cakes in amazement.

'I know, I know,' said Prudence, laughing. 'I dropped the whole bottle of green colouring into the icing mixture!'

As they bustled about Hoana gave Hope the guitar. 'Sing us a song, *e hoa,*' she said.

'Give us a drink,' said Hope.

Hoana produced a flagon of sweet sherry and she poured

out glassfuls for anyone who wanted it, balancing the full glasses rather precariously on a pile of land files. Hope sang in her plaintive, bluesy voice

Pokarekare ana
Nga wai o Rotorua

The other women joined in, some of them singing in harmony, *the troubled waters of Lake Rotorua would grow calm if you crossed them, my darling*, the cheap Victorian ballad whistled by the whalers, the one even Franco the Italian fisherman knew.

Maggie, singing too, hugged a secret: she had persuaded her parents to let her stay at Prudence's place tonight so that she wouldn't have to run for the last tram, and so that they could practise French next morning as it was Saturday. But it wasn't Prudence she was going to stay with. She had decided, daringly, to take her fate into her own hands and stay with Manu. She didn't even mind staying in his funny untidy house with all those kids and clothes and no furniture if that's what he wanted. At the thought that he might hold her, properly hold her and what she might learn at last, her heart jumped.

Ka mate ahau i
Te aroha e

I am quite ill with love, she translated to herself, singing gleefully, thinking of the pretty nightie and her toothbrush at the bottom of her satchel. Before she started university and working at the Bureau she knew all girls were virgins until they got married because everybody had said so. Now she wasn't so sure that this was entirely true. She didn't want to not be a virgin exactly, but she wanted to *know* about sex. Manu would know. She wondered what he would say when she told him she was coming to stay and she grinned and sang and drank sherry.

The old land files packed on the shelves along the walls stared down at her with their rustling silence but Maggie did not notice. As she piled up the bread and drank the sherry she looked about her, thought how different the courtroom felt, full now of women and bottles and food: how could it ever have seemed ominous?

There was banging and shouting out in the street.

'Must've gone six,' said Hope drily.

The men walked up the stairs in groups, all carrying wooden crates of beer, lots of laughing and banging down of bottles and lighting up of more cigarettes, the strum of guitars in the background. Then other people started arriving: wives with more plates of food, some rugby players, the bosses in their suits, Maoris, Pakehas, two Samoan nurses, some Rarotongan girls who sewed handbags in a factory and wore flowers in their hair. The Land Court crushed and vibrated with people and smoke and noise.

'Where's Manu, where's Manu?' shouted Maggie to Rangi. He was opening beer bottles two at a time with his teeth, a feat they all practised.

'He had to see his grandfather,' he shouted back, 'he'll be here later.'

'Good!' cried Maggie, laughing and drinking her sherry fast.

'Maggie, this is Bay Ropata,' said Paddy, 'he's the head of the Welfare Department.' *Oh, God yes, the maniac who's supposed to have given the prisoners of war a big feed before he shot them dead.* The stocky, grey-haired Maori man she'd seen in the office and marching in the Anzac parade pressed his nose against Maggie's twice as he took her hand. She leaned back from him, deeply alarmed.

'You're Tiny Bennett's girl, aren't you?' he asked her, and

she nodded, still breathless from having her nose squashed by a person with a much larger nose than hers who was meant to be a maniac. 'Aaah, great prop forward, I remember him way back in those All Black trials, what does he say about you learning the Maori language, eh?'

Maggie looked at him in surprise, fancy him knowing that. 'Um – he doesn't mind,' she said rather inadequately, hoping he never met her father in the street. And then she burst out, 'I love it, I *love* learning it, I love the sound.' And then she blushed.

He looked at her for a moment, shrewd eyes. '*Kia kaha e hoa*,' he said which she knew meant, 'be strong'. Then he introduced her to his Maori wife Rima, and his two teenage boys. He didn't seem terribly maniacal.

'*Kia ora*,' said Maggie shyly and shook hands with them all.

At the other end of the room someone banged on one of the tables for silence and Mrs Tipene grabbed the bread as it started to slide from its high buttered pile. Maggie had only seen the Head Boss about twice, a remote pale man in a suit even on the hottest days, no shorts and long socks for him.

'Ladies and Gentlemen –' the Head Boss cleared his throat, 'Ladies and Gentlemen, it gives me great pleasure, ladies and gentlemen, to welcome everyone here tonight to celebrate the birthdays of Paddy O'Rourke from Housing and Gallipoli Gordon from Alienations. They are two of the men in this office that we could not do without, indispensable. Nobody remembers better than I do when they arrived to work here. Those days, after the war, when we all returned from overseas, when we came back to God's Own Country – and by God it *is* God's Own Country, we found that out after our adventures on the other side of the world *blah blah blah blah . . .*'

Emily's blonde hair, and then Emily herself emerged at

Maggie's shoulder through the crowd, carrying a huge sherry flagon with a yellow ribbon round it.

'This is the one I won from the boys for wearing Elvis on my leg,' she said and she grinned, filled Maggie's glass; they crossed their eyes at each other at the droning voice and the boring, favourite subject: 'The War'.

'Have you seen Manu?' whispered Emily, searching the crowd.

'He's got to see his grandfather, Rangi said,' Maggie whispered back, 'He's coming later.' There was a ripple of applause at something the Head Boss said. *I'll tell Emily*, Maggie thought. *I'll tell her about Manu.*

Underneath the applause Emily said, 'Don't laugh, Maggie, I'm in love with Manu. I want to marry him.'

Maggie dropped the glass of sherry, it didn't break, just rolled into a corner. Orange liquid trickled along the courtroom floor.

'*What*?' said Maggie, staring at her friend. Then she bent down automatically, scrabbling around people's feet, 'Sorry, sorry,' retrieving the glass. '*What*?' she said to Emily again.

'Here, have some more,' whispered Emily as the boss still droned on. 'I know I know, he's a Maori, I'm at university and he's only got school certificate, don't remind me. But honestly, Mags, if you knew him like I do you'd understand and not be shocked. Don't be shocked, you're my friend.' A burst of applause again and this time people waved their empty glasses and started singing 'Happy Birthday,' and cheering. Maggie stared in disbelief at Emily's back in her yellow dress that matched her hair as she filled people's glasses from the yellow-ribboned flagon, smiling and chatting, the belle of the ball. Then Bay Ropata, the maniac, began speaking in Maori: his eyes shone; beautiful, resonant words rolled off his tongue and filled every corner of the courtroom, flowed under the trestle tables, up to the ceiling, along the shelves and shelves of files.

'Doesn't it sound lovely,' whispered Emily reappearing, leaning her elbow on the sherry flagon, listening to Bay. 'Even if I don't understand a word of it, if my Manu and I had children I'd make sure they spoke it. Don't stare at me like that Maggie!' and she grinned and disappeared again to pour more sherry.

Maggie watched her blankly. *Her* Manu? There had to be some misunderstanding surely? Manu who had unlocked Maggie's feelings? Who made her laugh? Who smoothed her skin with his warm, warm hands, down by the sea? *I've brought my nightie.*

Bay finished his speech and Mrs Tipene began singing another old ballad whistled by the whalers and Bay and lots of the others joined in; something mournful about it, like their kind of blues.

Tangi mai e te tau
Mohou kua wehea nei

'Now come along everyone,' cried Mrs Tipene when the song ended, 'everybody eat something now, come along, *haere mai ki te kai*. Bay, will you give the blessing please.'

And the room went slowly quiet as Bay Ropata said grace and then everyone crowded round the tables and Mrs Tipene and Hoana appeared with huge steaming saucepans.

Maggie emptied another glass of sweet sherry automatically.

'Oh, boy, pork and *puha*, have you had this Maggie?' and Tane the geologist, his spectacles quite steamed up, thrust a plate of pork ribs covered with something green like spinach into her hands.

Harry Beans who already had a plateful said to her. 'You might quite like this hori food you know; it's only sort of watercress, the green stuff,' and Maggie stood there with a steaming plate seeing Paddy and Gallipoli looking round the throng at their fiftieth birthday party, drinking beer and smiling and smiling. On the far side of the room Emily still stood with the sherry flagon, laughing with some of the rugby players and watching the door.

Maggie looked down at the plate in her hand. 'I think I'm drunk,' she remarked to Hoana, shaking her head vigorously, trying to make her thoughts fit in there, not spill out and make a mess on the courtroom floor.

'Don't shake your head like that, eat more porkbones,' said Hoana, 'that'll soak it up. Nothing can survive porkbones,' and she actually put her hand out to Maggie, 'Stop it! your brains'll fall out,' and she laughed. So Maggie laughed too and just at that moment Manu came into the courtroom.

He looked terrible.

'*E hoa*, what's wrong?' said Hoana to Manu, 'you look as if you've been crying mate.'

Maggie had never seen a man look as if he'd been crying before; his eyes were swollen and Maggie could see that he was very drunk. He didn't see Emily; he avoided Maggie's eyes and spoke in a surly voice to Hoana. 'Meremere is *hapu*,' he said and his words slurred. 'My grandfather is mad at me and says we have to get married in the church in three weeks.'

'Well that's all right,' said Hoana, 'I thought someone'd died! What're you crying for, you big sookey, it'll be lovely to have a baby; is Meremere crying?'

'No, she's pleased,' said Manu, 'she's been wanting to get married for ages.'

'Well then,' said Hoana.

Finally Manu looked at Maggie. She shrugged and made herself smile at him. He looked relieved at her smile, half smiled back, shame-faced. And then she saw him look towards the door uneasily as if to escape, as Emily came eagerly towards him through the people.

Maggie Bennett laughed a little stiff laugh, the way she had laughed before she knew him, and thought of her pretty nightie at the bottom of her bag. '*Kia kaha*,' she said to Manu as Bay Ropata had said to her, *be strong*.

Emily in her yellow dress, the belle of the ball, came up to Manu, laughing, putting out her hand to touch his face and she said to him, 'Where've you been, Manu?'

Maggie moved away quickly, seeing just for a moment the sea in the darkness, and the shapes of the sandhills and the cutty grass moving in the wind as her unruly hair fell across his chest.

The noise rose and rose. The court was so hot all the men had taken off their jackets and loosened their ties and rolled up their sleeves; women's cardigans were draped neatly over the judge's bench. The fat, grey-haired man named Sinatra who everyone called the King of the City arrived in a bright red shirt and almost at once began to sing, as if true to his name, but he sang Maori songs not Frank Sinatra songs. More and more people joined in: *Me he manu rere*; *if only I was a bird*, they all sang. The strum of lots of guitars became more and more insistent, Hope and Rangi and Hori and Roimata and Hui all playing together, urging each other on, singing song after song; other Maoris with guitars appearing, joining them.

> My tears have washed
> I Love You from
> the blackboard of my heart,
> It's too late to clean the slate
> and make another start

and the group around them getting bigger and bigger, the tables pushed into a corner, the women clearing the plates and the debris, more and more people singing.

A space was clear for the Samoan nurses who danced twirling their hands and their feet. Then the Raratonga girls – just finished their shift at the bag factory – got up. All the guitars immediately began strumming faster and the girls moved faster in time to the strumming, their eyes smiled and their hips moved, faster and faster, and it seemed to Maggie the flowers shone in their shining hair. Everyone was flushed and smiling and drinking, empty sherry flagons lay everywhere and empty brown beer bottles rolled along the courtroom floor. Someone took Hope to the lavatory, Maggie saw how she looked up smiling at the electric light as she was led away.

Hui propped his wooden leg on a chair, strummed, began to sing.

Pa mai to reo aroha
Ki te pae o Aotearoa

and at once Bay Ropata gave a great leap into the air and then stood, poised, his hands outstretched and quivering and other Maoris joined him until a whole group of them were singing and doing strange graceful actions in unison and leaning backwards and forwards as they sang. *It's different dancing again,* thought Maggie, *their hips move differently and I think it's something to do with sex, not that I'll ever know anything about sex.* Gallipoli Gordon's Mario Lanza voice soared up. Maggie saw that Paddy was doing the actions shyly and not very well from where he was standing across the room and the Maoris called out to him, beckoning him over as they sang, but Paddy's thin body just swayed drunkenly where he was, his wig only very slightly askew, smiling and smiling, his good birthday party. Bay Ropata, and Sinatra in his red shirt, led them all; to Maggie's surprise other Pakehas had now joined the group. *Prudence* of all people knew the actions, and the Head Boss with his jacket off, and even her boss of the Land

Records office who was always so rude about Maoris had joined in. Manu was singing too Maggie saw, his eyes still swollen but laughter back in his face and holding his head high the way they all did and she looked away from him quickly; she had no secret now. She thought how their bodies changed as they danced, took on quite different shapes: Mrs Tipene was a bustling, leaning-forward little person but she seemed graceful and somehow very neat as she gestured with her arms; Roimata the telephone operator, who was so fat, looked graceful and actually elegant as her hips moved; Hui didn't look as if he only had one leg: he stood there full of energy and pride.

Maggie had seen these action songs on newsreels at the pictures when the Queen came to visit, she'd never seen them live in front of her eyes before: at school they'd only learned 'Nut Brown Maiden' in English.

Titiro ki nga hoea kua wehea nei

something about soldiers and separation she roughly translated for herself. Oh it's a *war* song, no wonder Paddy and the Head Boss and the others knew it; funny Prudence knowing it, though. They sang on together, people she knew, people she didn't know, perhaps some of them didn't know each other but they sang together in harmony with the guitars strumming in the background as if they'd sung together all their lives as perhaps they had, in memory.

When the song finished everybody in the room stamped and clapped and whistled and people mopped their brows with handkerchiefs and laughed and lit up more cigarettes and drank and Maggie drank and drank too, once looking at Manu's laughing face one more time.

Somehow the ordained times had come to cut the iced birthday cakes on the judge's bench, more speeches and singing, and the courtroom quite literally shuddering as the men finally did a wardance, a **haka**, stamping their feet and rolling their eyes and Bay Ropata putting out his tongue in the traditional way. Maggie looked vaguely for his famous bayonet wound but it remained concealed under his blue shirt. Fruit cake with bright green icing – *Prudence, how did you make it that funny green colour!* – was handed around and for Maggie the evening merged into one long, hot, spinning, sweating song.

She noticed vaguely that Hori, even though he was a Married Man, kissed the **divorcée** behind the judge's bench. She noticed vaguely that Manu and Emily disappeared. She noticed vaguely that she was sitting with Prudence and Rangi and Hoana and Harry Beans and Tane and Sarah and Paul in a big pile on the floor and even then she hoped Paul wouldn't have an epileptic fit. She thought she remembered that Gallipoli Gordon had sung *the party's over it's time to call it a day* which sounded so sad to Maggie that she had actually cried, was that why she was crying? *Was she crying?* She never cried, but she couldn't remember, who would ever love her anyway? Sarah's long pony tail had come undone, seemed wrapped around Tane the geologist's neck in some way. She absolutely *definitely* remembered coming back from the lavatory and talking to Mr Porter, the unfrocked Methodist minister, about his gramophone recordings of 'The Early-Morning Calls of Native Birds'. And hadn't he talked to her about something he called 'The Other'?

'There are spirits,' Mr Porter had said, emerging through the smoke of the cigarettes, his kindly eyes magnified by his spectacles, 'and there are *intentions* all around us,' and she had looked at everybody drunk or singing or asleep, and the smoke and the brown beer bottles and the sherry flagons.

'Well, I know there are radio waves,' she said helpfully, staggering against him, 'Sorry, sorry.'

'Something more,' said Mr Porter, 'I think.'

'Yes, yes, Hori and Rangi believe it,' she perhaps said, but the room was spinning and dancing and laughing, the electric light bulbs looked complicated and fractured as she stared at them the way Hope stared at light. She was sure she had a memory of Paddy falling asleep in a corner, his head in his red wig resting gently in an unfinished bacon and egg pie but later he wasn't there.

Lying on the courtroom floor next to Harry Beans, with her head on Rangi's stomach which moved gently in time to his snores, she saw two old Maori land files float very slowly past her, in the beer.

SIXTEEN

'The bugger's finally realised he's finished!' cowed John Evans in triumph to his lawyer. 'Now, watch me!'

And early the following week, just as Parliament was reconvened (all the farmers hurrying to the city to take up their other occupation as MPs) it was announced officially that the Leader of the Opposition, at present in England, had informed his party that, due to ill-health, he was having to resign as an MP. They didn't even wait for him to come back.

John Evans, ex-sheep farmer, was elected as the new leader. Editors wrote respectful articles in the newspapers:

> Mr Evans's long career as a sheep-farmer makes him ideally placed to understand the needs of our great little country. His record as a serving officer in Egypt with our battalions shows he has the right qualities of leadership and courage, and his time overseas in Britain just after the war means he has contacts with our allies and the Empire.

There was an official photograph of him with his wife and daughter, all smiling, on the front page of all the country's main newspapers. There was an election due at the end of the year but it was surmised it would be called earlier by the incumbent prime minister, before the opposition party could properly be expected to get themselves organised after this sudden change. But the present government was unpopular: the newspapers gave proper weight and seriousness to their profiles of the man who could be their country's next prime minister. There was a small paragraph about Emily and the fact that two years ago she'd had the highest examination marks of any school pupil in the country.

'It's good to have his daughter as your friend,' Mr and Mrs Bennett said to Maggie.

That week, as the winter rain set in, Burt Lancaster appeared in tights in 'Trapeze' at the Rialto Picture Theatre. At the Bureau staff had a collection for a present for Manu's very imminent wedding. Maggie gave two shillings. Roimata went out and bought a big clock and the Head Boss presented it with a short speech in Housing before rushing off to a meeting. Mrs Tipene, who to Maggie's surprise turned out to be Manu's aunt, looked proud and a little triumphant. She hadn't liked the way Emily Evans had run after her nephew with her nail polish and her blonde hair. Meremere was from a very, very good Maori family and Mrs Tipene was pleased.

Manu, leaning on his trolley of files, made a short speech of thanks in English and Maori, not laughing much. He did not look at Maggie.

Maggie did not look at him either; looked, rather, out of the window at the heavy, grey sky.

Emily was away sick.

Down the street the wind blew sodden leaves along the gutters and Paddy leant over to Maggie when Manu had finished his speech and told her she had been transferred to his Housing Department.

She closed the last land register with a grimace of relief; Harry Beans pulled at her arm one final time. 'Ask Prudence

McDonald about her parents,' he said but in all the delight of leaving the interminable land files Maggie forgot.

She saw at once how efficient Paddy was in Housing – dear, bumbling, stumbling Paddy with his wig askew at parties. At work he was a different man; no wonder they were all so fond of him. His vision was of little Bureau houses popping up like magic, all over the city.

'Look, look, look,' he said to Maggie after she'd only been in his department an hour, 'it's brilliantly simple. We want as many Maoris as possible to own their own houses when they come to the city, it's hard to make a big transition like that when so many landlords say NO MAORIS. So we build them houses. We arrange 3½% mortgages and take their child benefit for a deposit. If you're satisfied that all is in order all you have to write on the application form is: "this man seems to be a good provider." Watch Emily, copy Emily, she's a wizard at this stuff; I hope she'll be better soon.'

So on her second day in Housing, because Emily was still away, Maggie found herself showing couples the pretty booklets with the pastel drawings of the neat little houses with trees and children. 'It's *easy* to have a house,' she found herself saying, hoping they didn't realise this was her second day in Housing and she was seventeen. She wrote THIS MAN SEEMS TO BE A GOOD PROVIDER on every form she could find.

But Mr Porter, the unfrocked minister, who had loaned her his gramophone record of 'The Early-Morning Calls of Native Birds' as promised at the office party, shook his head sadly. He was the arrears clerk.

'I'm afraid it doesn't always work out,' he said. 'Sometimes the man turns out not to be a good provider, after all. But we try never to take a house back again if there are children, it wouldn't be right. Look, I've got a new gramophone record for you to listen to. I thought you might find it interesting.' On her desk he placed 'The Sounds of the Mudpools and the

Geysers'. On the cover of the record there was a picture of brown mud, bubbling ferociously.

'Thank you so much, Mr Porter,' said Maggie.

Mr Porter sometimes read the Bible in his lunch-hour, even if he was unfrocked. He brought sandwiches and an apple in a lunch tin every day. He was short and round and kind and Maggie couldn't think what he might have been unfrocked for. He hadn't mentioned 'The Other' again and Maggie wondered whether she had dreamed that bit, had Mr Porter talked to her at the office party about spirits and intentions in the air?

'I like being in Housing,' she said to Paddy at the end of the second day. 'I feel as if I'm actually doing something. And to herself: *it stops me thinking about Manu. What a fool I was. I won't be a fool again. I won't let anybody see that I'm sad. Fancy thinking I loved someone like Manu. How ridiculous I was. How ridiculous.* She still blushed to herself when she thought about the pretty nightie packed at the bottom of her bag. Blushed, huddled over her housing files.

'Just ask Emily if you've got any problems,' said Paddy. 'She's the bee's knees. I hope she'll be better soon and back in the office. I miss her a lot.'

Maggie hoped Emily would stay away forever.

She and Prudence walked up the hill to lectures. Maggie kicked pohutukawa tree roots that pushed up the pavement.

'What's the matter?'

'Nothing. I'm sick of everything. It's all too hard. Maori's too hard.'

She kicked the next tree they passed. 'Land and love, land and love, blah blah blah, Maoris keep going on about them all the time as if nothing else in the world matters. *He whenua, he wahine, ka ngaro te tangata*, that's a proverb that means men are destroyed by land and women, I'm sick of it, why don't they say women are destroyed by stupid men instead?'

Prudence looked at Maggie carefully as she kicked yet another tree. 'Those trees are older than you,' she said gently. But she saw Maggie's miserable face. 'Why don't you ask someone like Bay Ropata to help you with your Maori?' she suggested. 'Go into Welfare one day and ask him, he'd probably be pleased.'

Maggie didn't answer. *Actually, I don't want to take Maori lessons from a maniac, thank you very much.*

But when she got into the library she immediately immersed herself in the one Maori textbook, the present tense, the imperfect tense, the narrative tense, the future tense; *who would ever love me anyway.* She missed Manu and his sunshine smile with a funny pain she'd never had before. She breathed in the smell of the Maori dictionary, holding her head in her hands. *Manu made me stop feeling lonely. I could talk to him. He listened to me.* Over and over she turned the pages of the textbook. *He made me laugh.* She wrote everything she learned in her pavlova notebook. She saw she had written, from one of the old Victorian ballads, **taru kino**, the dangerous vine that the song said making love was.

She finally found a proverb about the sea and she remembered how happy she had felt, the day of the fishing trip. But this proverb was different from the feeling about land; there was a warning rather in the words:

> *Kaore ana te au ahi*
> *Ka pa he au moana e mate*

smoke from a fire is soon gone but a current from the sea causes death.

And for some reason, as the light outside the library windows darkened, Maggie shivered.

The days and nights became even colder.

'Beowulf' and Dr Samuel Johnson appeared on the English syllabus: the pleasures of Keats and Coleridge were replaced by translations of Old English and the history of the development of dictionaries. Manu, married, suddenly left the Bureau to join the police force and Emily looked pale in the Housing Department but Maggie was glad Manu had gone, had hated the flying trolley appearing now round a corner. They gave the trolley to Rangi. He moved with the files more slowly, smoking and whistling.

On her way to her Maori class she observed that the snooty Maori man who was also doing the Maori examinations was sitting, his legs neatly crossed and a university scarf around his neck, on the plinth of the English duke and the snorting horse.

'**Kia ora**,' said Maggie cautiously.

He looked up. She saw he was reading a German textbook.

'Are you studying German *as well*?'

'And French,' he said calmly.

'Heavens, you're a language freak!'

He shrugged but made room for her on the plinth. 'What are you studying Maori for?' he asked.

'I love it!' she said. 'I love the sounds,' and her face lit up and her eyes shone.

He stared at her for a moment. And then he smiled. 'I'm Kara Rikihana,' he said, '*kia ora*.' He shook hands with her limply across the horse's forever-prancing feet and then they walked up the stairs to the small, high room.

After the class Isobel Arapeta looked at her three special students carefully. 'I think you three better come up to my place once a week as well if you're going to have any chance of passing this university examination. We'll start next week, I won't charge, of course.'

So Maggie trudged up the hill against the wind to Isobel's

house which overlooked the harbour. It was so blustery she almost lost her balance and her coat flapped around her legs in the darkness. At the corner she leaned on the wind for a moment, like the seagulls, supported there. And then she turned and pushed on up the hill. The wind seemed to blow the streetlights backwards and forwards, front gates banged shut and she heard the clock on the old fire station tower strike seven.

One of Isobel's daughters, half-Scottish, half-Maori, opened the door. The paint was peeling from the big wooden house with the verandahs, inside the lino was coming up from the kitchen floor and someone had started taking wallpaper off in the hall but had never finished. They sat by the fire: Isobel with her Scottish accent and her red lipstick; Timoti Pou with his waistcoat under his suit jacket; Kara Rikihana with his elegant, dark green trousers and his snooty manner; Margaret-Rose Bennett wearing a blue full skirt over a white petticoat, and a blue twinset and black ballerina shoes.

'Now then,' said Isobel Arapeta.

They worked and worked, not noticing the time or the wind howling outside. They pored over the one textbook and the dictionary, and the language hooked into their hearts. They translated the Bible, they translated the old handed-down chants, the *waiata*.

> *Ka mea e koro ka unga mai i ahau*
> *Kia tika i te hiwi*

were you, beloved, to invite me, straightaway by way of the hill I would come.

Maggie sighed. *Love, love, love* she thought, *just like the songs we all sing at the parties. How boring.*

From the kitchen the taxi driver Tom Arapeta laughed with his daughters as they did the dishes. Later he brought them a cup of tea and some Maori bread he'd made for them and at Isobel's prompting sang to them, quite unselfconsciously, an old song from his home village.

Tom Arapeta had a high, soft voice and Isobel held her hand under her cup and looked at him as he sang, then half smiled to herself and looked away. And Maggie thought how teachers took a risk, bringing pupils into their homes and their lives, showing themselves as real people. She wondered what Isobel was thinking as she stared out again, down towards the city and the boats by the wharves, all the lights twinkling below them in the darkness.

Down the hill the wind clamoured about them and the garden gates clanged and the fire station clock chimed nine as the three students, their heads full of the Maori language, were buffeted down into their city.

In the library Maggie found an old Maori poem that said:

> *Ko taku tangata hokoi tera*
> *I ako ai au te ai rape ei!*

There was no English translation. Maggie consulted the Maori dictionary. The proverb seemed to mean *that was my beloved man who taught me tattooed-bottom intercourse, oh!*

She gave a nervous embarrassed giggle, half out loud. *What does that mean? Whatever is tattooed-bottom intercourse? Maoris don't have tattooed bottoms, Manu didn't have a tattooed bottom, what can it mean?* But then she paused in her mind: she hadn't ever actually seen Manu's bottom in the dark by the sea. Perhaps Maoris all had tattooed bottoms and Pakehas had never, ever, realised. *Heavens.* She looked around the library in case her face showed what she was thinking about, but people were busy with their own work and their own thoughts. A few desks away a fat, rather dishevelled Maori sat over a book. His shirt had come out of his pants. Maggie looked surreptitiously at where his big bottom was but even though she could see a little bit of it, it was too covered by his trousers to get a proper look. Then she realised what she was doing, and looked away at once, deeply embarrassed.

And at the next class she looked surreptitiously also at Timoti and Kara in the high room wondering if they had tattooed bottoms. Was it some special Maori custom? But they didn't come to the tattooed-bottom-intercourse poem, and she was much too embarrassed to ask. She saw that Timoti was looking at her, was so mortified that he might have seen her looking at his *bottom* that she blushed deep red and wished the wooden floor of the small, high room would open up and engulf her.

And always the guitars strumming, always the honeysuckle bushes shadowy in the darkness, in the rain and the wind, always the parties. Sometimes, now, Bay Ropata was there, the boss of the Welfare Department. Maggie didn't think she could any longer file him as a maniac in her mind. She saw again how the boys deferred to Bay: the war hero, the man with the bayonet wound in his stomach.

> Slowly I'm falling more in love with you,
> Slowly I'm learning that your heart can't be true

Hope sang, and Maggie, lighting a cigarette, grabbing another beer, knew she would never fall in love. She wouldn't make a fool of herself again. She wondered, cruelly, how Hope could fall in love. Blind since birth how could she *see* to fall in love?

> Now I can't hide my feelings, no matter what I do,
> Slowly I'm falling more in love with you

sang Hope. Paul the epileptic sat next to Hope, nodding in time to the music.

All those old songs, about love.

So that when Emily, white-faced in the empty Housing office after work, told Maggie and Prudence that the night of the office party she had *gone all the way* with Manu and that now she was pregnant, what could they do but put their arms around her in despair.

'I *loved* Manu,' Emily sobbed, her shoulders hunched up under her bright, brave jacket. 'I never loved anyone before, even when he had to get married I loved him. I've still been seeing him, of course I have, you didn't realise, did you? He makes me laugh, and he makes me feel –' She banged both her hands down on her desk. 'They're different from us. Maoris are *different* from us. People don't understand what it is they can give us. I think it's better, they're not like us always worrying about money and security and doing the right thing and what the neighbours say. I think I was learning another way of looking at life and other values, it was more generous, and it was more fun and it was more – *warm*,' and her whole body shook as she sat there and wept over the housing applications, tears falling on strangers' signatures.

Yes, thought Maggie.

Finally Emily said, 'My father will kill me.'

Prudence and Maggie knew that the daughters of Members of Parliament didn't get pregnant. Especially pregnant to Maoris. Especially a Member of Parliament who had suddenly become Leader of the Opposition and was planning to be the country's next prime minister. They both stared at Emily as they saw the consequences of all this.

'Does Manu know?'

Emily shook her head. 'What's the point?' Tears ran down her face. 'What can he do? Get divorced before his other baby is born? 'Course he can't. I – I told you I've been seeing him still, since he got married. But I haven't told him I'm pregnant, I just wanted to be with him. I love him. My father will kill me.'

Prudence and Maggie looked at each other, at Emily weeping. Maggie gave almost a groan: was so glad and grateful it wasn't her. And she blushed once more to think she had taken a pretty nightie to the party.

'Where will you go?' asked Prudence gently. She and Maggie had heard of course about the places in the South Island where girls were sent to have their babies, before giving them up for adoption.

Emily sat for so long, her face in her hands, that they thought she hadn't heard. Finally she looked up at Prudence.

'I love Manu,' she said, and the tears were wet on her face. 'God, I would so like to have this baby. It could be my part of Manu, to keep. You know how spoilt I am, I always think of myself, and that's what I want to do.' Just as Maggie thought: *she's going to keep Manu's baby, she's not going to have it adopted*, Emily's whole body gave a small quiver and she began talking again.

'But I'm not going to do it.' She stared unseeingly in front of her. 'I could damage my father's career, that wouldn't matter. Why should I care about him after all the damage he's done to my mother? But I would damage Manu's marriage; you know how Maoris always know everyone's business. Meremere would soon find out. And I just – isn't it silly? – I just can't in the end, bring myself to do that.' Then she looked up at Prudence. 'I've been stupid, but I don't have to be cruel. What's the point of saying you love someone if you can't do what's best for them? Love isn't just a word.'

All the housing files lay silent.

'He already looks after his own family,' said Emily. (*And Maggie saw the children in the bare house calling Manu! Manu!*

and looking for food.) 'And now he'll have his own with Meremere. I've thought and thought. And I've decided. I'm not going to some far-away convent in the South Island to hide my head in shame.' She stared down at her desk. 'Look – look what arrived for me this morning. Manu and Meremere's application for a house, and I've filled it in. I've written THIS MAN SEEMS TO BE A GOOD PROVIDER and I've signed it. So just don't –' and her voice broke, '– ever *ever* ask me to do the right thing again.'

Prudence grimaced. She had looked everywhere for that file, trying to make sure it stayed on her own desk.

'Love is easier said –' and Emily tried to laugh while she was crying, '– than done.' And then she said, 'I'm going to get rid of it.'

Her words filled the shocked space of the empty Housing office, that winter in the South Pacific in the 1950s, where all the songs were about love.

And in the old wharfies' hotel down at the far end of the city by the docks her father had another drink with the man he'd met before. Again they talked, heads together, in leather armchairs by the window just at dusk, before the hotel closed at six o'clock. Just as they parted, some money again quietly changed hands.

'And there will be a job for you in my office after the elections,' John Evans said expansively, and he walked out of the lounge bar smiling to himself. He stood on the wooden verandah for a moment, looked up into the cold, clear, darkening sky and rubbed his hands together. Life stretched out in front of him, shining.

Sinatra, in his wharfie's duffle coat had just finished the afternoon shift and was going into the hotel. He paused in the dusk; he'd seen the car, now he looked carefully at the man rubbing his hands and staring up at the sky. *So here was John*

Evans again, thinking no one at the wharfies' hotel would know him. Well, well. When an MP in a suit came to a run-down building by the docks, Sinatra always knew about it. It was his city.

John Evans got into the waiting Austin Princess.

In the back seat a very young blonde woman leaned forward out of the shadows and kissed him eagerly as he got in. Then the car drove away.

Well, well.

Sinatra simply noted what he had seen, as he noted many things in his city.

SEVENTEEN

Anyone passing the university on the hill at seven minutes past eight on a grey winter's morning could have looked up and observed, through one of the long windows, a tiered lecture-hall of students, uninterested almost to a man, struggling to read out loud, in unison, 'The Battle of Beowulf with Grendel the Monster'.

'Why do we have to say Anglo-Saxon sentences out loud when nobody even knows what it sounded like; why can't we just read it to ourselves?' muttered Maggie sulkily to her neighbour. 'It's so *boring*.' Her teeth ached to bite something.

Then a voice rang out above the battle, loud and recalcitrant. 'Why are we *doing* this?' It was the bearded poet who kissed with his tongue.

The old lecturer looked shocked, stared at the questioner over his glasses, rubbed his hands up and down his academic gown. 'Because, young man,' he said, 'this is the fountain, the beginning of our literature. This is our literary history.'

'*Is* it ours?' said the poet. He was sitting next to the girl in black, the one who painted black round her eyes. 'Look at us, so far away from it all. We are new. We need our own history. Our own literature. I want my poems studied, not an anonymous Anglo-Saxon's!'

The lecturer's face turned quite red, he pulled a large handkerchief out from somewhere, wiped it across his face.

He had made the study of 'Beowulf' his life's work, had lectured at Oxford in England. 'This is our *language*, English is our language, it doesn't matter how far away we are. This is where our language comes from. Our Shakespeare and our Coleridge and our Keats and our Wordsworth *and* let me stress to you our Katherine Mansfield.' *And all you little tin-pot, untalented, would-be poets,* he wanted to add, but didn't. He put the handkerchief away, very angry: no one had ever questioned 'Beowulf' before.

'This is our first piece of recorded literature. It is so important understand where you come from; the importance of understanding the roots of your language cannot be stressed enough.' Maggie suddenly thought of Timoti Pou, struggling to learn his own language that was dying. And of Manu, strapped for speaking one language at school, then strapped for not speaking it at home. Manu. And then she suddenly stared at the girl sitting next to the poet and her heart began to beat. The one with the black-painted eyes.

The old man went on intoning the language that nobody had ever heard.

At the end of the lecture she waited on the concrete steps by the ivy, dried up and dead now on the brick walls. When the girl with the black eyes came out through the door, Maggie put out her hand, very hesitantly. 'Excuse me,' she said. 'Excuse me.'

The girl dressed in black stopped.

'Excuse me,' said Maggie in a very quiet voice, swallowing nervously. 'I was wondering if you could help me. I need to find out how to arrange an –' she stumbled on the word,' – an –' but she couldn't say it. 'It's not me, it's a friend of mine, she's in trouble and we need help and I thought maybe you – maybe you would know.' She had reasoned, staring at the girl, that if you kissed poets in public you probably knew about things. She felt that she was blushing but held the eye of the girl in black, did not look away. 'Please,' she said in a very small voice. 'We don't know what to do.'

Students brushed past on the steps carrying books and satchels and laughing and talking. 'What's your name?' said the girl in black.

'Maggie Bennett, I work at the Bureau, in Housing, I'm a part-time student, I'm in your English class.'

'Listening to that tedious old bore who should've been put out to grass years ago.' The girl paused for a moment and then said, inconsequently, but Maggie understood at once, 'How long?'

'I think, no, I, I don't really know for sure.' There must have been something in Maggie's face, of desperation, or of truth, for the face of the girl in black softened slightly.

'It's dangerous,' she said. 'And it gets more dangerous the longer you leave it.'

'Yes.'

'It can be very expensive.'

'Is it?' They hadn't talked about money.

'I'll phone you at your work this afternoon,' said the girl in black, 'I'll see if I can find anything out,' and she walked away down the concrete steps. It was a grey, foggy morning and she seemed to disappear almost at once. Maggie stood there for a moment. And then she too disappeared down the steps and into the mist.

Roimata the telephone operator, listening in to other people's telephone calls at the Bureau as she did most afternoons when business was slack, heard Maggie Bennett receive a call from a woman who said she was sorry she was not able to help her friend after all. The call was very cryptic, but Roimata, so used to listening to voices, understood. She had watched the pretty, blonde, Pakeha girl whose father might be prime minister flirting with her cousin Manu for months. She had particularly noticed how very pale she was lately, how she looked as if she cried a lot.

The last thing Maggie Bennett's caller said was, 'Remember, it can be very dangerous.'

Roimata understood.

She heaved her weight out of the chair by the Bureau switchboard, leaving the phones to answer themselves, and swayed down the green-walled corridor to the Adoptions Department.

'Auntie Hinemoa,' she said to Mrs Tipene, leaning against the doorway and breathing heavily the way she did, 'Auntie Hinemoa, I think Manu's been a naughty boy.'

'We'll find someone,' said Prudence.

It had been raining all evening and the streetlights shone in the puddles.

The small cargo boats that went up and down the coast bumped gently against the wooden wharves and the sea smelt of tar and rope. The far wharf was lit up by a visiting American ship, the *Dwight D. Eisenhower* which, as the morning paper had said with a back page photo, was on a Goodwill Mission to its Allies.

Maggie and Timoti walked to the tram station. Timoti was wearing his grey three-piece suit under his raincoat; she realised he had two suits and alternated them each week: one was grey and one was navy blue. They discussed Maori personal pronouns but Maggie was thinking, *Who can we find? Who can we find?* Thinking of the girl in black's warning: '*Remember. It can be very dangerous.*' As they walked a Maori girl passed them with an American sailor; they rolled together down to the *Dwight D. Eisenhower* with their arms entwined, goodwill indeed. Timoti Pou stared after them, the look in his eyes unfathomable.

He put his hand under her arm as they crossed the street and her heart fluttered, feeling his hand so close to her breast. *It doesn't seem to matter who touches my breast, it feels like that* and the thought made her ashamed. They walked on in silence. Finally she said, feeling she ought to be polite, 'Where do you live?'

'In the Maori Men's Hostel down behind the railway station,' he said shortly. 'No women allowed.' Somehow the words disturbed her even more and she manouvered away from his arm. She knew he had noticed. She saw Emily in her mind, automatically pushing back her blonde hair with her hands, her bleak, pale face. *I don't want to learn about sex anymore* thought Maggie, bleak also.

They walked through the empty city streets, dodging puddles in the dark, stepping over a discarded newspaper, walking under sagging wooden shop verandahs. 'Limelight' starring Charlie Chaplin was on at the Rialto and there was a lone doughnut going stale in the dark window of the White Daisy milk bar. The only people they passed were more sailors going back to their ship, some with girls, they were almost all Maori girls. Timoti didn't talk; he seemed angry.

'At least the sailors got off the ship,' she said brightly, making another effort. 'Did you read that when the *Capitol* docked for a day only *twenty-five* of the one hundred and sixty-seven passengers got off to have a look, the rest couldn't be bothered, we're too boring.' Timoti didn't answer, just walked along. She thought he was rude, not to talk. He didn't seem to have any manners.

'Is it the Maori girls with the sailors?' she asked finally. 'Are you angry with them? Are they your relations?'

He still didn't answer. And then he suddenly said quite unpleasantly, 'Learning our language doesn't mean you know anything about us.'

They had reached the tram terminus. He politely helped

her on to the waiting tram car and then walked away. It had just started to rain again. *Hope he gets wet*, she thought. *He doesn't have to be so rude.* And her mind immediately went back again, to Emily.

But then she saw him turn back in the rain and just as the driver got on at the front Timoti jumped on the tram, kissed her on the mouth, and then jumped off again as the bell clanged and they began to rattle off into the raining darkness.

'Bloody stupid Maoris,' said the tram conductor several moments later as he came to punch her ticket. 'Bloody stupid Maoris can never make up their minds. I reckon this country'd do a damn sight better without them, couldn't run a second-hand butcher's shop.' He glared at her. 'Do you know what I think girlie? I think they ought to go back where they came from.'

EIGHTEEN

John Evans's sleek, handsome face stared out from every newspaper.

John Evans's daughter Emily sprawled on her bed defiantly painting her nails an even brighter red.

The Platters sang loudly from her gramophone about smoke getting in your eyes and she stared out at the bush at the back of the big house. The wind blew through the dark ferns, and the manuka, and the karaka bushes.

There was a knock at the door and her father walked in.

'You're never home,' he said. 'The papers wanted another picture.'

'Well, here I am, home. And here you are, home. And I'm sure Mother is home too. Our dear little Happy Family.' And she turned the music up slightly.

'It won't be long now,' he said. 'Before the election is called.'

'Looking forward to being prime minister?' Her flippant tone always unsettled him.

'Listen Emily.' He leaned across and turned the music down. Then he sat in the chintz-covered armchair in the corner. He cleared his throat. 'Emmy. Lots of things will come with this. Our lives will be very different – your mother's too. There'll be overseas trips and parties and meeting interesting people. And I need you. Don't let me down now. We –' and he had the grace to look slightly embarrassed, 'we have to look like a happy family. That's what politicians do.' She snorted with a kind of laughter but, even immersed in his own plans, he saw too that it wasn't laughter exactly and that she was very, very pale. 'What's the matter? Is something the matter?'

'Will you give me some money, Dad?'

His face relaxed. 'Of course I'll give you some money, Emmy, you only have to ask. Actually, actually I want to give you something else.' He leaned forward suddenly. 'Listen. I've bought you a big piece of land further north. It's absolutely beautiful, a huge piece right along the coast, completely unspoiled. Its commercial potential is staggering, absolutely staggering. Handled in the right way, of course. I'll deal with everything, of course.'

Emily looked puzzled. 'Why?'

'I want you to have your own security, your own freedom, whatever happens to me. I'm not getting any younger –' but Emily saw that he preened himself slightly in her dressing-table mirror, turned his head slightly. *He's got another girlfriend.* Then the telephone rang and his wife called and he got up at once, energetic, powerful.

'Phone my secretary about the money,' he called back into her bedroom where the trees shone dark in the night outside. 'Whatever you need.' Then he actually put his head back around the door. 'Whatever you need, dear,' he said magnanimously, glad to have her at last beholden.

It did not occur to him to ask what the money might be for. Which was perhaps a pity, for it was the only grandchild he was ever to have.

The wind blew, shaking the dark ferns.

*

In the high room Isobel Arapeta said to her students:

Kaumatua is a Maori word meaning old person. Maoris respect age, believe wisdom comes with age, they respect and treasure their old people in a way some other cultures do not. They believe that their old people are wise simply because they've been around for so long.

*

Mrs Tipene called her three sisters around to her house to play cards. She lived in a Bureau house in the same suburb as her father, and as her nephew, Manu Taihape, but several streets away. Once there had been seven sisters and four brothers: after the war there was only one brother: Manu's father. One daughter had died of TB, one had died of cancer and one had died of a heart attack. So now there were the four of them.

Mrs Tipene filled the big metal teapot and brought it to the kitchen table. She had put on the electric heater. The evening meal had been cleared away, the four sisters, all plump except Mrs Tipene, sat and smoked and drank cups of tea.

'It's about Manu,' she said, as she dealt the cards.

'*Ae, tera tamaiti,*' sighed the eldest sister, Alice, and she scratched at her white hair with a pencil.

'He's a good boy,' said Carmen. Manu was her favorite. 'He's so good to the family, he hasn't had it easy. He'll settle down now that Meremere's starting having babies, it was a lovely wedding.' She threw down the ten of diamonds.

Mrs Tipene looked at her hand, put her cards face down on the tablecloth. 'He's made another girl *hapu*,' she said.

'Oh he's a bugger like his father,' said Bubs, the youngest, 'you can never tell where he'll put his *mea* next, come on Hinemoa, play!'

Mrs Tipene threw down the Jack of diamonds.

'His father was spoilt because he was the youngest of all of us,' said Bubs, 'that's our fault. Do you know I heard he was off up the coast staying with that woman again, just took off on the car, left them all again. If it wasn't for Manu that family would starve.'

'Lucky Manu's there,' said Carmen, the peacemaker. 'He looks after all the kids; he's a good boy, *ka pai*, it was a lovely wedding.'

'Listen,' said Mrs Tipene, 'listen. It's a Pakeha girl.'

Alice put all her cards out on the table. 'Is she going to have it at the same time as Meremere?'

'Listen, *e hoa ma*, listen. This girl's father is probably going to be the next prime minister.'

Bubs put all her cards down too. '*E ki?*' she said, her eyes wide, 'is that so?'

After a moment Mrs Tipene gathered the cards across the table, shuffling, dealing. They poured more tea and then they began playing again. For a moment there was just the sound of the cards on the table and their cigarettes being inhaled and exhaled in the kitchen. An alarm clock ticked on top of a cake tin.

'Seven spades,' said Alice.

'Seven clubs,' said Mrs Tipene.

'Bloody Manu,' said Bubs.

And all four of them started to laugh.

'Maybe *we'll* get a prime minister in about thirty years' time then,' said Bubs, 'and he can get us back on our land.' The sisters laughed and laughed together, leaning over the table, and against each other. And Alice the oldest, began coughing, as she often did when she laughed.

'I'll take it,' she said finally, wiping her eyes, lighting another cigarette, handing the packet around. 'We've only got one *mokopuna* with us now that Wikitoria's gone. It'll fill the days. I'll take the baby.'

Mrs Tipene shuffled the cards, dealt again.

Bubs said: 'It won't be very nice for Meremere, just married and that. Her family can be trouble you know, that bloody high and mighty tribe, think they're royalty.'

Carmen sucked her teeth. 'Manu is a good boy,' she said again.

The card game went on. The women smoked and yawned.

'I've missed the last tram,' said Alice, who lived in a different suburb, 'never mind.' And she took off her shoes.

'I'll stay too,' murmured Carmen, dealing, and Mrs Tipene put the kettle on again, got out the Amber Tips tea and removed the alarm clock from the top of the cake tin. The tin was full of peanut biscuits and she put some on a plate on the table beside the cards.

'I'm off then,' said Bubs at last. 'Arthur will be back from the taxis. See you fellas in the weekend.' They were always in each other's houses at the weekend.

'Hooray, Bubs,' they called to her from the front door, waving as she drove off in her big old car.

Mrs Tipene brought pillows and blankets, settled Carmen on the sofa, helped Alice into the single bed that used to be her daughter's. '*Kia pai ta korua moe*,' she said. 'Sleep well, you two, I'll bring you up a cup of tea in the morning before I leave for the Bureau.'

'That'll be nice, Hinemoa,' said Carmen.

'I expect I'll be gone,' said Alice, 'I'll walk down to the tram stop, catch the first tram. I wake too early.' And then she added. 'I'll take the baby. That's fine. Tell Manu.'

Maggie was late for a lecture, couldn't find a housing file. 'Well, for heaven's sake, who dealt with you last time?' she said in exasperation to the Maori man at the counter.

He looked at her, puzzled. 'I dunno,' he said, 'you fellas all look the same to me.'

Paddy appeared at her shoulder with the correct file. 'Off

you go to your lecture,' he said. But she saw that he was disappointed in her, had heard the tone she had used to one of his beloved clients.

'Sorry Paddy,' she said, hurriedly gathering her things.

At the front door of the Bureau a young Maori woman carrying a broken electric heater stopped her.

'Are you Emily?' she said.

'No,' said Maggie. 'I'm Maggie.'

'Where's Prudence then?'

'She's still in the Housing Department, she hasn't got a lecture tonight.' Maggie looked puzzled: was this Maori girl with lots of lipstick a housing client? Still you never knew, and she had already been rude to one of them. 'Can I help you?' she said politely even though she was late.

The woman looked embarrassed and stared up the street, biting her lips together. Then she said, 'Give this telephone number to Emily,' thrust a torn-off piece of paper at Maggie and went into the Red Rose Parlour next door.

It was Prudence who had rung the bell of the Red Rose Parlour where the sailors visited, and disappeared inside to talk to the girls who would know.

NINETEEN

Maggie put polish on the furniture, polishing quite late at night sometimes as if to say: look at me. I'm a good girl.

Look at me, I'm a good girl, she wanted to call out, rubbing vigorously at the legs of the dining-room table. But she knew she wasn't a good girl at all.

She felt it could so easily have been her, not Emily, who waited for the massage girls next door to arrange an abortion, felt herself constricted and cold. She did not go to Prudence's every night. She came home early more often: 'the library's got a bit noisy,' she said to her parents. Not only did she polish, she did the dishes, vacuumed the house. She tried some evenings to sit with her parents by the radio with her textbooks but the silent sound of the embroidery unnerved her, as it had always done. She did not think about Timoti Pou very much, even though he had kissed her on a tram car. Something had happened to her heart. She worked late into the night in her bedroom, bent over the Maori words and the English poems and even 'Beowulf'. As if knowledge might keep her good.

One night she had to go to the library. She sat over the books she needed, silent and concentrated, until the librarian said, 'the library is closing now.'

The 9.30 tram noisily approached the tram stop; she could

see its big front light shining in the dark as it clanked towards her.

'Would you like to come to the University Ball with me?' said Timoti Pou to Margaret-Rose Bennett. He had materialised out of nowhere in the night: she realised he must've been waiting for her. After the first shock she had nodded and smiled, of course, that's what women always did. But she sat numbly on the tram, knowing it was impossible. She would never be allowed, never, she could just imagine her mother's face if she even broached the subject.

Next day, as all the men threw down their pens, pulled on their coats and hurried down the hill to the Prince of Wales, Mrs Tipene came into Housing. She passed Rangi, at the door.

'*Kia ora e Rangi*,' she said.

'Goodnight Auntie Hinemoa,' he called back over his shoulder. Mrs Tipene was wearing her raincoat and carrying her bag and her umbrella. Only Emily, Prudence and Maggie were still there, just finishing their work, this was the one night none of them had lectures.

'*Kia ora*, Emily, I'd like to talk to you,' said Mrs Tipene.

Emily froze.

Prudence looked from one to the other. 'Perhaps Maggie and I should go,' she said hesitantly.

'*No!*' said Emily.

'No, it will be nice for you to have your friends here,' said Mrs Tipene, 'stay, you girls.' Maggie and Prudence sat down silently at their desks again, obediently, like schoolgirls. There were big spaces between all four of them; Mrs Tipene stood near the closed door in her coat. Their faces were dim under the harsh office lighting and outside it was almost dark but Emily's face was as pale as the white housing files. Maggie wished she was anywhere, *anywhere*, but here. She thought of Manu, his warm, sunshine presence in this Housing office a hundred times, laughing past with his trolley. He wasn't even handsome, just warm, and smiling. *Some people should tie in their personalities, not spill them out all over the place, causing havoc. Or* – and suddenly a darker thought came to her – *is it that people like me and Emily come from families where there is something missing?* She examined the thought. *Something – about loving?* The idea shocked her and she pushed it away at once.

'I've been talking to my sisters,' said Mrs Tipene. 'My oldest sister, Alice, has said she'll take the baby.'

Emily looked at her in horror. At first she could not speak.

'Alice will take it,' repeated Mrs Tipene.

'What are you *talking* about?' Emily almost spat the words across the room at the old lady.

'Manu's baby,' said Mrs Tipene.

Emily somehow recovered. 'Meremere's having Manu's baby,' she said coldly. 'I suggest you talk to her about it if you want to put it in your Adoption Office.'

'No, I mean your baby,' said Mrs Tipene firmly.

'I'm not having a baby,' said Emily.

'Does Manu know?' said Mrs Tipene.

'I'm not having a baby,' said Emily.

'Does your father know?' said Mrs Tipene.

'*I'm not having a baby!*' screamed Emily across the desks, 'I'm not having a baby and even if I was it would be nothing to do with you and your bloody sister, Alice, whoever she is, do you hear me? How dare you come and talk about this! This is none of your business and *nobody* knows about it,' and she burst into tears.

The door to the Housing office opened. 'Oh, hullo, Auntie Hinemoa,' said Roimata, the telephone operator, breathing heavily. 'I was waiting to walk to the tram stop with you.'

Emily picked up her coat and ran out the door, pushing past Roimata. Her pile of housing files fell all over the desk and on to the floor. The other women remained silent but both Prudence and Maggie began automatically to pick up the files, tidy them, straighten all the papers.

Finally Mrs Tipene sighed. 'We're all Manu's aunties,' she said, 'of course it's to do with us. You talk to her, Prudence, you're a sensible girl, we'll be pleased to help.'

Prudence tried to smile at Mrs Tipene but she did not say anything at all, and at last the old lady and Roimata went away. They heard their feet along the corridor and then silence. And there was no sound at all of the hidden music, of the snatches of song from behind a door, or of a guitar strumming, somewhere almost out of earshot.

Prudence said slowly, 'Someone told me once that Maoris bury the afterbirth under a special tree. We throw it away.' She shrugged.

'It's illegal what we're going to do, isn't it?' said Maggie. 'What if we get caught?'

'What Emily is going to do is her choice,' said Prudence. 'I think she should be allowed to make it.' And Prudence sighed, and then smiled her gentle smile at Maggie. 'Come on, let's go up to my house, you haven't been for a while, come and have a drink. The boys'll be there soon, and Hope will be wondering why no one's come to collect her from the typing pool.' As they were putting on their coats, looking out at the dark evening, Prudence said quietly: 'I admire Emily in a way. She had the guts to be very honest about herself and I don't think that's very easy. Most people don't know how to face the truth of themselves at all.'

That night at the house on the hill Maggie sang very loudly.

> My blue crazy heart
> Is lonely for you
> It dreams in the moonlight
> It drifts in the dawn light

She sang louder than the others, as best she could. Emily wasn't there. And she thought of what Prudence had said: 'most people don't know how to face the truth of themselves.' *I'm never truthful to myself or other people*, thought Maggie. *I'm always too frightened.*

She drank much more beer than usual, swayed down to the tram stop as they were all leaving, tripped on the footpath. She realised then that she'd left her purse behind, ran back up the hill, looking anxiously at her watch, *my blue crazy heart*.

On the verandah under the honeysuckle Bay Ropata, the boss of Welfare, who they said had killed Italian prisoners, and Prudence, sat on two kitchen chairs, staring down at the city. Bay's arm was resting very lightly across Prudence's shoulder.

'Tuesday,' said Prudence, passing her desk next morning. 'She's to go there after work on Tuesday.'

On Tuesday Emily screamed again and again, late in the night in the bathroom of Prudence's place under the hill where the honeysuckle grew wild and the neighbours never complained, for there were no neighbours. Prudence sat with her in the bathroom, Maggie sat on the floor outside with her head in her hands. She had never spoken to Emily about Manu. She sat there praying, praying for this to be over, praying that nothing awful would happen to Emily: *please, God, don't let her die*; guiltily sending up a grateful prayer too, that it wasn't her, that what had seemed so natural and so new should come to this, over and over in her mind the rain on the windows of the car and the sea crashing against the sandhills, Emily screaming.

They'd taken her to the secret address arranged by the massage girls and waited for her outside, standing uneasily near a dairy where old people shuffled. A woman, Emily told them when she came out, had stuck some wire in her and told her to go home but it would take a few hours.

'Let's at least have a party as usual,' said Emily, pale. 'Please Pru. I need a party.'

So Prudence had had a party, as usual; the men had gone home drunk about 9.00 PM, as usual; cars wobbling very slowly down the hill to the main street, voices and laughter echoing goodnight in the dark. Emily had laughed a lot, and said she had had the flu but was feeling better when Paddy asked worriedly why she wasn't at home when she looked so pale.

Maggie wondered if they all knew really, had Roimata told people? If Rangi – who everyone knew was crazy about Emily – knew, really, when he sang:

> too late now to forget your smile

Maggie had stared at Rangi from under her eyelashes. Perhaps they knew, perhaps they were pretending not to know. Who knew with these funny people from another culture, who knew? Or perhaps it was just that they were men, and embarrassed.

Or perhaps they simply didn't know that Emily was having an abortion while they all sang love songs.

E noho ra, they had all called, Goodnight. *O Danny Boy the pipes the pipes are calling.*

Prudence and Maggie had cleared away the fish and chip papers and washed the glasses and then, at a loss, had scrubbed the kitchen floor. Maggie had told her parents she was keeping Prudence company because the brother she lived with who was an accountant was away for the night. There was a cricket broadcast at midnight from a place called Headingley in England; the familiar crusty voice of a cricket commentator called John Arlott, whose voice they had grown up with in the nights, spoke of silly mid-offs and maiden overs and other voices discussed the visitors' chances rather dismissively. They left the radio on. The English voices crackled in the empty sitting room from twelve thousand miles away and then Emily began to scream.

For hours it seemed the three of them kept vigil: mostly Emily screamed, sometimes she was silent, sometimes Maggie, outside the bathroom door, heard her crying: great wrenching sobs of unhappiness as well as pain.

It was over just before four o'clock in the morning as the cricketers in England stopped for tea. Prudence half carried Emily, pale and shaking, to her bed; Maggie filled a hot water bottle.

'Come here Maggie,' called Prudence quietly from the bathroom. In the lavatory bowl there was a lot of blood and something white and Maggie turned away quickly. *No, look* said Prudence, *don't ever let this happen to you.* And then she pulled the chain.

The white thing didn't disappear at first and even Prudence looked disturbed that they might have to take it out and wrap it in newspaper and put it in a rubbish bin. When the cistern filled up the third time she pulled the chain and the white thing broke up slightly and the remains of Manu's and Emily's baby disappeared.

Emily fell asleep at last, Prudence went to sleep on the couch. Maggie smoked cigarettes where Hope, staring at the light bulb and singing love songs in her beautiful, plaintive voice, always sat. It was just beginning to get light and the cricket match was finishing when Maggie vomited in the kitchen sink. Over and over again she retched over the sink and a worm wound round her heart: it was *this* that happened if you didn't follow the rules.

On the early-morning news the Prime Minister grandly announced he was Going to the Country.

TWENTY

'What's your address, and what time shall I pick you up?' said Timoti Pou. 'My cousin will take us in his uncle's wife's car.' They walked down the hill from Isobel's house after the Wednesday evening lesson, Maggie had not been to sleep, saw Emily's face, heard Emily's scream, saw the white thing in the toilet. Isobel had told them: *Mamae is the Maori word for pain. As in English it can mean physical pain, of course. But in the old poem-songs physical pain seems not to be important. It is the emotional pain that seems to be meant, most of all.* Maggie had written all this down in her pavlova book.

'Oh,' she said to Timoti. She had neither told him she could not come to the University Ball, nor told her parents he had asked her. The Ball was on Friday. She had pushed it out of her mind but now her mind would not be pushed, Emily's pain was imprinted there. The worm wound tighter, trying to crush her: *this is the consequence of being bad,* said the worm, *of not obeying your parents, of not being a good girl.*

'Oh,' she said to Timoti again. And then, as a tram rattled towards them out of the darkness, she heard herself say, 'What time should I be ready?'

'You look very pale,' sad Timoti, 'are you all right?'

'Yes,' she said.

'Seven-thirty,' he said, and she gave him the address of the house by the sea as she got on the tram. He didn't kiss her, there was something in her face that stopped him.

Down her street she heard the sound of the sea and her face was tight and closed as she opened the wooden gate by the letterbox and walked down the path past where the cinerarias grew.

Her parents were sitting in the lounge listening to the radio. Her father was already in his dressing-gown and he had unscrewed his hand and put it down on the carpet.

'You're early,' he said, adding 'for you,' as he teased her. And then, 'You look tired, Maggie, what were you and your friend doing last night?'

'Talking French,' said Maggie shortly. She turned to go out of the lounge and then she turned back. 'And now I have to write an essay, it's about "Beowulf". You know, that's the first piece of writing in English that's ever been found. Well it's not English, it's Old English, doesn't sound anything like English really, it's just like translating a foreign language, all about monsters and battles. And I've been asked to the University Ball,' and she gave a tiny little half-laugh, 'my first ball. Lucky I've got the pink dress you made me, Mum.'

'A ball?' said Mr Bennett, 'aren't you a bit young for a ball?'

'Who asked you?' said Mrs Bennett.

'It's the University Ball and I'm at university so I suppose I'm old enough, they have it in the Town Hall, I think they take out the seats. Timoti Pou, he used to work at the Bureau, he's very nice, he's a lawyer.'

They heard the name only. There was a shocked silence before they spoke.

'You're not going to a ball with all those university people with a *Maori*?' Her mother's voice, tight and high.

'Well – well, he asked me and he's a very nice boy, I didn't like to say no.'

'I absolutely forbid it,' said Mrs Bennett. 'Look, just look where all this Maori business is leading, just as I expected.'

'I think it's a very bad idea,' said Mr Bennett, 'I don't think you should go. You could say no politely without hurting the bloke's feelings, surely?'

Maggie stood there in the doorway of the lounge with her weight on one foot as if she would run away, but she did not run. Something about what Emily had lived through, what Maggie and Prudence had witnessed, hovered around her head.

'It's only once,' she said quite coldly. 'Another time I'd be more prepared, would know how to say no. But I couldn't think of an excuse, he took me by surprise.'

'You don't need an *excuse*,' said Mrs Bennett,' with a *Maori*.' And Maggie saw how angry her mother was and knew she would pay for this, later. 'What do you think the neighbours will say, seeing a Maori walk in here and then walk out again with you on his arm.'

'Maoris are just people in the end,' said Maggie tiredly. 'Like us.' She didn't care if she went to the ball or not.

'They're not at all like us, they're very, very different.'

Emily screaming, hovered.

'Emily Evans will be going with a Maori,' said Margaret-Rose Bennett to her parents, 'and her father doesn't mind. He's going to be prime minister, he's coming with us, to make a speech, I think. We'll be with him, he said he's looking forward to seeing me there.'

'Do you mean Emily Evans has a – *Maori boyfriend*?'

'Heavens, they're not boyfriends, we don't have boyfriends, just friends. She has a friend at the Bureau, his name is Rangi Cox, he looks a bit like Humphrey Bogart, and her father likes him, and we're going to be in his party because he's going to make a speech.' Lies poured out of Maggie's mouth like nails, pointed and dangerous and sharp. She saw her parents' faces.

'I still don't think it's a good idea at all,' repeated Mr Bennett, 'and I'm disappointed in you, that you've put us in this position.'

But she saw that, by mentioning Emily's father, she had won. A kind of winning.

In the hall the grandfather clock ticked loudly.

'We'll say no more about it this time,' he continued, looking for a moment at his wife, 'but your mother and I categorically forbid you to ever go anywhere with a Maori again.'

'Maoris smell,' said Mrs Bennett and she picked up her embroidery. Maggie saw the crinoline on the pretty lady, and the roses.

Why is it like this?

'It won't happen another time,' she said in a small voice and she found that her strength had ebbed away and her knees were shaking. 'Goodnight.'

In her bed she lay awake and Emily's screams echoed round and round in her head.

Timoti Pou arrived in a dinner suit carrying, in a little box covered with cellophane, an orchid spray for her to wear; that was the custom. He was the most handsome man, and the only Maori who had ever stepped inside their front door. Maggie had instructed him nervously: *My parents think I'm doing French, not Maori, please don't mention the classes.* And she had seen his face then, blank over. In the way she recognised.

'Heavens!' said her father, 'I recognise you, you were in the Under-Twenty-One Rugby Squad!'

'And everyone knows you, Mr Bennett, from the All-Black trials. My father always talked about you.'

'Maggie tells us you're a lawyer.'

'Yes. Well, not quite yet. I'm in my last year, I'm doing conveyancing, and procedure, and evidence and family law.' He didn't mention Maori. 'I work for Appleyard, Stonewall and White.' He spoke confidently, and smiled a great deal, and laughed stiffly. Maggie saw his brown hand shake slightly as he moved past one of the floral armchairs in the lounge. And as he moved, his raincoat, which he hadn't been invited to take off, caught her mother's pink china tulips on their small table. He turned, looked down in dismay to where they lay on the pale green carpet. 'It's all right,' said Maggie quickly, 'they're not broken,' and she knelt on the floor in her pink evening dress, net over satin, matching the orchids and the china tulips.

Maggie's father cleared his throat. 'Please have her home by half-past twelve,' he said. For, of course, all balls ended at midnight.

Timoti's cousin was waiting outside in his uncle's wife's Ford.

'Your mother doesn't say a lot,' said Timoti.

The ball was held in the Town Hall with the seats taken out; the balcony was draped with streamers and there was a big Union Jack on the stage behind a four-piece band and a master-of-ceremonies. Students in evening dress ran inside, escaping from the rain, Maggie's corsage fell on to Captain Cook Street and one of the flowers broke off. Men huddled in groups, quickly draining flasks and bottles hidden in their cars before dashing across the road and up the steps to the concrete entrance portals. There were about four hundred people there, a buzzing of excitement: running in the rain, and illegal alcohol, and pretty frocks and dinner suits, and sex.

Maggie came through the entrance portals and suddenly stared. She looked about her in amazement and saw *at once* that she was the only white person there with a Maori. That Timoti was the only Maori there with a white girl: the few other Maori students had come with Maori girls. Then she saw one of her English lecturers looking at her oddly and a boy from her primary school who didn't even bother to hide the look of contempt on his face as he turned away and whispered to his girlfriend. People turned away and whispered: Maggie could not believe it when two friends from her school actually giggled into their hands.

'Hello Maggie,' they called, still giggling.

People stared, all around her.

With a shock she realised she had got used to the Bureau and the Maori classes and the parties at Prudence's house under the hill. *But the city wasn't really like that at all.*

She had forgotten. Or pretended.

Her face burned. A photographer took a photo of each couple. (The burning face, the orchid, the dinner suit.)

Timoti introduced her to three of his Maori friends who were at university, they were to sit at the same table. Their Maori girlfriends smiled hello.

The band began to play 'The Tennessee Waltz', a piano and a saxophone and a guitar and some drums. Maggie and Timoti, who had never danced together before, who had kissed once on a tram, looked at each other shyly, knowing they would be stared at. Then they got up and began waltzing round the Town Hall floor. They danced, feeling their way through the crowd, his hand on her back where the satin and the net joined, her hand resting on his shoulder like she'd been taught at school dancing classes with the old-maid teacher and the piano thumping, 'Some Day My Prince Will Come.'

Timoti spent a lot of the evening talking to people, smiling at people with his beautiful smile and his blue eyes, being popular. Maggie had to follow him around, and smile quite a lot also. He *was* popular, she could see, especially with all the rugby players, they slapped each other on the back and laughed and sometimes disappeared to find bottles hidden in

the old Ford Prefects and Austin A40s and the occasional
sports car that lined the streets outside. Some of the time
Maggie sat with the Maori girls at their table. All the time
people stared. Their table was almost foggy with cigarette
smoke, they all smoked, they all drank ginger beer which was
easier for hiding whisky in when the boys smuggled it in.
Although she wasn't used to whisky Maggie was glad of it, it
made her feel less conspicuous. She and Timoti danced the
Supper Waltz like everyone else, queued to eat their ham and
fruit salad like everyone else. Timoti politely helped her to the
ham while swapping reminiscences about last Saturday's
rugby game with the President of the Students' Union.
Maggie smiled at them, showing an enormous interest in
rugby, while they talked. Only once, suddenly, the sound of
Emily screaming filled her head. The sound was so terrible
and so lonely that she had to lean against the supper table for
support, just for a shocked moment. *But it's over now* she
thought to herself. *Emily is all right. It's all over.*

At five minutes to midnight the drums rolled, the lights
dimmed and the master-of-ceremonies cried out, 'Ladies and
Gentlemen – the Last Waltz!' and two hundred couples
smooched around the floor kissing, bodies very close, in time
to 'I'm in the Mood for Love,' not a waltz at all really. In the
dim light Timoti Pou turned Margaret-Rose Bennett's face up
to his and kissed her.

'I love you,' he said.

Then the lights came back on again and everybody stood at
attention for 'God Save the Queen'. And then the ball was
over.

'Well?' said her mother, waiting up for her in the lounge at ten
to one in the morning, looking at her flushed face.

'Well – it was nice,' said Maggie breathlessly. 'Sorry I'm a
little bit late but there were so many cars it was hard to get

away from the street by the Town Hall. Timoti wanted to come in and explain but I said you'd understand,' but she looked away from her mother's eyes, her weight poised in that way she had.

Her mother moved quickly towards her, hit her hard across the face: once, twice. 'Don't you ever *ever* do this to me again,' she said in her quiet voice.

After her mother had gone Maggie stood there in the room of the china tulips, in her nineteen fifties pink evening dress of net and satin, her orchids squashed flat where Timoti had held her and kissed her, her hand up to her face where her mother had hit her.

Nobody, ever before, had said *I love you* to Margaret-Rose Bennett.

TWENTY-ONE

All weekend she vacuumed and studied: the very image of a good girl.

On Sunday afternoon, while her parents were working in the neat garden, the telephone rang.

'*Kia ora,*' said Timoti Pou.

Maggie's heart almost stopped.

'How did you know my number?' she asked clumsily.

He sounded surprised. 'It was in the phone book, of course.'

'Oh. Yes, of course.'

There was a silence on the phone.

'What are you doing?' asked Timoti finally.

'I'm just – studying. The usual.'

'Oh,' said Timoti. 'Well, that's good. I am too.'

Then Maggie's voice came out in a rush. 'Did you mean it, that you *loved* me?'

'Yes,' he answered. 'I meant it.' And a soft, sigh came back to him.

Then she heard her parents walking up the path. 'I have to go now,' said Maggie, putting down the receiver quickly.

In her pink bedroom she felt very peculiar: as if her stomach was dancing.

Strange, swooping tangos were still being executed

somewhere near her diaphragm when she went to work in the rain on Monday. Then she saw Emily's pale, pale face.

But it's over now. Emily is all right. It's all over now.

Timoti telephoned her at her desk, his voice actually there in the Housing Department. 'I have to go to court over on the coast,' he said, 'but I'll see you at Isobel's place on Wednesday. I'll definitely be back on Wednesday.' She felt numb with gratitude, he was *making arrangements* with her, as if she was his person, telling her where he'd be, when he'd see her. She was aware of Roimata listening at one end and Paddy and Prudence and Emily at the other.

'I'll see you on Wednesday then,' she said, rather sternly. She hung up blushing, leaning over the housing files, hiding behind her hair.

The phone rang for her again almost at once and she gave a little apologetic smile to Paddy. It was Eddie Albert, her cousin.

'Gidday,' he said. 'You haven't visited for a while.'

'No,' said Maggie.

'Well, we all have to go away on a weekend advertising course the weekend after next. Will you stay at our flat and feed the damn cat?'

'Is that horrible Peter going away with you?'

'What do you mean horrible? Yes, yes he is.'

'Are you sure? Are you sure he won't be there?'

'What's the matter with you? Stop being a batty sheila or they'll come and take you away to the loony bin. We're all going, I told you. Peter's certainly going, he's just won another award, he pinched my idea of musical commercials, did a musical one about a firm that fixes false teeth.'

She couldn't help herself. '*What?*'

Eddie Albert began to sing on the phone to the tune of 'Little Brown Jug':

My false teeth jumped when I smiled,

My dear wifie, Finns she dialled.
Ha ha ha hee hee hee,
Finns fixed my false teeth for me.

'Everybody's singing it.'

He took Maggie's disbelieving silence as approval. 'So you can come then?'

She spoke at last. 'All right. Will you fix it up with my parents?'

"Course. Good on you.'

'Sorry, my cousin is very loony,' she said to Paddy.

And then, during the lunch-hour, Mrs Tipene brought her sister Alice into the Housing Department.

Outside it was raining hard, rain fell against the windows. The radiators in the office were on. Some people had gone out to lunch or to other parts of the Bureau. Paddy was upstairs in Alienations. Rangi and Hori were lounging on the desks drinking Coca-Cola and talking about rugby. Harry Beans had gone to buy some sports shoes, the man who drank Baxter's Lung Preserver out of a bottle had gone to the pub. Maggie was eating a peanut butter sandwich and trying to write her 'Beowulf' essay and Prudence was bent over a housing file eating a banana.

Emily was silent and pale, eating nothing, staring at nothing.

And then Mrs Tipene brought her sister Alice into the Housing Department. The three girls didn't notice them at first; people were always coming and going.

Rangi said '*Kia ora*, Auntie Hinemoa, *kia ora*, Auntie Alice.'

Prudence, and then Maggie, raised their heads in disbelief.

Emily was very, very still, at her desk.

Mrs Tipene walked between the desks with her sister.

'Hello dear,' she said, to Maggie. 'Hello Prudence.' And then she stopped beside Emily's desk. 'Hello dear,' she said. 'My sister Alice was just passing; we thought we'd come and say hello. Why don't you come and have a cup of tea in Adoptions, I've put the kettle on. All of you,' she said to the other girls, 'come and have a talk to Alice.'

Maggie prayed that Rangi and Hori would go on talking about rugby and after a moment they did, dissecting again the tries and penalties of Saturday's game.

But Alice was staring at Emily's pale, stony face.

Almost at once something, some knowledge or recognition, passed between the two women; between the old, brown woman with the white hair and the young, pale, defiant woman with the blonde hair and the red fingernails; Maggie could actually feel it in the air as they stared at one another.

And then Alice began, very softly at first, to make a sound.

It was like no sound Maggie had ever heard and she began to shake slightly. The sound got louder and louder and then faded again, loud and then fading; a kind of eerie, shivery weeping pulled out from some ancient pain. Maggie saw moss in dark forests where no sun ever shone and mouldering dead leaves in the earth. There were no words, only the grieving, weeping, shivery sounds in the Housing office as the big, white-haired woman stood there. Tears poured down Alice's face and she breathed them into herself as she wept. To Maggie's horror she heard herself make a kind of involuntary sob and felt tears on her own face. Then Mrs Tipene, understanding, joined in: sounds of a terrible, and yet somehow formalised, grief. It fell there, across the desks, and the packets of cigarettes, and the housing files for the Maoris coming to live in the city.

Rangi and Hori had become quite still.

Nobody did anything or said anything or shouted, *Stop this at once.* Just the rain against the windows and the sound of the crying voices, inexorable, keening on and on.

The door opened and Paddy walked in. He stood, shocked, in the doorway, listening. Mrs Tipene saw him, touched Alice's arm.

'**Kaati**,' she said. *Enough.*

Alice took a handkerchief out of her pocket. She wiped tiredly at her wet face, still making crying sounds. And then with great dignity she walked out of the office with her sister, looking at nobody.

Not a sound in the Housing office when they were gone.

And then Paddy, his face pale in a way Maggie had never seen it before said: 'Come along everybody, lunchtime is over, get on with your work now. Hori you should be back in Land Records. Rangi, go and collect all the files from Accounts and –' he paused for an infinitisimal second, 'Prudence, you take Emily and make her a cup of tea. Only ten minutes, mind.' He walked rather heavily towards his desk.

Harry Beans came through Housing, grumbling and mumbling about the rain and shaking his coat, went out again.

Maggie looked, at last, at Emily.

Her pale face looked as if it was sculpted in stone. She looked ahead of her as if she could not see. Prudence finally touched her shoulder.

Then Emily got up and went out of the office with Prudence as if she was walking in a dream.

Paddy saw Maggie continually watching the door. 'I don't want all you girls coming down with flu,' he said. 'You better get out of the office. Go with Terry.'

Rangi busied himself with files, his head down low over his desk. He did not look at Maggie. The man in the corner drank from his bottle of Baxter's Lung Preserver. Harry Beans whistled by with land files, oblivious.

Terry and Maggie drove to one of the outer suburbs of the city in the blue government van with the Bureau's name on the side, eating TIP-TOP hokey-pokey ice-creams because Terry insisted, even though the day was so cold and grey and wet. Terry was what they called a field officer, they hardly ever saw him in the office; a large easy-going man who had also been in the war, he was odd among the others because he did not drink, was teased often for always drinking Coca-Cola. 'I like the taste better,' was all he ever said.

Maggie's face was tight and pale. No matter how she looked out of the window, no matter how she licked the ice-cream, crunched the hokey-pokey, no matter where she turned her head – still she heard the awful cry of the old women as they stared at Emily. She felt as if she was mad: she could not get that sound out of her head. She tried to pull herself together. She never cried, yet tears had poured out of her eyes.

'Who builds the Bureau houses, Terry?' she asked in a high, tight voice.

'We employ people to work for us and we make them employ young Maori apprentices and train them. Lots of good young Maori builders are coming out of our scheme, lots of them, good blokes.' And vaguely she saw in his eyes the same enthusiasm as in Paddy's, a kind of true idealism, believing in the importance of the Bureau, thinking up schemes themselves; caring.

'Where are they from, the apprentices?'

'All over the show. The Bureau arranges for them to come into the city and the churches help run special Maori boys' hostels so they won't get into trouble.' He tooted his horn and two young Maori boys on the roof of a house waved at the van. In the light rain they stood at crazy angles on the roof, in singlets.

They drove along by the sea. The ubiquitous rain fell so gently it was like mist and seagulls wheeled round the rocks and an old lady poked among the shells, bent over them with a rain hat on but no coat. Maggie talked a lot to keep the sound of the crying out of her head, she asked Terry every question she could think of. He answered her good-naturedly; if he noticed anything strange he did not say so.

And every now and then Maggie felt a feeling of unexplained panic. She kept saying to herself, to make herself feel real: *somebody loves me.*

'There's a couple of sections up the hill here I'm thinking of buying,' said Terry, pointing. 'We haven't bought any round here. Have you heard of pepper-potting?'

'Pardon?' said Maggie politely. *It's Monday now. He'll be back on Wednesday.*

'We have a policy. We just buy one or two sections here and there for our houses. We don't want too many Maoris living together as a group, causes too much trouble. We like to have a little Bureau house here, a little Bureau house there, know what I mean?'

'Is that pepper-potting?'

He nodded.

'So if you put a few Pakehas in a street where mostly Maoris live, you'd call it salt-potting, I suppose?'

He laughed. 'Salt-*cellaring* I suppose,' and slowed the van down as they drove up a hill where there were houses on one side of the road, wild tall grass on the other and some FOR SALE notices stuck into the grass, leaning sideways.

'Here's where I was thinking of,' he said.

She looked around as he turned off the motor and saw a woman peering out of the window of one of the houses. A few moments later she came running down her neat concrete path in pink, fluffy slippers. She was followed by a man from another house running and waving his arms.

'Oi!' shouted the man. 'Oi!'

Terry got out of the van and stood in the light rain, throwing his cigarette butt into the long grass.

'Good afternoon,' he said.

'You're not going to buy any sections here, are you?' said the woman, gesturing in dismay at the Bureau sign on the side of the van, 'surely you're not going to buy any sections round here?' Maggie got out of the van too, stood in the rain.

'Listen, mate!' said the man, puffing from running and waving his arms and shouting. 'Listen mate, we don't want you buying sections round here. 'Course I've got nothing against the Maori's personally –' and he leant on his knees for a moment to catch his breath, '– but they lower the value of our houses, you people know that. I saw your van here the other week and I said to the wife, "Hell's teeth they're not buying round here, are they?" You're not, are you?'

All four of them stood in the soft rain.

'Look,' said the man urgently to Terry, who still hadn't said anything, 'is there any way we can talk about this? Come to, you know, some arrangement? D'you want a beer?'

'No thanks,' said Terry pleasantly. He looked at the long grass and the FOR SALE notices and rubbed his chin with his hand. 'The thing is,' he said, 'we just want to build a few houses. We just want to have a little house here, a little house there, know what I mean?'

'But they have parties and get drunk and don't look after their gardens,' cried the woman. 'And they have all their relations to stay, our houses will be worth nothing, you're going to simply ruin our lives! We don't want Maori neighbours, you wouldn't want Maori neighbours, would you? Would you?' she repeated shrilly as the rain fell on her frock and her fluffy slippers.

Maggie looked at Terry's inscrutable face. She remembered

him singing 'When Irish Eyes Are Smiling' with Paddy at the office party.

'The thing is,' said Terry slowly, 'the thing is, people in a country have to live somewhere, don't they?'

'Yes, but not next door to *me*,' said the woman, hugging herself, and she was so agitated she actually did a little dance in her pink slippers on the wet road, her feet jumping from side to side. The rain became heavier. 'Oh, please don't misunderstand me, they're lovely people, the Maoris, we all know that and here we are living in God's Own Country happily together. But they're *happier* living back in the countryside all together in their dear little Maori villages. They can live their own way there.'

'That so?' said Terry. He rubbed his chin again. 'What can they do back there? There's not a lot of work in the country these days if you haven't got land and a lot of capital. I expect they want chances for their children, education and jobs. Just like you do.'

'But you wouldn't want them to live *next door*!' repeated the dancing woman.

'Funnily enough,' said Terry, 'where I live I had a bit of trouble the other way round, there was a Maori family objected living next door to me.'

'What do you mean?' said the man. The rain was making him so uncomfortable that he kept pulling his shirt away from his body, and now he and the woman were looking at Terry in further alarm.

'Well,' said Terry, 'the thing is, my wife is an Indian and they didn't like the smell of her cooking. Maoris can be quite prejudiced, you know, they can be quite fussy about their neighbours.'

There was an appalled silence on the hill.

'Still, there it is,' said Terry. 'We've all got to live somewhere. But I do assure you, it's only a little house here, a little house there, that's all we're planning.' And he and Maggie got back into the blue van and drove away, Terry patting vaguely with his handkerchief at the water running slowly from his bald patch down his face. Maggie took off her wet shoes.

Neither of them spoke as they drove. The old lady in the rain hat was still poking at the shells by the sea. Maggie puzzled over Terry. She'd met his son at the office party. He was training to be a vet and he wasn't an Indian.

'I didn't know your wife was an Indian,' she said finally.

'She's not actually, God forgive me,' said Terry. 'I just like to wind the buggers up.'

On the roof of the house the two young apprentices in singlets were drinking Coca-Cola. They waved again at the van. The light was beginning to fade and Maggie hoped they'd get off the roof soon.

'Hang on a minute,' said Terry as they came towards the docks. He stopped the van, called out of the window.

'Sinatra!'

He jumped out and caught up with the fat, grey-haired Maori who had been walking back along one of the wharves. The white man and the brown man stood oblivious of the rain; they had their heads together and spoke to each other intently for a minute or two. And then they both laughed. They shook hands and Terry came back to the van, wiping the rain off his bald patch again with his handkerchief.

'Good old Sinatra,' said Terry, 'Dunno what we'd do without him.' He started up the van. 'One of our apprentices got into a bit of trouble, Sinatra goes up to the prison to see him every Sunday.' Water from his coat dripped on to the van floor. 'Good man that.'

Maggie looked back, saw Sinatra walking alone back along the wharf. The rain fell.

'He seems to be everywhere,' she said.

'Some people,' said Terry after a pause, 'try and look after the world. Instead of looking after themselves.'

Maggie glanced at him, surprised again. But he only stared out at the rain, his face impassive, as the van turned up the hill towards the Bureau.

'Oh look,' said Terry as they passed a corner dairy. 'The Prime Minister has panicked.' There was a billboard outside.

ELECTION:
EARLIER DATE ANNOUNCED

Maggie thought at once of Emily and the crying sound started again, in her head.

Prudence, but not Emily, was back in the office. Maggie had only been back a short time when the firebell gave its little call and the men took off like rockets, looking down at their shoes, avoiding the girls' faces.

'Is Emily at home?' said Maggie, not looking at Prudence.

'She didn't want to go home. We sat on the wharves for a while but she wouldn't talk.'

'It was raining!'

'She wanted to sit in the rain. Finally, I took her to the railway station.'

'The *railway station*?'

Prudence shrugged. 'She insisted. She asked me to leave her there. So I came back to the office.'

'Will she be all right?'

Prudence looked out at the dark rain. 'I don't know,' she said.

'It was nothing to do with Mrs Tipene and that loony old sister,' Maggie's voice got higher and higher. 'They were just busybodies, it's bad enough that Emily had to – go through what she did – without them getting involved. It was nothing to *do* with them.'

'I suppose they thought it was to do with them.'

'What were they *doing* anyway, that terrible crying?'

'That's their lament.'

'It was nothing to *do* with them,' Maggie repeated angrily. 'I can't bear to think of something so private and terrible like that being made everybody's business.'

'That's how Maoris are.'

'What do you mean?'

'They talk about things. They share things. They're Manu's aunts, they think it is their business.'

'You mean gossip?' Maggie's parents had a deep aversion to gossip, kept themselves very much to themselves.

'You can call it gossip. Or sharing.'

'But Rangi and Hori and everyone knows now. And *Paddy*. He knows, doesn't he?'

'Yes.'

'Poor, poor Emily,' said Maggie wildly. 'I couldn't *bear* for people to know things about me. I never tell anybody *anything*. I don't talk to my parents about things, certainly not my one *aunt*,' and her voice rose even higher at such an improbability. 'I hardly ever see my aunt, she knows nothing about me, they live in the South Island. I talk to myself. Well, I think to myself.' She picked up a pile of files, took them to a cupboard.

'Well what about your friends?' said Prudence. 'Don't you talk about things to them?'

'You don't discuss everything with friends. Do you? Should I, do you mean? Is that a – um – psychology thing?' She looked at Prudence uncertainly. 'My best friend Susan, I never see her now. She was coming to university with me but she went to be a nurse instead, so's she could marry a doctor.'

Prudence gave a kind of snorting sound, brought another

pile of housing files over to the big cupboard but said no more, waved goodnight suddenly, was gone.

Plodding up the hill to the university, past the pohutukawa trees in the rain, Maggie thought: *there isn't anyone. I don't talk to anyone.*

Faintly in her head the sound of the crying voices began again.

In the library she hurriedly took a book about Dr Johnson from the shelves, passed the gurgling heaters, found a seat in the corner. But the words began to dance almost at once.

What would it be like to have someone that you can actually tell things to? She imagined Timoti's handsome face across the library desk, his suit and his waistcoat and his blue eyes. But he would be away for two more days. Would Timoti become her person, the person she found at last to talk to? Would they get married like everybody did, if he loved her? She saw the woman in the pink fluffy slippers dancing on the wet road and Terry talking about pepper-potting. Perhaps she and Timoti would be a pepper-potted family, sprinkled over the city.

But inside her head, the insistent sound of the old Maori women crying became suddenly so loud that she was forced at last, there in the library, to listen.

She knew of course. Manu's aunties did think it was their business. They were crying for, they were *mourning* for – she could not keep the thought out any longer – *for the white thing in the lavatory.*

They had been saying goodbye.

Quickly she picked up her books and her coat and ran out into the rainy night. She ran down the hill from the library, ran through the empty wet city streets, past the old rusty trucks in the disused yard where a guitar might sometimes strum and then up the hill behind the city to Prudence's place, it would be all right at Prudence's place. Rain fell on her coat and on her wild, wild hair.

Prudence's house on the hill, where the honeysuckle grew so wild, was in darkness. No sound of a guitar, no voice singing about love.

TWENTY-TWO

There was a very large photograph in the paper on Paddy's desk next morning of Emily and her father at a political meeting. They were both smiling. Emily's smile was loud and wide. Her desk at the Bureau was still empty.

'Isn't she coming back?' said Maggie, fearful suddenly. Her face was pale under her wild hair. Wild, uncontrolled dreams had haunted her night: she thought she had heard a crying sound: half awake, half asleep she wondered if it was her mother she could hear.

'She phoned and said she'd be here later, I expect she has to help her father.' But Paddy's face was bleak, as if he had lost something. 'You're going, too,' he said to Maggie.

'What do you mean?'

'You're being transferred to the Welfare Department. Bay Ropata's asked for you.'

'Welfare?' She knew nothing about welfare. Bay Ropata was supposed to be a maniac. Emily's words: *we won't go there. There's always mad people and murderers in Welfare shouting and screaming*, and sometimes Mr Porter the unfrocked minister had to take files there when a Good Provider stopped paying his mortgage. 'I don't want to, Paddy, I want to stay here.'

'Hori's coming here from Land Records. They like to move you youngsters around.'

Mad people and murderers. 'I don't *want* to,' said Maggie again.

Paddy's face was blank. 'This is a government department,' he said. 'The bosses decide.' And Maggie knew: Paddy too was one of the bosses, maybe he was moving her because she wasn't very good at her job.

Outside the rain poured down.

Emily appeared in the afternoon. Her hair had been heavily blonded and her nails were very red.

'Emily!' everybody said, 'Emily!' and Rangi skidded from his file trolley over to the coat rack and took her wet coat. She held her head very high. 'Did you see my picture in the paper?' she said to the room in general. And murmured to Maggie as she sat down, 'I told you I'd have my roots "Secret-sinned" when my big moment came. I was ready just in time, fifteen minutes to spare!'

'Are you all right?' whispered Maggie later.

'Of course!' said Emily and her eyes shone with anger and scorn and she looked away from Maggie. 'Party tonight?' she said to Prudence blithely.

Just for a moment, later, trudging up to the house on the hill behind the city after her lectures, because that's where her feet were automatically taking her, Maggie panicked. Her heart began to pound unpleasantly. *Is there a party tonight? Last night there was no one there. There's always someone there. What if the parties are over?*

But she heard the singing and the guitars as she got round the corner and she smelled the rain on the honeysuckle bushes and she sighed with relief. It was all right. Of course it was all right. Everything was all right.

Prudence's place was warm and welcoming as it always was, although the roof was leaking quite badly in one corner and she'd put a bucket there to catch the drips. Rangi was smoking and strumming the guitar in time to the drops falling. And Emily stood there, a glass of whisky in her hand, singing along with him loudly.

'G'day,' Rangi said, and he stopped playing. 'Welcome to Paradise. Have a beer, we're having such a great time here, Tane and Sarah are celebrating, Emily's celebrating, we're all celebrating.' And he looked down at the guitar, his normally open, laughing face a mask. Maggie saw that he was very drunk.

What's wrong? What's wrong? Maggie looked about the room she knew so well. Something was different, some feeling in the air.

Tane the Maori geologist and Sarah the Pakeha typist told her they were getting married; in a fortnight they said and Sarah, pale, flicked back her long ponytail and smiled at Tane and the others, and then suddenly looked away, ashamed.

'What do your parents say, Sarah?' Maggie asked.

'They've kicked me out,' she said, 'I'm living with Tane's sister and the kids, we're going to go and live on the coast.'

Maggie looked at Tane. 'On the coast?' There were no universities out on the coast. 'Are you still going to be a geologist Tane?'

He pushed at his glasses. 'No. I've decided to leave Varsity. And the Bureau. We're going to go to the coast and live with Mum.'

Maggie remembered Tane's eyes shining behind his glasses on the day of the fishing trip, telling her how he wanted to understand his country's history, his people's history, through studying the land. 'What'll you do?' she asked him.

'I've got a job in the Four Square grocery store at home,' he said, and he pushed at his glass and laughed.

'But, but why can't you still go to university, work at the Bureau?'

'More money at the Four Square if I do stocktaking on the weekends. And we don't want to have to come across Sarah's family in the street. Her father's threatened to shoot me, and he's got a hunting rifle.' And still he laughed. 'I'm sick of it here,' he said, and his face exploded with laughter and he turned away quickly from Maggie's stare and looked for another beer.

And Prudence murmured to Maggie: 'They're going tonight, from here. Sarah's father is apparently very serious. He has got a gun. He says he's going to kill Tane for making her pregnant; she's only seventeen.'

Kill Tane? Maggie stared at Sarah, who looked half frightened, half triumphant. *This is the nineteen fifties, people don't **kill** people. I'm seventeen too but Mum and Dad wouldn't **kill** Timoti, no matter what happened.* She suddenly grabbed another beer very quickly.

'You haven't asked me what *I'm* going to do,' said Emily to Maggie. Maggie saw that she, too, was very drunk, much drunker than usual. They usually got happy-drunk, not angry-drunk.

'Become an MP?' said Maggie, trying to make a joke.

'No, no, no, I'm going overseas. I booked my ticket on the *Rangitane* at lunchtime. I'm going at the beginning of September. Eureka!' And she threw up her hands dramatically.

'But, but that's soon,' said Maggie, shocked, dismayed. 'What about your exams?'

'I'm not going to sit them. Why should I?' Emily swayed against Rangi's shoulder.

'But you must!' Maggie said.

'Must? *Must*,' said Emily mocking her. 'We aren't all good little girls like you, Margaret-Rose, little Princess. I'm not bloody interested actually, I hate this boring country and its boring government departments and its gentility and its pretence and its –', she searched angrily for a word, grabbed at something, ' – *gloves.*'

'*Gloves?*' repeated Maggie uncomprehending. She looked round for Prudence.

'Go,' said Paddy, 'Go.' Maggie saw that Paddy too was very drunk indeed. Drunk in a different way. Everyone seemed different. As if a mirror had been smashed.

'Gloves?' said Maggie again.

'Oh you know how women wear *gloves* when they're going to meet each other for afternoon tea. Doesn't your mother wear *gloves*?'

'Yes,' said Maggie.

'What are they *doing*?' said Emily, more and more angry, 'wearing gloves to catch a tram down the road. What are they doing with their lives? Do you want to end up like them?' and she shuddered.

Rangi stared at Emily expressionlessly, strumming his guitar, to late now to forget your smile, said the song.

'Go,' said Paddy again, drunk, his wig askew.

'What does your father say?' said Maggie.

'I can twist my father round my little finger,' replied Emily. 'He's bought me acres of beautiful land because he wants me to be rich! I'm going to be a millionaire!'

Hope's voice, whisky-filled, floated up from the corner where she always sat, where Paul the epileptic was also sitting. 'I thought you disapproved of your father,' Hope said mildly.

'If you can't beat them, join them, Hope,' said Emily and she laughed very loudly.

'Won't he want you to finish your degree?' The deep, deep voice of Gallipoli Gordon came rumbling across the room.

'I've told you all, all of you, I don't care. I can't bear to be in this country any more, it's full of liars and cheats and bores, I want to be somewhere where things happen to people. Do you think –', Emily was shouting now and the whole room listened to her, even Hope in the corner stopped strumming, 'do you think I want to spend the rest of my life drinking DB bitter and eating fish and chips and not getting anywhere, not *doing* anything? Well, just look at us, *look at us!*' And with her arm she made a large, wild gesture at the room they all knew so well, where they all sang and laughed and the roof leaked.

'I'm getting out of here,' said Emily. 'My father will be able to get me a job over there, when he's prime minister, when I tell him I'm going. He'll be prime minister any moment now!' She laughed angrily. 'Sing, Hope.'

> *Tahi nei taru kino,*
> *Mahi whaiaipo.*

sang Hope, smiling at the light, *making love is like a dangerous vine.*

In Maggie's dreams the dangerous vine wound itself around the wooden planks on the dark wharf and deep in the sea a white baby floated.

TWENTY-THREE

Men's voices boomed out along the tram lines, up the hills, through the suburban streets: VOTE FOR ME. Cars drove slowly round the city with loudspeakers attached. The rain kept falling. Sometimes something went wrong because of the weather: cars stalled, banners drooped, loudspeakers crackled and broke. Some people didn't care about any of it.

'There's free medicine and free education,' said Harry Beans, 'neither party will ever change that. If one of them says they'll raise my wages or have more rugby I'll vote for them, otherwise why should I bother?'

Emily and Maggie and Prudence and Rangi and Hope and Tane and Sarah were all too young to vote. You had to be twenty-one to vote. The election only interested them because Emily's father was probably going to be the next prime minister.

'What party do you vote for Paddy?' asked Maggie.

'Ask yourself,' he said. She asked herself, but did not know the answer and gave up thinking about it, waiting for the evening, for the Maori class at Isobel Arapeta's house. It was five days since the ball: *will he love me still?*

Still in her head, if she wasn't careful, the crying sound echoed.

She was the first one there; Isobel, on the telephone, waved her in to the sitting room by the fire to dry out. She looked deep into the fire and suddenly saw houses and witches and waves. And diamonds.

Her heart jumped when the doorbell rang; she sat very still. Timoti and Kara took off their coats in the hall, then came in; the room filled with their voices and their bodies, talking to Isobel about a Maori they all knew who had died and drying their trousers by standing close to the fire. Steam rose from them.

'*Kia ora*,' said Maggie brightly.

They glanced at her. '*Kia ora*,' they said, and went on talking.

She found it hard to concentrate in the class: *not once* did Timoti look at her.

'Come on,' said Isobel once, quite sharply. 'Wake up, Maggie, *he aha to mate*? What's wrong? We've had this one before.'

Maggie read aloud:

Ka mea, e koro, ka unga mai i ahau
kia tika i te hiwi.

and translated slowly, remembering now, this was a love song, like the songs at the parties: *were you, beloved, to invite me, straightaway by way of the hill I would come.*

'Good,' said Isobel.

The three students hurried down the hill in the rain, Kara jumped on a tram and waved. Timoti turned at once to Maggie and kissed her hard, clumsily almost, forcing her mouth open with his tongue, rain on their faces.

When she had extricated herself she said breathlessly, 'I thought you didn't love me any more.'

'Why?'

'You didn't look at me at all all night, or smile at me, I haven't seen you since the ball.'

'There were people there. I'm not going to look at you while there are other people there,' and he kissed her hard again. 'I've been waiting to see you again, I've got something to show you.' He took her hand, turned a corner into a dark side street near the fire station.

'I have to catch the 9.30 tram.' Her voice was at once anxious.

'There's time,' he said.

There, down an alley, a small sign glowed with one word: PEPITO'S. Timoti pushed at the dark door and it swung open.

Maggie gasped. There was music. There were people sitting at low tables lit with candles in beer bottles and the wax ran down the sides of the bottles, making patterns. On the walls there were posters of sun and sea and smiling people. A man in a fisherman's smock, like the one Franco the Italian was wearing on the fishing trip but clean and ironed and not smelling of fish, showed them to a table. He lit their candle.

'Two coffees please,' said Timoti, and when the man had gone away he took Maggie's hand in the dim, flickering light.

'I thought,' he said quite shyly, 'this would be a nice place to say I love you.'

She stared at him, feeling herself smiling. 'Where *are* we?' she said.

'It's a coffee bar.'

A record was playing. *When the deep purple falls*, a woman sang. Maggie's face felt as if it would burst from smiling: at Timoti's words, *he loves me*, at the music, at the coffee bar, at life.

'I've never been to anything like this ever, ever,' she whispered. 'It's wonderful. Oh look, there's one of those poets, look, talking to one of those girls they kiss.' A saxophone echoed across the dark, shadowy room and the words of the song whispered into their hearts.

From the mist of a memory
You wander back to me
Breathing my name like a sigh

The man in the smock brought two cups of coffee in beautiful, bright yellow and blue and red cups. Maggie had never seen a yellow and blue and red cup before. She had never drunk coffee before.

She smiled and smiled at Timoti. The crying voices in her head faded away at last.

'It's not so noisy in the library now,' she told her parents, 'and so many of the books I need are there.' She and Timoti arranged to study together in the library. She was glad to have a break from going to Prudence's place so often. Something had happened there. Something had broken. So now, instead, she would wait at their library table for her boyfriend. Sometimes she had stew at the university cafeteria, sometimes she ate a squashed chocolate fish from the bottom of her bag. He would come later, often his white raincoat was dripping with rain. He would hang it on a chair near the radiator along the wall and come and sit beside her, undoing the bottom buttons of his waistcoat.

'Hello,' he would say, and get out his law books and smile at her with his blue, blue eyes so that her heart opened. She actually felt it opening, like a flower, or a starfish. The bad dreams faded.

They would sit close beside each other, bent over their books. The thick radiators gurgled and sometimes the lights flickered, affected by the weather. The crippled boy sat at a side table in the corner, his crutches rested beside the big window. Other couples sat together in the library too: lovers whispered, sat with their feet and legs touching under the tables as if sex and learning were somehow intertwined, books and hands and glances. In the bushes near the library, in the darkness, Timoti would kiss her and put his hand on her breast: 'I want you,' he would say over and over again, before she had to run for the 9.30 tram.

One night in the library he whispered. 'I have to go home again this weekend. I've tried and tried to get out of it and I just can't,' and he sighed. 'It's my uncle's eightieth birthday and he insists I come. He won't allow them to have the party unless I come. So I want you to come with me and meet my family, who knows when I'll be back there again.'

An angel flew over, smiling; the one who had arranged for her to stay at Eddie Albert's flat and look after his cat.

'I love you,' said Timoti to Maggie as he kissed her hard that evening at the tram stop. 'Do you love me?'

Maggie practised. 'I love you,' she said as the 9.30 tram loomed into view out of the rain. She waved as the tram rattled off; she saw that people stared.

At home her mother was scrubbing the kitchen floor.

'Mum, it's late to be tidying up.'

But Mrs Bennett went on scrubbing. 'Eddie Albert phoned you,' she said. 'To remind you he wants you to cat-sit this weekend.'

'Oh, yes, he said,' said Maggie. 'All right.'

The scrubbing brush made a harsh, rhythmic sound backwards and forwards across the green linoleum.

'I hope you're not seeing anything more of that Maori.'

'I told you, Mum,' Maggie said. 'It was just the once. I haven't got time for boyfriends.'

*

In the high room Isobel Arapeta said to her pupils: *tito is the Maori word meaning 'to lie'. Or, a liar. I think it is important to understand, when you're learning this language, that sometimes Maoris and Pakehas have different ways of looking at the truth.*

*

Angelique Benson had been to seven balls.

Saturday night after Saturday night the white, floating, strapless dress, so daring and so beautiful, shone; was featured in the newspaper more than once. Eligible young men vied to accompany her, encouraged by ambitious fathers: *she's the catch of the season, with Benson as your father-in-law, you'd be set for life.* Not that they needed encouraging: up close the pointy bra and the strapless dress were mesmerising and their mothers kept saying anxiously: *girls who go strapless are fast.*

The young men cut in during waltzes, took the white-gloved hand nervously in theirs, placed their other hand sweatily on her bare back. Angelique smiled and smiled for hours on end, pointing her bosom. The young men twirled if they knew how, shuffled if they didn't, sometimes silently cursing that rugby practice had interfered with ballroom dancing classes. They had not understood that waltzing, even briefly, could be so important.

The young men secretly found Angelique cold, not fast: she still smiled but was strangely unmoved by their enthusiastic advances towards the pointy bra in dark, parked cars. As if – one wiser than most, thought – she knew more than they did and was bored. But they persevered, of course, egged on by their fathers and Angelique listened to their talk of rugby all over again while she smiled and smiled.

And, always, the powerful Mr Benson was not far away, watching over his precious little jewel carefully, looking the young men over, looking for a suitable husband for his beloved. She would appear again, beautiful, in his newspapers.

And in the same newspapers, next door to the floating white jewel, there were sometimes photographs of Emily: she had become a feature of her father's election campaign. She was photographed with him at meetings. She shook old people's hands, hardly came to work, never went to lectures. Her brightly smiling face shone out at them from the morning newspaper on Paddy's desk.

'Why is she doing this, she *hated* her father's party,' Maggie asked Prudence. 'She said it was anti-Maori.'

Prudence said nothing till she had finished writing THIS MAN SEEMS TO BE A GOOD PROVIDER on a file and then she spoke.

'Perhaps,' she said slowly, 'Emily's anti-Maori now.'

She could not have shocked Maggie more. '*Emily*?' she said. 'She can't be, she's –' and she felt around for the right words, '– she's one of us.'

Prudence said nothing. And Maggie thought, *what did I mean: 'one of us'? What was I thinking? What did I mean?* And she thought of Emily weeping in her bright, jaunty jacket and the cries of pain and unhappiness that terrible night. And then she saw again Emily's frozen face, as the old ladies cried.

Just then Bay Ropata came in the door. His presence was so large, his personality so huge, that the whole office stopped.

'G'day, Bay,' said Paddy.

'Where's my girl?' said Bay, and Maggie thought he meant Prudence, was shocked.

'That's you, Maggie,' said Paddy.

'Me?' And then she remembered. 'What, *now*? It's eleven o'clock in the morning, I'm in the middle of things.'

'No one is indispensable,' said Paddy, smiling slightly, 'give your files to Prudence.'

Bay lumbered over to where Prudence and Maggie were. He rested his hand very gently on Prudence's shoulder as he said to Maggie: 'We need you right now.'

She followed Bay sulkily, sighing loudly; dragged her raincoat behind her along the long corridor she hadn't been down.

She had a desk and a phone.

The rest of the office was empty.

'What do I *do*?' she cried, as Bay put on his hat.

'Order,' he said, making a grand gesture in the room. 'Create order out of chaos, and put it in statistics, the bosses want statistics,' and he disappeared.

Mrs McMillan, the woman from Yorkshire who Maggie remembered from the fishing trip, came in, drying her hands on a towel.

'Oh, good, there you are at last Maggie,' she said.

'What do I *do*?' asked Maggie again.

Mrs McMillan perched on her desk and sighed. 'Bloody Bay, hasn't he explained anything to you?'

'No.'

'Well. This is the Welfare Department. Your job is to answer the phone and take details of a problem and tell people a Welfare Officer will call as soon as possible. If anyone comes to the public counter with a problem, take details and tell them a Welfare Officer will call as soon as possible.'

The phone rang. Maggie looked at it.

'It won't bite,' said Mrs McMillan.

'This is the Welfare Department,' said Maggie.

Her first telephone call was to say a Maori man was bashing his wife up outside a hotel. Maggie's eyes widened and she looked at Mrs McMillan in panic. 'Bashing his wife up where?'

Mrs McMillan took the phone. 'Call the police,' she said. 'This is a police matter, and we have no way of getting there in time.'

'The police won't interfere in domestic disputes,' cried the caller hysterically, 'he's going to kill her, it's my sister.'

Mrs McMillan sighed. 'What's your name, where's the hotel?' she said.

She hung up, got off the desk. 'I'd better go,' she said, 'but it'll be long over by the time I get there.'

'*Hurry*!' said Maggie.

'Hello dear,' called a very old lady from the public counter.

'Oh hello, Auntie Aroha,' said Mrs McMillan glancing over. 'Bay's not here.'

'Never mind, dear, I'll wait.' And the old lady sat down on the bench beside the counter.

'This is Maggie,' said Mrs McMillan, putting on her lipstick in a small mirror. 'She's the new clerk.'

'*Hurry*!' said Maggie to Mrs McMillan.

'Pleased to meet you, dear,' said the old lady. 'Any chance of a cup of tea?'

'The tea's there, on that small table,' said Mrs McMillan, and she was gone. The old lady looked at the tea and then looked at Maggie hopefully. The telephone rang.

'This is the Welfare Department.'

'I've lost my daughter,' said a voice. Maggie anxiously took details.

Rangi came in through the back, his cigarette drooping, wheeling the trolley of files.

'Oh Rangi, help!' she yelled, and he laughed.

'The thing is to just keep calm,' he said. 'This department can't solve every problem in the city. You can only do what you can do. *Kia ora*, Auntie Aroha, I'll make you a cup of tea,' and he plugged in the kettle, looked for the milk, lit a cigarette.

'I don't even know who the other Welfare Officers are except Mrs McMillan,' said Maggie desperately, 'and a man rang and said he's lost his daughter.'

'I expect he'll find her again, eh, Auntie Aroha?' said Rangi.

'*Ae*,' said the old lady. 'Yes, my dear. People often find again what they have lost.' And she started murmuring in Maori over her old handbag.

'Is she going to stay here?' whispered Maggie.

'Why not?' said Rangi.

'I dunno,' whispered Maggie, starting to giggle in a kind of hysteria. 'I have no idea why I'm here or what I'm doing.'

'This place is nothing like Housing or Land Records,' said Rangi. 'You should be honoured to be here, they have all the high-flyers here, the *crème de la crème*.'

'Don't you *dare* start talking French to me, Rangi Cox!' said Maggie.

'One of them's young like us. Bubs Gordon.'

'Bubs? What a dreadful name to give a grown-up.'

'I've got an old auntie who's seventy-three who's called Bubs. The youngest in the family is often called Bubs. The one in this office is a Mormon, that's why he doesn't come to our parties. Mormons are not allowed to drink, so he rows instead. He's in the university rowing team.'

'Rowing?'

'Well, that's how we got to this country in the first place,' said Rangi. 'In the olden days. It's probably in his genes. And there's Glory Ngahuia Brown, the most beautiful woman in the Bureau. And Errol Flynn.'

'Pardon?'

'Yeah. Errol Flynn. Their name used to be Whinihi but they were posh Maoris and changed it to Flynn and called their son Errol,' and Rangi was laughing again. 'He thinks he's God's Gift to the World,' he added, still chuckling.

'Kettle's boiling,' called Auntie Aroha.

'Here,' said Rangi, handing Maggie a little government booklet he'd found in a pile of papers, 'that's a list of what Welfare does,' and he went to the table in the corner to make the tea.

The list read:

marital breakdown problems
housing mortgage arrears
adoption problems
education problems
employment problems
alcohol-related problems
police reports
escaped prisoners
released prisoners
and all related matters appertaining to the above.

'Oh, my goodness gracious me!' said Maggie, and Rangi laughed.

Maggie took twenty-seven calls and tried to understand the filing system.

It was clear almost at once that there wasn't a filing system.

A man came to the counter asking for money in what Maggie thought was a rather sinister manner. Auntie Aroha, still sitting with her handbag by the counter, talked to him in Maori and after a while he went away. A young girl walked in and asked Maggie to help her get a job.

'Um – what are you good at?' asked Maggie.

'Doing dishes,' said the girl.

'Have you got a phone number?'

'No, I don't live anywhere yet, I've just arrived.'

Auntie Aroha knew where there was a church hostel and gave the girl two shillings.

Bubs, the Mormon rowing fanatic, rushed in in a rowing jacket carrying files, gave a big, friendly grin to Maggie, refused a cup of tea because it was against his religion and rushed out again. The other two Welfare Officers came in together later: Errol Flynn, who seemed to think he actually was a film star and Glory Ngahuia Brown, the most beautiful woman in the Bureau. Glory was very beautiful: Maggie looked at her fearfully, *hope Timoti doesn't know her*. The two collected files, went again, spoke nonchalantly to Maggie in passing. She was only the clerk. They had degrees, they were the *crème de la crème*: Errol and Glory.

Auntie Aroha waited till about three o'clock in case Bay came in, then said she must catch her tram. 'I'll come another day,' she said cheerfully. 'Nice tea, dear.'

A fat, grey-haired Maori man in a black singlet came in and leaned on the counter. Maggie knew she had seen him before.

'Good afternoon,' she said politely, nervously, hoping, now that she was alone in the office, that he wasn't a murderer or a mad person. 'Can I help you?'

He smiled at her. 'You're new,' he said.

'Yes. I'm Maggie.'

'*Kia ora*,' he said, and he put out his hand across the counter. 'I'm Sinatra. My mother named me after Frank Sinatra before she buggered off.' His slow, lazy smile lit up his whole face, and Maggie smiled back, caught in his warmth.

'I remember you,' she said. 'You were at the office party in a red shirt, and Terry told me you visit a Maori apprentice up at the prison.'

'And I saw you going off on that office fishing trip that morning. You caught your first fish, didn't you?'

Maggie looked at him in surprise. 'I did,' she said. 'But how did you know?'

He smiled again. 'I'm the King of the City,' he said, 'I know everything,' and she did not know whether he was joking.

'Where's Bay?' said Sinatra, getting down to business.

'I think he's gone to make a speech at the Rotary Club.'

Sinatra laughed. 'Good on him,' he said. 'He'll catch them in his net with his war stories and they'll find they've got a Maori office junior!' Then he took a large bundle of pound notes, some coins and a piece of paper out of his pocket. 'This is money some of the wharfies owe on their mortgages,' he said. 'I knew it was payday so I waited for the buggers as they came out of the office before they went to the pub, wanted to save Bay the trouble. Tell him Sinatra came,' and he was gone.

The piece of paper was torn from a notebook. On it, in pencil, were neatly printed names and beside each name a sum of money. It amounted to the exact sum of money he had given her across the counter.

This is a very peculiar place, thought Maggie, her hands full of notes and coins. *I could abscond to Timbuktu with this.* Some of the money had sand on it, or bits of tobacco.

Bay wandered in again at last, looking as if his tie was throttling him. He was humming and carrying a sack. '*Kia ora*,' he said to Maggie.

'Your Auntie Aroha was here, and a man called Sinatra collected all this money down at the wharves,' she said, anxiously handing him the money and the names.

He grinned as he saw what was written there. 'Good old Sinny,' he said, 'he saves me a lot of work. Some of our people are a bit slow paying their mortgage, we find it easier to go and take the money off them, me and Sinny! He's a kind of cousin of mine.' Bay handed the money back to her. 'Give all this to Housing,' he said. 'Good old Sinny, King of the City.'

'That's what he said.'

'Did he, the skiting bugger? Well, don't forget to put it all in our statistics,' and he laughed. 'And Auntie Aroha will be a great help to you, you'll see.'

Aunties and wharfies she thought, putting all the money in a big envelope. *What a bizarre way to do government business.* She stared at Bay's sack.

'Mussels,' he said. 'I got them down at the bay when the tide was out after I'd addressed that meeting of employers at the Rotary and showed them my bayonet wound, does wonders.' He opened the sack on top of some files on her desk. 'Want some?'

'No thanks,' said Maggie, shuddering slightly.

He opened mussels with a small penknife, eating them as he opened them. 'Go on,' he said, 'try one.'

'No thanks,' said Maggie.

'*Kei te pehea tou mahi i tenei ra tuatahi, e hoa?*' he said *How did you get on with your first day?* Sucking the mussel out of its shell.

'It's very – um – hectic,' she said nervously, watching the mussel juice fall on the files.

'Hectic,' he repeated thoughtfully. 'Yes. Well, we're only a sticking plaster of course. Till the explosion.'

'What do you mean, explosion?'

'I mean explosion,' said Bay Ropata. 'You know what an explosion is.' The telephone rang on his desk. He sauntered over to the phone, the sack of mussels still under his arm.

'*Kia ora*,' he said. And launched into a conversation in Maori. Maggie listened, understood a little. He was talking about a young boy who kept getting into trouble and was likely to end up in prison.

'Keep him there,' said Bay in Maori. 'Now. I'll come and get him and put him on tonight's paper bus and send him home to the coast.'

And then Maggie realised.

At last she was hearing the language used as a real language of transaction and communication, as if it was not dead at all. Perhaps it would be a good thing to work in this department after all, well, as long as there weren't too many murderers and mad people; perhaps she would learn a lot.

'*E noho ra*,' Bay said to her after he'd hung up, 'see you tomorrow, you'll get used to it.' He put on his hat and he left the office, humming.

It was only then that she noticed he wasn't wearing shoes.

'I've been transferred to the Welfare Department,' she said dubiously to her boyfriend as they sat, legs touching, in the university library.

TWENTY-FOUR

Newspapers said day after day NEW BLOOD NEEDED TO LEAD THE COUNTRY (so that people ended up saying to each other: *we need new blood to lead the country*). Lots of bands enthusiastically played the National Anthem at John Evans's election meetings.

When the day of the election came John Evans's party was resoundingly triumphant.

Before midnight, photographers flashed at the exultant new Prime Minister of the country together with Mrs Evans and their daughter Emily, waving from the tall steps of Parliament Buildings. Emily was wearing her best yellow frock and laughing out into the night. The National Anthem played and Sinatra walked past, mixing with journalists and party supporters, talking and listening and watching.

John Evans, victorious, talked live on the radio about the Greatest Little Country in the World and how his new government would help make everyone in this country more prosperous. The National Anthem played.

'When that man says *everyone*,' said Hui Windsor at Prudence's place, lifting his wooden leg on to a chair, grimacing because the rain made it hurt more, and because he was drunk, 'he doesn't of course mean *us*. That man –' and he looked around again to make sure Emily wasn't there, '– that man would sell his own mother if he could make money out of her. I'm telling you, they've been interfering and making nuisances of themselves in the Alienation Department, and the Consolidation Department, they want Maori land *sold*. And now they're the government. I don't trust the buggers, they'd close the Bureau if they could, and build petrol pumps on the graves of my ancestors.' He grabbed Rangi's guitar, began to strum, sang angrily:

> *He puru tai tama e,*
> *He puru tai tama hoki*

we're wild bulls, we Maori warriors, watch out.

John Evans should have been listening, perhaps.

*

There were two small interview rooms in the Welfare Department and sometimes Bay Ropata would disappear into one of them and Maggie would hear humming. Once she put her head round the door. He sat alone, leaning on the empty desk. He kept humming for a moment and then looked up at her.

'I'm composing an oratorio,' he said.

She did indeed learn a great deal, as she had forseen. Not just about the language but about the city where her mother wore gloves to town. John Evans's city now.

Sinatra's city.

She learned that just underneath the respectable surface there was pain and anger and danger and trouble.

'I told you,' said Bay Ropata mildly. 'We are only the sticking plaster till the explosion. What else can we be? They're trying to demolish a whole culture here.'

'What do you mean?'

'Observe,' said Bay. 'Look at most of our warriors, our proud people. Fat, broken-down, drunk, in prison. That's how you demolish cultures. Lucky you fellas don't understand how our roots wind round the land.'

'What do you mean?' said Maggie again.

Bay was lumbering about the office, taking bits of paper from files, putting them in his pocket, writing notes to himself with a pencil. 'You fellas nearly wiped us all out, you know,' he said. 'I know it's not quite what you learned at school, but that's what happened. War and disease. You took our land, you changed our laws, we were demoralised and decimated – no, decimated only means one in ten – *destroyed*; we were very nearly destroyed. Not counting all the fighting over land you know what you gave us? Dysentry. Influenza. Tuberculosis –'

'Measles.'

'Measles. VD. Whooping cough. All that stuff. We were nearly finished, we'd given up. But, a group of my people, the first graduates and doctors; they saw it happening, they saw their race literally disappearing in front of their eyes. And you know what they did? They got on horses and went round the Maori settlements all over the country – all the desolate, broken-down, diseased villages. My grandfather told me about it, he was one of the doctors, riding up to places in the dusk and seeing children coughing and the hopeless faces.

'And they *exhorted* them. That's the word my grandfather used. They said: it's now or never and never is almost here. This is what you have to do. Take what you can from these white fellas. Get drains, believe the doctors, don't throw the medicine in the river. Have more children.' And Bay grinned. 'They told them to have *lots* more children. But my grandfather told me that then, having bashed and bashed their message, then they'd sit in hundreds of meeting houses long into the night and *exhort* again, exhort the people not to lose a sense of themselves. To hold on to their sense of themselves. That's what happened.' Bay stuffed the last bits of paper into his jacket pocket.

'Of course the country is full of casualties, all the people who couldn't begin to join the two cultures together, who fell down a hole in the middle. It's like a war. The casualties are either dead, or mad, or in prison – all the ones we deal with here.' And he picked up his hat and wandered off. 'But we've kept our roots, *e hoa*, and we're dangerous.' He smiled amiably at her from the doorway. 'We might still outsmart you buggers, you know; it's not over yet.'

But before he could get out the door another old auntie came in to tell him about a death in his large, unwieldy family. They spoke in Maori, the old lady cried for a while and Bay cried too, wiping his eyes with a big white handkerchief, blowing his nose.

Emily turned up at the Bureau again in a new frock. 'I've handed in my resignation,' she said to Paddy, 'I leave for England in three weeks.'

'Did you tell your father?' asked Rangi.

'I told him on election night,' she smirked. 'He was so intoxicated with becoming prime minister, so self-satisfied and so jubilant – well, of course he just agreed. He'd have agreed to anything! We're going to build a fishing lodge and a boat harbour and a luxury hotel on my land so that I become extremely rich, that's what he said. I'll never be working in a dump like this again.'

Paddy bent over his beloved housing files, hurt in his eyes.

Timoti said he would pick Maggie up from Eddie Albert's flat at eleven o'clock on Saturday morning to go north and his face lit up when he realised at once that they could both stay in the flat, alone, on Sunday night when they got back.

'Thank God, *at last*,' he said to Maggie and he held her even tighter in among the dark trees by the university: she felt again something hard, pressing against her.

TWENTY-FIVE

She opened her eyes and thought: *today is the day that I'm going to a Maori village with my new boyfriend who wants to make love to me and I don't really want to, because I don't want to get pregnant like Emily.*

Her heart beat fast in her safe, pink bedroom.

She arrived at Eddie Albert's flat with her satchel of books. Hidden in a brown paper bag her party dress and her pretty nightie were rolled into a small ball. Eddie Albert was on the phone to his girlfriend, Shirley, who was very sulky that he would be away till Monday evening.

'I'll see you on Monday as soon as I get back,' Eddie Albert said.

'This is *Saturday*. The weekends are *ours*,' said Shirley. Maggie could hear her shrill, hurt voice.

The other advertisers were laughing and joking, all the Boys, going on a trip together, determined to have a good time. Maggie glanced at Peter the oxymoron from under her eyelashes, thought how fat and ugly and white he was, with too much Brylcreem on his hair. Peter greeted her cheerily, as if he'd never had his finger up her vagina. He'd probably forgotten.

'How's work with the Natives?' he asked, joshing her.

She said what she had found: that there was trouble and pain.

'Don't give me that stuff!' said Peter, standing at the door in his expensive overcoat, waiting with the others for Eddie Albert to cut short his phone call. 'They're great fellas, the Maoris, of course, but it's their own fault. We certainly don't discriminate against them: this country has the best race relations in the whole world, everybody knows that. Look at America, look at South Africa, look at the poor bloody Abos in Australia. There is no discrimination in this country, never has been. They've got the vote, they were always treated like us.' (Peter, too, had drawn bare-footed Maoris smiling at Queen Victoria when he was at primary school.) 'But Maoris are lazy. And they eat the wrong kind of food and they're all fat and they all die of heart attacks. They come to the city because they can live on social security, that's the root of it all. They should stay on their land; they're happier there.'

There was a general chorus of agreement from the others.

'Come on, come on,' called Eddie Albert, off the phone at last, 'leave my loony cousin in charge.' The other advertisers started piling into the taxi that was waiting outside.

'Eddie. Don't call me "loony" all the time.'

'Well, you know how it runs in families.' He was putting on his coat. 'And you're such a dozy sheila. It wouldn't surprise me.'

'What do you mean?' There was such a look of puzzlement on her face that just for a second, one arm in his coat, he looked genuinely taken aback.

'Well, you know.'

'What?'

'Don't you remember? You must remember.'

'What must I remember?'

'Well – Auntie Norma and all that.' He pulled on his coat properly.

'Mum?'

'Yes, of course. Well, you must remember when she was in the loony bin!'

The taxi tooted.

'When?'

'When Elizabeth died, of course. For a year and a half. Your Dad came back from the war and she was already in there. You came and stayed with us for months. You must remember.'

'No, I don't.'

The taxi tooted again.

'Oh, well. We never talk about it, of course. But your mum was in the loony bin.'

Maggie stared up at him. 'Cheer up, it's a long time ago, I won't tease you again. Come and wave us off,' and he hurried out to the taxi. She called him back.

'Eddie!' He slowed for a moment, irritated.

'Eddie, do you remember Elizabeth?'

'Oh, come on, it's years ago,' he called over his shoulder.

'Eddie!'

He half stopped on the path; then saw her face. The taxi tooted for a third time. But Eddie Albert turned and walked back towards her.

'Yeah. I do remember her actually,' he said slowly, and he had an odd, concentrated look on his face. 'I missed her like anything when she died. We used to come and stay with you sometimes, me and all my sisters. She was brave, that's what I remember about her. She was the bravest of all you girls. She was the only one who would play on the trolley with me and go fast down hills. I've never forgotten her.'

'Come on Eddie!' called the advertisers.

And his face changed back to normal, he waved to his colleagues, was gone down the path.

She waved and smiled brightly at the departing taxi.

'Don't forget to wash my socks!' called Peter, and he

winked and they all waved, 'Yeah! Do our socks!' and the taxi roared off.

She stood quite still at the end of the path, almost in shock for a moment. *Someone had talked to her about her sister.*

And then she seemed almost to shake herself.

And then she went inside.

Quickly, holding her nose, she collected all the dirty socks she could find in all the rooms, took them into the wash-house at the back of the big flat. She turned on taps. She got out the box of Rinso washing powder. She poured it on to the socks. She saw her hands, scrubbing and scrubbing. *I shouldn't be surprised about the loony bin.* Scrub, scrub, went her hands. *Perhaps it explains things, sort of.* Scrub, scrub. *How weird to hear Eddie Albert actually talking about Elizabeth.*

More and more hot water came out of the taps; sock after sock got scrubbed against the wooden washing board. *I'm glad she was brave.*

The socks got rinsed in cold water. *It was all a long, long time ago. I mustn't think about it too much. I shouldn't be surprised about the loony bin.*

Then she hung all the socks on the back verandah. There were thirty-seven.

She put out four saucers of food for Jingle the cat who immediately finished two of them. 'You can't starve in twenty-four hours,' Maggie told it. 'It's a biological impossibility. It'll be your own fault if you're hungry.' *I shouldn't be surprised about the loony bin at all.* She went and stood, quite motionless, waiting, by the front gate.

At eleven o'clock Timoti arrived, in his cousin Henare's uncle's wife's car; all morning since seven he'd worked in his law office.

Inside the empty flat Maggie felt almost uneasy as they kissed: nobody there, nobody watching them. It was the first time they had ever really been alone. And nobody waiting for them. It was so silent, she could hardly breathe as he held her, nothing but the occasional rumble or jolt of the very old refrigerator. Otherwise silence and she could feel Timoti's heart beating as fast as hers.

'Feel our hearts,' she whispered.

He felt her heart, her whole breast and she gave a little gasp; he laid her on the landlord's horrible orange sofa but she struggled to sit up.

'Shouldn't we be going, won't we be late, it's a long way and I feel a bit – nervous,' she said.

'It's all right. I won't do anything much, we'll go in a minute, we won't do it properly.' But he was pulling off her cardigan and her blouse, pulling her skirt down and her petticoat down and taking off his trousers.

And then he held her. 'You're the first Pakeha I've ever kissed,' he said.

She didn't answer, pushed Manu's laughing face away.

Gradually their hearts slowed down as they got used to lying there together although she still felt stiff in his arms. Her white arm lay over his brown one, her thin legs looked white and pale next to his big brown ones. They lay with their faces very close together: both of them had dark curly hair. They breathed in time to each other, listening to the Saturday city silence.

Very, very shyly, she said to him. 'What's tattooed-bottom intercourse, Timoti?'

'*What?*'

'Well,' she said, 'it's from one of the *waiata*, it talks about tattooed-bottom intercourse and I – um – just wondered what it was.' She squirmed round the orange sofa, out of his arms. 'Well, actually I was just wondering if you had a tattooed bottom?' and she looked quite politely under the leg of his underpants.

Timoti looked nonplussed, saw her peering. 'You haven't,' she said.

'Well, *of course* I haven't, do you think we all tattoo our bums?' He looked offended for a moment and then he started to laugh a bit and Maggie gave a little giggle, wished he laughed more: it smoothed his face. And it suddenly occurred to her: *he's like me, he finds it hard to laugh, too.*

'I suppose it's an old poem,' she said, 'I just wasn't sure, I mean how was I supposed to know.' And then lying down again, wriggling, getting comfortable against his body, she said, 'I've never lain down with a boy before.' And, shyly, 'It's nice isn't it? Nice and – sort of cuddly.'

'Yes,' he answered holding her tight.

'But,' and she fidgeted again, 'it's quite hard to find places to lie down. You can't lie down in a car.'

'We used to lie down in the long grass at home and show girls our things.'

'Yes, but we live in the city.' Then she added suddenly: 'On this sofa one of Eddie's friends – touched me. It was horrible.'

She felt him tense immediately. 'Were you lying down here with him?'

'No no,' she said, and she wriggled again so that he could see that she was telling the truth, 'we were listening to the "Lever Hit Parade" and he suddenly –' she screwed up her face in distaste, 'touched me.'

Timoti whispered, 'Lie still.'

And, uncertainly, he touched her too.

They arrived in Rangimarie late in the afternoon, driving north from the city for nearly five hours, down roads finally that the bus from the city didn't take. At last they wound down an unpaved, very dusty road behind a row of macracarpa trees and blackberry bushes and Timoti stopped the car outside a small old church.

'Let's have a stretch ' he said, 'before they grab us.'

The winter sun had shone stronger and stronger the further they got from the city and it shone still on the peaceful gravestones and on the grass that grew up between them and on the newly mown lawn by the church door, even though the day was almost ended.

They walked between the gravestones; a few were broken, a few had poems on them, many had photographs encased in glass. On one of the graves a small bunch of fresh daisies lay.

'That's Ngaio,' said Timoti. 'That's my sister.'

Maggie looked down at the photograph of a laughing young girl. 'The one who was seventeen? Whose unveiling you went to?'

'Yes.' And he stopped, smoothed the new stone, sat awkwardly beside the grave.

NGAIO POU

Aged 17 years

Moe mai e hine i to moenga roa

sleep gently in your long sleep.

'She was named after a beautiful tree,' said Timoti. 'A *ngaio* tree.'

'She looks beautiful in the photograph,' said Maggie shyly.

'Until Ngaio died, I hadn't been here for years,' he said. He had his eyes closed, feeling the warmth of the sun. 'I don't come home much. I just don't like it. I don't belong. I find it all depressing, nothing happens, everything's dying.'

She closed her eyes too, feeling the sun on her eyelids, that feeling of colour that bright light can push through the eyelids. And she thought of her sister, of Elizabeth. *How awful. I don't even know where they buried Elizabeth.* And, quite unexpectedly, she felt a great, sad feeling of loneliness suddenly, for her brave sister that she didn't really remember.

'I suppose we better go,' said Timoti, getting up.

Further down the road on the other side from the church, past more blackberry bushes, was the meeting place for the local Maori people. There was a place to park cars and a bright yellow hall, and vague smoke seemed to be drifting at the back as the sun set. Above them in the distance, right up on the hill, she could see part of a carved roof, silhouetted against the sky.

'Is that your – like, your meeting house, right up there?'

'Yes, but they don't use it any more, it's falling to pieces. They use the hall for everything.'

They crossed the road. He said suddenly, turning to her abruptly, 'My house isn't like your house.'

And then he walked up the steps and inside the yellow wooden building and into the big kitchen at one end. Maggie followed. About eight women were working there.

'Timoti!' they all cried.

'There you are at last, Ti, where've you been? Oh, lovely to see you again so soon, usually it's so long between visits. Look who's here, look who's here! *Haere mai, nau mai, haere mai*, welcome!' They kissed him and hugged him and small children ran round his legs but she saw he found it all difficult.

He introduced her. 'This is Maggie.' She gave a nervous, polite smile. 'This is my mother, Grace. This is my Auntie Rose; you have to shout or she won't hear you. This is my niece, this is my cousin, this is my cousin too.' Everybody smiled and some of them kissed her, including Grace, Timoti's mother.

'Where've you been, Ti? Your Dad's been waiting for you, and Uncle Heke, he's so pleased you could come, he'll want to talk to you. Where's your suit? Where's your shirt? We'll iron them.'

Shrugging apologetically to Maggie, Timoti was borne

off by his mother and a cousin and she heard the car start up.

'Where are they going?' she asked, disconcerted.

'Oh, it's just down the road, their house. Grace'll be back in a minute.'

'Here you are, dear,' said Timoti's Auntie Rose, who was making scones. She handed Maggie a big knife. 'You cut up our apples, eh, for the fruit salad?'

'All right, where're the apples?' Maggie shouted in her ear.

'I'm not that deaf, dear,' said Auntie Rose, her eyes twinkling.

'Well –' and Maggie took a deep breath and plunged in. **'Kei whea nga aporo? Homai ki ahau,'** she said nervously, *give me the apples.*

'Gee, look at that, good on you, *e hoa,* listen to that!' and the women smiled in amazement.

And Auntie Rose handed her the apples in a sack. **'Kia ora e hoa,** where did you learn that?'

'I'm learning Maori at university. For my degree. That's where I met Timoti.'

Auntie Rose watched her lips, stared at her in disbelief, and then burst out laughing. 'You don't mean to tell me you fellas sit down and study it these days?' Maggie nodded.

'You don't! You study it?' Maggie nodded again.

'Well, I'll be damned. Boy, I was strapped, no kidding, if I spoke Maori at school and now you fellas are learning it at the university, you Pakehas, well I'll be damned!' and she wiped her eyes on her apron.

'You mean to say Timoti's learning too? said Marama, Timoti's cousin. Maggie nodded. 'Well, bugger me. He hasn't lived here for years and years of course, too busy getting Pakeha-fied and posh, eh Auntie Rose?'

Auntie Rose spoke sharply to Marama, in Maori, spoke too fast for Maggie to understand.

'I don't care,' said Marama in English. 'He hardly ever comes home, he's a city boy now. He always wanted to be a Pakeha really. I know him. He's ashamed of us.'

Auntie Rose said firmly, 'He's a good boy, he's going to be a lawyer.'

'He's a Pakeha,' Marama insisted.

'His boss wants him to learn Maori,' said Maggie. 'He thinks it'll be useful for business.'

'Is that so?' said Auntie Rose, and she shook her head.

And all the time the children ran in and out and the women sliced bread and cut fruit and laid tables at one end of the hall.

'Is this your first *hangi*?' asked Auntie Rose.

'Yes, but I know it means an oven in the earth.'

'*Titiro*,' said Auntie Rose, *look*.

At the back of the hall the smoke rose in the dusk from beneath stones and earth and sacks laid across a hole in the ground.

'There's a whole pig in there, and spuds and sweet potatoes and cabbage.'

'A *whole* pig,' said Maggie uncertainly.

'Moana shot it; that's Timoti's dad. He and Timoti's brother, Pumpkin, went up the hills a couple of days ago and shot a big one.'

Maggie swallowed hard. Her mother went to the butcher's shop by the tram terminus.

'Sit down, Grace, sit down,' they said to Timoti's mother as she came back into the hall, a large woman in an apron, puffing up the dusty road. They put more tea leaves and more boiling water into a huge brown teapot and they all drank out of thick white cups.

'Look at this girl of Timoti's,' said Auntie Rose, 'she can speak Maori, what do you think of that?'

'That's good,' said Grace, huffing down on to a chair and smiling at her and Maggie saw: the blue eyes belonged to her.

Maggie sat there among the women, the friendly women, as they lit up their cigarettes and chatted together and finished preparing the food. *Why am I here with the women? I want to be with Timoti.* They talked now about babies and who was pregnant and who had died and who was getting married. They talked mostly in English but with smatterings of Maori words, like the boys in the office. If the children cried they hugged them or slapped them, depending, and gave them big pieces of bread and butter. 'Come here Peter! You stop belting Shireen or I'll *patu* you, you hear me?'

A crackling wireless played in the background but no one was listening. They drank endless cups of tea; Maggie noticed that both Grace and Auntie Rose held their cups with their little fingers extended. Maggie's mother had taught her that this was vulgar, only done by people who were trying to be genteel and showing their ignorance.

'Have you got a frock, Maggie?' asked Grace.

'Yes, it's in my bag in the car. But it needs ironing.' She saw herself: making the white dress a small ball with the pretty nightie early that morning, avoiding her mother as she packed her books to go and stay at Eddie Albert's place which was now hundreds of miles away. And Eddie Albert telling her that her mother had been in the loony bin.

'Come on then, come back to the house with me and we can fix Timoti's clothes too,' and the other women called, 'See you later then, see you later.'

It was night now, and colder. They walked down the dirt road together in the dark. There were no streetlights but the lights from the hall warmed behind them and there were lights from a small group of houses further down the road. Grace walked slowly in her slippers, puffing slightly; Maggie clip-clopped along beside her in her stiletto heels, sometimes stumbling on pebbles. She could see Grace's breath in the frosty, quiet darkness.

'Are you cold, dear?'

'No,' said Maggie, 'I'm lovely.' There was the faint scent of the manuka trees, and stars shone. They walked in silence for a while.

'*Rangimarie*,' said Maggie, 'that's a good name for this place, *rangimarie* means peaceful, doesn't it?'

Grace laughed and puffed. 'I'm not so sure that it'll be peaceful much longer,' she said.

'Why?' said Maggie.

Grace sighed in the dark, didn't speak at first, breathed heavily, as if talking and walking were a big effort.

'There's so many people coming through,' she said finally. 'Suddenly there always seem to be people looking, moving around here, it makes me feel nervous somehow, as if things will change. It's beautiful here. But that's because there's just us here.' She seemed almost to be talking to herself rather than to Maggie.

'Is it Maori land?'

'Of course,' said Grace.

'Well, that's all right then; it can't be taken. I used to work with all the land records. At the Bureau.'

'Oh, yes,' said Grace, non-committal. Again she waited a long time before she spoke again, puffing and breathing. 'The government wants to put a main road through, behind the church straight to the main road south. And the men say it'll make the journey through to the meatworks easier. Lots of them have to travel there for work – my husband had to make that long journey all his life. I suppose it's a good idea in a way. The kids don't care of course, there's nothing for them here. They can't wait to get to the city.'

Their footsteps crunched and the stars shone.

'But what happens to our graves, our *tipuna*, my Ngaio, with cars and trucks roaring past? And why should they want a road to come here? It doesn't lead anywhere else.'

'I'm sorry about – about Ngaio,' said Maggie, feeling clumsy.

'*Ae*,' said Grace, *yes*.

For a while they walked in silence.

'My mother,' said Maggie hesitantly, 'my mother lost a daughter too.'

'Oh,' said Grace, 'I'm so sorry. How did she die?'

''I'm not – not exactly sure. They never talk about it. It's – it's as if they can't. She fell at the beach. Something like that.'

'How old was she?'

'Seven,' and she heard Grace's intake of breath.

'Oh, your poor mother.' And she said something in Maori then, but again as if it was to herself. Perhaps she was thinking of Ngaio. 'She must love you very much then.'

'Yes,' said Maggie. Grace heard the bleakness of her tone. The soft sound of their footsteps went on up the road.

Above them the old, ruined meeting house loomed and Maggie heard Grace sigh.

'I went into a meeting house once,' said Maggie. 'It was in the museum.'

'Ah – ours was so beautiful once. But now, the roof's fallen in, everything inside is damaged. The weaving of the wall panels, the *tukutuku* panels was so fine, like lace, all made of reeds, and thread made from flax. All damaged now.'

'How did it happen?'

'The same as everywhere, I suppose. Too many people leave, go to the cities and don't come home. Nobody cares enough, it's too expensive. Not many people can do the special carving now, or weave the dried flax like lace.' Grace sighed again. 'My generation didn't go away from here, except the men of course, to the war. But everything is so different now, things move so fast.' She stopped, turned, looked back at the shadowy ruin in the distance. 'So much of my past is in there, and there it is, my past: falling to pieces.'

'And Timoti's past?'

Grace shook her head in the darkness, walked on. 'Timoti is the new generation. He can't be held by the past. We sent him away to school early on, it was a Pakeha school. He was clever and we managed to get him an educational grant, and then a scholarship. We knew it was for the best. He has to make his way in the Pakeha world. We understand that and we're very proud of him.'

For a while they walked in silence and Maggie thought: *it's beautiful, and it's like the end of the world. Of course Timoti couldn't live here, no wonder it depresses him. What do they do here?*

'But sometimes I've begun to think . . .' and in the darkness Grace stopped again for a moment. The sentence remained unfinished, hanging there. She looked across at Maggie's dark, white shape. 'You know our word?'

'Which word?'

Maggie felt that Grace was weighing her carefully in the darkness, wondering whether to go on, and then deciding to. '*Turangawaewae*. This is my *turangawaewae*, my home, the place to put my feet.' Maggie followed Grace up a path leading to, Maggie recognised, a Bureau house, where lights shone in the windows.

'I suppose you could say,' said Grace, 'that it's the place you carry around with you, in your heart.' And just before she opened the front door she added quietly, 'Timoti might find it is there one day. Inside him.'

Inside, Timoti and his father sat on either side of a welcoming, crackling fire; there were knitted patchwork blankets, green and pink and yellow, thrown over the old fireside chairs. His two brothers sat on a sofa with an old grey blanket over it and they all drank DB bitter, brown bottles on the floor beside them, just like her father. *But it's not like our lounge with the china cabinet and the three-piece suite.* The father, Moana, an imposing-looking man with white hair stood up and shook her hand quite shyly.

'Pleased to meet you,' he said.

Maggie used the more formal greeting: '*Tena koe*,' she said.

'Oh that's nice,' said Timoti's father and smiled at her and Maggie remembered the pink china tulips when Timoti came, and her mother, silent.

The two brothers shook her hand. Paatu, older and heavier than Timoti, looked relaxed and sure of himself, but Tumatauenga who was younger, the one they called Pumpkin, looked embarrassed. He didn't quite look at her, sat down again quickly and drank more beer. He was very fat. Timoti had told her about Pumpkin, something about him coming home on parole from the nearest town where he'd gone to live, some trouble. And Maggie saw almost at once how Pumpkin looked at his brother who was going to be a lawyer. Something in his eyes, some longing, which part of Maggie seemed to recognise but she did not know why.

The same photo of Ngaio that was on the gravestone looked cheerily down at them all from above the fireplace.

Grace picked up Timoti's suit. 'Come on then, we'll do the ironing in the kitchen,' she said, smiling, handing Maggie Timoti's trousers. Maggie smiled bravely. She had never ironed a pair of man's trousers in her life.

Paatu lived next door, went home to get his pregnant wife, Noelene. A Pakeha. Maggie felt disturbed, odd, looking at the heavily pregnant white body as Noelene smoked and leaned against her brown husband. She pushed away the white thing in the toilet. Paatu laughed and drank DB bitter as Noelene leant against him.

When everyone was finally ready, when they'd all had a cup of tea and put on their ironed suits and shirts and frocks, they all piled into a truck, women in the front, men standing on the back.

'Now you boys mind your suits,' called Grace as she revved and revved the engine till the motor at last turned over.

On the stage at one end of the hall a small band played guitars and sang. They called themselves The Wayfarers and had Brylcreemed their hair like The Platters and wore red shiny jackets over their drain-pipe trousers.

> Doo wop
> Doo wop
> Love love love

they sang.

The hall was crowded with people, mostly Maoris, everyone saying hello and drinking and smoking and laughing. *It is true, they always laugh* she thought, *even if it isn't funny, it's just their way. They laugh.* And she thought suddenly of Tane, laughing because he had to give up being a geologist to work at the Four Square grocery store far from the city.

There were light bulbs hanging from the ceiling and they flickered every now and then, as if they were a long way from the source of power, as if they were just hanging on, might peter out at any moment. Some old women in black, with black scarves round their heads, sat near the stage in a group.

'Come on,' said Timoti, 'let's get this over with, these are my aunties.'

'*Aiiiiiii, tetahi Pakeha,*' said one of them, staring at her openly and curiously. There were five of them sitting there in black, one had a tattoo on her chin. Almost all of them had no front teeth. '*Nau mai, haere mai e Timoti,*' they cried over and over again, *welcome, welcome.* 'He's our best one,' they said to Maggie proudly, 'he needs a really good girl to look after him,' and they stared at her, weighing her up.

How they clung to Timoti, how they loved him and kissed

him, how he was *theirs*, she saw. But she saw too how he was embarrassed by the way they touched him and seemed to own him, how he soon managed to move away.

At last she and Timoti danced and she felt his arms around her again like they had been that morning that now seemed so long ago. The Wayfarers strummed their guitars and sang 'The Tennessee Waltz'.

'Tennessee Waltz', 'Carolina Moon' – the American place names come even as far as Rangimarie thought Maggie. *Music joins the world up.* Her dress was white, in a new material with little bumps on it, called Everglaze. Her mother had made it. Maggie pushed away any thought of what her mother might say if she could to see where her meticulous sewing had landed. They danced over to the joined-together wooden tables where the men congregated, drinking; Paatu, his eyes shining, leaned against the tables with a bottle and Maggie saw that he staggered as he gave her a sherry and his brother a beer. Timoti pulled a piece of paper out of his back pocket, looked at it nervously. He gulped some DB bitter, lit two cigarettes, passed one to Maggie.

'I'm going to say a short bit of Maori to my uncle. Kara Rikihana helped me with it before Maori class the other day, I hope I can remember it. Keep the old man quiet.'

'Which is your uncle?'

Timoti looked around the hall. 'He's not here yet. But when he comes in you'll know. G'day Harry!' and he grabbed a small boy who was chasing someone round his legs.

Suddenly the lights went out. There was some desultory whistling but obviously this was nothing new. People lit kerosene lanterns they'd brought with them, hung them on nails on the wall and from the rafters and the hall took on a sort of flickering fairground air, lights and music and people enjoying themselves. Maggie liked it better, liked the smell of the lamps, and the shadows.

When Heke Pou came in, tall and white-haired, Maggie thought she'd never seen such a straight-backed, handsome old man. A kind of charisma – in Maori the word was *mana*, she knew – seemed to float around him, near him *or perhaps it's the lanterns*, she thought, *they make him look like a kind of ancient warrior*. And he was *eighty*. She could see why Timoti felt he had to do what Heke Pou said.

'*Kia ora e Heke*,' murmured voices all around her, '*Kia ora e Heke.*'

The boys in the band with their Brylcreemed hair and their red jackets stood respectfully at the back of the stage. Timoti's father climbed on to the stage and waved the old man to join him. The two handsome white-haired Pou men stood there and Timoti's father began to speak and the noise of the crowd in the hall died down, though not entirely, as children ran and mothers scolded and people drank and laughed quietly in corners where the lamp light didn't reach. Pumpkin was standing near Timoti, watching him. The small boy called Harry ran past again, stopped when he saw Maggie, and gave her two squashed, melting, chocolate pineapple chunks.

'Oh, thanks Harry,' said Maggie. She leant against a wall in her white dress with the melting chocolate and the glass of sweet sherry, watching and listening, understanding only a little, wondering how much Timoti understood.

'They like talking, the Pou men,' said a voice beside her, 'this'll go on for bloody hours.' It was Paatu's pregnant wife, Noelene.

'Would you like to sit down?'

'No, it's more comfortable standing tonight,' and the two Pakeha women leaned together against the wall. It was true the Pou men liked talking; there seemed no sign of an end.

'Would you like a chocolate pineapple chunk?'

'No!'

Maggie ate them both and then drank her sweet sherry and then felt a bit sick.

'Do you like living here, in Rangimarie?' Maggie asked Noelene diffidently, speaking quietly as the men talked on, not looking at Noelene's stomach.

Noelene shrugged. 'I don't mind. I'm used to being bored. I only come from five miles away. My parents used to run the pub at the crossroads. Why, you thinking of coming here?'

'No!' said Maggie, horrified. 'I just wondered. Where do all these people come from?'

'Oh – just round and about. People always turn up from somewhere at these things.'

Just then the lights jumped into brightness again. There was an ironic cheer and the women doused the lamps as the speeches went on and the smell of the kerosene drifted upwards with the cigarette smoke.

Heke Pou spoke, not of one war, but of two. Maggie thought again how extraordinary it was that such an old man could still be so straight and so handsome. In the harsher light of the bulbs she saw how parchment-like his face was, how the bones showed.

'Did your parents mind?' she said to Noelene.

'What, about me marrying Paatu?'

'Yes.'

Noelene laughed. 'Nah. My Dad ran off with a Maori girl half his age, how could he mind!'

Grace bustled up with a wooden chair. 'Sit down, Noelene,' she said, 'you shouldn't be standing.' Noelene obeyed her, called her Mum.

I wonder if I'd be able to call her Mum too, thought Maggie.

Finally Timoti's father motioned Timoti to come up on the stage and Maggie saw him wipe his hands nervously on his trousers. He began speaking in Maori. His uncle listened, his expression unreadable. Timoti wasn't like the older men, couldn't speak like them. He forgot a bit and it didn't sound quite right, but Maggie saw him persevere until his short speech was over and her heart contracted for him, knowing how hard he found all this.

'Gee,' said Noelene, 'even he's at it now. I didn't know he spoke Maori. God, he'll be as bad as the old boys, I hope they don't get Paatu at it!'

But Paatu was swaying and laughing at the bar.

'Well, what did he say, Mum?' said Noelene to Grace. 'Anything new?'

But Grace was looking proudly at her son in his ironed suit who had been trying so hard, and so haltingly, to speak his own language. And she began to sing just from where she was standing, her song for his speech. She had a beautiful, full, high voice; the notes rang out clear and loud and true in the hall and even the children stopped running and crying and playing.

Te taniwha i te moana
Maranga mai ki runga

a wonderful creature came out of the sea, sang Grace in her navy blue dress, her hair tied back in her bun, her hands neatly folded over her fat stomach. Maggie thought it was the most beautiful voice she'd ever heard: a large, grey-haired woman standing alone, unaccompanied, singing a Victorian ballad in the crowded smoky hall. She caught sight of Pumpkin's face. He was staring up at the stage, some feeling of exclusion in his eyes, something she couldn't decipher.

Then the speeches were over at last and the *hangi* was opened outside and the men passed around the pork and the potatoes and the cabbage in the electric light shining out from the hall on to the grass.

'*E Pa, whakapaingia enei kai,*' *bless this food O Lord*, said

Heke Pou and then everyone said *Amine* and then everybody ate. Maggie gingerly ate a very small piece of the pig.

After the eating and the singing and the dancing and the talking, Timoti and Maggie finally walked back along the unpaved road, a few cars tooting slowly past, people calling out goodnight, carrying their kerosene lanterns. Some walked along the road with Maggie and Timoti, looking at the stars and the moon shining in the bright winter night. In the darkness Timoti took her hand.

'I was proud of you doing your speech,' she said.

'That's the one and only time,' he said grimly. 'I'm not turning into one of them. I'll never live here.'

'No, of course not,' she said. After a moment she asked, 'Where's your sea, Timoti? You said you were by the sea.'

'I'll show you.' As he passed their house he called out to Grace. 'We're just going for a walk, Mum.'

'All right, dear. You're sleeping in the sitting room, I'll make up the couch. Maggie's sleeping with me.' And she went inside.

Maggie let go of Timoti's hand in alarm. 'I can't sleep with your *mother*!' she whispered.

Timoti looked surprised. 'Why not?'

Maggie didn't know what to say. 'I – I just *can't*,' she said. 'I've never slept with a woman before.' Timoti looked quite puzzled. 'I've never slept with anyone, Timoti, I *can't*!'

'Well, you must've slept with your mother before?'

'No, not really. When I was little, I suppose. Not much – I mean not the whole night. I've never slept with anyone the whole night.'

'Well, there's not enough beds. And you can't sleep with me. They're just like your parents, they wouldn't let us. Don't be silly, Maggie.' She tried to think of her aunt, Eddie Albert's mother, sleeping with Eddie Albert's girlfriend Shirley. It was impossible.

'Come and look at the sea,' said Timoti. And then he whispered: 'Tomorrow night you'll be sleeping with me,' and held her hard for a moment, kissed her hair. Her stomach jumped in something like fear.

Where the unpaved road ended, tracks in the long grass snaked round the cliffs, or up the hill. They climbed upwards, past gnarled and twisted old pohutukawa trees, stumbling in the darkness against the roots that pushed up the ground just as they did in the city. And then suddenly, below them, the stars shone on dark water and they stood beside the old, ghostly meeting house that nobody used any more. From the doorway half a carved face seemed to stare at her, sideways, indistinct.

'Oh,' said Maggie softly, uneasy. She stared at the shadowy, broken-down building, heard the sea below.

'They say there are *kehua* in there,' said Timoti.

'Ghosts? You don't *believe* that!' After all he was a lawyer. An educated man.

'Who knows,' he said shrugging. She saw that part of him might believe it, after all. She thought of Rangi and Hori and Manu talking about monsters and spirits. How superstitious they all were. Even Timoti.

She tried to think of them: Maori ghosts flitting about under the leaking roof, past the cracked old carvings, hiding behind the panels of broken reeds in the darkness.

And heard the sound of the sea, below them.

Without warning, the feeling about Elizabeth that she'd felt in the churchyard came back: a great, sad feeling of loneliness for her sister. And then, at once, as if they had been superimposed on the shadows of the meeting house, she saw, quite clearly, Eddie Albert with his trolley standing at the front gate of their house. And Elizabeth – with unruly, curly hair blowing in the wind – was standing on tip-toe to see if there was anything in the letterbox. Quite clearly Maggie saw them. *And then Elizabeth turned and looked at her.*

Maggie stood transfixed, looking at her sister's face and she could hear the sea at the end of her street. The moment stayed and stayed. Then there was a spinning, falling feeling in her head and Elizabeth faded away. Just the darkness, and the shadows.

She had no memory of Elizabeth, she didn't remember Elizabeth. Only the photographs. *I'm starting to see things. I don't remember Elizabeth at all.* The thought went further. *Am I a loony too? Like my mother?*

'Timoti,' she whispered, hardly able to make her voice speak, 'Timoti.'

He turned, put both hands on her breasts and kissed her as the sea fell against the rocks below.

And he whispered back. 'Tomorrow. Tomorrow night you will be sleeping with me.'

In the little house Mr Pou had put on his pyjamas and climbed into bed with his youngest son.

All night Maggie lay close to one edge of the big soft double bed, listening to Grace's gentle snoring beside her. Something about the closeness of Grace's big, warm body stopped her panic. *It's all right. It's all right. Perhaps ghosts are memories we forget. Perhaps I remembered a memory of Elizabeth, up on the hill by this sea here. Perhaps the sound of the sea tricked me, or perhaps it was because Eddie Albert talked to me about her this morning.* Sometimes Grace turned and the old springs of the bed squeaked and twanged and then settled again. Twice someone went to the lavatory, a loud fountain and then the chain. *Of course there's no such thing as ghosts really. Not for people like me.*

The winter dawn of Rangimarie drifted past the window.

Next morning they went to the little wooden church. Grace wanted to take the truck but Timoti persuaded her to walk, *good for you Mum*, so Grace puffed up the dusty road. The service was mostly in English but the hymns were mostly in Maori: '**Whakaaria Mai**' turned out to be 'How Great Thou Art'. *Why are hymns always sung too high*, thought Maggie. Only Grace's beautiful voice slid up there easily.

Coming back along the road, Grace and Moana sang an old Maori song they remembered, one of the whistling whalers' songs.

E kui ma, e koro ma
Kaua e riri mai

old people, don't be angry with us, you used to do this too.

Maggie was enchanted, parents singing along the road; it was so alien to her it made her feel as if she wanted to laugh and sing herself. But even as she was humming along the road, she suddenly felt a choking feeling in her throat, had to drop back, pretend to look at a fern. She had never, once, heard her mother sing; felt a sudden pang of terrible pity. *A year and a half in a loony bin? Poor Mum, poor Mum.*

I will, vowed Maggie along the unpaved road, *sing to my children*.

As they got home they could hear Paatu and Noelene arguing in the house next door.

'Leave me alone, you randy bastard!' shouted Noelene, and Grace pursed her lips and bustled about basting the lamb that had been slowly cooking in the oven. Maggie helped Grace put on the potatoes, cut up the cabbage, while Timoti sat on the back steps with his father, who was polishing everybody's boots and shoes. Pumpkin appeared. 'The Sunday Request Session' crackled on the wireless. Pumpkin slowly insinuated himself into the kitchen, and then slowly out on to the back steps, sat beside Timoti, his arm resting against Timoti's arm. Timoti moved away to light a cigarette and Maggie saw something in Pumpkin's eyes that she again almost recognised, quickly dismissed. She almost recognised it because Pumpkin was looking at Timoti with a look in his eyes that was often in Maggie's eyes, when she looked at her beautiful, unobtainable, mother.

'Dinner's ready,' called Grace.

A dog barked first, and then they heard it themselves.

From far above them, on the hill, came a sound that Maggie immediately recognised. It was the crying sound. Grace came at once to the door and looked out across the fields. She shaded her eyes against the bright winter glare as she tried to see where the sound was coming from and a small, cold wind ruffled her skirt and her apron.

'Moana,' she said to her husband. At the tone of her voice he heavily picked himself up from the doorstep.

The two of them stood there for a moment and Maggie heard it more clearly: that sound; the lament. The crying sound.

Far above, on the hill, where Timoti and Maggie had walked last night and Elizabeth had come, where the broken roof of the old meeting house leant up towards the sky, a figure appeared, moving along the skyline. The figure looked so small and odd, silhouetted, seeming to stumble as it came closer.

'It's Auntie Kura,' said Mr Pou.

Timoti's mother began to run first and the others followed. Maggie ran too; as she did so she saw people coming out of other houses, all running towards the crying, stumbling figure.

As they got nearer, running upwards, catching their clothes in the twisted trees, Maggie saw it was one of the old ladies from the birthday party, the one who had a tattoo on her chin. She was again dressed all in black and her thin white hair streamed out behind her. Maggie thought she looked as if she was a very small witch.

'*Aue te mamae te mamae.*' Maggie heard wailing words, then the same painful crying sound with no words that Mrs Tipene and Alice had made in the Housing office as they stared at Emily.

As the old lady reached the crumbling meeting house she tripped in the long grass. A young girl reached her first, picked her up; Grace came behind her puffing heavily, calling to the old lady.

'Auntie Kura, Auntie Kura, what's the matter?' Grace bent down, panting, then knelt down clumsily beside the old lady. Maggie was near enough now to see that the old lady had tears streaming down her wrinkled cheeks.

She began at once to speak in Maori, clutching at Grace; she spoke so fast and so incoherently that Maggie could not follow.

'When? When did he come? *Kaua e tangi*, Auntie Kura, please stop crying, *he aha he aha*, what did he say?' And Grace used her apron to wipe the old lady's face.

And then Maggie at last heard a word being repeated a word over and over. 'Rates,' Auntie Kura kept saying in bewilderment. 'Rates. Rates.'

Timoti moved through the long grass, knelt beside his mother.

'Who came this morning, Auntie Kura?'

She answered in Maori, and he looked at his mother.

'She's saying a man came and said her land has been taken.'

'Have you had rates demands, Auntie Kura?'

She answered again in Maori.

'Didn't you pay them? You have to pay them. It's the law.'

'*Ko taku whenua, ko taku kainga!*' cried the old lady. *It's my land, it's my home.* And Maggie saw how puzzled her face was, looking at Timoti and Grace, uncomprehending.

Timoti looked around at the other people angrily. 'Where's her sons, why didn't they explain she has to pay the rates?'

But everyone there knew that the old lady's sons had gone to the city years and years ago; had lived in the city so long that the grandchildren would not know their way home. Just like Timoti had gone.

'*Ko taku whenua,*' she kept crying, '*ko taku turangawae-wae,*' and Maggie remembered Grace's explanation: a place to put the feet.

A very thin, middle-aged woman came up to Grace. 'It's all right' she said, 'I'll take her.'

'But you have to pay rates,' repeated Timoti to Auntie Kura. 'That's the law.' And Maggie saw again that the old lady had no idea of his meaning.

But over and over again she said in Maori: *it is my home.*

'Come on, Auntie Kura,' the thin woman said, 'I'll make you a cup of tea.'

And after a while, when everybody had got up and brushed the grass seeds away, the thin woman and the little old woman in black with the wild, white hair walked very slowly, arm in arm, down the hill past the old trees, to one of the box-like houses at the bottom.

The Pou family talked about what had happened over the roast lamb.

'They can't take her land. Can they?' Grace kept saying.

'She's the only one still alive,' said Timoti's father, all the time speaking slowly, working it out. 'All that land along the coast would have been in her name only. But the land has always belonged to her family.' He looked at Timoti. 'She wouldn't have any idea about rates, rateable value, all that stuff. Her husband died a long time ago, she's probably put everything in a drawer since he died. There's only the few little shacks on all that land. She wouldn't move round here when nearly everyone else did years ago, she said she didn't care about running water, she wanted to hear the sea.'

'But that doesn't mean they can take the land, does it?' said Grace, and she turned to Timoti. 'Does it, Ti? You study law. Surely that can't be the law?'

His face was tight and angry. 'I don't know,' he said.

'We should have thought,' said Grace. 'When all those rates surveys were done here everything changed. We should have thought to look after her better, make sure the rates were paid.' She shook her head. 'But surely they can't take her land?'

'It seems a funny time to come,' said Maggie. 'Sunday morning.'

'Pakehas often do things in a funny way,' said Pumpkin angrily. It was the first time he had spoken. 'Pakehas have ruined our lives,' and Grace and her husband both turned to Maggie in embarrassment but she smiled at them quickly, embarrassed herself, shook her head to say she didn't mind. Pumpkin pushed his plate away, stared down at the table.

Timoti ate his lunch very quickly and then put down his knife and fork. 'I'll go and see her,' he said.

When he came back, his blue eyes were dark with anger. 'She never paid rates,' he said. 'Someone from the Council left a letter with her this morning saying the whole block had been seized in lieu of the rates she owed. She doesn't even know what *in lieu of* means, of course, let alone rates. The letter's signed by someone called Alvin Fitzgerald. It says a receiver has been appointed. Last Friday. She doesn't know what a *receiver* is either. I can't believe this can be right, but it probably can.' He started collecting up his things. 'Dad, listen. I can't take time off. There's absolutely no way I can come back again for the rest of this year, you've got to call a meeting, make sure nobody else can get caught like this. Go round everyone. Make sure they've paid.'

'What are we paying rates for?' said Pumpkin, surly, still not looking up.

Grace answered. 'Roads and – well, roads.'

'*They* want roads,' said Pumpkin. 'We don't need roads. There's no sewage, there's no rubbish collection, the dump stinks. I hate it here.'

'And electricity,' said Grace firmly. 'We've got electricity now.'

'It's always going off. Anyway I'd rather have lamps,' Pumpkin said. He didn't say anything else before Maggie and Timoti left, sat in a corner, a fat boy sulking and kicking at a chair.

As the car pulled out from the crossroads, Maggie said, 'I love your mother's name, Grace. I never thought about *grace* before, about what it means. What a beautiful word it is.' Again they drove for hours. Sometimes she dozed. 'Your mother's lovely,' she said, waking suddenly. Sometimes she stared out of the window. 'I like your mother,' she said dreamily. The rain came again as they got nearer to the city, the wipers swished backwards and forwards in the rainy night, on down the road to the city.

Finally they drew up outside Eddie Albert's flat in the darkness.

'I'll have to get the car back to my cousin tonight,' said Timoti. 'His uncle's wife needs it for work, I'll come back on a taxi.' But he ran in the rain with her into the flat, they turned on the lights, pulled down the blinds as the cat cried bitterly round their feet. Timoti kissed Maggie and left.

She saw the thirty-seven socks. She fed the lonely cat with mince from the fridge. Then sat on the rug in front of the empty fireplace, rocking slowly backwards and forwards, hugging her body. *Prudence made me look down the toilet. I don't want to do this really. I'm scared. But – he is my boyfriend, and he loves me.*

The wireless sang about a blue moon and she thought of

her narrow, safe bed with the pink candlewick bedspread. The song changed.

> Gonna make a sentimental journey
> Gonna set my heart at ease.

And then the doorbell rang.

All the songs they sang at the parties were about love, not about wondering if you did it quickly or only sort of did it, whether you wouldn't get pregnant; not about sleeping in your cousin's bed anxiously trying to use, for the first time, a rubber sheath that Timoti – determined not to be irresponsible like most Maoris were – had brought shamefaced and proud from the barber's shop near the Wong Fu Café. He fumbled, trying to put it on and Maggie lay quite rigid, trying not to look. They weren't confident enough to laugh. Neither of them was good at laughing. *Blue smoke goes drifting by* sang the wireless.

'I love you,' said Timoti and Maggie.

And clung fumblingly together because nobody had ever explained to either of them, how love worked.

Afterwards Timoti fell asleep almost at once. After a while Maggie got up. Gingerly and with enormous distaste she picked up the rubber thing that had white stuff in it that now lay on the floor beside the bed; she padded along the cold, lino-covered hall to the lavatory, pulled the chain several times till the thing disappeared. Shivering she got back into the bed and curled up against Timoti's back. He woke and turned and put an arm around her tightly.

'Hello, darling,' he said. 'You are my darling, go to sleep.'

Maggie took his brown hand in her smaller white one.

She smoothed her own hair, her own face, very gently, with his hand.

'Stroke me,' she said shyly. Timoti was almost asleep again.

'What, as if you're a cat?' he said, smiling and yawning in the darkness but stroking her hair, as commanded.

'No,' she said, 'no.'

And suddenly the ghost of Elizabeth filled the inside of her head and she held his hand tighter.

'No, as if I am *me*.'

TWENTY-SIX

One of Sinatra's cousins worked as a security guard at the Town Hall. Sinatra observed that the new Prime Minister was to make a speech at a businessmen's supper there, about the future of the country. Entrance was by invitation only.

'I want to come and hear that speech,' Sinatra said to his cousin, 'to keep an eye on the buggers. Get us in, *e hoa*.'

'OK, what you want to come as, Sinny?'

'What d'you mean?'

'Well, you can't come as a wharfie, *e hoa*, you know business hates the wharfies since the strike. You gotta come as a sort of businessman. Gotta suit?'

'Yes,' said Sinatra, 'but do I have to? I could be a chef.'

'If you want to hear the speech you gotta come in a suit. I'll get you in the bottom door, by the stage, so you can have a good view.'

Heads turned at the appearance of the impressive-looking, grey-haired Maori. Most guests thought he must be one of the four Maori MPs, some shook his hand. John Evans smiled graciously at him, knew he had seen him somewhere.

In his speech the Prime Minister spoke of the future of the Greatest Little Country in the World and how he was going to give business more freedom, loosen up constricting government regulations. There was great applause.

And Sinatra, in his suit, talking politely to all sorts of people, ('I'm in the export business,' he said) saw an interesting thing over the sausage rolls. He saw the young blonde girl who was the Prime Minister's daughter, the one who he knew worked at the Bureau, sitting with a sad-faced woman, the Prime Minister's wife. And he also saw the young blonde girl who was *not* the Prime Minister's daughter, the one who was not allowed to be Miss World, the one who had been kissing John Evans in the Austin Princess. She was the daughter of the Chairman of the Business Association, the most powerful businessman in the country, the man who owned newspapers. Sinatra saw the protective and proud way the businessman escorted his daughter, introduced his daughter, treated her like a piece of fragile, priceless china. The Prime Minister shook his hand, smiled at her, passed on.

Sinatra noted this, as he noted many things.

A hint of spring drifted with the scent of hyacinths in the lighter evenings and sex lay around them all, everywhere.

The poets who knew all about sex came, with the women dressed in black, to the Maori Community Centre down by the docks where bands played: smoking strange-smelling cigarettes, dancing in the night, knowing where the good times were.

Now that Maggie knew, now that sex was something she too had experienced, she felt that sex was absolutely *everywhere*, she couldn't think how she could have missed it. Wherever she turned people were kissing each other. In trams, in the street, up trees in the park (some first year students, exuberantly), in the library, in the office. Errol Flynn, the pompous Welfare Officer named after a film star, kissed his beautiful colleague Glory Ngahuia Brown in the interview room: Maggie bungled in looking for Bay, bungled out again giggling and blushing, knowing Errol Flynn was married, thinking how silly they looked, caught kissing. 'Sorry!' she had called back cheekily over her shoulder. *That snooty Glory Ngahuia Brown knows all about sex, she's an adulteress!*

She sang 'A-DULT-ERESS!' loudly in the office, to the tune of 'Jealousy'.

All the same she felt uneasy about Glory Ngahuia Brown, watched her suspiciously from her desk. She had seen Glory Ngahuia Brown talking to Timoti on the concrete steps of the university, by the ivy. *I know she's sexy even if I don't quite know what that means exactly. I hate Timoti talking to her; she smiles up at him in a certain way, I'm sure she's interested in him.* Glory held her head very high. Glory's father was a well-known minister who had preached to the young Queen when she came to visit a few years ago; it was only a matter of time before he became a knight, everybody said so. And one day Glory, because of her family, would be a Member of Parliament in one of the Maori seats, even though she was a woman, that's what everyone said. *And* she was the most beautiful woman in the Bureau.

I really hate her, thought Maggie.

Prudence came in to Welfare from Housing with some arrears files, leaned on the desks, humming. *How pretty she looks. She is not an adulteress, I'm sure. She was just sitting with Bay on her verandah after a party.*

When she took Prudence's files with Welfare Officer reports back to Housing she saw Emily, bright-jacketed and blonde and nail-polished. Haughtily, boredly, she was finishing up her files, unable to disguise her impatience to be elsewhere, her impatience with them all.

'I'll be gone in thirteen more days,' was all she said.

Stay here, don't go, Maggie wanted to whisper to her; *spring is here, just around the corner*. But Emily's eyes were cold and distant, as if spring was not for her.

Maggie could hardly wait for the evenings in the library,

sitting in their usual seats at their usual table, her leg warm against Timoti's leg as she translated old words, his arm resting along the back of her chair. Sometimes he touched her hair.

But in her safe, pink bedroom she admitted to herself that she didn't quite, yet, understand about sex *exactly*. That there was a piece of the puzzle still missing.

At midnight her mother walked into Maggie's bedroom in her nightdress. Maori textbooks, the dictionary, papers, books that were Maori not French, lay everywhere like guilty secrets; her mother looked round the room in horror.

'What's this? Where are your French books?'

'Oh – oh I'm just doing a bit of – revision.'

Her mother moved quickly forward and slapped Maggie's face, hard; Maggie, trapped, sitting at the small desk by her bed could not move her head quickly enough, the blow caught her neck, she put her hand up to her head as her mother hit her face again. And then Mrs Bennett quickly stretched forward and grabbed Maggie's home-made Maori dictionary, the one with the pavlova cake on the cover. She ripped at it, ripped pages out, tore them, all Maggie's carefully written words, all her laborious work, all the Maori words she had learnt.

'No!' cried Maggie instinctively, 'No I need that.'

Her mother threw the torn pages at her and left the room. She had not said another word.

Maggie crouched down, not noticing her marked face, scrabbled at the torn pages, smoothed them against the soft carpet.

In the hospital where Mrs Bennett had spent one and a half years, (the place everybody called 'the loony bin'), mad people walked about the grounds (which had very nice trees and flowers) wearing shoes without laces and with cardigans sometimes done up on the wrong buttons. In the night, from the locked wards, the sound of screaming could sometimes be heard, and sometimes shouting. Mrs Bennett was one who screamed. She screamed at what she remembered: at the red bathing suit and the sea and the sunshine. Finally she was given electro-convulsive therapy: electrodes clamped to her head hurtled electricity through her brain. She became calmer and at last Mr Bennett was allowed to take her home. 'I'll be responsible for her, I'll look after her,' he said. 'She needs to be home with her family.' He loved his beautiful wife very much and believed he could love her back to health. And, indeed, she did not scream again.

Mrs Bennett's daughter, Margaret-Rose Bennett, screamed in the Bureau.

'I can't make sense of any of this! No one's ever made sense of it, how can I be expected to? How can anyone make statistics out of this mess, you're always losing files and reports or putting them back in the wrong place or not telling me where you're going or what you're doing!' Finally she bit a housing arrears file and then wildly shoved all the papers and files off her crowded, untidy desk. She knocked the telephone and the receiver clattered to the ground; the black cord swung backwards and forwards among the scattered papers.

Bay wasn't there.

The other Welfare Officers looked up with varying degrees of interest: there was always a lot of violence of one sort or another in this office: they were used to it. Only Mrs McMillan noticed the bruise on Maggie's face.

Outside the rain fell.

'I need to go home to sleep,' she said to Timoti.

'I need you to come with me to the Maori Community Centre,' he said. 'There's a talent quest on. One of the boys from the hostel is singing, I have to go.'

'I'll have to catch the 9.30 tram,' she said.

'I *know*,' he said and his face got that blanked-over look. 'I also know not to phone you at home. I know all the rules.' And then he looked at her carefully. 'What's wrong with your face?'

'Nothing.' She shook her hair forward. 'I knocked into something at the office.'

In the darkness as they walked along in the rain he kissed her where she had knocked into something at the office, and for a moment they clung together.

The Maori Community Centre was a dilapidated wooden hall near the railway station, down by the docks, a bit like the wooden hall at Rangimarie, only this hall was bright pink that had faded. Where the poets came with their girls, knowing where the good times were.

When they got there four Maori boys in shining silver suits were singing.

> Japanese Rhumba ay ay ay
> Turn out the lights
> Pull down the blinds
> I'm coming up slowly.

The audience was sitting on long benches, clapping and laughing.

While the next group was getting ready to play, someone turned on the jukebox and Maori women in cardigans buttered scones and refilled a big teapot. Someone else arrived with a big bag of mussels, running in from the heavy rain. The cardiganned women, singing along to the jukebox, *my tears have washed I Love You from the blackboard of my heart*, began buttering bread and making mussel sandwiches.

Maggie and Timoti found a place to sit in the crowded hall, squashed on a bench, everybody smoking, wet raincoats piled on the billiard table in the corner. A trio of Maori girls came out and sang 'Blue Smoke' in harmony and then a blind man in dark glasses sang "Georgia on My Mind" exactly like Ray Charles and the audience whistled and cheered and stamped.

Suddenly above the cheering another sound was heard: shouting, a bottle smashing against the jukebox, then the sickening sound of someone being smashed against a wall. Women screamed and the caretaker hit one of the men with his big, wide broom. Somehow, before it could be stopped, the police arrived. All Pakehas. The fighting men were taken away, one covered in blood and Maggie saw a policeman wrench a Maori man's arm up behind his back and heard a cracking sound as they pushed out of the door. She was shaking violently. Timoti was gone, out of the door with the police.

A tall young Maori girl in a short white dress was quickly sent out on to the stage. A band played at the back of the stage, she stood alone at the front, holding the microphone. She stood like a thin tree and her voice echoed round the subdued hall.

> Now you say you're sorry
> You cried the whole night through
> Well you can cry me a river
> Cry me a river
> I cried a river over you.

When Timoti came back his tie was undone, and his shirt, his hair and his trousers were wet, and she saw his face was tense not just with anger but with a kind of bleak knowledge. As if he suddenly understood what the future might bring him. *Because he was a Maori.* And that that wasn't what he wanted, that wasn't how he'd planned his future. He didn't want to be a *Maori* lawyer: he wanted to be a big city lawyer, one of The Boys. Like the other lawyers.

On the 9.30 tram in her wet raincoat Maggie sat, almost

asleep, thinking of her mother ripping up her dictionary, thinking of Timoti, ashamed she had screamed in the office. She sat leaning back against the seat of the tram and sang very quietly.

Cry me a river

how silly. No one could cry a river, and then she opened her eyes and saw the conductor looking.

Down the street in the rain, towards the sea, towards her home, she kept singing as if to comfort herself. The rain was still heavy, but she stopped outside one of the wooden houses down the street. She could hear a trumpet playing. She stood quite still by the low fence and the hydrangea bushes and listened to the sound wafting out into the night and the rain. It was a rather unsteady version of 'Praise My Soul the King of Heaven' and she knew it was Mr Lomond practising. Mr Lomond was a member of the Salvation Army Band. The sound was emerging from the Lomonds' lavatory because that was the only place that Mrs Lomond, who hated the sound of the trumpet, would let him play.

Her heart beat as she opened the back door quietly.

Her mother's bedroom door was tightly closed, her father was listening to the wireless.

'You'd better have a hot bath,' he said absent-mindedly, listening to his programme, 'You look like drowned rat.'

She kissed her father goodnight and closed her bedroom door also.

She tried to dream of books.

But when she fell asleep she dreamed that she was standing outside the old, broken-down meeting house at Rangimarie. She peered in to see the torn woven panels that hung, shadowy, in the darkness, like old lace. She was looking for something: for ghosts. Or memories. All the women she had met the day she'd gone there with Timoti were standing slightly apart from her. She knew they could see the bruise on her face even though her father hadn't noticed it and she tried to hide behind her hair. The carved, shadowy, half-face in the doorway stared, sideways.

Could somebody solve me? she said in her dream. *I'm an oxymoron* and she heard the singing: *cry me a river*.

Then Grace, Timoti's mother, hugged her. 'Never mind about all that, dear,' said Grace. 'We'll make some pavlova cakes for everyone, and iron the trousers.'

TWENTY-SEVEN

She ran down to the bookshop in her lunch-hour and bought another indexed recipe book. This one didn't have a pavlova on the front, it had a leg of lamb with mint sauce. It was all they had left. All day she collected words, filled in words, copied words from the torn pages, asked Bay for words.

After work, before the night class in the little room at the top of the university with the nuns and the Indian and the French woman, she saw Kara Rikihana sitting on the statue's plinth by the dead ivy, his scarf draped elegantly, his knees crossed neatly. It had stopped raining at last, people could hardly believe it; breathed in the fresh, cold, night air. Maggie and Kara sat there in their coats, glad of the freshness in the air too, waiting for Timoti, knowing he would run up the hill any minute in his flapping white raincoat. Maggie clutched her new recipe book. Kara was looking at some German grammar and leaning against one of the snorting horse's noble legs.

'You are a language freak, Kara,' she said, lighting a cigarette, looking down the hill.

He shrugged, that way of his. 'My father was a German seaman, passing through, two nights I believe, maybe that's why German is easy. My Maori granny brought me up. I didn't speak English till I went to school, that's why Maori is easy.' He shrugged again. 'I found French easy too. I like

languages, I like the way they all have – very formal rules.
Like mathematics.' He moved away irritably from Maggie's
cigarette smoke, looked down at his German book again.

'Oh, sorry,' and she brushed at the smoke with her hand.

'Anyway, I believe people in this country should be forced
to learn another language. Anything – French, German,
Maori – it probably doesn't matter, just something *else*.'

'Why?' asked Maggie. 'Tell me what's the point of learning
French?'

Kara didn't answer for a minute. Then he said slowly,
'We're so far away from everywhere, in this country. We're too
cut off. It's dangerous to be so far away from the rest of the
world, it will stunt us if we're not careful. We need to know
about other people who think differently from us, express
themselves differently from us, but nevertheless have a valid
point of view.'

'You mean froggy French?' said Maggie scornfully, 'but I
don't care about their point of view.'

'Listen to yourself,' said Kara equally scornfully. 'That's
just plain prejudice. Prejudice comes from ignorance and fear.
You, of all people, should know that,' and when Maggie
turned her head sharply to see what he meant he looked at
her slyly.

Students passed them, chattering and laughing and hurrying in the night.

'Yes. You're right,' she said slowly. 'Sorry.' And then she
went on quickly, 'But sometimes, don't you think learning
another language can make you feel so –' and she hunched in
her duffle coat looking for the word she meant. And into her
head again came the broken-down meeting house at
Rangimarie and Timoti Pou, a student of law, saying g*hosts
live there* the night she saw Elizabeth; as if ghosts lived there
indeed, as if ghosts existed, as if all her life what she had been
taught was wrong.

'Muddled,' she said finally, lamely.

He seemed immersed in his German grammar but he said, 'Are you muddled because you're learning another language, or are you muddled because you're muddled?'

'Ha ha, Mr Smart,' said Maggie morosely. After a while, stubbing out her cigarette and aiming the stub at a tree trunk, she said: 'Do you think the Maori language will die soon like everyone says, that it's a dead language?' As the university clock struck seven more students ran past up the steps, smooched past in couples, walked alone.

Kara shrugged again but then he sighed. 'It's almost too late.'

But just as Timoti hurried up the path towards them in his navy-blue suit with the waistcoat and his flapping raincoat – they saw him glance at his watch – Kara spoke again. He was looking at Timoti.

'But maybe not quite,' he said.

'What do you mean?'

'There are a few more people like me and Timoti.'

'But – Timoti doesn't even want to learn Maori! He wants to be a lawyer, an ordinary lawyer.'

Kara looked at her shrewdly. 'You've seen something of my people,' he said. 'Do you really think we'll let him escape so easily?' and Maggie looked at him, puzzled, as Timoti joined them by the noble, marble duke.

'It's a very, very *formal* language in lots of ways,' said Isobel that night, quite out of the blue. 'The culture is hemmed around with formalities and rules of etiquette and politeness, it's a hazardous place, remember that.' And she stared out of the high window, down to the dark city below.

'Hazardous?' questioned Maggie, thinking she might have misheard.

'Hazardous,' repeated Isobel, and her students saw that

she was very pale tonight, had more lipstick on than usual, and rouge on her cheeks.

Isobel turned to Kara Rikihana, said to him again what she said to him every week, but this time urgently, almost angrily. 'Kara, it's a sin you working for the Justice Department. You're wasted there. I've told you, you should be teaching Maori language while there's still time.'

Kara shrugged, said nothing.

That night they looked at another old *waiata*, an old song-poem.

> *Taku aroha ki taku whenua*
> *I te ahiahi kauruku nei*
> *He waka ia ra . . .*

my love alas for my own land, as the evening shadows come, if only there was a canoe . . . And Maggie saw the old lady dressed in black, her white hair streaming out behind her, running along the top of the hill, crying for land, for her home.

'Such beautiful words,' said Isobel dreamily, 'my love for my own land, in this evening of shadows, if only there was a canoe . . .'

And her pupils saw that, brightly rouged as if for courage, she looked out again over the lights of the city, over the dark harbour and into the distance, through her own dreams.

Something's wrong thought Maggie suddenly.

'I tried to find out something about that Alvin Fitzgerald who took the Council papers to Auntie Kura,' said Timoti as they walked down to the tram terminus after the class. 'I rang the Council, and the Bureau up north. But I can't find out anything more than we found at Rangimarie. Alvin Fitzgerald has left the Council, he doesn't work there any more. Someone there just confirmed the land has been confiscated for non-payment of rates and the Bureau didn't seem to have any papers about it at all. It's so –', and he stopped and searched for a word to convey what he was feeling, '– *ugly*. My family keep ringing me from Rangimarie and saying, "Do something," but what can I do? I want to pass my exams, I can't get caught up in all that.' And he suddenly grabbed Maggie and kissed her hard, held her very close to him, kissed her again. 'Oh, God we've got to be properly by ourselves again,' he said angrily. 'I hate this, I'm twenty-three years old and I have to kiss my girlfriend on street corners. I can't come to your place, I can't even phone you. You're ashamed of me.'

'No,' she cried, 'I'm not ashamed. It's just my parents – oh you can't possibly understand, I'm sorry it's like this, but they wouldn't, they –' She stopped. She did not know what to say. She had not told him about the dictionary.

'I know,' he said angrily, 'it's because I'm a Maori, I know.' She saw the naked pain in his face. 'Let's go somewhere in the weekend, let's borrow Henare's uncle's wife's car on Saturday, drive somewhere, a hotel somewhere – ,' he paused for a moment and then concluded, '– somewhere.'

They both knew what he meant. Somewhere where Maoris wouldn't be unwelcome.

Maggie told her parents she'd been invited to stay with Prudence, to help her spring clean. 'We thought we'd scrub and dust and clean out cupboards and speak French at the same time, because *surely* spring must get here soon.'

They leaned, shivering slightly, on the wooden verandah that ran round the second storey of the small-town hotel, staring at the misty winter stars: at the Southern Cross, at the huge ceiling of the Milky Way. There were no streetlights here, only the stars in the clouds. The public bar of the hotel had closed hours ago. One light from a house much further down the road, nothing else. The darkness of those small country towns on a winter night.

But from somewhere they could hear an old gramophone record, scratchy and badly recorded.

'Oh,' breathed Maggie. 'Oh, it's the song from the coffee bar.'

A woman's crackly, pure voice sang:

> From the mist of a memory
> You wander back to me
> Breathing my name like a sigh

And then the saxophone soared from the cook's bedroom at the back by the pile of empty beer bottles, cried in the darkness, whispered finally along the verandah.

Timoti and Maggie leaned there, trying so bravely to join their lives, their arms round each other on the dark hotel verandah saying *I love you* as if that could solve everything, and a saxophone playing.

In the frosty darkness, almost echoing the saxophone, a sheep cried out from the paddock across the railway line and it sounded so plaintive they both half laughed, those two who found laughter so difficult; but their laughter was such an odd, disturbing sound that they guiltily stopped.

'There's fifty million sheep in this country,' Maggie murmured in Timoti's arms, 'and about two million of us, did you know that?' and she felt him smile and they kissed in the darkness and turned back into their room.

The brown and white arms and legs intertwined, making love. But, in the way of the times, constricted, the sheath tearing, withdrawing *no, no, you musn't do that*, hoping Maggie wouldn't get pregnant, as if it was all luck, as if pregnancy was a kind of lottery. And then they lay still. The dark hair of their heads lay together on one pillow, a white face and a brown face breathing together, fast asleep. And in the night did she hear him turn and groan, and say, '*I don't want to be a Maori*' in his sleep?

Next morning early the sheep were loaded into a huge lorry to be taken to the freezing works, dogs biting at the spindly sheeps' legs as they ran, frightened, in circles. They bleated in terror, knowing. The breath of the farmer lay on the frosty winter morning as he shouted and swore.

When the loading of the animals was finished the farmer came into the hotel for a cup of tea, rubbing his cold hands together. Maggie saw the cook put some whisky in the teacup. The dogs sat, panting and thin, by the back door.

Timoti and Maggie self-consciously had Sunday breakfast in the hotel dining room. Maggie wore a curtain ring on the third finger of her left hand. It was a bit big and she had stuck a piece of blotting paper at the back so it wouldn't fall off.

Timoti drank his tea with his little finger crooked, the way his mother and his auntie did.

'Don't *do* that,' mumbled Maggie, half embarrassed.

'Do what?' He looked surprised.

'Hold your cup like that, with your little finger like that. It's, it's sort of vulgar. Someone trying to be genteel.'

Timoti stared at her for a long moment. And then he said, and his voice was very cold, 'Your grandparents taught my grandparents to do this. The missionaries and the teachers taught us this was good manners. It's changed, has it? Now it's not good manners? Is that right?' He left his little finger where it was.

But when she had turned away, he pulled his little finger down: another Pakeha lesson learned, unlearned; relearned.

TWENTY-EIGHT

Just as he was getting ready for work, sitting on the side of his bed and bending down to tie his shoe laces, Gallipoli Gordon from Alienations, who sang better than Mario Lanza, had a heart attack and died. The night before he'd been eating fish and chips and drinking DB bitter and singing old songs.

Bay took the phone call from Gallipoli's wife; Maggie heard him speaking in Maori gently on the telephone, his back to the rest of the office but his body swaying backwards and forwards as he spoke, in a kind of keening.

'They all die of heart attacks,' said Harry Beans at lunchtime, biting at his meat pie on the grass outside the Bureau where Maggie sat in her duffle coat eating a peanut butter sandwich. 'They eat the wrong food.'

'No,' said Maggie, 'it's not just the food.' And she said: 'I think – I think sometimes they die of other heart troubles.'

'What do you mean?' said Harry Beans.

'I mean, I think they die of – hearts that hurt.' She looked away, embarrassed.

'What a load of rubbish,' said Harry Beans. 'Any problems they've got are their own fault. The same laws have applied to them and us since we all signed the Treaty of Waitangi in 1840. You're getting like a hori too, that's your trouble.'

The Bureau was to send a busload to the funeral on the

second day. Sinatra, who it transpired was related to Gallipoli's wife, was in the office, phoning relatives, telling them Gallipoli's wife wanted him buried in the north, not in the south, calming everybody, arranging everything with Bay. '*Kei te pehea koe*, Maggie?' he said, and she wondered how he knew she could speak Maori.

'I'm fine thanks, Sinatra.'

The old ladies who often sat in the corner and had cups of tea were already gone; as soon as they'd heard they had immediately begun weeping; had gone north at once on a nephew's truck or a cousin's car.

'You surely don't mean,' said Mrs Bennett, the needle going in and out, in and out, 'that anyone can go, that people turn up in busloads and stay? You hardly knew him. You shouldn't be going to his funeral, funerals aren't for strangers.'

'I did know him, Mum. He worked in the Bureau. But I'm not going with them tomorrow, I have to look after the office. I'm just telling you about it. Their funerals all take three days, that's their custom.'

'They all die of heart attacks,' said Mrs Bennett. 'They eat the wrong food.'

Maggie had finished remaking her dictionary in the lamb and mint sauce book. She had made a statistics chart and stuck it on the wall, but nobody gave her much information to put on it. She looked at it and shrugged. *I can probably get a lot of work done on bloody old 'Beowulf' since nobody'll be here all day.*

But she didn't read 'Beowulf'. She sat instead in the empty office, answering the phone if she had to and thinking of Gallipoli Gordon and his beautiful voice. As Bay put his hat on to leave for the funeral he had said to her, 'Gallipoli got accepted at the Royal College of Music in London. But he didn't want to go. He said he'd miss the mountains.'

The night before he died he'd sung the old song they always asked him to sing

> Just a song at twilight
> when the lights are low

She thought of his deep voice telling them about the south where he came from, that colder, lonelier island. He had lived in the north for many years, because that's where his wife came from. But he had always talked about the mountains near his home, and of the *pounamu*, the green jade found there. She remembered the day of the fishing trip, his story of his ancestors dying of measles.

But what she was really remembering as she hunched over her desk behind her hair, trying not to remember, was how she'd shivered on the fishing boat in the sunshine seeing his closed eyes, like a premonition, when he'd spoken to her in Maori: *te tatau o te po*; *the doorway to the night*.

Death.

She shivered again, although the office radiators were on.

For the first time in months she went home straight after work and her father was on the same tram.

'Good heavens!' he said, seeing her.

'Come for a walk along the beach, Dad, just for ten minutes. It'll be nice, it's not raining for once.'

He looked surprised but walked with her.

The first heady, fragrant scent from the daphne bush in the first neat garden drifted in the dusk, telling them spring really was on its way. In number twenty-seven Mr Lomond was practising the trumpet again: 'Silent Night' jolted out of the small lavatory window, bar by bar.

'Oh dear. He must be getting ready for Christmas already,' said Mr Bennett.

'I suppose the Salvation Army don't like to be *too* critical,' said Maggie and they grinned at each other.

They leaned over, put their bags just inside their gate and walked to the end of the street, to the sea. The beach was totally deserted, the tide was out. They walked along the firm, damp sand towards the Heads. The wind was stronger here, pulling at the cutty grass behind them, blowing at the sand-hills. *Where Manu used to park.* Quickly she pushed the thought away. For some time she and her father just walked companionably, enjoying the freshness after the city, and the smell of the sea. It was already dusk.

As they walked the wind rose, blew sand along beside them, unsettled the receding water.

'There was no one in my office today,' she said at last. 'They all went to that funeral I was telling you about.

'Oh yes?'

'Maori funerals are long things.'

He nodded non-committally.

Maggie took a deep breath. 'Did Elizabeth have a funeral, Dad?'

She saw that she had shocked him. He pulled his coat around him with his good hand, but she could not give up.

'Why don't we talk about her, Dad? Do you miss her?' He did not answer. On and on the two pairs of footsteps were imprinted in the sand.

Finally he said, 'I was overseas. You know that.' And he hunched his big front-row-forward shoulders down into his coat and she saw that the conversation was over. The wind tore at their flapping coats now, spray caught their faces as they walked and the light was almost gone.

'Let's go back,' he said. She saw him put his hook in his coat pocket. But she did not see him glance at her bleak face. They walked in silence, following the two sets of footprints back along the dark, empty shore.

The sea crashed behind them as they turned away and up to the street.

Her father said, 'You know the bookcase in the dining room?'

'Yes.'

'The left-hand side?'

She could feel her heart suddenly beating fast. 'Yes.'

'On the very top shelf there is a drawing Elizabeth did of two whales dancing. The teachers at your school gave it to me when I got back from the war when – when your mother was in hospital. They thought I might like to have it.'

Maggie could hardly breathe.

'It's probably faded now. It was the most beautiful child's drawing I ever saw. But – I had to help your mother get well again so I put it up there where she would never see it.' Maggie could hardly hear him. It was completely dark.

'I missed her more than I could say,' said the father.

They picked up their bags and walked down the path to the back door, past the cinnerarias, where the sun never shone.

She waited until they had both gone to bed. Then very quietly and carefully she climbed on a chair, felt for the drawing. It was folded in four. She laid it very gently on the carpet. In the corner still, neatly placed, were five gold stars.

But the paper was fragile where it had been folded, almost worn through. And the crayon had almost faded.

Two shadows danced gracefully on a blanched, white sea.

Maggie saw that Bay looked exhausted. 'Didn't you sleep all the time you were away at the funeral?'

'A *tangi* isn't necessarily for sleeping,' he informed her. 'Did you know your mates were sick on the way home? That Emily better get better soon, she's going overseas on Saturday.'

'Were they car-sick?'

'No. The food from the earth oven, from the **hangi**, so they said.'

'You don't –' she looked at him, puzzled. 'Do you *eat* at your funerals?'

He looked very surprised. 'Of course we do. People sometimes come hundreds and hundreds of miles to pay their respects. We look after them, *e hoa*, that's part of it.'

Emily and Prudence were both away from the Bureau for several days with food poisoning. They thought maybe the pork from the **hangi** hadn't been cooked properly.

'Pakeha stomachs,' said Bay Ropata. 'None of the Maoris got sick. You fellas don't eat properly, your stomachs are too genteel.'

For some reason Maggie sent up a little silent prayer that Bay and her mother, such experts on each other's eating habits, would never meet, but the smiling angel must not have been listening.

TWENTY-NINE

Emily was leaving God's Own Country.

There was one, final, spectacular storm. Gales lashed the city. Down their street the sea hurled itself over the sand and the cutty grass and came right up to the road, swirled there, menacing. The mournful foghorn could be heard in the distance in the daytime as well as at night and the bad-tempered houses built into the hillside jutted out angrily, battling with the wind. All over the city there was the sound of rain on corrugated-iron roofs, a wild drumming, drainpipes broke with the weight of the water. The insides of tram cars ran with rain as they clanked along the flooded streets and – a most unusual and devastating experience for the whole country – the Saturday rugby was cancelled. The wind tore at the city, as it had always done.

And, on Saturday, down at the docks, the *Rangitane* was loading for England.

Umbrellas blew inside out as they ran up the hill on Saturday afternoon; they put newspapers on their heads to try and keep dry, past the drenched, battered honeysuckle and up on to the verandah of Prudence's place. Where, despite the weather, Rangi, a cigarette drooping from his mouth, sat on an old wicker chair, strumming his guitar, looking out at the rain.

'Come inside, Rangi,' said Prudence for the third time, 'the verandah's leaking.' Maggie thought how odd it was to see the old house in the middle of the day, the peeling paint and the rotting wood.

All Emily's friends from the Bureau came to say goodbye. She was wearing sunglasses. She danced and drank and smoked and regaled them all with stories of her parents' big farewell for her.

'We weren't invited, eh?' said Hope.

'*Course* not!' said Emily scornfully and Hope, smiling at the electric light, sang

> *Tahi nei taru kino*
> *Mahi whaiaipo*

making love is like a dangerous vine.

Emily told them that Members of Parliament, her father's colleagues, had given her the addresses of British politicians, and cousins of royalty, and old great aunts in Kent.

'Just think of all the free meals I'll get,' she laughed glee-fully, angrily, 'because my Dad's Prime Minister. And I'll be so rich, with all my real estate and my fishing lodges, I'm going to have a wonderful life!' She already had a job in London. 'Selling sheep!' she crowed.

Nobody could see her eyes, behind the glasses.

Paddy sat getting very drunk, staring moodily into his beer.

Bay Ropata called in with his wife and two sons to say goodbye, on their way to another funeral.

'How long does it take?' asked Bay's wife, Rima.

'Six weeks,' said Emily; 'well, it's forty days actually; forty days and forty nights at sea playing quoits and drinking rum, so I'm told,' and she whooped about the crowded, singing room, pouring sweet sherry, drinking it.

'I expect,' she went on, 'the Cold War will hot up when I'm

gone. Perhaps the Russians will drop an atom bomb on this place, you know, like the Americans did on Hiroshima. And everything will disappear, these islands, just disappear, nothing, none of you left. And I'll be on the other side of the world, a woman without a past.' And Maggie and Prudence caught each other's eye, and turned away, and sang loudly with everybody else.

> What do you want to make those eyes at me for
> When they don't mean what they say

Hui pulled his wooden leg up on to the sofa, grimacing, the way he did when it rained. 'You're a fool,' he said angrily, 'you're a fool to go, looking for a life somewhere else, this is your home, whatever's happened,' and Maggie thought *he knows; they all know.*

Emily sparked at Hui across the room. 'I hate this place,' she said.

'You hate yourself,' Hui murmured but Hope and Rangi and Hori were singing louder and louder and Emily did not hear.

'This place,' she called across to Hui, 'is the end of the world. If you go any further than here you start going back again!'

'Back to *where*?'

'To Europe, to where things happen. Do you realise people read books there, when did you last read a book? And have their own opinions and don't believe in superstitions and stupid myths. At least I won't spend the rest of my life drinking DB bitter and singing sentimental songs!'

Hui turned away from her, grimacing again at his aching, non-existent leg.

Wind tore at the roof of the old house, rattled the windows. Paddy opened another bottle of DB bitter. 'Go!' he said and his wig lay quite askew on his head and his face was sad.

Prudence had made another of her cakes. It said, GOOD-BYE EMILY COME BACK SOON, in bright red icing.

Rangi and Hope and Hori sang in harmony.

> Blue smoke
> goes drifting by
> Into a deep blue sky
> My memories of home
> will never die.

Emily suddenly hugged Prudence tightly and her tears fell from behind the sunglasses on to Prudence's jersey.

They all drove through the storm to the wharves, stumbling in the rain with Emily's trunk, standing in the doorway of one of the big tin sheds as Emily was buffeted towards the gangway.

A grey-haired Maori in a black oilskin waved as they passed. He was supervising huge boxes being loaded in the rain.

'There's Sinatra,' said Hori.

'Oh, I know him,' said Maggie, pleased, and she waved to him also.

'*Kia ora*, Maggie,' he called as the cranes swayed over the deck of the ship.

Just then a official looking black car swept on to the wharf and drew up alongside, blocking the boxes that were being loaded. The Prime Minister of the country got out. He held his daughter to him as cameras appeared from nowhere, flashed in the afternoon rain. Emily at once ignored her friends, smiled and smiled at her father and his colleagues and the cameras. She was swept up the gangway, turned and waved once more to her father. As she turned away she saw Maggie standing in the rain with wet streamers.

'Next time we meet I'll be frightfully affluent,' she called grinning. 'Millionaires only at my place.' The wind whipped at her words but Maggie heard.

'Where is it?' she called back up. 'This place for millionaires that is going to make you so rich? The South of France?' If Emily heard she didn't answer.

Prudence and Hori tried to throw streamers up to the deck but the rain and the wind kept tearing them away as they sang 'Now Is the Hour'.

Rangi strummed his guitar in the rain until they'd finished the English version and then he started singing the older, Maori words that he remembered his grandparents singing when the soldiers went away across the sea.

> *Haere ra*
> *Ka hoki mai ano.*

One of the whistling whalers' tunes, a song from another country.

Finally the boxes were all loaded, the *Rangitane* hooted one last time and the gangway was hauled up by sailors in oilskins. They shouted and undid big ropes. Just as the ship began pulling away from the wharves Emily called down to Maggie. Maggie could not hear, shrugged up at Emily, waved.

Emily called again and the wind, this time, caught the words, carried them down on to the wharf where Maggie was standing, delivered them to her.

'It's called **Rangimarie**,' was what Emily said.

The ship, shrouded in mist and falling rain, pulled away and the gap of water widened between it and the wharves. Emily Evans, standing at the rail in the rain in her sunglasses with a glass in her hand, melted almost at once into the gloom.

Maggie was to come straight home that Saturday evening. Eddie Albert and his girlfriend Shirley were coming to dinner. She ran in the rain to where she knew the Maori Men's Hostel was, near the docks, down the street of old, high, wooden houses, once grand, now run-down boarding houses. A hand-written notice in one of the windows of the houses said:

ROOM TO LET
BREAKFAST PROVIDED £2/10/- PER WEEK
NO CHILDREN MAORIS OR DOGS.

and a few doors away a sign said: PRESBYTERIAN MAORI MEN'S HOSTEL.

The front door of the hostel was open and she hurtled in. Because the rugby had been cancelled the men sat around the big bare dining room with bottles of DB bitter; some still wore their sports clothes; some wore suits, going somewhere; some had bare feet. There was a guitar in the corner. Timoti sat at the dining-room table, his arm resting on a big pile of law books. He had once told her he hated this place, longed to live somewhere by himself.

He looked extremely surprised to see Maggie, who had never been here, soaked to the skin, standing shyly by the door, trying to catch her breath. But she saw too that his face lit up.

'Come on,' he said and they walked, the others whistling behind them and laughing, but not unfriendly, past the notice that he'd told her about: NO FEMALE VISITORS WITHOUT PERMISSION. Maggie looked automatically at her watch, it was ten to five, she should be home, helping with the dinner, she would have to hurry. Timoti's room was small and cheerless with the narrowest single bed Maggie had ever seen. The blind was torn and outside the window the wooden fire escape led upwards to other floors. His two suits, the grey one and the navy blue one hung behind the door on coat-hangers.

'Oh,' she said.

Timoti took a thin, worn towel from a drawer, rubbed her hair as he spoke. 'Come to a party,' he said, 'the boys are having a party,' and he kissed her hard and put his hand on her breast.

'I can't,' she said helplessly when the kiss ended. 'You know I can't,' and his face closed. He handed her the towel.

'I don't want to live like this any more,' he said. 'I'm going to get a girlfriend I'm allowed to meet on Saturday nights like other people,' and her heart jumped with panic and with pain.

'But I love you,' she said, standing there with the wet towel, looking at him beseechingly. But his face was completely blank. Like the little girl in the street when her father hit her; like Manu when he undid the pins in her hair. He had blanked her out. That's what they all did.

Maggie took a deep breath. 'Listen,' she said, 'I have to go home, you know I have to go home, because of my cousin and his girlfriend coming. I love you. I know it's horrible, my parents not inviting you, but I do love you. But listen, I had to run here before I got home, to tell you, it's about Rangimarie.'

'What about it?'

'Well, I might be jumping to all the wrong conclusions but I think it might be about your Auntie Kura. I think it must be about that Alvin Fitzgerald who signed those Council papers. It's about Emily.'

'What? What are you *talking* about?'

'Her dad gave her some land. She's always talking about how rich she's going to be and how they're going to build a fishing lodge for rich people and a luxury hotel but I always thought it was somewhere else, somewhere in the main world. But she said it's in Rangimarie.'

'*What?*'

'She told me today.'

Timoti grabbed his white raincoat. 'Where is she?'

'She's gone,' said Maggie. 'The boat left. I have to go now, they'll have arrived. I must go home.'

'What did she say? What did she say *exactly*?'

'She just said that the land her Dad had given her, that they were going to turn into fishing lodges and millionaires' paradises, is in Rangimarie. I just wanted to tell you. But I have to go now, I have to, my cousin will have arrived.'

He looked silently at her for a long moment. Then he put the white raincoat on over his running trousers and his jersey.

'I want a girlfriend I can *be* with,' he said. 'I'm going to get another one, and when her cousin comes to visit, I'll be introduced, just like you were introduced to mine.'

'Will I see you on Monday, in the library?' she asked and she heard her own voice, high with alarm. But he had gone, and she was left by herself in the small bleak room. Her clothes had made a little puddle on the wooden floor. She wiped the water with the thin towel and laid it neatly on the windowsill to dry. The other Maori men looked at her as she made her way alone back along the wide corridor to the front door. She ran to the tram terminus in the gloom.

'Change your clothes and set the table please, Margaret-Rose,' said Mrs Bennett. 'I was expecting you before this. Shirley's already here.'

'The ship was delayed,' said Maggie immediately, 'because of the weather.' She saw Emily call out the name of the place where Timoti came from, and then the boat pull away and Emily, in her dark glasses, disappear.

Emily had said: *it's called Rangimarie.*

'Was the Prime Minister there?' asked Shirley.

'Oh, yes. There'll be photos in the paper, I expect.' And then the lies poured out like nails again, unstoppable: 'He asked me up to their house. To a cocktail party.'

There was a surprised silence.

'When?'

'Tonight. But – I said I couldn't come because we had visitors. So he said come next Saturday. Any Saturday. I suppose I might.' *That way I could see Timoti.*

'I asked you to set the table,' said Mrs Bennett.

'Where's Eddie Albert?'

'He'll be here soon,' said Shirley hopefully. 'He's having a drink with the boys.' A Drink with the Boys. All the women in God's Own Country knew that expression. Eddie Albert banged in loudly half an hour later, telling them how he'd nearly won one hundred pounds on a double.

All evening Maggie thought of Timoti's angry, hurt face; all evening Shirley smiled and smiled while Eddie Albert and Mr Bennett talked about business and about advertising.

'I was going to work in a bank after school certificate,' said Shirley to Mrs Bennett and Maggie, 'but I'm glad now I changed my mind and did another year's commercial and went into advertising and met Eddie.' And she smiled more.

But Maggie saw that what she was really saying was 'I'm twenty. I'm twenty. And I'm not engaged.'

THIRTY

On Monday evening Timoti Pou waited till all the other lawyers and clerks and secretaries had gone; till only his boss, the powerful lawyer that everyone so admired, remained. They were often like this in the early evenings: the boss and his young student lawyer working in separate parts of the office; the boss watching Timoti carefully, seeing how hard he worked on things that were quite alien to him, how he would not give up.

Timoti heard the lift clanking, someone else in the building going home. Then he walked into his boss's office.

The powerful lawyer listened in silence until Timoti had finished.

Damn. For a moment he said nothing, just stared at the young Maori, who nevertheless held his gaze.

'First: what you're suggesting is pure guesswork. Second: what you're suggesting can never be proved boy, never.'

Timoti kept to himself that he now had proof. 'You're his lawyer, sir,' said Timoti. 'I thought you'd probably know about it.'

'A man like the Prime Minister can have twenty lawyers.'

'You're the best,' said Timoti.

'Third: you're a clever fellow. But I wouldn't pursue it any further if I were you.'

'But it's *illegal* what happened, taking my auntie's land. That land has been in her family for hundreds of years. She didn't understand about rates. She's about eighty years old, she hardly speaks any English.'

The lawyer signed, shrugged, sat with his fingertips touching. Timoti was standing at the other side of the desk, the lamplight shone only on the bottom half of his boss's face. Timoti could not see what he was thinking.

'I wish,' said the lawyer, 'that you wouldn't talk about your *auntie* that way, as if you were a kid, it sounds very peculiar and immature in a grown man. *Auntie.* Actually it is not illegal. The Council were perfectly within their rights. When a charge has been imposed on Maori land and hasn't been paid the land can be seized, in lieu of payment: that is the law.'

'Whose law is *that*?' said Timoti Pou, bitterly.

'Let me give you a word of advice, boy,' said the half face in the darkness. 'You could go far. To go far, you have to learn what to accept and you'll have to accept this, and forget you ever even heard about it. Don't let your emotions get in the way of your work; you'll never make a lawyer if you do. I've got high hopes of you but you haven't got a hope in hell of pursuing this – business – without losing everything you've got. You can't go round making accusations against the Prime Minister of this country, you'd be pulverised.' He paused. And then he leaned forward so that his whole face was in the light.

'Listen to me. Let me give you the most important piece of information of your life. Even if you wanted to throw away all your chances, go out on a limb, make a stink, there is –' and he paused for a moment again. 'Timoti, there is – a network. Lawyers and politicians and newspaper owners, they have a *network*. They – assist one another. You'd be surprised at the information the press knows and doesn't print: there's nothing sinister in this, that's just how governments work all over the world – governments often tell the newspapers what to print, what not to print. You'd never get your story off the ground. And anyway, a bit of Maori land up in the wop-wops – oh, please! Who'd be interested?' He leaned back, half his face in shadow again. 'You're a *Maori*, you're not part of the network, don't you forget it.'

'I never forget it,' said Timoti Pou.

'Let's leave it then.'

Then suddenly, in a total acceptance of Timoti's story he said: 'It was extremely clever of you to have unravelled it, to have followed the threads. I'm very impressed, to be honest. But, remember this: the Prime Minister has already employed the one Council official who knew about it – that man, Alvin Fitzgerald, has been promoted beyond his wildest dreams, just begun work in the PM's office as a kind of minder, he'd do *anything* for John Evans. And *I* know because I'm his lawyer. But that's it. So if anyone ever got even a whiff of it, it could only be through you. And then of course there would –' and the threat was gentle and kind, '– be no place for you in our firm. Or any other firm, come to that.'

And he leaned back right in his chair and his face was out of the light altogether. His voice was soft.

'You're doing fine, Timoti. You know damn well I'm interested in you doing well, interested in making you our first Maori partner. Do you want to be our first Maori partner?'

'I do, sir, yes. I want it very much.'

'It may not ever make you part of the network, but you'll come a damn sight closer than you'd ever get otherwise. It'll shock the legal brethren, but that'll be good for them. I've got plans for you, Timoti, that you don't even realise. But you've got to be on our side. Don't let me down now. Forget this. Forget all about it.'

'Thank you, sir,' said Timoti Pou.

And he gathered his books and came down in the old

clanking lift from the office and walked out into the dark streets of the city. He lit a cigarette, turning into a doorway, sheltering the flame from the wind. For a moment he considered going up to the university library. But then he turned and walked down to the docks, to the old run-down part of the city, where he lived.

In his small bleak room he did not turn on the light.

He sat on his narrow bed.

He thought about how much he wanted to be a lawyer, to be part of the real world. To be like one of them.

He thought about Maggie who he wanted to marry. He thought about Maggie's parents and how they would never accept him *because he was a Maori*. And about the heavy burden of other people's expectations *because he was a Maori*. And about how he could – should – tell his Uncle Heke what he knew but how it would *involve* him when he didn't want to be involved.

He thought about how hard and how long he had worked, to get this far.

The streetlight shone in: he hadn't pulled down the torn blind. The fire escape was a shadow outside his window. The timber in the window frame was rotting. He thought of Maggie dancing down the street singing, *I've got a good ear*, and how it had somehow enchanted him, lifted his heart. He thought of the signed papers he'd seen in the Council office while the caretaker whistled outside and of the land files that had been mislaid in one of the Bureau offices for a little while. He thought of his Auntie Kura running along the hillside calling for her home.

He suddenly put his head in his hands and wept.

On that same Monday evening Margaret-Rose Bennett sat in the library, at the table they always sat at, until it closed at 9.00 PM. The seat next to her was empty. He hadn't come. He didn't love her. For a long time she remained there, bent over her books, not seeing the words as other students read and whispered and flirted. She looked up over and over again, less and less hopefully, when someone walked by. Then she caught the 9.30 tram home.

Down her street trumpet sounds of 'Good King Wenceslas' faltered out of Mr Lomond's lavatory window, were picked up by the wind, spiralled away.

She walked past her house and down to the sea. Tonight it was wild and angry, waves crashed against the sand, dull and booming; pulled back over the pebbles and the shells and the hidden rocks, rasping and shrill. And then boomed back again.

The sound hypnotised her. She stood watching the sea in the darkness.

Her parents were asleep; nobody was waiting, or called, or opened a door, or stared at her as she came in the back door. Her head ached. She had forgotten to eat again. She got a glass of milk, and a bottle of aspirin from the bathroom cupboard.

In the night she woke suddenly with tears pouring down her cheeks. It gave her such a fright, so unused was she to crying, if this crying. It seemed to happen without her help, as if her tears and her eyes were separate from the rest of her body. She lent over to the bedside table in the darkness, took the lid off the aspirin bottle, poured them into her hand. She felt liquid between her fingers. Putting the bedside lamp on she saw that she had unscrewed, not the aspirin bottle, but the bottle of ink for her fountain pen and that great blots of blue-black ink were soaking into her neat, pink candlewick bedspread.

THIRTY-ONE

'Look,' she said, pointing dramatically at the university walls, speaking too loudly, 'look, the ivy's beginning to sprout again, spring *must* be coming, it *must* be.'

Kara Rikihana shrugged, ignored her, read a German text-book.

Pale in her duffle coat, glad of the fresh, windy air, she sat with him on the statue plinth under the noble duke, where they often waited for Timoti to come up the hill for the Maori class. But she was trying to look anywhere but down the hill, where Timoti would surely appear. She would surely see him tonight. She kept staring at the new leaves of the ivy as if she had suddenly become interested in botany.

'Do you think Isobel is – all right?' she said to Kara after a while.

'What do you mean?' But she saw at once from his face that he had noticed too.

'She looks – pale, lately. Wears more make-up than she used to.'

'Yes. I don't expect her life is easy.'

'Why? What do you mean?'

'It's a very long way from Scotland,' said Kara.

'I just thought she looked pale,' said Maggie again. And both of them saw their teacher in heavy make-up, staring out at the dark harbour.

'Do you think she might be sorry she came? Or –' Maggie hesitated, '– sorry she married a Maori?'

He stared at the moving, rustling trees across the path. He did not answer.

'She is such a wonderful teacher, she should have classes of hundreds. I wish more people could speak Maori,' said Maggie finally. 'The boys at the Bureau, they don't know lots of the grammar and stuff, but I sort of feel they know the language really.' She thought of Manu's old words: *those fellas know it really, in their hearts*.

'They *don't* know it,' said Kara angrily. 'It's got to be more than a soppy feeling and singing a few songs, being a Maori. There's a whole generation that doesn't know it. It's not good enough, knowing some of the words and thinking you're speaking your own language. All those Maori parents who wanted their kids to do well in the Pakeha world, like Timoti's parents wanted for him, stopped speaking it in the home. It's lost. It's as good as lost.'

Kara so seldom did anything but shrug, as if he didn't care. Maggie saw how angry he was. His eyes flashed.

'Where I work, in the Justice Department, the prisons we're in charge of are full of Maoris. Full of them. And we've got a few Maori policemen now – they made a special fuss about getting Maori policemen because there's so much Maori crime – but the police can't speak it. Your friend Manu Taihape is the only one who can actually speak the language properly.'

Maggie looked at Kara in surprise. 'What do you mean my *friend* Manu Taihape?' she said sharply. 'Manu Taihape is not my friend.'

He ignored her. 'We have these Maori cops going round with hardly a word of Maori between them. You can pretty much work it out mathematically: almost any Maori who's educated enough to get a job as a policeman can't speak

Maori.' He had almost ripped the German grammar. She had never seen him so worked up.

'Do you know what *education* means, for Maoris?' he said. *'Education for Maoris means losing their language and losing their culture.'*

His words shocked Maggie deeply. She stared at Kara, took in the meaning of what he was saying. And at that moment Timoti appeared, hurrying up the hill. Her heart beat fast, immediately, in the wrong way, too fast. His white raincoat flapped in the dusk as he ran up the university steps.

'Hello, you two,' he said.

Maggie sat submissively beside Timoti in the high classroom.

As soon as the class was finished Timoti said to her, 'Come on,' and walked down ahead of her. The crippled boy was climbing down awkwardly past the new ivy as Timoti and Maggie came out into the night. Maggie's full, blue skirt swished by. He watched them go, expressionless.

At the corner of the park, where the trees whispered, Timoti turned to Maggie but instead of saying anything he clumsily, his books in the way, tried to hold her close to him. She put her bag of books down on the grass and put both her arms round his neck.

'I love you I love you I love you,' she cried and she buried her face in his neck, in his waistcoat, turning her head from side to side with hurt, running it to and fro along his chest trying to put herself together again, burying her heart in his life. 'I'm so sorry about my parents. But I'm not my parents.' Again and again she pushed her head into his heart. 'Please don't leave me again,' she said in a muffled voice, 'I need you to love me. I get frightened.'

When she finally looked up she saw his face, creased with pain.

Then he picked up her books from the dark grass and took

her arm quite firmly and in silence they began to walk along the edge of the park and down the hill. At the taxi rank she got in quietly as he gave the address of his hostel; she sat leaning against him slightly as he hunched over his knees. When they got to the shabby wooden building with its verandahs and peeling paint and fire escapes she walked with him past the sign that said NO FEMALE VISITORS WITHOUT PERMISSION, past the old warden who was nodding over *Best Bets* and didn't even look up. In his room, where his other suit, his grey suit, hung on the back of the door Timoti pulled down the torn brown blind, locked the door. The light from a streetlight shone in where the blind didn't fit the window. The wind, calmer now, caught the blind occasionally and it rattled against the glass. He looked at her, took off her coat and her cardigan and her blouse, her blue skirt that had swished past the crippled boy, her petticoat, her nylons, her suspender belt, her flat shoes. Not until her white body stood there did he even take off his raincoat. Still they hadn't spoken.

Then very quickly he took off all his clothes and he and Maggie were lying on the thin bed. He was so tense, so passionate, that part of the rubber sheath tore. When he hurt her she bit, not him, but her own arm. He finally gasped aloud on this bed in the Maori Men's Hostel down by the docks without any words at all.

When it was over he got off the bed and put on his raincoat. And then, standing in the bleak room, looking down at the naked girl he said, 'I get frightened too.'

The shaft of yellow light from the streetlight fell across the bed. She stared at the room. She would hate to live in a room like this, no wonder he hated it, how pretty her pink room was with its bedspread and dressing-table and neat desk. *I must never get pregnant or I'll be trapped in a room like this.* Her own thought shocked her. She shivered involuntarily.

'I always know I'm a Maori,' he said. 'Your parents are only doing to me what I get done to me every day of my life, did you know that? I always know. I know it when I get to the office, I know it when I go into a shop, when I'm in the rugby team, when I sit exams. *I'm a Maori*, that's what I say to myself. It's impossible for you to understand. People look at me differently, treat me differently. It affects everything I do. I hate that pressure, it's there all the time, *always*.

'And my own people pressure me too. I just want to be a lawyer, like other lawyers. I don't want to be a *Maori* lawyer. I just want to be a person,' and pain cried out in his voice. He fumbled, found a cigarette in the pocket of the raincoat, lit it, inhaled almost desperately. 'I think I've found out what happened to Auntie Kura's land. But I've been warned that if I pursue it, I'll lose my job.'

'What happened?' She had pulled the blankets around her. Her wild hair and her pale face peered out. His beautiful brown skin shone against the white raincoat and his blue eyes glittered and the blind rattled again against the window.

'A Maori caretaker I know let me in some offices up north on Sunday to look at the Council papers.' He again breathed the smoke deep into his lungs. 'They think they're the only ones with a network,' he said bitterly, more to himself than to Maggie. 'That Alvin Fitzgerald worked for the Council and he now works for the Prime Minister. He took it on behalf of the Council because the rates weren't paid and then, just as he was leaving, he somehow sold it on. There are some papers missing, no doubt they'll turn up, eventually. When people have forgotten. It's dicey but he could probably argue they were legally entitled to sell it. But what does that say about the *law*? What kind of rotten law is that? There's no appeal, nothing. It's all there in the Act: "land can be taken in lieu of debt". It doesn't say it can be sold on, but it can be taken. Then somehow they managed to have a lot of buyers one after the other so that the original transaction is hidden. I'd never have found it if I didn't know what I was looking for. But they can't hide the *dates*. It became your friend Emily's less than six weeks after it was Auntie Kura's and the Prime Minister's name isn't even on it. We would never have known. The Bureau won't know.'

He had been standing in the dark all this time. He suddenly put on the light and they both blinked in the ugly room. Then he went to a chest of drawers, took something out, came over to the bed. In his brown hand he had a small box which he gave to Maggie. Inside was a ring with one diamond in the middle, the sort her friends wore when they got engaged.

Maggie gasped.

Timoti said: 'Will you marry me?'

This was the moment all girls dreamed of. She leaned forward, the blankets fell off. She sat naked on the bed. The pale, white body and the unruly dark hair and her clothes all over the floor. She slid the ring on her finger, turned it round and round. He loved her. He loved her so much he wanted to marry her. *She would never feel unloved again.*

'We can keep it a secret now if you want,' said Timoti. 'But as soon as exams are over, I'll ask your father if I can marry you. At least you'll be eighteen then. Plenty of girls get married when they're eighteen. If your parents don't agree, we'll find a place so that we can be together and we'll just announce it in the paper and see what they do. And it doesn't matter if you get pregnant, you can go back to Rangimarie and live with my mum and dad when it starts showing. They like you. They accept you. It would be nice to have a son.'

Round and round went the ring on her finger and then she turned her tight, pale face up to him, staring at him, this man who loved her.

How could she live without him?

'I know you'll make me a good wife,' said Timoti. 'And I

love you, Maggie.' He was standing by the bed looking at her. She could see his brown chest under the raincoat, breathing in and out anxiously, waiting. 'Will you? Will you marry me?' he said again.

'Yes, Timoti, of course I'll marry you,' she cried, on the thin bed in the Maori Men's Hostel. 'Of course I will. Thank you. Yes. Oh, thank you for loving me.'

And she jumped off the bed and threw her cold white body against him and he quickly put his arms around her and pulled her under the raincoat and she put her arms around him and held him tight, feeling the warmth of his body. And they both gave a long sigh.

They stood together in the small room, clinging to each other. A door banged, a clock chimed. The blind rattled sometimes. Still they stood there, not speaking, just holding on. Hours might have passed, or minutes, as they clung to each other to save their lives.

Time stopped.

She caught the 9.30 tram home, as usual. On the tram she took off her new, shining diamond engagement ring and put it in her purse.

THIRTY-TWO

Margaret-Rose Bennett walked differently.

She was an engaged person. Although she was an engaged person who kept her flashing diamond in her purse, she was nevertheless an engaged person. She sat at her desk, contained, secure: waiting for her first telephone call as an engaged person.

'Good morning. Welfare Department. How can I help you?'

'Has the bugger done it?'

'Pardon?'

'The report, the bloody Annual Report.' It was the Head Boss.

'The Annual Report? Ah – no. I don't think so.'

'The Minister's waiting for the Bureau Report. Every department has put in their stuff except that bugger, Bay. Where is he?'

'He's in the interview room with a client.'

'Bugger the client. Put him on.'

'She'll be jake, mate,' said Bay, who was carrying a basket of oysters.

'By the end of the week.' She heard the Head Boss's voice crackle on the other end of the phone.

'Right,' said Bay, 'right.' He called all the Welfare Officers to sit around his desk, opened oysters with a penknife. Maggie felt the space on her finger where the ring would be.

'Here's our oysters,' said Bay, handing them around. 'Now.' He bent his head briefly, uttered a short Maori prayer. 'Now. Have you fellas all got your statistics and your comments? We've got to do this report.' The phone rang. It was the police. A young Maori boy was threatening to jump off the top of the main post office. Bay was gone.

Glory Ngahuia Brown leant over Mrs McMillan's desk. Her beautiful eyes were flashing. 'I'm trying to get a very clever girl with university entrance a job with a big electrical firm. Her name is Jean Forbes and she's got wonderful references and they said how much they were looking forward to meeting her. But when she went to her interview and they saw she was a Maori they said it had already gone to someone else.'

'Racist bastards,' said Mrs McMillan, rubbing her lips together where she'd put on her lipstick.

Maggie sorted through files. She knew she had to try and find some statistics. 'Why didn't you keep statistics *before*?' she said to them all angrily.

Glory Ngahuia Brown looked up, stared. She had seen Maggie with Timoti Pou, disapproved strongly of one of their best young men going out with a Pakeha, especially someone as handsome and clever and high-flying as Timoti Pou. 'You're the clerk,' she said coldly, 'it's your job.' She and Errol Flynn left together.

'A – DULT – ERESS,' sang Maggie loudly as she gathered up the oyster shells. *I hate her. But she won't get Timoti now* and triumphantly she thought yet again of the diamond sparkling in the bottom of her purse.

An old Maori lady in black came to the counter to see Bay, one of his regulars.

'He's at the police station,' said Maggie. 'I don't know when he'll be back.'

'Never mind, dear,' said the old lady, 'I'll wait.' And she sat at her usual place on the bench in the corner and slowly rolled herself a cigarette from her big old tin of tobacco.

'Do you want the paper?' asked Maggie.

'No, never mind, dear.'

'I could make you a cup of tea.' She liked having these old ladies here, it meant the office wasn't empty if a frightening person came in; and often they came up with solutions, gave other Maoris advice, or sometimes money. They were much better than the pompous Errol Flynn at the job, in Maggie's opinion.

'That'd be nice, dear, three sugars,' and the old lady pulled the tobacco off her tongue with her gnarled brown fingers.

Later in the morning Mr Porter, the kind arrears clerk – the unfrocked Methodist minister – came in with some files. He placed them neatly on a corner of Maggie's untidy desk and she smiled at him.

'Good morning, Miss Bennett,' he said. 'Did you enjoy the recording of "The Sounds of the Mudpools and the Geysers"?'

'Oh, yes, I meant to bring it back ages ago, sorry, I'll bring it in tomorrow. It was very – interesting and – bubbly,' and Maggie smiled again at him and Mr Porter smiled too, his magnified eyes shining behind his glasses.

'The Maoris say,' he said, 'that there are spirits in those mudpools.'

'Mr Porter,' said Maggie, glancing across at the old lady who was now asleep by the counter. 'Mr Porter,' she couldn't keep the words inside her a moment longer, 'Mr Porter, I'm engaged. I got engaged last night.'

'Congratulations, my dear. I hope you will be very happy,' and he beamed at her again.

'But it's a secret at the moment. Till exams are over.'

'Of course,' he said.

'But I'll show you my engagement ring.' She got out her purse. The little diamond shone.

'Very nice,' said Mr Porter. She slipped it on her finger, flashing it, turning it and then, unable to stop herself, she kissed it. Mr Porter smiled benignly.

'Mr Porter, can I ask you something?' She put the ring back in her purse.

'Of course.'

'Mr Porter, do you think Maoris are more religious than Pakehas, I mean apart from praying at funny times, have you noticed that they are religious and superstitious *at the same time*? Don't you think that's a peculiar combination?'

Mr Porter straightened the housing files even more neatly, rubbed his nose under his spectacles, cleared his throat. 'Well, you can never generalise about any race,' he said. 'People aren't all the same, whatever race they are. But –' and he stared down at the files, 'Well, I like to think of it like this. Maoris are sort of used to gods, it's part of their culture; they're used to something outside themselves that perhaps doesn't come so naturally to us. I think it sits easier on them, religion, they don't feel they have to question it and intellectualise it the way we do. Also,' – and he pushed again at his spectacles which had begun to slide down his nose – 'also, I don't really think of it as *superstition*, the rest of it. I feel they are correct, I believe I have mentioned to you before that there are spirits, intentions, all around us. In my opinion that is,' he added politely.

'Do you mean ghosts?'

'You can call them ghosts if you like. I rather think of them as – feelings – in the air, drifting around us whether we are tuned into them or not.'

'Do you think,' said Maggie very hesitantly, 'that they could be memories that have been forgotten?'

Mr Porter looked at her curiously for a moment.

'That's interesting, my dear. Maybe. Or maybe it could be – a very highly charged instinctive feeling about something, intuition, that we hardly know we possess.'

'Do you think Maoris have this feeling more than we do?'

'No. No I don't actually,' said Mr Porter. 'I feel it is a very personal thing, nothing to do with which race we belong to. But I feel they are more *attuned* to these things around us; they're more used to the idea.' He stared into space. 'We would be very foolish to think we Anglo-Saxons have all the answers to the mysteries of the world. I don't know where such things come from – these ghosts, or intuitions, or memories. What I am so sure of is that we ignore them at our peril.' And then, as if he'd caught himself talking too much he said, 'Well, I must get back to my desk.'

Suddenly she remembered the dead body on the wharf and the sailors talking about a 'native curse'.

'Are there Maori curses?' she asked. 'Do you believe that? I once saw a man who was supposed to have been killed by one.'

'I think,' said Mr Porter, 'that a curse is something you bring upon yourself.'

Maggie looked at him for a moment. *I wonder if this is why he's an unfrocked minister? He doesn't talk at all like a frocked one.* 'In my family,' she said, 'thinking along these lines is known as an Over-developed Imagination.'

'People often say that,' said Mr Porter, 'when they are frightened of what they might find. Don't be frightened.' And he turned back to her from the door. 'Congratulations again my dear, on your happiness.'

Prudence rang from Housing. 'Look out your window,' she instructed. Maggie looked, and saw the sun shining.

'Ye Gods, a miracle!' *It's because I'm going to marry Timoti*, she thought.

'It's nearly lunchtime, meet you in ten minutes,' said Prudence. 'We'll buy Hope some Winning Post chocolates. It's her birthday tomorrow and she loves them. She told me that by pressing the centres from the bottom she can feel which flavour it is!'

Prudence and Maggie ran down the hill: the horrible winter was almost over, they could feel it in the light, soft air. They bought the chocolates, then ate sandwiches on the wharf, tossing crusts to the seagulls, throwing off their cardigans. In the distance a group of wharfies loaded a tanker. Prudence and Maggie sat there feeling the first sun on their faces, feeling the spring. They leaned against the wooden posts, and closed their eyes, and dreamed. *Timoti and I are going to get married. I'm going to be Mrs Timoti Pou. I will tell Prudence, I will tell her I'm engaged. Maybe she can tell me how to talk to my mother.*

'Where does your mother live, Prudence?'

'My mother's dead.'

Maggie sat up at once, embarrassed. 'Oh, Prudence how terrible, I'm sorry. How awful, you're only young. I didn't realise your mother was dead too, you poor thing. You haven't got brothers or sisters, have you?'

'No.'

This must be what Prudence had meant when she talked on the fishing trip about 'Only Adults'.

But Prudence was getting up, shaking the crumbs off her skirt. Suddenly Maggie remembered Harry Beans: *ask Prudence about her parents*, he had said in his insinuating, nasty voice.

'When did your parents die?' asked Maggie shyly.

Prudence looked at her for a moment and then she said: 'They were murdered.'

Maggie gasped.

'They were murdered on a farm down south where we lived when I was a kid. Years ago.'

'Oh, *God*. Oh, I'm so sorry Pru, I'm so sorry. I'm so sorry. Oh, how – awful.'

Prudence looked at the water, screwed up her eyes. Maggie wished the wooden wharf would swallow her up, felt her heart beating, looked away. But then Prudence, still standing there looking at the water, her green cardigan hanging from her hand and trailing on the wharf, said: 'Remember the Rabbit murders?'

Of course Maggie remembered the Rabbit murders, everyone on these islands remembered the Rabbit murders. Murder was part of their folklore. These islands with such few people, such isolated communities, were full of murders. People still said: *Remember the Bayly murders – he chopped up one of the bodies?* Or, *remember Minnie Dean who murdered little children and was the only woman to be hanged?* Or, *remember the Rabbit murders, he was a mad soldier?* And of course, just lately, *what about the Parker-Hulme murder, those schoolgirls who murdered the mother?* Remember? Of course people remembered.

At the time of the Rabbit murders Maggie had been busy doing addition and subtraction and multiplication and spelling; hadn't really understood as adults talked quietly, pointed at the fuzzy photograph in *THE FACTS!* Maggie thought the man had killed rabbits. People remembered because of the funny name: Rabbit, Mr Rabbit. He shot a married couple on a remote farm: he said at his trial they were laughing at his name. A wild-looking man, the grainy photographs in the newspapers showed: back from the war; one of the soldiers who had not recovered.

'Of course I remember,' said Maggie, and then, incredulously, 'was that your *parents*?'

Prudence nodded. Maggie was so aghast she could hardly speak. She felt she should stand, not sit on the wharf; scrambled up, felt her hands all sweaty, could not bear the idea of such horror in her familiar world. This was *Prudence*, who had *parties*.

'Were you there?' she almost whispered.

Prudence spoke in a flat voice, unemotional. 'I was nine. I got off the school bus, I had to walk about a mile from the bus stop. I found them.' She grimaced, shrugged. 'I found them on the verandah, shot. There was lots of blood running down the steps on to the grass. Our dog was dead, too. It was tied up by a back fence, it had tried to jump over, it hung itself. It was just dangling there from the barbed wire.' Prudence stood bleakly on the wharf. Maggie put her hand very awkwardly on Prudence's arm.

'I rang the telephone operator. We had a party line, so you had to pick up the phone and turn the handle.' Prudence shook herself slightly. 'It's all right. It isn't a secret or anything but I don't talk about it much, what's the point?' She wasn't looking at Maggie, but at the harbour, at the boats. She had curly, fluffy, pretty hair: she looked like a curly, fluffy, pretty girl. The two girls stood for a moment in the midday of their city, listening to the sounds of the wharves: a crane lifting, men's voices calling, ropes straining against the side of the wharves and the gentle sound of the water slapping at the wooden posts beneath them.

Then they walked slowly back to the Bureau. The spring feeling was gone. As they came up the hill to the grass where the old pohutukawa trees grew under the pavement Maggie said very carefully. 'Studying psychology, does it help with all this?'

Prudence walked for a while before she answered. 'For a long time I had that thing that soldiers get. Shell shock. They said Mr Rabbit had shell shock. Or a nervous breakdown or something. I used to shake and cry a lot. But when I was about thirteen I met a doctor who – she sort of helped me to accept it. Because I didn't have any brothers or sisters I didn't have anyone to share it with. I'd gone to live with my grandmother but she kept pretending it hadn't happened, she wouldn't let me talk about it.' She slowed on the pavement. 'Isn't it funny that people think *silence* cures things? When silence so obviously makes things much worse.'

Maggie nodded. 'Yes, I know,' she said. And they continued walking up the hill.

'But of course it's why I decided to study psychology, yes. I still see her, the doctor. It isn't over but I'm all right. Well, you know me, you know that I am. And the studying probably helps. And I met a man who understands about demons and how they come back to haunt you and sometimes overwhelm you.'

Maggie thought of Prudence smiling her sweet smile at all those parties. And of Bay Ropata, sitting with her on the verandah in the dark.

At the door of the Bureau Maggie very shyly, very stiffly, still holding the Winning Post chocolates for Hope, put both her arms round Prudence and kissed her cheek, very embarrassed. She had never kissed one of her friends in her life.

Back in the office she sat at her desk, almost motionless. *People's lives are so different from what one thinks.*

Bay Ropata burst in with a Maori couple. 'We're just going to have a bit of a rehearsal of my oratorio,' he said. 'Don't mind us.'

The woman began to sing, reading the music that Bay had given her. There was one repeated tune that Maggie could catch; the rest sounded like kind of disharmonic opera. The woman sang on and on in Maori, unaccompanied. Her voice soared around the office: strange, intense notes and Bay conducted, waving his arms about, holding a pencil.

Maggie felt anxious, uncomfortable, oppressed by a feeling of violence everywhere, of unreality, echoed somehow in the music, in the strange singing of the woman in the government office. She could not stop thinking of Prudence, her face as she told the story. *People's lives are so different from what one thinks.*

She wanted to feel safe, that life was *safe*.

She felt in her purse, held the engagement ring in her hand for a moment, felt it against her palm, then put it safely away.

All afternoon the discordant, anxious notes echoed her discordant, anxious feelings.

Perhaps that means the music's good, she suddenly thought, surprised. As if Bay were somehow tapping into the discordant feelings of his people.

He lumbered off at the end of the day, office papers sticking out of his pockets as usual.

'Bay.'

He turned at the door, hearing the tone of her voice.

'Bay, did you know about Prudence's parents?'

And Bay sighed. '*Ae. Ka mohio ahau.*' *I know.*

In the library, she leaned against Timoti, wearing her ring.

'I'm so glad we got engaged,' she whispered. 'You don't know how glad I am.'

He whispered back, 'So am I.' And their legs touched under the library table.

She wanted to tell him about this strange day; about Prudence. But he had a law test the next day and his face was strained and tired, he bent over books about conveyancing. She kissed him at the tram terminus, ran her hand down his face, smoothing it; watched from the tram, putting her engagement ring back into her purse, as he walked off carrying armfuls of books. He stopped to light a cigarette. The match flared, lighting his beautiful face.

After Maggie's tram had gone, Timoti went into one of the red phone boxes. He had a lot of shilling pieces in his hand and he telephoned the operator to put him through to his Uncle Heke in Rangimarie.

THIRTY-THREE

Warm spring winds blew across the city, blowing winter away, lifting skirts at street corners, sending people's newspapers flying into the air: unruly newsprint kites disappeared over the roof tops.

Maggie picked some of the first flowers from the garden before the morning dew had gone – freesias, hyacinths; and then, going up the street, she did something she'd never done before – stole a piece of daphne. The fragrance engulfed her on the tram. Getting out her tram ticket she looked carefully again in her purse, saw the diamond sparkling there. She knew Prudence would still be at a lecture: she went into Housing and laid the flowers on Prudence's desk. The scent of the daphne drifted, receded, as she walked down the green corridor to the Welfare Department.

Timoti phoned her to say he wouldn't be at the library.

'Where will you be?'

He sounded evasive. 'Oh, well, I've got a bit of extra work to do. Do you know it's only five weeks till exams?'

'I do. I do.'

'We'll decide about things after that.'

'Yes,' she said. *Yes*.

In the later afternoon Bay Ropata came into the office, his grey hair blown wild and no coat. He was clutching his stomach with both hands.

'I've split my wound,' he said. 'We were practising the *haka* for the Governor-General's birthday.'

Bubs gently pulled off Bay's shirt. '*E hoa*!' he said.

Maggie stared nervously. So this was the famous bayonet wound received at El Alamein when the Maori Batallion was there. No wonder he was called Bayonet. The huge join had burst and the flaps of skin hung loose right across his stomach. She thought there was every chance his innards might fall out.

'Bloody thing,' said Bay, looking down at it. 'I s'pose I'll have to get it sewn up again at the hospital. I don't like your Pakeha hospitals.'

'We've got really good hospitals,' said Maggie indignantly so that she wouldn't have to look any more. 'We were the first country in the world to have free health care for everybody, don't you forget that.'

'I don't like your Pakeha hospitals,' repeated Bay stubbornly, holding his stomach together as Bubs persuaded him downstairs to the car.

I've got an English lecture, Maggie muttered to the green walls. *Innards and statistics, what a life! You'd think somebody might remember I've got an English lecture.* When Mrs McMillan appeared in the office Maggie grabbed her bag gratefully, ran up the hill and slipped into the lecture hall at the back as the professor discoursed on Dr Samuel Johnson, telling them that this man who made the first dictionary also rolled down a grassy bank in his suit in Greenwich Park, in London, having first removed his gold watch from his waistcoat pocket. Maggie laughed to herself, picturing the fat man rolling in the grass and thinking about dictionaries. And then a surprising thought jumped into her mind. *I love all this learning about people and what they did and what they wrote and what they thought. Not everyone has an ordinary life like those girls I went to school with. Prudence's life isn't ordinary. Perhaps my life doesn't have to be ordinary. I don't want to get married if it means living in a room or going away to Rangimarie and having a baby. I want to learn more, like Timoti does.* When she caught herself she was so deeply shocked at what she was thinking that she actually blushed in her English lecture. She didn't know thoughts like that lurked at the back of her mind. She tried to push them away at once. Of course she wanted to get married and have a family, like everyone did.

After the lecture she hoisted her bag over her shoulder and trudged off to Prudence's place, *at least I can drink and sing there and don't have to think stupid thoughts.* Turning into the back streets of the city, away from the tram routes, passing the old disused motor yard, she suddenly, definitely, heard a guitar coming from the shadowy wrecks of old rusty cars. Just for a moment she stopped, listened carefully. Quite clearly then she heard a woman's voice drifting through the windows, singing,

> **Tahi nei taru kino**
> **Mahi whaiaipo;**

making love is like a dangerous vine.

The wind blew her up the hill, to Prudence's place. But on the way up, the honeysuckle in sight, she stopped, stared at the cold stars. *It is **love itself** that is like a dangerous vine,* she thought suddenly. *I need so much to be loved that I never, ever think clearly.* For a split second she recognised that she had understood something about herself. But then she shook her head in the wind as if to clear it of all thinking and ran up the hill to the house where a guitar was calling.

*

They met Timoti off the bus in the darkness. It was raining, the windscreen wipers screeched across the truck window as they drove down dark roads to the yellow hall.

His Uncle Heke had absolutely insisted: 'You owe it to your ancestors' land,' he had said. He would have to miss half a day's work in the morning. He was missing important law lectures. He was hungry.

He ran from the truck through the pouring rain into the hall; the electric lights flickered nervously the way everybody was used to. Unlit kerosene lamps hung from the rafters, in case. *How I hate this, how – primitive – it all somehow seems. And why are we even meeting about this? There's nothing to be done.*

Grace embraced him, made tea, gave him scones and chops she had brought from the house. He ate them at once, greedily.

And as he ate he counted that there were eleven people in the hall, waiting for him. He did not at first see the twelfth, that his young brother Pumpkin was sitting on the floor in a corner. He finally saw the fat shape, almost in darkness.

The old, old man, and Timoti's father, waited in front of the small group in two wooden chairs. When he saw that Timoti had finished eating, Uncle Heke indicated with his carved walking stick to Timoti, to sit in a third chair; Timoti did so, wiping his mouth and his fingers on his handkerchief.

Heke made a brief prayer in Maori and then he looked at his nephew in silence for a moment. For once he spoke in English to Timoti. 'It has started,' he said. 'The chain men have already been. The surveyors put in their pegs. They measured up the land.' And then fixing Timoti with a terrible gaze he said forcefully, 'We *need* you.'

'I can't,' said Timoti. 'I told you. I told you, I told you. I have my exams next month, I can't risk failing them.'

'They are bringing bulldozers,' said Heke Pou.

'I must pass,' said Timoti. 'This is my last year. I'm no use to anyone if I don't pass.' *I have to stay out of this. Why did I allow him to persuade me to come?*

'What's the use of exams, of all your Pakeha learning, if they can take our land?' The old man's voice was sarcastic. He resented having to speak in English to be sure his nephew understood. 'I went up on the hill while they were putting in their pegs. They didn't even notice me.' And he spat on the floor of the hall. 'I could have been a tree.'

Timoti's father intervened. 'He will give us the information. And then we must let him go. He must pass his exams, *e Heke*. Everything depends on these next few weeks. He's going to be a lawyer. They're going to make him a partner if he passes. The first Maori that huge firm has ever had.' Such pride in his father's voice. Then the two brothers spoke to each other in Maori angrily. *Arguing about me. As if I am not my own person, but belong to them.*

'Tell them,' said Heke Pou, finally. His back was straight and proud. He sat with his carved stick supporting him, his white hair shone as the lights flickered. And the rain drummed on the corrugated iron of the hall while Timoti told the small group of people what he understood to have happened to Auntie Kura's land over the hill.

'But I can't get involved,' he said again. 'My boss knows what I've found out because I told him. If he even knew I was here tonight he would change his mind about making me a partner. He's warned me off. I can't – we can't – fight the Prime Minister. It's ridiculous to even think about it.' He and his Uncle Heke sat like two opposing forces as the rain clattered on the roof.

'Do you know the story of Te Whiti?' Heke Pou's voice still held the sarcastic note.

Timoti looked impatient. 'Not really,' he said. He did not want to hear another old story.

'Te Whiti gathered his tribe. They lay down in front of the advancing army. They did not move.'

Auntie Kura sat in black, smoking her thin, hand-rolled

cigarettes. She said, in English also, a language she hardly ever spoke: 'This land cannot be theirs. It has always belonged to my family.' She coughed and then began to sing in Maori of her ancestors and of their right to the hills that ran alongside the ocean and it was just as she was singing that the lights finally went out. Auntie Kura's voice went on eerily in the darkness, the strange, atonal chanting. Timoti felt odd, uneasy; tried to push the feeling away. Timoti's mother lit two of the lanterns; the Maori faces were shadowed and flickering in the half light as they leaned forward and listened to the past.

Timoti tried to see the time on his watch. He wanted to sleep. He would be getting the early bus back to the city in the morning. How impatient all this made him feel, this is what always happened, old people *singing* while there was business to be discussed. How he wanted to do business in an orderly way (in a *Pakeha* way he realised he was thinking). But this was a lost cause – and they probably knew it.

And then, at last, he made up his mind for good.

No matter what happened he would not come again. Somehow, having made the decision finally, he felt better.

On and on the small group of Maoris spoke, discussing what Timoti had told them. Sometimes, finally, Timoti dozed. But his young brother Pumpkin, smoking incessantly in his corner of the hall, listened intently.

The expression on his face in the lamplight was unreadable.

THIRTY-FOUR

'*Distance has the same effect on the mind as on the eye,*' Dr Samuel Johnson said, '*And when we glide along the stream of time, whatever we leave behind us is always lessening, and that which we approach increasing in magnitude.*' Margaret-Rose Bennett thought about her mother, and of Prudence. *I'm not sure if that's true.* She was walking along the green corridor that led to the Welfare Department after her early-morning lecture.

'We were just waiting for you, *e hoa,*' said Bay, and she saw he had his hat on. Bubs picked up an armful of files.

She struggled in her mind to adjust Dr Samuel Johnson to Bayonet Ropata with his hat on. 'Where are we going? What about the phones?'

'Bugger the phones,' said the Assistant Head Boss, who was jiggling his car keys in the doorway. 'We want your statistics.'

He drove them to the Maori Community Centre in a very posh Bureau car, 'I bet this is the Head Boss's car,' whispered Maggie to Bubs in the back seat. 'We don't get these up at Prudence's place.' Bay hummed in the front, Bubs and Maggie held piles of files, looked at each other, made faces at the stiff, unsmiling neck of the driver. They were dropped off on the corner. As they crossed the road over the tram lines two policemen walked past.

'Hey, it's Manu!' said Bubs.

Manu grinned his wide, sunshine smile, shook hands with Bay and Bubs.

'*Kia ora, e Makareti*,' he said to Maggie.

For a split second, seeing the smile, she felt an odd, bleak feeling of loss. He and Bay spoke in Maori. Maggie understood he had a daughter now. They joked about his policeman's uniform, they were all laughing. She thought of Emily weeping in the bathroom, and what she had seen.

She turned away without saying anything and went into the old wooden building.

It looked so different in the daytime, empty and big, with dirty windows. The caretaker, expecting them, stood leaning on his big, wide broom. He walked with a limp and wore a khaki beret from the war.

'Well, we'll get some peace, here,' said Bay cheerfully, seeming not to notice at all that the jukebox was playing loudly. They settled themselves in the room beside the stage where the loudspeakers and the microphones were stored.

'What happens now?' said Maggie.

'Right,' said Bay. 'Right. Now let's see. Let's start with – let's see the list – Adoption Assistance. Now then let's see, let's see.' Maggie handed him her records book and her chart. Bay ran down her lists with his thumb.

'Mmmm-huh. Mmmmm-huh. Hmmmmm.' He stared at the ceiling, lit a cigarette, tapped a nearby pile of tangled electric plugs with his shoe in time to *my tears have washed I Love You from the blackboard of my heart*, which could be clearly heard through the wall.

'Twenty-nine!' he said finally, in triumph.

Maggie and Bubs looked at each other, Maggie wrote down on a clean sheet of paper:

ADOPTION ASSISTANCE
Cases dealt with by the Welfare Department: 29.

'Now then,' said Bay, 'Housing Mortgage Arrears. Mmmm-huh. Mmmmm-huh.'

'Tell me something about that Sinatra person whose mum named him after Frank Sinatra,' said Maggie, 'the one who brought in all that money for mortgage arrears. He turns up all over the place.'

'Ahhh,' said Bay, and he grinned. 'Sinatra. Sinatra owns the city, I told you. He's the King.'

'I know, but who *is* he? Why is he always everywhere?'

Bay shrugged. 'He's a city Maori,' he said. 'We need the city Maoris. They know their way about.' Maggie waited but Bay said no more.

'His wife –' began Bubs.

'Never mind about that,' said Bay quickly. 'Never mind about that.' He began humming his oratorio in earnest, firmly ending the conversation about Sinatra. Maggie recognised the tuney bit that the woman had sung in the office.

'Are you going to get your oratorio performed, Bay?' she asked.

'*Ae*,' said Bay. 'We'll do it in the Town Hall, we've got plenty of good singers. A Maori oratorio, that'll be something new,' and he broke into Maori operatic song.

The door opened.

'*E hoa*,' said the caretaker, 'That bugger has locked the front door!'

'*A wai*?' Bay stopped singing most reluctantly.

'Your boss, that Pakeha. He's locked the door so you can't get out. But I can't get out either, he's told me I have to stay here till you've finished your business. How long you gunna be?'

Maggie knew that her father and Bay were on the same level in the government. She tried to imagine, and failed, someone locking her father into a hall. But Bay didn't seem to be concerned. He looked at the ceiling.

'Mmmm-huh. Mmmmm-huh. Mmmmm-huh.'

After a while he said: 'Thirty-two, mmmmm-huh. We won't be long, make us a cup of tea, *e hoa,*' and Maggie wrote it down on the clean sheet of paper.

HOUSING MORTGAGE ARREARS
Cases dealt with by the Welfare Department: 32

Then Bay got into the swing of things: 'Domestic Violence, forty-eight,' he cried, 'Financial Problems, ninety-four. Truancy, nineteen, Prison Visits, fifty-two.' He began again to sing.

> Court Attendances thirty-one,
> Landlords thirty-seven,
> Visits to schools fifty-five,
> Tangis hundred and eleven!

'Go and have a dance,' he said absent-mindedly.

Maggie and Bubs looked at each other in surprise.

'Dance,' said Bay. '*Kanikani*! Dance!'

'Well, OK,' said Bubs.

The jukebox was now playing 'Blue Suede Shoes'. Maggie and Bubs shrugged in slight embarrassment, took each other's arms politely. At first they tried to dance neatly. But their quick-step got faster and faster and turned into the new rock and roll as they danced round the empty hall, *one for the money two for the show*; danced and spun to the famous voice while a partly deflated green balloon floated inconsequentally past. '*You can do anything but lay off of my blue suede shoes*' they cried, breathless and laughing and finally Maggie leaned helplessly against a wall, her uncontrollable, loud laugh echoing in the emptiness. Tears poured down her cheeks. *I'm crying with laughter* she thought *I'm **crying** with laughter and*

Bay's singing the statistics. Bubs danced about the hall by himself chasing the balloon, laughing and hiccupping and whistling in his rowing jacket.

'This is God's Own Country!' Maggie hooted, 'we're locked in a hall and we're singing about blue suede shoes in God's Own Country!'

'Listen to your *laugh*, Maggie,' Bubs said, 'you sound like a mad horse.'

'Here you fellas,' called the caretaker, limping out of the kitchen. 'I've heated up some meat pies and some pork bones left over from a wedding.'

At four-thirty-five in the afternoon the Assistant Head Boss came back and unlocked the door.

The caretaker and Bay and Bubs and Maggie were playing billiards next to the kitchen.

'She's jake, mate,' said Bay. 'Statistics all finished.'

THIRTY-FIVE

When the phone rang on Sunday Maggie heard her mother answer it.

Then she heard her mother say: *No, she is not here. Please do not telephone this house again under any circumstances. You are not welcome here. Please keep away from my daughter. She is forbidden to have anything more to do with you.* Then there was silence.

After work next day Maggie went at once to their meeting place in the library

She placed her books on the usual desk. She did not go and eat anything in case she missed him, though she knew he would come of course. Of course he would. He loved her. He must not blame her for her mother. She read again the twenty-third psalm in Maori, she almost knew it by heart but tonight the words muddled up. She changed over to her English books, read 'The Ancient Mariner.' She liked Coleridge the best because Coleridge went to lots of parties like her, and got drunk like her, and talked nonsense – like explaining to Dorothy Wordsworth the different notes of the nightingale. And most of all because the Ancient Mariner's ship sailed right past these islands and Timoti *would* come. He knew how frightened she got when he didn't come. He musn't blame Maggie. She wasn't her mother.

At half-past eight looking at her watch for the umpteenth time she found she was trying to translate 'The Ancient Mariner', *the ice was here, the ice was there, the ice was all around*, into Maori. She needed him. She needed him to love her so that the world would feel safe.

All evening he did not come, though she stayed till the tired librarian was turning out the lights.

Outside the closing doors of the university she stood trembling, her weight on one foot, her arms full of books, almost unable to move; *I cannot – I cannot – I cannot live without Timoti*. People passed, some of them glancing at her, but mostly students going home, pale with their own worries and problems. People often looked pale before exams; stood, looking mad, outside the university doors. Moonlight shone across her wild hair as the path emptied, but she did not know that as she stood there.

Timoti watched her for a long time before he came out of the dark shadows and the whispering trees beside the path. His arms too were full of books but he managed to take her arm. She gasped – 'Timoti' – as he pulled her back towards the trees.

'I am not a dog. I am a person. You parents treat me as if I were a dog.' His voice was low and harsh. 'Where do you think my dignity is? How do you think I hold on to it?'

'I know, I know, I am so sorry.' She threw her arms around his neck, her bag of books banging them both. 'I love you Timoti, I love you. It doesn't matter about them.'

Somewhere there, in among the branches and the shadows and the darkness he pulled her to the ground. Their books fell, Maori books and law books and books of English poetry, but the ground was soft and there was no noise, only their breathing, they had not spoken again. One of Maggie's shoes came off, he pulled at her skirt and her pants, undid his trousers, pushed himself on top of her, inside her. Her suspender belt dug into her hip. He thrust into her body over and over again.

'Are you going to marry me, are you going to marry me?'

'Yes,' she cried desperately, 'I am going to marry you. I am quite sure now. I cannot live without you.'

'As soon as exams are finished?'

'Yes.'

'We'll get a room somewhere, till you have a baby.'

'Yes.' She saw the notice: NO CHILDREN MAORIS OR DOGS.

'I love you, Maggie,' he said as he fell still at last against her, 'I love you Maggie, I love you Maggie,' and the words pierced her heart and tears poured down her cheeks so that she, too, had a climax, of a kind. *He loved her. Somebody really, really loved her.*

'I love you too, Timoti,' she said, and she stroked his dark hair, 'I cannot live without you,' and he held her very tightly for a moment, there on the ground.

'I'd better go home,' she said, after a while. They sat up, pulled on their clothes, smoothed their hair. As they stood up, as Maggie hopped in the darkness putting on her shoe, Timoti took some twigs out of her hair. Then out of his pocket he brought a long, green stone pendant.

'This belonged to my grandmother. But you don't have to have it if you don't want it, my mother gave it to me for you. I've told her we are engaged.' Although it was dark she could feel its long, cool smoothness. She held it in her hand.

'Thank you,' she said. And thought of Grace: motherly, motherly Grace.

They walked down to the tram stop. The library had closed at 9.00 PM. She looked up at the town hall clock. It was 9.55. She caught the 10 PM tram, waving to the still, stoic man at the tram stop who watched her go.

But even though she was late she didn't go home. She

passed their house and all the houses and walked on down the street that eventually just stopped, at the sea.

The tide was out. Along the damp sand she walked in the darkness, her hair tangling in the wind, blowing across her face, her bag of books banging against her legs as she walked. She didn't hear the sea, yet it was quite loud as the wind caught at the waves and broke over the rocks that at low tide were not hidden by the water, the rocks that shone there in the moonlight. Sometimes she stumbled on some driftwood. There was a car parked right at the far end of the beach, where she and Manu used to park, by the cutty grass and the sand-hills, underneath the cliffs. Manu. Manu. He was different.

Timoti holds me in desperation. And that's how I hold him. We hold each other as if we are desperate. What's wrong with me? I should be happy now. **E kore ahau e hapa.** I shall not want I shall not want it is an Ancient Mariner and he stoppeth one of three. *Did I get pregnant tonight? Emily got pregnant and it spoiled her life.* It is an Ancient Mariner he stoppeth one of three I shall not want. *I do want, I want to go on learning and studying but I want someone to look after me. I don't know what I want.* It is an Ancient Mariner it is an Ancient Mariner I shall not want. *What does love mean? What does love mean? Does it mean loving someone else or does it mean what you want for yourself? Other girls get married. Everyone gets engaged when they're eighteen. Emily said love isn't just a word. I don't want to go to Rangimarie and have a baby but I love Timoti, I do love him. I* **need** *him. I need him to love me.*

On the beach in the darkness, the moon covered by cloud now, her hands and arms began suddenly to tingle and she felt a sharp pain in her chest. And the knot of cold knowledge forced its way up again to the surface from the depths where she never dared look. *I need to be loved so much that I never, ever think clearly.*

'I want someone to *talk* to,' she cried aloud.

She turned jerkily, as if she'd suddenly heard her own voice; her head spun and she was at once frightened, felt herself suddenly panicking, dizzy in the darkness. Ran the wrong way, ran into the sea, stumbled, gasped, felt the cold cold water in her shoes and catching at her skirt. Ran, her bag still banging hard against her legs, back along the beach past the driftwood. *What's wrong with me?* Back, gulping at the air, along the empty street, catching despite herself, the heavy fragrance from the daphne bush, to the house of her parents. *Cry me a river* said the song. At the gate she stood shaking, trying to open the catch by the letterbox where Elizabeth had stood, stumbled down the path past the cinerarias. The house was in darkness but as she opened the back door her mother called, 'Is that you, Margaret-Rose?'

She could hardly breathe, standing in the dark kitchen. The light suddenly went on. The kitchen looked jerky, pointed, her feet and her skirt were wet.

Her mother was standing in her dressing-gown in the doorway to the hall, her hand still on the light-switch, staring at her. At once Maggie felt invaded, her body felt invaded by the way her mother looked at her.

'Where have you . . .' The voice sounded very far away and Margaret-Rose Bennett saw her mother step towards her. She saw her own hand rise slowly, to shield herself, but her mother did not hit her.

'What's the matter with you?' And she suddenly called back down the hall, 'Richard!'

Her daughter did not make it to the kitchen sink before she vomited. Hanging from her hand as she slid to the floor, her mother saw, was a piece of ugly Maori green stone attached to a long dirty chain.

They put her to bed in her thin, safe bed with the pink candlewick bedspread neatly arranged; her heart stopped beating so wildly, her hands stopped tingling. Her father had already unscrewed his hand when he'd gone to bed, was awkward as he brought first her books in with his good hand, and then a cup of tea.

'Are you pregnant?' said her mother. The shocking word hung in the room.

'What's that pendant?' said her father, deeply embarrassed.

'Oh – someone gave it to me to take to the office.' She looked straight at her mother. 'I'm not pregnant. I don't want to be pregnant. That's not what happened. I forgot to eat. I got all the poems and the twenty-third psalm all muddled in my head.'

They both looked puzzled. 'The twenty-third psalm?'

'Oh. Oh, yes it's for – the French, we translate it into French, I've got all the French and the Ancient Mariner and Dr Johnson mixed up in my head. I walked on the beach to try and get better and I – I saw a car and it got – muddled.'

'It's too much. You're doing too much. It's all this Maori rubbish.' Maggie looked at her father but saw he meant the office, or Timoti, or the green stone pendant sitting on the bedside table looking so out of place, not the language. 'It's damaging you, you need to pull yourself together or you won't pass your English and French exams.' They wanted her to pass. It was important to them that she passed.

But her mother stood by the window still, looking at her, looking her *over* it felt. Maggie felt quite clearly again the invasion of her mother, in her body.

When they finally left her in the darkness she listened desperately for the sea, the shussssssshing and sighing of the sea, she breathed in time to the sound, calming her heart until at last, exhausted, she slept.

At dawn she woke with a start, trying to remember something, grasping at something as it slipped away, something about Elizabeth and the sea. It was something red, she tried hard to hold on to it in her mind. She had seen Elizabeth again. She knew she had seen her again.

And then as she lay there, quite clearly in her mind as the first birds tried the first notes and the light began to filter behind the blind at her bedroom window, she saw Prudence asleep with Bay Ropata in the house under the hill where the honeysuckle grew. The greenstone pendant stared at her malevolently, as if it could read her thoughts.

'I think I'm going mad! I'm seeing things, things are coming into my head all by themselves without me putting them there!' cried Margaret-Rose Bennett, aloud in her bedroom, and she shook her head over and over, tried to shake the thoughts out of her mind. She covered her face with her hands in despair.

'Mum!' she called again and again.

Her father phoned the Bureau and said she had the flu.

THIRTY-SIX

They assembled at dawn, just as the first light touched the broken roof of the old meeting house.

Heke Pou had impressed on everyone that they must arrive before it was light. They had arrived from neighbouring settlements in trucks, in old cars. One old man came on a rusty motor bike with his sheepdog running along beside him: he told them the bulldozer transporter had arrived the evening before at the crossroads. The drivers had been drinking in the small hotel (which only closed when the policeman rang to tell them he was coming), talking of the road they were to make at Rangimarie.

In the hall they had cups of tea and thick pork sandwiches made by Timoti's mother, Grace. Heke Pou, white-haired and upright, standing for hours, welcomed the people as they came trickling in, explained what they were going to do over and over again. Women brought children asleep in sacks and shawls; people settled on the floor of the hall to drink their tea, gossiped among themselves; some dozed off briefly. Pumpkin had brought his mother and the sandwiches in the truck; he too stood, waiting behind his uncle, watching everything carefully. He and his uncle had been on the hill last night until it was too dark to see any more, cutting the chains with butcher's tools, burying the surveyors' pegs under manuka and ferns. Now his uncle had ordered him to make sure all the cars and trucks were at the back of the hall, not the front.

Finally, as he saw that the light was coming, Heke counted the people. Not counting the children there were thirty-one.

And in his own language he sighed his thoughts to himself. *Aieeeaieee*. Thirty-one people to defend their land and most of them women, or old men like himself. The young men were in the city, or at least at the freezing works. Te Whiti had had many hundreds, so the story was told. Heke Pou sighed again. He looked at Grace and Moana, talking to people, making sure they had eaten something. Their son Timoti should be here, taking his place. How deeply he disapproved of the way they had 'Pakeha-fied' him. Then he raised his hand for silence and in his own language asked the god that the missionaries had brought to his land, to watch over their actions and guard them from harm. And then he walked out into the first light and an old woman's voice called eerily into the dawn to her ancestors who had, for so long, called this place their home.

> *E nga wairua o nga tipuna*
> *arahina matou, tiakina matou*

*

The sound of the two bulldozers could be heard first, and then they arrived, rolling in to Rangimarie, clanking noisily and slowly past the church and the empty hall just before 7 AM. Both the drivers, one Pakeha, one Maori, were smoking, flicked their butts lazily into the grass at the side of the dusty road. The little chimneys at the front of the huge yellow machines belched out black smoke into the spring morning. A truck followed the bulldozers, the driver consulting a piece of paper every now and then. They knew there was no road round to the sea, that would be part of their job. First they would negotiate a path round the side of the hills, leaving the truck by the houses. They were to start bulldozing a road down to the sea.

Usually children heralded their arrival, excited little Maori children who'd never seen a bulldozer before, totally in awe of the huge, loud machines, staring in amazement with their big eyes, then running alongside, barefoot, laughing, waving at the drivers. The first bulldozer driver, a Pakeha, stopped his vast vehicle, leaving the motor idling, where the dusty road ended outside the little cluster of houses.

'Funny, eh, Hori, no one here?' he called back to the Maori driver on the second bulldozer.

The boss parked the truck, kicked at its tyres and then climbed up on to the first bulldozer. 'Come on,' he said, 'the sea's round the hill according to this.' He waved some instructions on a piece of yellow paper. 'We'll get round to the sea and then we'll have a smoko. They're probably all at the social security, or the pub.'

The two bulldozers started off across the land with lowered blades, slowly but inexorably cutting at pohutukawa roots, laying down swathes of tall grass and fern and manuka as they rumbled and clanked along, raising pollen and dust and seeds and leaves and causing small birds to fly suddenly upwards, startled. The sun had begun to rise in the sky now but hadn't yet caught the houses: dark windows stood like empty eyes, watching.

Just around the side of the hill, just where they caught a glimpse of the beautiful long coastline and the sea and the trees, a small group sat on the land in front of them.

At first the two men in the front vehicle didn't understand what they were seeing, because there was no noise and no movement and what they saw looked so peculiar. The front huge vehicle clanked noisily to a stop again.

Some people were wearing old coats and hats and blankets. A wizened old man sat with a sack around his shoulders and his dog sat alert, ears pricked up, beside him. The barefoot children who usually ran along the side of the huge exciting vehicles crying *gizza ride mister* sat silent, staring upwards with big dark eyes. The two men on the front bulldozer gave each other uneasy looks: *old sheilas with tattoos on their chins, young sheilas, kids, what's all this?* The second bulldozer rounded the bend. The Maori driver couldn't see at first why they had stopped but the group had seen him, had seen that one of the drivers was a Maori and a high-pitched sound filled the air. **Nau mai, haere mai**, called the voice: **nau mai ki to tatau marae o Rangimarie**. And in the voice was a cry, a sound, that sent a shiver up his spine. He didn't know what they were saying, he was a Maori from the city, but somehow he knew at once what was happening.

The boss had had time to pull himself together. It all looked so stupid, all sitting on the ground, women and kids mostly, it must be some ritual. He spoke quite kindly above the ticking over of the motor, no point in causing any ruckus.

'Youse folks are in our way,' he called. 'Move outa the way please, having a prayer meeting or some mumbo-jumbo like that, are ya?' And he laughed and looked back at his mate who laughed too.

A fat young man, one of the few young men, stood up. 'Go away, you bloody buggers,' he shouted. 'Go away from our land.'

And then the drivers saw that an old white-haired man suddenly seemed to rise up out of the little group; tall, white-haired, old enough to be the drivers' father or even grandfather, but tall, taller than any of them. He nodded at Pumpkin to silence him, stood there in the middle of the group leaning on, but not bending over, a carved stick. Nobody spoke. A baby cried suddenly, was hushed, the sea shushed below them and the bulldozers' engines idled and coughed. Then from the shore two seagulls suddenly dived over the little crowd and one of them bombed the boss who felt, rather than saw, a blob of something land on the top of his head.

The group of Maoris burst out laughing. Little children who had been awed into silence opened their mouths and laughed and pointed at the boss's head; old ladies cackled, it seemed to the drivers, the few young men laughed, *sitting there on the land*, the boss recounted later to his superiors, *sitting on their bums and laughing*. And the old man standing in their midst smiled and said something in a language none of the drivers understood.

The boss was furious. 'Shut up!' he shouted. 'Shut up!' He took a handkerchief out of the pocket of his dungarees and wiped at his head. 'Get off this land, it doesn't belong to you. I've got instructions to bulldoze a road through and that's what I'm gunna do,' and he waved the yellow piece of paper. 'I'll run youse over if you don't move.'

The group of Maoris stopped laughing as suddenly as they had started. Again the tall old man seemed to separate from the others, seemed to rise up out of them as if they were lifting him.

'We will not move,' he called politely. 'This is our land. It has been taken from us illegally. Perhaps you don't realise that so we do not blame you. There are thirty-one of us here for you to run over, and the children,' and it seemed to the three drivers, a sound like a sigh seemed to echo through the small crowd, in agreement, or perhaps it was the sea.

The boss looked nonplussed, then suddenly turned round to the Maori driver. 'Hey, Hori, come and talk some sense into your relations, can't you?'

'I don't know them,' muttered the Maori driver, staring fixedly at the sea.

'Well you're all horis, aren't ya, for God's sake, talk to them, tell them to move!' Hori climbed down from his bulldozer, walked forward reluctantly, looked away from the old man, unwilling to catch the eye of an old person like him, to show him any disrespect. He looked back at the boss. 'Perhaps there's a mistake,' he mumbled.

'Don't be so bloody stupid!' shouted the boss, 'look, it's all here, all the instructions, tell them, GET THEM OUT OF THE WAY!'

But Hori, between his boss and his people, literally could not move; stood awkwardly, head down, breathing unhappily. Someone from the little crowd called to him a Maori, a few small laughs, but he shrugged, still looked away towards the sea. A small boy suddenly ran forward, unable to contain himself, touched the huge treads of the bulldozer that towered over him. The group watched him carefully but no one called him back, and he stood there, looking up in awe at the boss.

'Jesus,' said the boss, and he roughly pulled at the gears of the bulldozer which bucked as it roared into life. The small boy was hastily pulled back, the crowd braced itself.

'Back off, Hori, you hopeless bugger,' the boss called angrily. Hori got back onto the second bulldozer. Very slowly and carefully, he backed it along the track so that it disappeared from sight.

As he prepared to do the same, motioning the other man out of the driver's seat, the boss shouted at Heke Pou: 'We'll be back tomorrow, mate, with the police. You'll be locked up, you're all barmy!' And then he leaned across, pulled roughly at the gears and backed clumsily round the track and out of sight. The sound of the bulldozer's engine and the clanking of the treads very slowly faded into the distance.

It was five past nine on a beautiful spring morning.

THIRTY-SEVEN

It was five past nine on a beautiful spring morning.

Maggie did not run down the hill after her lecture, but walked, pale and concentrated where she used to dance and giggle with Emily. How long ago that seemed. No one had heard from Emily.

They had had, at last, a lecture on indigenous writing.

The lecturer was a young man they hadn't had before. He wore a gown but it didn't fit him, kept falling off as he waved his arms, then he'd hitch it up again automatically. He talked very fast as if he knew time was precious.

'We have our own writers,' he had said. 'We must support them and honour them. They are our future, the rest is our past. The further you take your English studies at this university, the further, I promise you, we will look into our own literary history. We are on the march, looking at ourselves at last.' The poets in the class cheered. When the lecturer got to Katherine Mansfield he said: 'She wrote in a new way. She influenced, and was influenced by, writers in England like Virginia Woolf, who became more famous, because Katherine Mansfield died so young. But this country was imprinted on her mind. Never, never forget, she took her country with her, when she left it.'

Maggie walked slowly down the hill thinking of Grace's

word: **turangawaewae**. *The place you carry around with you, in your heart.*

The empty Welfare office stared at her: she sighed as she saw the papers piled high on her desk. Then she heard humming coming from one of the interview rooms: Bay was at his oratorio. There were dirty cups everywhere, and a milk bottle with old milk in it. The phone rang.

'Welfare Department,' she said.

'I've been worried about you. You've been away from work. I didn't want to ring your home. Are you all right?' It was Timoti. 'I've been worried about you,' he said again.

'Oh, Timoti.' *O Timoti.*

'Have you been ill?' Roimata would be listening, of course.

'Just a few days. The flu. I'm fine now.'

'Are you better? Will you be at Isobel's tonight?'

'Yes.'

'You must look after yourself. After this week it's only two weeks till exams.'

'Thank goodness lectures finish this week and we can just study.'

'Thank goodness,' said Timoti. There was a kind of silence between them. Neither mentioned what had happened in the trees in the darkness. But as if he was reading her thoughts Timoti said: 'We'll work everything out when exams are over.' She had a sudden, weird feeling that Time – which had seemed to stop when they'd clung together that night in his room – now raced on, unstoppable: the moment she had finished her last exam the Future would start. 'See you tonight, darling,' he said, and hung up.

Darling. He cared about her. He was looking after her. He loved her.

Bay had heard the phone and her voice, came ambling into the office.

'You better, *e hoa*?'

'Yes, thank you, Bay. Just the flu, I think.'

Bay looked at her shrewdly the way he sometimes did. And then he moved across to his desk which looked unusually tidy. 'Our Annual Report's gone in,' he said. 'I signed it yesterday. They were very –' and he paused to find a good Pakeha word, 'affable.' And then he looked across at Maggie again, his eyes twinkling. 'We should get a medal,' he said. 'We beat the buggers.' Maggie began to laugh and Bay laughed too, their laughter egged each other on and when Bubs and Errol Flynn walked in the door they heard the loud neighing of a horse that was Maggie's way of laughing and the deep chuckles of their boss echoing around the office.

'You might at least make us some tea,' said Errol Flynn in a wounded kind of voice, as if he believed they were laughing at him.

'Well, you go down to the dairy and get us a pint of milk,' said Bay. 'Our girl has to conserve her strength for her exams,' and Errol Flynn, furious, could do nothing but obey (for, of course, they always always obeyed him) and Maggie walked off to the ladies' with the dirty cups and the sour milk, her loud laughter dying down at last. *I'd nearly forgotten how to laugh*, she thought as she poured the milk down the toilet. *I musn't forget that.* And then: *Bay was making me laugh on purpose.*

In the mirror a pale, anxious face stared out at her, with wild hair.

When she came back into the office with the clean cups Bay was talking over the counter in Maori to Sinatra, the King of the City in the black singlet. Sinatra acknowledged her with a wave, but they went on talking. The two grey heads were close together, but this time Maggie noticed how young Sinatra's face was under his grey hair. *He's a young man* she thought, *he's not old at all*. She was struck by the oddness of the couple and yet their closeness: Bay in his respectable shirt and tie that always looked as if it was strangling him, Sinatra in his black singlet, with a black wharfies' duffle coat over his arm. They looked as if they were plotting but she tuned into their language and realised they were trying to find a young boy who had disappeared. She dried the cups, opened another packet of sugar, turned to offer Sinatra a cup of tea. But he had gone.

'You know, I do like that Sinatra,' she said to Bubs later. 'I like him because he's always somewhere there, always helping someone. I sometimes feel like giving him a big hug,' and she smiled to herself sheepishly at such an unlikely event. 'No wonder they call him the King of the City.'

Bubs paused beside her desk. 'They say he knows everything that goes on,' he said, 'because he's always walking through the streets, just saying hello to people, listening to people. And of course, lots of people know what happened to him.'

Maggie looked at him sharply. 'What do you mean?'

Bubs gave a small sigh. 'He used to live in a nice house, had a car and a lovely family. But . . .' Bubs paused, fiddled with some files on Maggie's desk, embarrassed. 'You know how sometimes women go funny when they've had a baby?'

Maggie looked puzzled. 'No. What do you mean?'

'Sometimes,' said Bubs, 'I think it affects their heads. My auntie used to say it could. It's not their fault, my auntie said. Anyway, Sinatra's wife went mad after she had a baby. She stabbed the baby and their little boy to death. And then she killed herself. Sinatra came home and found them.'

Maggie stared at him aghast. More violence. *She could not bear it: she did not want to hear.*

But Bubs continued. 'Sinatra disappeared for a while. No one knew anything about him. When he came back he'd sold his house and his car – everything. They said he came back with a little suitcase and two curtains. Just lives in a room somewhere and wanders round the city. That's why they call him the King.'

'Two *curtains*?'

'That's what they say. Curtains with cars on.'

Maggie began to wonder if she was still ill. 'What do you *mean*, curtains with cars on?'

'You know, Mercedes Benzes and Austin Princess cars and that.' Bubs was now picking up a big pile of files. 'I expect they were his son's curtains and he kept them, to remember him, he was only four.' And Bubs was gone. But Maggie sat at her desk, another picture imprinted on her mind as clearly as if she had been there: at the railway station a fat, grey-haired Maori man in a black singlet with a young, blank face stood by himself with a small suitcase, and under his arm the curtains with the cars.

She shook her head again and again, trying to empty things out of it; tried to bury herself in 'Beowulf'.

At about three o'clock Bay sent Maggie out of the office. **'Haere atu,'** he said, *go away*. 'You look terrible. Go out into this beautiful afternoon and say a prayer to God and thank him for it. Sit in the sun, go home, have a sleep, get drunk, stop worrying about passing the exams, anything.' And he did something unusual: leant across her desk, pressed her nose twice with his, formally.

'**Kia kaha e hoa**,' he said, *be strong*.

Tears formed immediately in Maggie's eyes. She took her books hurriedly and left.

She passed Paddy from Housing at the front door, his arms full of files.

'Bay's told me to go away for the rest of the afternoon,' she explained, shrugging. 'Exams. And I never see you, Paddy,' she added wistfully, 'now that Prudence is having no more parties till exams are over.'

'Exams have got a lot to answer for,' said Paddy. 'How's it going? The studying?'

'I think I took on more than I could chew,' said Maggie. 'I mean, bit off.'

Paddy stood there, in the doorway. The spring sunshine just touched his reddish-brown wig. Then he said. 'Don't get caught. Don't get caught in all this like Emily did.'

Maggie stood, shocked, as if Paddy had hit her.

But Paddy had gone.

There was no one sitting on the green by the Bureau to see the first sign of the red flowers on the pohutukawa tree. Down the hill Fords and Austins sat parked in the sunshine. She walked into the main street, trams clanging along, past her father's government department. She stared up. She knew which window was his, a hundred times she'd gone up in the clanking lift with the concertina doors to the top floor where he sat in his office, easily holding, between metal prongs, papers and files about government imports.

In a side street some sort of demolition team was very casually knocking down buildings. Most of the men were leaning against a fence and smoking. A steel ball attached to a crane nudged against an old wooden building which gently and almost silently disintegrated almost to dust in front of her eyes. Just like that. She walked on, right down to the harbour, on to the far wharves, sat on an old tyre. In her bag she had 'Beowulf', Coleridge's 'Collected Poems', *Nga Moteatea* and Boswell's 'The Life of Samuel Johnson'. She felt she had begun to be unable to differentiate between them. She opened one book.

> *Taku aroha ki taku whenua*
> *He ahiahi kauruku*
> *He waka ia ra . . .*

*my love alas for my own land as the evening shadows come, if only
there was a canoe*, Isobel's poem, and Isobel's pale, made-up
face swam into her mind. *What was wrong with Isobel?*

She closed that book hurriedly, opened the book about Dr
Johnson, began to read:

> Dr Johnson was visiting Bath and a gentleman
> expressed a wish to go and live in —

Maggie blinked and looked again:

> — live in Polynesia in order to obtain a full acquain-
> tance with people so totally different from all we have
> ever known and be satisfied what pure nature can do for
> man. Dr Johnson said: 'What could you learn, Sir? What
> can savages tell, but what they themselves have seen?
> Of the past, or the invisible, they can tell nothing.'

She re-read, disbelieving:

> Of the past, or the invisible, they can tell nothing.

'Dr Johnson had no idea,' she said aloud.

A shadow fell across the book.

'Excuse me, are you Elizabeth Bennett?' It was an American
accent.

Maggie raised her head very, very slowly and she had to
shade her eyes from the setting sun to look up at the woman
standing there.

'You are – are you?' The young woman looked uncertain.

After a long pause, staring at the woman who she had
never seen before, feeling that tingling in her arms, Maggie
slowly shook her head. 'I'm Maggie Bennett,' she said.

'Oh, but you're the little sister, the baby then, are you? Margaret-Rose after the second princess, that's right. It's just that – isn't it weird, after all these years I'd know that hair anywhere. Elizabeth had such lovely wild, curly hair and of course you must look alike. I'm Beryl Taplin, well I *was* Beryl Taplin, I'm married now of course, I used to live on your street when I was a kid and play every day with Elizabeth but my parents went to America. How is Elizabeth, I suppose she's married too, is she? Oh, my, I'd love to see her again, I've been thinking about her these last few weeks since I've come back. We were just too little to write letters, to keep in touch but I've never forgotten her, she was my first friend, you know? I sort of keep thinking she is my *past*, I know it's silly, how is she? How can I get in touch with her? What luck I bumped into you. What has she done with her life?'

'Elizabeth's dead.'

'*Dead?*'

'She died when she was seven.' Maggie squinted up at the woman haloed in the sun.

'*Seven?*' The woman suddenly looked as if she'd seen a ghost. 'Oh, oh, excuse me – oh, I'm so sorry. Oh, oh what a terrible – it was the hair.'

'Do I look like her, even now?' said Maggie surprised.

'Oh, *yes*,' said the woman. She stood uneasily for a moment and then rather reluctantly she squatted down, uncomfortable in her tight green frock and her stiletto shoes, looking at Maggie. 'I saw you from the corner of the wharf there as I was walking past. I haven't been back long and I was sure you were Elizabeth, grown up.' She paused and then said uncertainly, 'She must've died the summer we left. How did she die, I mean so – suddenly and – well, so young?'

'She fell,' said Maggie. And repeated it lamely. 'She fell, at the beach.'

'Oh, I am so sorry,' and she still stared at Maggie for a minute uncertainly, then stood up again, wanting to go.

'Wait,' said Maggie and she scrambled up herself. 'Can you remember her? What was she like?'

But the American woman had become anxious, this talk of death. She stared towards the end of the wharf as if longing to be there, but then she looked back at Maggie, saw her oddly desperate face. Finally she repeated: 'I've only been back a few weeks and I guess I was, you know, thinking of my childhood here. And mostly I remembered Elizabeth. She had that hair, just like yours. There was an old photograph of your granny wasn't there? With the same hair.'

'*Yes*,' said Maggie.

A sailor walking past saw two young women facing each other on the wharf. 'And, well, I guess we just played together a lot. And your mum used to play with us. She was so pretty, your mum and laughing, wasn't she, and you were in a little pushchair. Oh, and sometimes all your cousins came from the South Island, that boy and all his sisters. Your dad was at the war, wasn't he?' She paused and shook her head a little as if trying to loosen the old memories. 'What I remember most is being on the beach, every day it seemed, that summer before we went away. She had a red bathing suit, Elizabeth, and she was,' – and the woman smiled in spite of her anxious tone – 'She was a bossy little kid wasn't she, but she was – Oh, I did love her, we all loved her didn't we, we were always running after her, remember those long skinny legs she had, and playing hopscotch?'

Margaret-Rose Bennett stared silently at the woman in the green dress. Who gave another half smile and then made a little embarrassed gesture with her hand, a piece of her past gone with the death of Elizabeth Bennett. Finally, shrugging, she said: 'Well, I – I must go, I am so sorry, really.' She looked at Margaret-Rose once more, puzzled still in some way, and then she walked back along the wharf. As she got further away the green dress seemed to shimmer in the last sunshine.

Maggie sat on the wharf for a long time, 'The Life of Samuel Johnson' lying there on the wooden boards. That was the most anyone had talked to her about her sister in her life.

A policeman looked at her several times but she didn't look like one of the boat girls so he walked on. As it began to get dark, lights came on in some of the boats and a guitar strummed somewhere and then ropes creaked as the tide gently changed and the boats moved slightly. Further out in the harbour islands shone darkly.

The policeman came back, stood stolidly in front of Maggie.

'What's your name?' he said.

Maggie was so startled she scrambled up, blushing.

'Nice girls don't sit by themselves on the wharves,' said the policeman.

'Sorry, sorry,' said Maggie, 'I was just thinking, sorry,' and she gathered up her books apologetically, as if she was guilty. When she looked up at the fire station clock she felt more guilty, she would be late at Isobel's house.

When she got there, hurrying in, apologising, catching Timoti's eye, Isobel was talking to them about their oral Maori exam in two weeks' time, telling them they would have fifteen minutes Maori conversation each, separately, with an outside examiner.

'I *can't*,' said Maggie, and felt that tingling beginning again in her arms.

'Of course you can,' Isobel said briskly.

'Will they ask us to say poems and explain proverbs and talk about canoes and tribes?'

'No, no, that sort of thing will be in your written papers, this is just conversational Maori, nothing archaic, just like we're talking now.'

'I won't be able to understand, I won't be able to answer, oh I'm so tired,' said Maggie and she saw that Isobel and Timoti and Kara were all laughing at her.

'He aha to koutou mate?' she said angrily, *'What's wrong with you all?'* Tears came into her eyes quite unexpectedly and she blinked them away at once.

Isobel leaned across to her chair, patted her arm.

'It's just that you're having this whole conversation saying you can't do it, in Maori,' she said, in English.

And then Kara Rikihana stood up in Isobel's front room, because this was the last class in the house where the wallpaper was peeling, and began to speak in Maori.

He said to Isobel: 'You have given us your time and your knowledge and your love and we will use your knowledge and try to make you proud of us. And one day we will pass on everything we have learned from you, to other people who want to learn.'

'You *must*!' said Isobel, and all three of her students caught the urgency in her voice. From the kitchen they could hear the voice and laughter of Tom Arapeta, doing the dishes with his daughters.

Maggie knew now that a speech should be followed by a song. She looked at Timoti who nodded and they stood up beside Kara. They sang:

> *E kui ma, e koro ma*
> *Kaua e riri mai*

old people, don't be angry with us you used to do this too, the song Timoti's parents had sung down the road.

And Isobel Arapeta, who had been born in Scotland forty-four years ago, listened to her pupils with an unfathomable expression on her pale, pale, carefully made-up face and looked out over the dark harbour of the city.

Down the hill spring winds danced and an old bougainvillaea tree flowered early against one of the verandahed houses and the fire station clock struck 9.30 as Maggie kissed her boyfriend in the darkness and then got on the tram.

Her parents were still up tonight, sitting in the lounge on the chintz-covered couch, listening to the wireless. The embroidery needle went in and out.

'How did you feel today, back at work. All right?' asked her father.

'I'm fine,' said Maggie. 'I met a woman today who thought I was Elizabeth.'

She was shocked by the look on both their faces. Her mother dropped her embroidery on the carpet and did not pick it up, stared at her daughter. Her father reached to the wireless, turned down the volume with his hook, looked back at her.

'What do you mean?' he said.

Maggie explained.

Her mother stood up suddenly and Maggie backed away.

'You don't look anything like – Elizabeth,' said Mrs Bennett and she seemed to say the name with great difficulty. 'Nothing like her at all. She was always a stupid girl, Beryl Taplin, I remember her always following – Elizabeth – around, wanting to play, how would she know anything after all these years? How would you? Both of you following her down to the beach day after day, *oh God*,' and as if the past had come up and punched her Mrs Bennett went quickly into her bedroom and shut the door. Maggie saw her father's shoulders sag.

Mrs Bennett could not, even when she came out of the place they called the loony bin, get Elizabeth's face out of her head: it sat there, blocking every other view. She had loved her bold, adventurous first-born daughter so much, she took comfort from her when her husband marched away to war, when she had to have another baby, alone in

the city. In a strange way, in the way lonely wives sometimes do, she
leaned on a child. When the child died, that day in the sunshine, Mrs
Bennett went away to the loony bin.

'Your mother has left you some soup on the stove,' Mr
Bennett said and without looking at her this time he reached
across with his hook and turned up the volume on the wireless, picking up his wife's embroidery with his good hand.

Maggie dreamed she stood beside the sea. Just at the moment
she woke she clearly heard, for several seconds, a child's clear
voice, humming.

She *knew* it was Elizabeth.

Elizabeth was coming nearer.

THIRTY-EIGHT

On the second beautiful morning they sent two policemen with the bulldozers. The elder was the one who always phoned the hotel if he was coming past and it was after six o'clock, so they'd have time to close the bar before he arrived. But the younger one had been sent up all the way from the city. Someone in the city wanted this sorted out and quickly.

The police car arrived first at the turnoff to Rangimarie, bumped down the dusty road.

'I'll talk to them,' said the older man comfortably. 'I know them, they'll listen to me all right, don't you worry about that.' He walked up to the door of the house of Moana and Grace Pou. They were good old folk, gave him plenty of respect, wouldn't cause any trouble although that fat son of theirs was a problem, put him in the army and put him on a diet, that'd sharpen him up. 'They'll give us a cup of tea,' he said over his shoulder. At the same time as giving a brisk little knock on the door he opened it and walked in. 'It's only me, it's Jack,' he called. The house was very tidy, patchwork woollen blankets lay neatly over the chairs. But the fire was out in the stove and the house was quite empty.

He soon saw that all the houses were empty. The roar and the clank of the bulldozers could now be heard loudly and soon the huge yellow vehicles lumbered into view.

'Listen,' said the younger policeman. 'They'll be all round the hill again, like they were yesterday. We'll go round on the bulldozers. They'll soon move.'

'I think I should talk to them first, I know them, I'll be able to sort it out.'

'Can't talk to them if they're not here, can you now,' and the younger policeman had already turned back to the road, signalling to the bulldozers and the boss in the truck.

The boss and the young policeman were on the front bull-dozer with its driver, the local policeman was on the second one with the Maori driver as they rumbled and clanked along the track they'd made the previous day.

The group of Maoris sat where they'd sat yesterday. Perhaps they hadn't moved.

The bulldozers came to a halt just as they had yesterday. But the young policeman from the city jumped down at once. He looked at the little group and almost laughed. Old people and children mostly. A few fat Maoris. They should have gone ahead yesterday, what a waste of time. Still, someone in the city wanted it done properly. He brought a piece of paper from his jacket pocket. He raised his voice slightly above the idling motors.

'I have here,' he called, 'a legal document telling you all to move. This land has been quite legally bought and paid for and you are breaking the law by sitting here. Now off you go all of you, and let the drivers get on with their work and we'll say no more about it.'

A fantail darted past in the sunshine, darted back again and then disappeared up into one of the tall trees.

'Off you go,' repeated the policeman slightly more sharply and he clapped his hands, as if they were children and he was their teacher. 'Off you go.'

He was surprised to see a very old man, very tall, rise up from the crowd.

'Young man,' said Heke Pou politely, 'we told them yesterday. This land has been taken from us illegally and we will not let it go from us. It is our ancestral land, our people have lived here for generations.'

'I don't give a hen's arse how many generations have lived on it, GET OUT OF THE WAY!'

The older policeman had climbed down from the second bulldozer, came round to stand beside his colleague. He was appalled at the younger man's rudeness.

'*Kia ora*, Heke,' he called, greeting the old man politely in his own language. '*Kia ora*, Grace, *kia ora*, Moana. There seems to be some misunderstanding here. Why don't we all go back and have a cup of tea and talk this over.'

'*Kia ora*, Jack,' answered Heke Pou gravely. 'There is no misunderstanding. They took this land from Auntie Kura.' He indicated the old lady sitting in the group. 'We will not move. If you take the bulldozers out of Rangimarie we'll have a cup of tea.' Then Heke Pou looked at the younger policeman. 'We understand that your orders have come from the city,' he said. 'We understand who has taken the land, but we will not move.'

Because the young policeman did not know who owned the land he missed the significance of what Heke was saying, turned angrily to the driver. 'They'll move,' he muttered, 'they'll move when we start the motors up.'

The older policeman looked shocked. 'You can't possibly move the bulldozers while the people are here. Look how carefully they've chosen their position, at the narrowest, the most difficult place. It will be much too dangerous to go forward while there are women and children here, the kids could run anywhere.'

'Well, the women and children will just have to hop it. What do you expect us to do, go whinging back again and tell them a group of old girls kept us from our work? Start up!' he called to the drivers, and climbed up into the front bulldozer.

The drivers looked uneasy, especially the driver in the front machine.

'I don't think . . .' he said.

'START UP!' shouted the policeman again.

'I'll do it,' said the boss and he grinned and pushed the driver out of the way and smoke poured from the little chimney as he revved up. He knew the group would scatter as the huge vehicle lumbered towards them.

'You can't do this,' called the local policeman, moving between the vehicle and the crowd.

The boss put the bulldozer into gear. The bulldozer lurched. As the wide treads began to turn they caught the side of a huge pohutukawa tree. A big, sharp branch snapped and flew forwards, straight into the face of the older policeman knocking him under the lowering blade. A wild scream tore at the sunshine morning as the boss tried to wrench the huge machine to a standstill but for a moment it rolled inexorably forward. And then there was silence.

'Jesus Christ,' whispered the boss, clumsy with fright, sweating, trying at once to reverse. Sweat poured from under his arms as he stopped the machine again. The younger policeman jerked forward with the motion of the bulldozer, stared at the ground in front of him, transfixed. He saw a movement and looked up: Grace Pou was moving quickly towards the body. Neither the young policeman from the city nor the boss ever forgot the look of scorn in her eyes as she briefly looked up at them.

The ambulance from the nearest hospital had come and gone; the bulldozers had finally rumbled and clanked out of Rangimarie again belching black smoke but everyone knew it wouldn't be for long. Everyone had come back to the houses except for the old man. The one wild scream of the old police-man who they had all known echoed still in the valley.

Over and over again Heke Pou walked the ridge and turned, walked the ridge and turned. If they looked up they could see him, a thin figure against the sky, walking along past the old, ruined meeting house. Finally Grace went up to bring him down. Pumpkin followed her, some way behind.

He saw his mother walk towards Heke. They spoke only in Maori. Pumpkin understood Maori. He heard her telling him over and over again that it wasn't his fault; heard the old man say he had known Jack since he was a boy, had known his father.

Pumpkin heard Grace make soothing sounds with her voice. 'Come and eat,' she said.

'It should have been me,' said Heke. 'They will blame us, not the bulldozers. It should have been me. If it is the Prime Minister we are fighting they will not blame the bulldozers. Tell Timoti to come home.'

It was dusk now and the last light caught at the open wound of the earth, where the bulldozers had been.

'We cannot take on the Prime Minister,' murmured Grace. 'You heard what Timoti said, the law and political things are hand in hand. And he must make his way in the world he's chosen, *e Heke*, you can't keep calling him back. The bulldoz-ers will be back in a week or two, Timoti can't do anything, Jack's death won't even make any difference. We can't win this. Leave it now.'

Pumpkin turned and ran down the hill, a fat boy running, ungainly, through the bushes and the trees.

THIRTY-NINE

It was still dark next morning when Tumatauenga Pou who was known as Pumpkin, Timoti Pou's younger brother, started his journey.

He carried a sack: he did not own a suitcase. He could hear both his parents snoring gently as he quietly closed the door of the little house that nestled into the hill; as he walked up the unpaved road past the yellow hall, past the church, he heard, very faintly, the sound of the running stream from the hills that gave them all clear, fresh water in their tin tanks. He hoisted the long sack across his shoulders, his sandshoes crunched along the road. At the bottom of one sandshoe were two pound notes and his birth certificate which was the only important document he owned. He thought you might need your birth certificate in the city. It was a chilly morning, the sun not yet up from over the hills, and he wore an old coat that had belonged to his father. The lining was torn, hung down a little against his grey flannel trousers, his best pair, the ones he had worn in the yellow hall the night of his Uncle Heke's eightieth birthday party.

Rangimarie was still asleep.

A lone dog barked from a tin kennel, pulling at its chain.

'*Turituri e Tama*,' called Pumpkin quietly and the dog, recognising his voice, was still.

The first bell bird called: velvet, bell-like sounds coming from its throat as the first light streaked over the hill.

Pumpkin walked for an hour and a half until he came to the crossroads where the paved road began. Here, some of the people who came past would know him, they would stop and give him a ride. They would say *Kia ora, Pumpkin, where're you going, e hoa*? and he would say, *I'm going to the city to see my brother.*

And eventually, somehow, he would get there. He had never been to the city. He had been at the school in the nearest town: unsettled, straining to get out of the classroom, leaving the day he turned fifteen. He had stayed in the town, getting a job with the local butcher because he knew, from hunting with his father, how to quarter animals' bodies with neat, strong blows. He had lived with a cousin, he and Ngaio his young sister who was in her last year at secondary school and was going to train as a teacher. The night Ngaio had been run over by a drunk in a Ford truck, Pumpkin had smashed the window of the Four Square store: wild, out of control, heaving bricks at the Weetabix and the Bushells Tea and the mock-up cardboard model of the Anchor butter.

The judge wanted to send him to prison but the Welfare Officer explained the circumstances. The Pakeha driver did not catch Pumpkin's eye in the small court as he was fined thirty pounds. Pumpkin was bound over to live back in Rangimarie with his grieving parents; he had lived there since, for over two years, kicking the stones along the unpaved road, riding his cousin's horse along the desolate shore on the other side of the hill, occasionally hunting wild pigs with his father. On Friday nights, with some of his mates who had jobs at the freezing works, he went to the nearest pub, the one at the crossroads where they served him even though he was under age. Most Friday nights Pumpkin would fall, paralytic, against the bar rail. His mates would get him safely home.

Now he was going to the city he had never seen, carrying a long sack.

Only Maoris would pick him up, the fat boy in the sand-shoes with the torn lining hanging down from his coat, carrying a sack, but plenty of Maoris went past here.

'What you got in that sack, *e hoa*?' a farmer asked him as he heaved up into the front of a lorry, 'is that a guitar you're carrying?'

'Yeah,' said Pumpkin, and he laughed, showing his white teeth. 'I'm gunna be a rock 'n' roll star.'

'Like Elvis the Pelvis, eh?'

'Yeah, like him!' said Pumpkin, laughed again.

'Play your guitar, *e hoa*!'

'Nah. It's got a broken string.'

They sang 'Heartbreak Hotel', he and the farmer, until they came to the dairy factory, and the milk cans rattled along on the back of the lorry.

It was getting dark and still the city was miles away and cars roared past him as he walked along the verges of the main road. He'd walked all day since the farmer dropped him off. He'd eaten a bread roll the farmer had given him, and a water melon from a field. He had blisters on his feet. He hitched the sack up more firmly on to his shoulders, put one foot in front of the other: that was how he would get to where he was going. He was going to make Timoti proud of him.

A bus pulled up just ahead of him, waited for him to catch up; the driver's door opened.

'Hey Pumpkin, I thought it was you, what are you doing here, *e hoa*? Bit dangerous on these big roads, you might get run over.' It was the country bus from home, the one that went to the city every day. The driver was a cousin.

'I'm going to the city. To see Timoti.'

'*Haere mai, haere mai*, jump in. I'll drop you at the railway station.' Pumpkin got into the front seat, mumbled his thanks, not looking at the other, paying, passengers. He fell asleep at once.

At the railway station the driver woke him and pointed him towards the docks, where the hostel was, before disappearing into the bus office. Pumpkin looked up at the big hoarding with a smiling blonde lady that said:

MAKE A DATE
WITH COLGATE
AND YOUR DATE WILL DATE YOU AGAIN!

He stared at the buildings and the tram cars. There were lights shining all over the city: up on the hills, across the water, everywhere. *Gee, bet their lights don't go out*, thought Pumpkin. Ships lay beside the wharves. He could make out the shape of a big crane. People pushed past him, coming into the railway station to catch trains to their homes out in the suburbs. He clutched his sack and he felt his heart beating beneath it as he whispered to himself: *mahara he aha koe i haere mai ai*: *remember why you've come*.

When Timoti got back with all his law books from the library, from kissing his girlfriend as she got on to the 9.30 tram, Pumpkin was sitting in the hall of the hostel. Timoti was angry with surprise, did not notice how his brother's face had lit up when he came in the door, and then faded again at his angry tone.

'What are you doing here?'

'I want to be in the city.'

'This is ridiculous. What for?'

'Just for a while. I hate it at home. Maybe I can get a job.'

'You're on probation.'

'The two years is up.'

Timoti almost groaned, in exasperation and tiredness, knowing it would be him who would have to help arrange all this.

'Pumpkin, I've got exams in a week, I've got to pass, so much hinges on it. Can't we leave it till after that?'

'You haven't heard, have you?'

'Heard what?'

'The bulldozers came. They killed Jack Ryan.'

'Jack Ryan? The policeman?'

Pumpkin nodded. 'Uncle Heke arranged for everyone to sit on the ground round the hill.'

'*What?*'

'To stop them. He wants you to come home.'

This time Timoti did groan. He sat on the stairs with his brother and put his face in his hands and groaned. He stayed there for several minutes and Pumpkin just waited. Finally Timoti lifted his head. 'Do Mum and Dad know where you are?'

He shook his head. 'They won't worry till tomorrow. They'll think I'm staying with one of our cousins. You can ring them.'

'Have you got any money?'

'Of course I haven't.' The two pound notes were at the bottom of his shoe, he could feel them there with his birth certificate.

'What's in the sack?'

'My clothes.' Pumpkin held the sack close to him.

Timoti hardly knew him, hadn't lived at home since Pumpkin was a young kid.

'You'll have to have a bath. You smell.'

'I hitched all the way here. You'd smell if you hitched all the way.'

'It's your shoes.'

'They're the only ones I've got.'

'Oh, God,' said Timoti.

'I'm hungry,' said Pumpkin. 'I won't stay long, Ti.'

Boarders were allowed, at the Presbyterian Maori Men's Hostel, to make tea and sandwiches in the evening in the big kitchen; the two brothers ate big slices of bread and honey and Pumpkin told him again about the bulldozers and the branch rushing through the air like an arrow on the blade. Timoti's heart sank further at every word.

Pumpkin slept on the small bit of floor beside Timoti's narrow bed. He fell asleep at once as Timoti stared through the torn blind at the streetlight and the fire escape of the big city. Next morning while Pumpkin was still sleeping he put five pound notes beside the coat with the torn lining. He saw that Pumpkin was sleeping clutching his sack, as if he was afraid of the city.

*

At the very last class in the small, high room at the university Isobel Arapeta, her face so pale that it shone, told her pupils – the Indian man and the French woman and the nuns and the three who were working for exams: **pamamao** *is one of the many Maori words meaning distance, far away, somewhere a long way away. It is made up of two words:* **pa** *– to touch –* and **mamao** *– distance. So* **pamaomao** *means* (and the two nuns sitting loyally in the front row thought they heard her sigh) *the way distance touches one.*

*

Pumpkin had left a note for Timoti. **Kia ora**, *Timoti. Found a job, found a room. See you soon.* He didn't tell him he was sharing a room with a burly Maori he'd met in a pub by the docks who, when Pumpkin after a few beers told him why he had come to the city, had laughed, thrown back his head and laughed.

'You are a silly young bugger,' he said. 'Someone better look after you. Your brother's doing exams, isn't he? I've heard of him. You better come and stay with us.' When Pumpkin looked offended at his laughter the Maori clapped him on the back but in a kindly manner. 'You've been reading too many comics,' was all he said.

While they were walking home from collecting Pumpkin's sack from the hostel and leaving the note, Pumpkin's new friend, who told him his name was Sinatra – *my mother named me after Frank Sinatra before she buggered off* – said: 'Might get you a job on the wharves. Can you cook?'

Pumpkin looked startled, hoisted his sack higher up on his shoulder. 'I can do eggs and chops,' he said. 'Me and my sister used to do them. But I'm a butcher really. Well, sort of.'

'Well, I might get you a job as a butcher then,' said Sinatra.

As they walked through the streets at the edge of the city they met Bay Ropata who was walking with Prudence back to her house under the hills. The two burly men greeted each other, pressed their noses together and laughed and parted: Prudence did not know she had just seen Maggie's boyfriend's younger brother carrying a gun.

They placed the sack under the bed where Sinatra slept. 'I'll look after this,' said Sinatra firmly. Pumpkin slept on a camp-bed in the corner by the old kauri wardrobe with the door that wouldn't close. There was a basin with cold running water on one of the landings and the toilet was out at the back. The old wooden floors, also made from kauri, sloped and knotted precariously in the broken-down house where lots of drifting Maoris came and went. In Sinatra's room there were curtains made of thin, bright material: colourful sports cars and big, shiny, posh cars moved slightly in the breeze from the open window, and in the middle a bright yellow tractor. Pumpkin stared up at the curtains from the camp-bed, fascinated.

Across the road wrecks of old cars lay in darkness.

In the night, from one of the other rooms, Pumpkin heard guitars and snatches of the songs he'd known all his life. It made him feel less lonely and it made him feel sure of what he was doing.

Tahi nei taru kino
Mahi whaiaipo.

Up a street behind the city, near Prudence's place.

'I'll do it tomorrow,' said Pumpkin to himself as he fell asleep.

Timoti was so relieved when he got home from the last Maori class and saw Pumpkin's note that he asked no questions. He phoned his parents in Rangimarie, told them Pumpkin was staying in the city, looking for a job, tried to persuade them to stop mad old Uncle Heke doing anything else. On leave from work he stayed up every night now, bent over his law text-books as the days moved inexorably forward.

And in Rangimarie his father did not say that his hunting gun was missing, because he did not know.

FORTY

Sinatra was asleep, snoring with his mouth open, sleeping heavily, as he always did just before morning.

Pumpkin, who had taken a moment to remember where he was, that he was in the city, that he had a job to do, lay for a moment longer on the camp-bed. He looked at the light coming in past the curtains with the cars on them; a strong wind was blowing them inwards, red sports cars billowed into the room. If the light in the city was the same as the light in the country and he could think of no reason why it might be different, then it must be about five o'clock in the morning. He had no idea how many people were living here. The old house made some odd creaks, as if it was moving slightly in the wind but otherwise it was quiet now, except for snoring. He heard some Maori voices from the streets, and some clanging sounds. Very quietly he moved across to Sinatra's bed, and very, very gently pulled his sack out from underneath the sagging springs.

He walked in his torn coat, clutching the sack, ignoring the big blisters that had come up on his feet. Across the road old cars and trucks rusted quietly, old wheels rotted in piles, *must've been a garage or something once*, Pumpkin thought. The clanging sounds he'd heard were dustbins being emptied in

the city streets. In Rangimarie they had to take everything to
the dump in sacks and cardboard boxes, up past the village on
the way to the crossroads. Pumpkin watched as the three
dustmen, all Maoris, emptied rubbish bins on to the back of a
big truck, with their cigarettes stuck to the bottom of their
lips as they worked. When one passed near him he asked him
if he knew where the Parliament Buildings were.

'*E hoa*, hop on if you don't mind sitting with the rubbish.
We go past there later.' Pumpkin climbed over the newspapers and the fruit skins and the tins and the bottles and the
cardboard boxes, he sat on the top edge of the truck, away
from where most of the rubbish landed. Slowly they pro-
gressed, as the morning got lighter, along the main streets of
the city, over the tram lines, veering over to one side when an
occasional tram clanged its bell, past the newspaper offices
and the shops still closed, and past Timoti's office building,
though Pumpkin did not know that. Taxi drivers lounged
near the one early-morning café, yawning and scratching and
smoking. When they got to the railway station the dustmen
stopped at something they called 'the piecart' and Pumpkin
took one of Timoti's pound notes and insisted on buying all
three of them meat pies. They sat in the gutter and ate.

'What you going to the Parliament for, *e hoa*? Gunna get a
knighthood?' and they all laughed and Pumpkin said he was
going to play his guitar to the Prime Minister like Elvis the
Pelvis and they laughed again and began singing:

> Well it's one for the money
> Two for the show

sitting in the gutter by the railway station eating their mince
pies and singing and laughing and talking about rugby before
people came to work and the city became a different place,
belonging to different people.

'Where're you staying?' one of the dustmen asked Pumpkin.

He did not mention his brother who would soon be a lawyer. 'I stayed at Sinatra's house, near where you fellas picked me up. Do you know Sinatra?' and all the dustmen laughed.

'*E hoa*, everyone knows Sinatra, he works on the wharves. We call him the King. He got me this job. He helped my brother when he was in prison. Sinatra knows everybody.' Then they jumped back on to the rubbish lorry and drove up the hill and into the grounds of the Parliament.

There was no sun on the grey building yet. It stood there, dark and forbidding and cold. Pumpkin stared up at it and his heart beat oddly. The windows stared back at him, reflecting darkness. In front there was a statue of a Pakeha man in old-fashioned clothes pointing at the sky and there was a long flight of concrete steps leading up to the front doors, and coats of arms on the pillars. People were starting to walk up the path now, and up the steps into the building: typists, men in suits. Pumpkin saw that none of them were Maoris. The rubbish truck drove round the back of the big building. A couple of cleaners stood at the back with big, wide brooms, helped empty the dustbins into the truck; one of the cleaners was a Maori, they swapped words and laughter and the dustbins clanged. As Pumpkin jumped off the truck, waving to the dustmen, he threw the torn coat into the rubbish, and as the others threw empty dustbins into the air and called to each other, Pumpkin walked with his sack through one of the open back doors. He saw a pile of big, wide brooms and hanging on a hook was a brown coat like the cleaners were wearing. He put on the coat, took a broom, and with his sack over his shoulder he started walking along a wide empty corridor.

He just kept on walking. When anyone came towards him he pushed at the wooden broom in front of him, and swept.

He saw a funny lift, like a little cage, *you wouldn't catch me in that thing*! He walked up staircases to other floors, along more corridors, past photographs of prime ministers and statesmen and the young Queen of England. He remembered his father talking about Michael Savage, stopped for a moment and stared at the picture, otherwise the photographs were of Pakehas he'd never heard of. The corridors were dark, lights hadn't been turned on in parts of them and some of them had funny coloured windows so the light couldn't get in properly. The ordinary windows were dirty; for a split second Pumpkin longed to take a bucket of soap and water and clean them, he liked cleaning windows. Then he passed a photograph of a Maori wearing a feathered cloak across his shoulders. Pumpkin stopped, read the name underneath: Sir Apirana Ngata. Oh, yes, he'd heard of him too. Somehow he felt comforted: other Maoris had walked along these corridors, just like he was. He looked up and stared in amazement at the high ceilings. Sometimes, round dark corners, people were muttering to one another as if exchanging secrets. And all the time, he felt his heart beating faster and faster and he could taste the meat pie in his dry mouth.

At one stage, coming down a staircase with his broom and his brown coat and his sack, he passed the front door, looked down the huge flight of steps to the grass and the back of the statue of the Pakeha man pointing to the sky and the gate he'd driven through with the dustmen. There were funny words written into the marble floor outside, with lions and odd animals that looked a bit like deer but had an antler in the middle of their foreheads. Somebody must've made a mistake. DIEU ET MON DROIT he spelled out and HONI SOI QUI MAL Y PENSE, some foreign stuff, it meant nothing to him. Further on he went up more flights of stairs, along more corridors, past more photographs. He looked carefully for more Maoris but couldn't see any. Lots of people were walking along the corridors now, calling, talking together. All Pakehas. No one even glanced at him, a fat Maori with a sack. The broom and the brown coat made him invisible.

At last, right at the top, he found what he was looking for: a sign saying PRIME MINISTER'S OFFICES. People went in and out, carrying papers, hurrying here and there. Right at the end of that corridor he found a dark corner, in that building full of dark corners. He waited till the corridor was empty and then he took his father's hunting gun out of the sack and made it ready with the bullets he'd put in his trouser pocket, always trained by his father to keep the gun and the bullets in two different places. The rifle wasn't really suitable for short range but it would have to do. Pumpkin had no idea what the Prime Minister looked like, he realised. He'd probably glanced at photos sometimes in his dad's newspaper but politics was as remote to him as the moon. But his adrenalin flowed as he stood in his dark corner, knowing that somehow he would at last make Timoti proud.

John Evans, Prime Minister, arrived with several other men at about ten o'clock. As Pumpkin stood in his dark corner he heard a man call down the corridor: 'Prime Minister, can I have a word?' and the Prime Minister called, 'All right, Gordon, but we're off in fifteen minutes,' and the group of men in suits disappeared through one of the doors. Now Pumpkin's heart was beating very, very fast, he could feel it racing uncomfortably under the brown coat. Once he had lined up to the door several times he held the gun lightly, feeling the sweat on his hands and running down inside his shirt. He did not feel exactly scared: he thought of Timoti and his Uncle Heke and the bulldozer and the scream of the policeman. He waited.

When, about twenty minutes later, the door opened, he

stood in his dark corner and lifted his father's hunting rifle, the rifle they used for shooting deer and pigs.

And Pumpkin called, as he'd heard the other man call: 'Prime Minister.' John Evans turned, bemused at the odd voice.

'Give us back our land, you bloody bugger,' called Pumpkin, and he pulled the trigger.

There was a tremendous explosion in the small space. Concrete flew out of the wall beside John Evans as he fell. Men ran and shouted, someone was screaming. Pumpkin was good with a hunting rifle. He had hit the Prime Minister's arm, as he had intended. He stood quietly with the gun pointing downwards until they descended upon him, tore the rifle away, pinned him against the wall under the photograph of a forgotten statesman, kicking him, pushing his arms and his legs so that he fell heavily to his knees, hurting them.

The bullet had grazed John Evans's shoulder; he had also heard clearly the words Pumpkin had called. People raised him to a sitting position, but somehow he pulled himself on to his feet, swayed, holding his shoulder where he had been hit. Blood trickled through his fingers and down his suit as he walked towards Pumpkin.

'What did you say?' he said hoarsely.

'You took our land at Rangimarie.' Pumpkin, on his knees, almost on the ground, could hardly speak because of the way he was being held, one man had an arm under his throat. But Pumpkin saw then, quite clearly, a look of panic in the eyes of John Evans who turned and muttered something that no one else could hear to a man beside him, his assistant, Alvin Fitzgerald, and then allowed himself to be half carried into his office.

The man the Prime Minister had been muttering to stepped forward. 'All right,' he said, grabbing the rifle from another man. 'Leave this to me. It's only a fat dirty little hori who stinks, the Prime Minister's fine, there's no need for panic. Leave it to me, everything's under control,' and he nodded to people to leave the corridor quickly. Pumpkin was thrown onto the ground and somebody kicked him.

Reluctantly, still in shock, people complied. A woman was still crying; a sob could be heard disappearing down the corridor. The alarm was ringing now and voices were raised in the distance but before anybody else arrived the man cocked the hunting rifle, raised it and shot Tamatauenga Pou, known as Pumpkin, in the stomach. There was a second, loud explosion and the man threw the rifle at the body just before the security staff appeared running, looking bewildered, at the other end of the corridor.

'*Get rid of him very quickly*' was what the Prime Minister had said.

'Let's have just one more party tonight, it's so dreary living like this, just studying and working,' said Prudence, and the girls from the Bureau clip-clopped in their stiletto heels once more past the Prince of Wales hotel where the beer hoses raced up and down the counters.

'Timoti's agreed to come,' said Maggie, skipping in the road, 'He said he would just this once, just for an hour. He's got so much work to do but I said a couple of hours off would be good for him, only four more days.'

'Quite right,' said Hope, holding Prudence's arm, her head cocked to one side as if she was listening to the sky, 'parties are good for us.'

They had long finished the fish and chips on the floor and were reading out old upside-down sports results by the time Timoti arrived. There was an almost imperceptible change in the room. Rangi gave him a seat, Hori gave him a beer. Maggie smiled and sang and smiled, and watched carefully. And she saw that they were all very slightly in awe of him: he had a different *mana*. Soon he would be a lawyer and he was one of them; they owned him and would be proud of him: he was *theirs*.

And tonight she understood something else: he had lost something too. *He was less like a Maori than the others.* His laughter was more neat, he was less able to relax and enjoy himself, he was more *formal*.

> What do you want to make those eyes at me for
> When they don't mean what they say

sang Hope, staring at the electric light bulb. And instinctively, watching, just for a moment, Margaret-Rose Bennett, who loved Timoti Pou, felt she might, just, understand what it must be like for Timoti, the schisms, the chasms in his head: this burden to do well in someone else's world, with someone else's values. And his own world pulling gently at his sleeve, whispering. And she suddenly remembered Kara Rikihana's words, sitting on the plinth of the statue as they watched Timoti hurrying up the university path in his flapping white raincoat in the dusk: *do you think we will let him escape so easily?*

Hope's high, beautiful voice filled the room, Paddy's wig fell sideways, Hui Windsor had unscrewed his wooden leg and stood it in a corner. And Maggie saw Paul the epileptic kissing Hope, the blind typist.

At nine o'clock the grey Ford Prefects went slowly wobbling down the hill past the pohutukawa trees towards the sea.

Timoti waited with Maggie for her 9.30 tram and she saw again the circles of exhaustion under his eyes.

'I hope you sleep well,' she said.

'You get some sleep too,' he said. And as the front light of the tram beamed towards them he kissed her. 'We'll work out things as soon as the exams are over,' he said. 'I know you'll make me a good wife.' He waved as the tram clanked away into the darkness. Maggie saw his arm raised still as the tram swayed around the corner. She began re-reading 'A Life of Coleridge' at once.

Timoti walked slowly home, knowing he had hours more work before he went to bed, thinking of torts and constructions and law. On the wall of the hostel somebody had pinned a big note telling him to telephone his Auntie Rose whatever time he got home. Timoti screwed up the note in frustration – *why can't they leave me alone* – but the telephone was ringing again before he'd even got to his room. Wearily he turned back to the phone in the hall, *but whatever it maybe, I will not go back again*, and answered it.

At first they thought they might keep it out of the papers altogether. But one of the parliamentry typists told her boyfriend who was a typesetter on the evening paper and the news went round like wildfire. The Editor discussed things with the Prime Minister, agreed to make it a smallish paragraph on the second page tomorrow, which would say: UNKNOWN INTRUDER IN PARLIAMENT GROUNDS, MR EVANS SLIGHTLY HURT.

And Pumpkin, who was dead, who looked like another one of the lost Maoris of that city, would probably have been buried anonymously on government instructions, if somebody hadn't told the oldest of the four Maori MPs, shortly after the attack, that the intruder was a Maori and had committed suicide.

All day the Maori MP insisted on seeing the body, would not be put off. Finally the Prime Minister himself, who in fine John Wayne tradition had refused to take any time off despite his 'accident', called the Maori MP up into his private suite in the building. As the sun set, he poured very large whiskies with his good hand, said he didn't want some poor pathetic

Maori being made into a scapegoat, nobody knew what he was doing there this morning or what he was angry about. The Prime Minister's assistant, Alvin Fitzgerald, stood by the window. The Maori MP drank all the whisky and then insisted again on seeing the body.

'This is a terrible thing and my people are ashamed, but we don't leave our people by themselves when they're dead,' he said, over and over again.

'We don't want it in the papers.' John Evans's voice had become steely as he sat at his desk with his arm in a sling and his face pale.

'We don't leave our people by themselves when they're dead,' the Maori MP said from the other side of the desk and a touch of steel could be detected in his voice also. The whisky bottle was empty.

Finally it was agreed that the Maori MP should take charge of what was left of the body. It would be buried quietly by his family: another Maori who had come to the city and lost himself. But – and this was the deal – nothing was to be said to the family about him being inside Parliament Buildings.

If the MP guessed that there was more to this than suicide, he said nothing. At least he had arranged that the boy could be buried properly by his family. He had gone as far as he could. It was he who was given the birth certificate that had been found in Pumpkin's sandshoe.

And so it was that the old man Heke Pou had received a message saying: 'Come and get your nephew, he has killed himself.' And so it was that Auntie Rose instructed Timoti, who picked up the ringing telephone in the Maori Men's Hostel at 10 PM, to go down to the mortuary attached to the public hospital where his parents and his Uncle Heke would be waiting for him.

FORTY-ONE

In their wildest nightmares Maggie's parents could not have imagined that their daughter was going to a Maori funeral hundreds of miles away just as her first university exams were about to begin.

Timoti, upsetting his mother almost more than he could bear, said he could not go back at once to Rangimarie with the body, that he must keep studying for the exams that were to start in four days, that he would come on the evening of the second day of the *tangi*, and stay over to the third. His father understood, held him by the shoulder and wept; Timoti did not, could not, look again at his mother after he had kissed her goodbye.

And Maggie told her parents that she had to go and stay with Prudence for this last weekend before exams, that they had decided to spend a whole weekend speaking French to be ready for the oral examination next week. Lies poured out of her mouth like nails as she saw again Timoti's face, the lines of exhaustion and shock and strain as he stopped briefly in the library to tell her that Pumpkin had committed suicide. Her parents made no objection to her going to Prudence's place, as if life was waiting in a kind of truce until exams were over.

She could think of nothing of use to comfort Timoti on Friday evening after he had finished work as they drove northward in his cousin's uncle's wife's car. She offered to drive: he declined. Lambs ran and played in the warm early evening as they left the city, the air became sweet, smelt of clover and grass, felt like velvet – but there was nothing to say. Sometimes she stroked his sleeve and said, '*I love you, Timoti.*' She thought of sulky, fat Pumpkin, who had always looked at his older brother with such wistfulness and such love. Maggie still did not understand that she recognised the look exactly because it was how she looked at her mother.

She wondered what it felt like to be so despairing as to kill oneself, not *think* about it but do it, and felt again shocked that someone so near her own age could actually do such a thing. She tried to think that at least Pumpkin wouldn't grow old and Keats drifted through her mind; *when old age shall this generation waste, thou shalt remain*, and she would have liked to tell Timoti. Also she would have liked to ask him about what would happen, she had never been to a Maori funeral, a *tangi*. She remembered how they'd all gone off from the Bureau to Gallipoli Gordon's funeral, the big busloads, the old ladies hitching a ride with someone, Emily and Prudence getting food poisoning. But there was something about Timoti's stern, strained profile that stopped her asking anything about what might happen: she knew he blamed himself bitterly for not taking better care of his brother.

Occasionally they passed other cars but for hours they seemed to be the only car on the long road, a light moving northwards in the darkness. Finally they came to the cross-roads, turned off, and drove down the unpaved road to Rangimarie.

As they came nearer they saw a flickering light moving slowly ahead of them. A woman was walking along the road, carrying a lantern. Timoti slowed down to pass her but did not stop. More lanterns flickered and moved as they came nearer to the yellow hall, as people came and went along the road.

Something had been built at the side of the hall, slightly in front of it, some sort of tent or lean-to. As they got out of the car Maggie strained to see. It looked like a tent, she could see tarpaulin over the roof, but it seemed to be made of ferns. Lights flickered from inside.

'What's that?' she whispered to Timoti.

'I think that's where the coffin is,' he answered shortly.

'What's it doing there?'

He shrugged.

They walked past the raggedy fence on to the grass. Maggie expected them to go into the hall, sit down, have a cup of tea, but Timoti seemed to hesitate, to be waiting. A woman called out of the darkness, Timoti's father came forward and embraced his son. Uncle Heke spoke in Maori but Maggie could not see his face, only his shadow. And then they were ushered into the tent.

Grace and two other women sat beside an open coffin, sitting on some sort of straw that had been put on the ground. Uncle Heke was now standing just behind them, leaning on his carved stick, and beside him stood a minister in his high white collar. Manuka branches made a kind of frame, fern leaves filled in the sides, and the tarpaulin was the roof. Three lanterns hung from a branch of manuka strung across the top, and in the light of the lanterns Maggie saw there were several photographs pinned up on another branch, photographs of Pumpkin.

Timoti motioned her to stay where she was by the opening and walked forward towards the coffin, towards his mother. Maggie watched as Uncle Heke greeted Timoti, pressing his nose, then holding both his shoulders, as if he needed to lean on him. Timoti held himself slightly away as if, Maggie thought, he was trying not to get too involved. Grace's hair was not properly tied back as Maggie remembered it, but hung wildly about her distraught face and suddenly Maggie thought, *it's only two years since her daughter, Ngaio, died. How could Pumpkin do this to his mother?* As Grace put out her arm to Timoti, calling in Maori, Maggie heard everywhere the crying sound, the sound of the crying women, the sound she had heard that day in the office when Mrs Tipene and her sister came to see Emily. On and on it went, from the tent or the hall beside it, she could not tell.

The same crying that she heard over and over again, in her dreams.

After a while Maggie understood she should go forward to Grace: her heart sank but she moved forward of course, moved unwillingly towards the weeping women and the coffin.

Pumpkin's body – it could not be seen that it was only the remains of Pumpkin's body – was dressed in better clothes than Maggie had ever seen him in, a suit and a tie. His hair had been Brylcreemed over his face in a different hairstyle to hide a bruise. In a way it didn't look like Pumpkin at all. Her heart beat very fast; she would have liked to hold on to Timoti but he was not there, she looked around but could not see him in the flickering darkness. She looked at Grace's face, wanted to say something that would help but understood there was nothing at all. Finally, very shyly, she knelt down beside Grace and stiffly put her arms around her. She felt the heat and the damp of Grace's big soft body and pulled back after a moment, uneasy. Grace kissed her, tears fell across Maggie's face, she wished she could escape all this – *feeling*. Dimly, amid the sounds of the weeping, she heard someone explain in Maori to someone else that she was Timoti's **whaiaipo**, his sweetheart, and she found herself thinking (knowing it was an inappropriate thought at this moment), that all this Maori around her would be good for her oral exam in two days' time. Someone else arrived to talk to Grace, an old man wearing a wreath of leaves around his head. Maggie backed away out of the tent and into the fresher air of the night. From out of nowhere, gently, a woman took her hand. In the flickering light that shadowed out from the makeshift tent Maggie saw an old enamel bowl full of water on the ground. The woman indicated that Maggie should dip her fingers into the water.

'That is our custom, when taking leave of the dead,' she whispered. Then she disappeared.

In the yellow hall the bright, stark electric light hurt her eyes. Lamps were hanging from nails and rafters, but someone was going round turning them off: there had been a power cut but now that the electricity had come on again they were saving the kerosene. She looked around the hall: there were people everywhere, sitting on wooden chairs, sitting on the floor, standing and talking in corners; children were asleep under rugs and coats and sacks at one end of the room, tables were set up at the other.

Disoriented, tired, Maggie sat in a corner watching, listening to someone making a speech in Maori that seemed to be about the outside toilets. Someone handed her a cup of tea and a large piece of fruit cake: it was Auntie Rose, the one who was deaf and had got her to cut up the apples for Uncle Heke's eightieth birthday party in this same hall. Other women came up, hugged her, sat with her for a while, chatting inconsequentially of this or that.

Sometimes she thought she heard a bell ring from the church across the road but perhaps she only imagined it, sometimes she dozed. At last Timoti came and took her to the tables at one end of the hall where someone gave her some meat and vegetables that she didn't want to eat. Timoti pushed his food into himself in big ungainly mouthfuls. The minister, a man from another village sat beside Timoti, eating a huge plate of lamp chops. Maggie did the dishes, as it seemed to be expected of her: but even doing the dishes she could hear the crying drifting in. Timoti spoke to various

people who came in and out of the kitchen. Then his older
brother Paatu, who seemed as drunk as he'd been at Uncle
Heke's eightieth birthday, came to get him and they disappeared back into the tent outside. Auntie Rosie seemed
indefatigable: cooking, serving, washing, peeling, her hair
pushed back from her exhausted face. Someone had opened
the back door of the hall, people stood on the back steps
smoking and looking at the stars.

Finally, at about two o'clock in the morning, Timoti came to
collect her. 'We'll sleep at home,' he said. They drove wearily
to the group of houses at the end of the road, lights shone out
of almost every house. On the side of the hill, where the bulldozers had torn at the trees and the grass and the top of the
earth, the gash in the land shone in the moonlight. In Grace's
house lots of people were sleeping on the floor, or making
cups of tea in the kitchen; one woman was breastfeeding her
baby, leaning against the back of the sofa where a man lay
asleep. Finally Noelene, Paatu's wife, now more pregnant
than ever, took her arm.

'Come and sleep over at our house,' she said, 'you'll never
find space here, I know what it feels like. You can have the
sofa.' Maggie felt such relief to see her white face, smiled at
her gratefully, wanted to say something to Timoti but he was
talking to a group of men and in the end she was too tired to
care. On the couch at Noelene's place, in her clothes, Maggie
dozed and dreamed and heard the crying voices and saw
Grace's ravaged face, and saw Pumpkin lying in his coffin in
a suit. And could not get rid of, awake or asleep, the smell of
the bodies, Grace's damp body, the smell that her mother had
called the smell of Maoris.

Noelene was shaking her awake but it was not even light.
She'd hardly slept at all, but Paatu, who she had never seen
sober before, had made a cup of tea.

'Come on,' was all he said, 'you must come back to the coffin now.'

At Grace's house Paatu quietly but efficiently woke Timoti, asleep in Grace's bed. Timoti groaned: 'Leave me alone.'

'You have to come to Mum now,' said Paatu.

It was still dark as the truck crunched along the road, stopped outside the raggedy fence.

'Come on,' said Paatu again, urging the exhausted Timoti out of the truck. 'You know what happened when Ngaio died.'

Maggie was so tired she hardly knew what was happening, yet understood that whatever it was it was Paatu's decision – laughing, drunken Paatu: Timoti must be there; she should be there, with Timoti. The yellow hall was quiet and almost in darkness, most of the visitors were now asleep in there; only one light was on at the very back.

In the tent of fern and manuka and tarpaulin Grace and Auntie Rose sat by the coffin. One of the kerosene lamps was still burning. The soft keening sound drifted round among the fern leaves, but almost inaudible. Maggie could not see if it was Auntie Rose or Grace who was making the noise.

'Hasn't Grace been out of the tent?' whispered Maggie to Noelene, 'Hasn't she had a rest?'

'This is how they do it,' Noelene whispered back. The old white-haired brothers, Moana and Uncle Heke, seemed as if they had been waiting for the two sons, Timoti and Paatu. The two Pakeha women, part yet not part of this, stood together slightly further away. There was now almost complete silence in the tent. Very gently, Heke motioned to the two younger men, and they moved towards the coffin.

Out of the stillness a great cry rent the air.

'**Kahore.**' *No!*

Still the men moved towards the coffin. Grace threw herself across the partly hidden body of her youngest son. '**Kahore,**

kahore, kahore!' Her cries filled the tent, echoed out into the darkness before dawn.

Somehow Maggie expected someone to come running from the hall to see what was happening, but the hall remained still and dark.

And then Grace, tears streaming down her face, pulled herself back from the coffin and reached for her handbag. It was such an unlikely thing to do, as if she was going to powder her nose, so incongruous with the almost Greek drama being played out in front of her that a little noise came out of Maggie's mouth, of embarrassment, a snort, almost a laugh.

Grace pulled a small pair of nail scissors out of her handbag. She began at once, still crying, to cut at her long hair, to cut at it, cut big pieces off. And she threw her hair into the coffin beside Pumpkin. *Snip, snip.* Maggie could hear the scissors, saw the nail scissors snip and the greying hair fall. Moana moved forward to his wife, put his hands gently on her shoulders: she continued cutting and snipping and crying. And Maggie recognised that there was formality in all this in some odd way, that she was watching a ritual: as if, in the middle of all the informality and pain and grief, there was a rule of conduct being followed that only she did not understand.

Black hair streaked with grey fell on to Pumpkin's body.

Then as if at some invisible sign, Moana pulled Grace back from the coffin and Timoti and Paatu picked up the lid lying beside it and began screwing it down, closing Pumpkin at last from view. Grace fell across the coffin, calling Pumpkin's Maori name, **Tumatauenga** again and again; again and again Moana pulled her back and the two younger men screwed the top onto the coffin.

Finally, exhausted, Grace lay back, leaning on Auntie Rose. Her eyes were closed.

Somehow the next thing Maggie found herself doing was

cooking lots of eggs in the kitchen under Auntie Rose's direction. Big pots of tea were handed round as people woke up.

'How's Grace now? How's Grace?' She heard them
murmur and nod, as if they knew what had happened in the
tent. Two men were making a *hangi* outside. Maggie could see
them from the kitchen window, putting a pig in a smoking
hole in the ground, and sweet potatoes and big cabbages.
Sometimes she caught sight of Timoti's face as people talked
to him: and because she knew him, knew his face and his
expressions she saw how much he wanted to get away now,
back to his law books in the city. The exams began the day
after tomorrow. These people didn't understand about exams,
how you had to pass them. People spoke in English and
Maori all around her, automatically she translated what Maori
she could, searched for words. *I'm swotting*, she said to herself
and she looked longingly at the spring sunshine that shone in
through the window and across the kitchen bench where she
stood drying more dishes.

In the late morning the minister began his service, not in
the church across the road but in the tent made of manuka
and fern leaves and tarpaulin. There were prayers and hymns,
voices soaring in the spring morning as people stood inside
and outside the tent but Maggie felt she had seen Pumpkin
buried already.

Burned behind her eyes was the image of Timoti's father,
gently but firmly pulling Grace away from the body of her
son.

And burned onto that, was the bitter, unhappy face of her
own mother.

She, too, should have cut her hair, and wept.

FORTY-TWO

The Prime Minister considered the matter closed.

His daughter Emily in London was told her father had been shot, but not badly hurt, by an intruder.

'Should I come home?' she asked eagerly. She hated London. Winter was coming, and she would be glad to leave. But her mother said there was no need, it was a minor incident and nobody wanted such incidents to dominate the life of the new government. It would look odd if she came home again so soon, give rise to the wrong kind of speculation.

Emily hung up the phone in her small flat in Notting Hill, stared at the grey, darkening sky and the bare trees outside the window, felt the fog and the creeping smog in the chill dusk. The glass in her hand trembled as she turned away and drew the curtains.

The Prime Minister went on with business as usual.

A photograph appeared in the newspapers of him with his arm in a sling opening a new sports ground. A small paragraph on the fourth page said the intruder in Parliament Buildings had disappeared and that security had been tightened. The paragraph was so small, people were to understand, because it was such a minor matter. The All Blacks were beating South Africa. *That* was news.

But the Prime Minister had reckoned without Sinatra, King of the City.

Sinatra had woken and found that Pumpkin, and his sack, were gone. Pumpkin had left a little note on the back of a tram ticket he'd found in the room: in his round childish writing it said: *thanks Sinatra,* **kia ora,** *see you soon.*

Pumpkin had taken the hunting rifle and hadn't come back. But when Pumpkin was asleep Sinatra had checked the rifle, found it had no bullets. So he hadn't felt too worried, thought Pumpkin had probably changed his mind, hitched a ride home, as so many of them did. Sinatra was, after all, an urban Maori. He didn't understand the rules of safety that the country boys knew: *never carry a loaded gun, keep the bullets separately.*

But Sinatra did know his city.

He saw the photograph in the paper of the Prime Minister opening the new sports ground with his arm in a sling.

He read the small paragraph about the intruder who had disappeared.

He had seen Pumpkin's eyes shine when he talked of his big brother that day they'd gone to collect his sack from the Maori Men's Hostel, and Sinatra knew, because he knew many things, who Timoti was, that he was studying to be a lawyer.

So Sinatra walked down to the docks that spring Saturday morning, turned up the street past the end of the docks, walked into the hostel where he asked for Timoti Pou. Timoti would know where Pumpkin was.

'Timoti's gone to a *tangi, e hoa,* his brother's *tangi.*'

'His brother's?'

'Yeah. He came to the city and committed suicide.'

'Did he?' said Sinatra, and his big bulk was suddenly very, very still. 'Did he now?'

'Yeah. Sad, eh?'

'Sad,' repeated Sinatra.

That afternoon, in the hotel by the docks where the horse racing blared out through the open windows and the hoses went up and down the smoke-filled crowded bar, Sinatra found one of his cousins, who was one of the Maori policemen in the city.

'*Kia ora*, Gladstone.'

'G'day Sinatra, how'dja be?'

'I'm good,' said Sinatra.

They talked for a while about Gladstone's sister who'd just passed some nursing exams and about a horse they both fancied in the 2.45. Gladstone, off duty, went into the TAB next door to put on the bets and Sinatra bought four more jugs of beer. They stood at one of the high benches and drank fast. They only had till six o'clock.

The race blared out over the bar, their horse won, punters who'd put on the right bet cheered and a glass smashed somewhere, or a jug. Both men's eyes were red, their words slurred slightly. The noise rose and rose in the hotel as the afternoon wore on, coins slid across the wet counters, pound notes sometimes that they had to shake the beer off.

'What about the Prime Minister?' said Sinatra at last.

'Yeah,' said Gladstone.

'What happened?'

'The shooting? Some guy took a pot shot at John Evans with a hunting rifle.'

'A husband?' and they both laughed.

And then Sinatra said quietly, 'A Maori?'

'How did you know?' said Gladstone, surprised, 'They're keeping it quiet.'

'Why?'

'Dunno.' Gladstone emptied another glass, lit another Capstan. 'Race relations, I suppose.'

'Oh, yeah?' said Sinatra, 'God's Own Country?'

'Yeah. That stuff.' Gladstone paused. '*We* don't want him to be a Maori either. There's four of us Maori cops now. We want Maoris to be the good guys now,' and he laughed and Sinatra smiled his lazy smile.

'How'd he die?'

'He committed suicide,' said Gladstone easily, and then, despite the huge amount of beer he'd drunk, caught himself. 'Whaddya mean, Sinny? How do you know he's dead? He disappeared.' And Gladstone looked suspiciously at his cousin who he knew very well to be a crook, of a kind.

Sinatra looked blearily but steadily back at his cousin who he knew very well to be a crook, of a kind; one of the Maori policemen in the city. There was an odd tension in the air.

And then suddenly both men laughed again. They were cousins after all, in the Maori fashion. They'd gone and stolen half a sheep once, from a butcher's shop, when Gladstone first came to the city and Sinatra was showing him how the city worked. Sinatra had looked after Gladstone, made sure he was safe, didn't go down the black hole that a lot of the young Maori boys disappeared into. Gladstone knew he would never have become a policeman if it wasn't for Sinny. Still laughing, Sinatra slapped Gladstone on the back and went for more beer. But Gladstone knew you couldn't fool Sinatra.

The bar was almost blue now with the haze of cigarette smoke and outside the open windows the late-afternoon sun slanted on to the little tugs at the nearest wharf. From a corner of the bar someone sang:

> Gonna make a sentimental journey
> Gonna set my heart at ease.
> Gonna make a sentimental journey
> To renew old memories,

and the cousins joined in the raucous singing, then finished more beer.

'They shot him,' said Gladstone quietly in all the noise, wiping his mouth with the back of his hand, 'only they don't know we know. We'd lose our jobs if we knew. I was on duty.'

'Who shot him?'

'Dunno.'

'What did they shoot him for?'

'Dunno.'

'Didn't they say? Do you fellas go round shooting people all the time?'

'Come on, Sinny, we don't have guns, you know that. We didn't do it. We arrived when it was over. And the security guys didn't do it, it was all over by the time they got there too; you know that lot, hopeless. I don't think they've had a security alert since the Japs were sighted during the war. They thought they were testing the alarms, one of them even stopped for a slash on the way!'

'So, who did it?'

Gladstone shrugged. 'The Prime Minister's got his own heavies. Prime ministers always have their own heavies; they call them personal assistants. But I did think until now they were just there to buy the beer and the fish and chips and bring the women in. There's been a woman coming in, certainly, but what's new.'

'A very young blonde woman?' said Sinatra, suddenly very alert.

'Bloody hell, Sinny, d'you have to know everything? How do you know?'

'I'm the King of the City,' said Sinatra quite seriously. 'Go on, about the personal assistant.'

'Nobody saw what happened. But we could tell he hadn't done it himself, the boy. It was the wrong angle. It was impossible.'

'Well, didn't you say anything, for Christ's sake?'

'Come on, Sinny. They told us he'd done it himself, the *Prime Minister* told us. We're the new Maori policemen. We don't say to the Prime Minister's personal assistant, you fellas are lying. Anyway he was a crim, the Maori joker, a no-hoper.'

'He wasn't a crim, he was only a kid,' said Sinatra.

'I heard he was a crim. Escaped from up the hill. That's what they told us.'

Suddenly Sinatra's voice was very cold. 'What a fucked-up little place this is when all's said and done,' he said. 'They'll pay for all this one of these days.'

'Hey,' said Gladstone, putting his arm over Sinatra's shoulder, 'this is the Greatest Little Country in the World.'

But Sinatra's good humour had gone and his face was grim. Gladstone remembered Sinatra could be like this and you had to be careful. No one really knew Sinny. He'd changed when his wife and kids died, poor fella. Gladstone poured out two more beers, pushed one across.

'He was only a Maori kid from the sticks who was trying to please his big brother,' said Sinatra but when Gladstone looked at him in surprise he only said: 'Ah, forget it,' and drained the glass.

When the hotel turned off the taps to the beer at 6 PM Sinatra rolled out of the door, said goodbye to Gladstone, clapped him on the shoulder to show there were no hard feelings. Then he went back to the Maori Men's Hostel and left a note for Timoti Pou.

Maggie and Timoti began the long drive back to the city on the Saturday afternoon as spring sunshine fell through the trees and ferns on the side of the road, and small boys kicked rugby balls in remote paddocks. The food from the funeral feast stuck in Maggie's throat: all that eating and eating and eating, even in grief.

Exhausted, she wanted to get home to her thin bed with the pink candlewick bedspread, to have a good sleep, to have one more day for swotting tomorrow before the exams started. Timoti drove without talking much: Maggie understood he was trying to get everything out of his mind, to clear the grief and the pain and the *messiness* away. As it got dark small villages twinkled; it was warm enough for people to be lounging on verandahs; someone sang, hoeing outside from an old wooden house in a paddock.

Timoti drove straight to the hostel. Once more he took Maggie inside, past the hostel warden reading 'Best Bets' and listening to the wireless, down the dark corridor – NO WOMEN GUESTS ALLOWED – into the small bedroom. He picked up a note under his door, shrugged, slipped it into a pocket. Maggie stared out at the rotting wooden fire escape outside the window as they got undressed.

She suddenly threw her arms around his neck, violent and tight. 'Hold me,' she said.

'But I am holding you,' he answered, puzzled, his arms around her. She held him and held him, pushing her head against his chest and she felt his pain, in his body.

Then they lay together on the thin bed and he pushed inside her, as usual.

Although it was Saturday night, she caught the 9.30 tram home, as usual.

'I needed to get back to English,' she said to her parents who weren't expecting her back from Prudence's place till tomorrow.

And Sinatra did one other thing, late that Saturday night.

In the darkness, by the old falling-down sheds and garages of the disused motor workshop, Sinatra made his way, like a big cat in the dark, across the rusting cars and the old tyres and the bonnets and the engines.

Much later that night a cleaning truck drove up, unchecked, to the front of Parliament Buildings. Two men got out with a ladder and some tins of paint.

Such a thing had never, ever happened in the country before.

No one had ever defaced Parliament Buildings. By the time a team of painters and cleaners had been summoned to remove the words that had appeared they had been seen by a lot of people, including some deeply moral, deeply offended, members of the Prime Minister's own party.

And Sinatra had a particular piece of luck. The Editor of the *THE FACTS!* was on a well-earned holiday after all that had been required of him in the run-up to, and the aftermath of, the recent general election. He had gone fishing.

His young, keen, temporary deputy, new to the job, was shown a photo of the defaced Parliament Buildings and he was so excited he nearly fell off his chair. He would make his mark. He printed the photograph on *THE FACTS!* front page.

The editor was urgently recalled by the government. The keen young deputy was fired on the spot. The offending edition of *THE FACTS!* was recalled. But the damage was, irrevocably and calamitously, done. Copies had been glimpsed all over the city, changed hands, were passed on. And someone had delivered half a dozen copies to the six most important businessmen in the city. And the most important one of all saw, to his unforgiving horror, the name of his *daughter* painted on the front of Parliament Buildings.

It was the oddness of the words that stuck in the mind, people remembered them and repeated them to each other. Only a few Maoris who knew their language well made the connection with a Maori proverb, understood that a Maori must be behind this, talked about it among themselves in their own language. Sinatra knew so well that, on those islands, any hint of sexual impropriety, where sexual impropriety was always outragedly denied, was fatal.

On the grey front wall of the building had been printed in huge letters, in bright, white paint:

FOR LAND AND FOR WOMEN MEN DESTROY.
THE PRIME MINISTER OF THIS COUNTRY
IS A MURDERER.

And painted right across the top of the two central pillars at the main entrance, where you might expect to read a Latin homily, two words were printed clearly: RANGIMARIE; and the name of the young blonde woman, the very young daughter of the businessman, with whom the Prime Minister was having a very clandestine affair. ANGELIQUE BENSON said the pillar.

No one knew what Rangimarie was supposed to mean. But all over the city rich influential families recognised the name of the floating, white-chiffon-covered, beautiful debutante whose father so treasured her; who had curtseyed low to the Vice-Regal chair, and who had worn a dress that was strapless.

FORTY-THREE

All day Sunday Maggie hunched over her books for the last time. Her small engagement ring lay in her cardigan pocket. Sometimes she felt for it, held it in her hand. Outside, at the end of her street, the sea sparkled and danced in the sunshine, as if diamonds lay there.

Her Maori books and her English books were in two piles on her table. The writers in both languages agreed about two things: the importance of love and the importance of death. And Maggie had now witnessed both these things, believed she could answer questions about these things.

Maoris, of course, were always going on and on about land, land, land, there were sure to be questions in the Maori papers about land.

But re-reading Coleridge on the Ancient Mariner at last returning:

> Oh! dream of joy! is this indeed
> The lighthouse top I see?
> Is this the hill? is this the kirk?
> Is this mine own countree?

and Dr Johnson on London:

> A man who is tired of London is tired of life,

and Katherine Mansfield on the wind of the city:

> It is only the wind shaking the house, rattling the
>   windows,
> banging a piece of iron on the roof . . .

she understood that they too believed what the old Maori poets believed:

> My, love alas for my own land
> as the evening shadows come.
> If only there was a canoe . . .

The writers *all* seemed to believe – she had only just realised – what the Maoris believed: that there was love and there was death and there was one other important thing.

And that was the land: *home*.

FORTY-FOUR

And so the tense, quiet days began: the sun shining outside and the beating hearts inside. The printed papers of the examination questions were handed out by stern men in gowns and the clock on the wall ticked inexorably as thoughts jumbled and danced in students' heads and people sighed and pens scratched on paper.

In her first English paper Maggie wrote about Keats and frozen time, thinking about the picture of her and Elizabeth eating wedding cake; in that old fading photograph Elizabeth was alive forever, never growing older like Maggie grew older, that's what Keats meant. She wrote about Coleridge's singing language and whether it was opium that made the songs, the way beer made them all sing so sweetly at Prudence's parties. When she wrote about the influences on Katherine Mansfield's writing, like Chekhov and Virginia Woolf, she also wrote about the wind of the city. She wrote about love, and about death, and about home. She hadn't understood, until she got into the examination room and read the questions, that she had enough different knowledge now to answer the questions in her own way. So that instead of just quoting from the books she had read about the poets, obliquely in all her answers she used what she had also learnt, this year, from her own life.

She left the big lecture hall, found Timoti in the library, a pulse beating under his eye, surrounded by law books and a Maori phrase book: the oral Maori examination was that afternoon. Maggie was to go first, then Kara Rikihana, then Timoti.

'*Kia kaha,*' they said to each other, *be strong*.

While she was waiting for it to be time she saw Prudence sitting on the green with her psychology textbooks.

'I expect you know all the answers, Pru,' she said, sitting beside her on the grass in the sunshine. 'You always seem so wise.'

Prudence smiled her gentle smile, flicked over the pages of one of her books. 'I think Bay taught me most of what I know,' she said.

'About – about psychology?' Maggie was embarrassed, picked at bits of grass, didn't look at Prudence.

'He understands pain,' said Prudence simply. 'He understands that pain won't go away, and he has taught me how still to live and somehow be happy. I am so lucky to have known him.'

Maggie thought of Bay, composing the discordant, anxious notes in the interview room.

The oral Maori exam was held in the small, high room at the top of the university.

Maggie had never been in the room in the daytime. It was dark, the sun shining away from the room at this time of the day, she'd never noticed before what small panes of glass made up the high windows that looked down at the city, and a middle-aged Maori man sat waiting for her. Her hands were clammy and her heart beat fast.

'*Kia ora, e hoa,*' the examiner greeted her, the phrase she knew best of all.

'*Kia ora,*' said Maggie.

He asked her her name, how old she was, where she worked, if her family had a car, where was she born, if she had brothers and sisters. Maggie answered carefully and shyly, but correctly. No sisters, she said.

Half way through the examiner said: 'Could you sing me a song?'

It seemed such a strange request that Maggie gave her odd giggle, like a snort: what an extraordinary thing to be asked in the middle of a university examination: 'sing to me'. She didn't sing him one of the well-known ones: *I bet he expects me to sing '***Pokarekare ana***', the one tune everyone knows, even Franco the fisherman* – but the one that Timoti's parents had sung, as they'd walked back along the dusty road past the macracarpa trees that Sunday morning.

> *E kui ma e koro ma*
> *kaua e riri mai*

don't be angry with us, old people.

Only once in the oral exam did she hesitate, when he asked her what her ambitions in life were, what she wanted for herself in the future.

'Me?' she said, involuntarily, in English. She stumbled not because she couldn't understand the question. But because The Future was waiting there for her, as soon as the exams were finished.

Finally she said, because she had to say something: '**He kaiwhakaako.**' *I want to be a teacher*, because that was one of the things girls did.

Later she went to see Eddie Albert, to clean her teeth at his flat after smoking four cigarettes in relief on the grass outside the university in the sunshine, and saw him, just home from work, kissing a strange girl on the orange sofa.

'This is Ariadne,' said Eddie, 'though she's not Greek. She's better at the horses than I am. We've just won four hundred pounds and we're going to get married and buy a house. You're eighteen tomorrow, aren't you – here's a camera, I was going to drop it in to your dad's office.'

'Hello,' said Ariadne, pushing her hair back from her rosy face and laughing. 'Happy Birthday! Happy Life!'

Maggie went home on the tram.

'Eddie Albert says he's getting married,' she said to her parents in amazement, showing them her new Box Brownie camera. And saw that they knew.

'He had no right to go out with Shirley all that time and then suddenly to do this,' said Mrs Bennett. 'Shirley's been on the phone, crying, he had no right.'

'Perhaps,' said Maggie slowly, 'there's no right and wrong, in love.'

'There is right and wrong in *everything*, you know that, that is what we've taught you all these years. That's what life's all about. You do what's right, we have always done what's right. Eddie should do what's right. Shirley's left on the shelf now. She's nearly twenty-one.'

'And we hear the new girl bets,' said Mr Bennett gloomily. 'How was the exam?'

Next day Maggie (eighteen at last: not old enough to vote, or get married without her father's permission, or drink) translated 'Beowulf', and wrote an essay about Dr Samuel Johnson, stating that it was her belief that the great Doctor was not infallible. When she got home her mother informed her that Susan, who had celebrated her eighteenth birthday three weeks earlier, had rung to say she was now celebrating her engagement, as planned, to a doctor.

For the first written Maori examination, the papers sent from another city, Timoti Pou and Kara Rikihana and Maggie Bennett sat separated from each other in the high lecture room. Not Isobel Arapeta – who wasn't a university lecturer, merely a night-class tutor – but a man from the French department stood guard, walking up and down between the seats of the small room, looking at the three students, staring out of the small-paned windows to where their city lay.

> *Taku aroha ki taku whenua*
> *He ahiahi kauruku nei*
> *He waka ia ra . . .*

the poem that Isobel Arapeta from Scotland had so carefully translated for them as she stared out across the harbour.

Maggie no longer heard the clock ticking as she wrote: *My love, alas, for my native land as the evening shadows come . . . if only there was a canoe being launched at the headland . . . in this great longing is there no one who will share it? For there is no one more melancholy than he who yearns for his own native land.*

Poor Keats, thought Maggie suddenly, *dying in Rome.*

And then, out of nowhere. *Emily can't have that land at Rangimarie. Not ever.*

The days got warmer and warmer.

On the day of the last exam, the second Maori paper, Maggie excused herself from the Welfare office, went and shut herself up in the Maori Land Court with her textbooks. She was wearing her white Everglaze dress to sit the last examination in. And to look nice afterwards. Because afterwards was when her new life would begin.

She did not know she looked like a white shadow in the dark room. She opened her books but she had forgotten the strange, rustling silence. She stared up at all the dusty land files piled on the shelves, felt them whispering, still, the secret: *land, land, land.*

The examination paper said: GIVE A PROVERB ABOUT LAND, TRANSLATE AND DISCUSS.

> *He whenua, he wahine,*
> *Ka ngaro te tangata*

she wrote: *for land and for women, men are lost.* She thought of the interminable hours she had spent filling in land records. She remembered the day of the fishing trip and saw again Gallipoli Gordon from the south, lying in the sun, the wood of the boat vibrating to his deep, dark words. And Grace, talking about the place you carry round with you, in your heart. And the Maori Land Court, the shelves and shelves of documents and the strange, rustling silence, of old papers, and of dust. As for doomed romances, the old song-poems were full of them. Her pen flew along the paper.

Afterwards the three of them sat in the high room talking excitedly about the paper, comparing answers, not realising quite yet, that it was all over.

Kara Rikihana suddenly looked at his watch. 'I have to go back to all my policemen. I'll leave you two love-birds,' and he waved and ran down the stairs.

It was then that Maggie looked at Timoti and remembered.

This was the moment. Her future had to begin now. Her heart beat fast and she felt she could hardly breathe. *Now.*

'Shall we dance in the moonlight?' she said softly. 'Or shall we walk beside the still waters?' and she moved towards him and her eyes glittered with hope and fear and love.

'I'm going for a drink with the boys,' said Timoti. 'I said I would. We finished the law exams this morning, they'll all be there already. See you tomorrow, Maggie. We'll go to the pictures and you can come back to the hostel and we'll discuss everything.' As he bent to kiss her Maggie hit him hard across the face.

He grabbed her arm violently at once: it was hard to tell who was the most shocked. Just for that moment there was silence in the small room, except that the sound of the slap seemed to echo on and on and on. Then Timoti shouted at her.

'Don't *ever* do that again. What do you think you're doing? What's the matter with you?'

She said nothing, stood there.

She had not known she was going to hit him. It was the first time she had hit anybody in her life.

She was like her mother.

She knew it. She knew it when everything got muddled in her head and she heard voices as if she was crazy. She knew it when she pulled away from Grace in the fern and tarpaulin tent, trying to get away from the bodies and the smells and the feelings. She knew it when Timoti made love to her and she didn't know how to respond, when she lay stiffly in his arms and somehow disappointed him. Without understanding why.

She was like her mother: *that's what's wrong with me.*

Timoti's face was an angry, frozen mask. She had hit him. And then she saw that it was much, much more than that she had hit him.

She was a Pakeha.

And he was a Maori.

And she had hit him.

He turned on his heel and he walked away.

So Maggie in her best white dress was the last person in the small, high room where they had learned what they had learned.

Finally she picked up her bag and her books and ran, ran

all the way, down past the park, past the statues of the early explorers, along the tram lines, puffing and shaking, up the other side of town, past the disused motor workshop, the rusty trucks; running, sweating, running up to the honeysuckle and the house under the hill in the evening sunshine. And because it was summer at last the scent of the wild honeysuckle flowers lay everywhere on the air, everywhere on the hill, everywhere.

She heard the guitars and the singing voices.

At the hotel where the law students were drinking Timoti Pou got extremely drunk. He had finished his exams, seven years of hard, hard slog: if he passed this year he would be a lawyer at last. He would join the boss's firm as the first Maori partner and be part of the world, the real world.

He did not think about Maggie at all.

He drank with the Pakeha law students in a hotel in the centre of the city. Most of them had been drinking since early afternoon; they all shouted and smashed glasses and vomited in the urinals. He drank so that he would be one of the boys, not someone who people called boy. They all drank very fast, there was only an hour's drinking time left here and Timoti was behind most of them. The boys drank more and more and made crude jokes about women although quite a few of them were still virgins and knew more about torts and contracts than about women. The noise grew louder and louder.

Staggering to the toilet Timoti found Sinatra's note stuffed in his trouser pocket. All it said was: *Come to the wharfies' pub and ask for Sinatra, it's about Pumpkin.*

Staggering back into the bar Timoti agreed to meet the boys again later, at the rugby club where they had arranged to take crates of DB so they could keep on drinking.

'Just got a bit of business,' he said.

One of the other law students laughed. 'With a *white* girl, eh boy?' he said and slapped Timoti on the back. 'Make it snappy, you know how to make it snappy, don't you mate, up against the wall and just let the weapon loose but keep your trousers on!' and the bar exploded into loud male laughter and Timoti lurched out into the main street in the evening sunshine and hailed a taxi from the stand, automatically looking for one with a Maori driver.

In the wharfies' hotel he asked for Sinatra, saw the fat Maori man in a black singlet drinking in a group, went over, pushing through the shouting, sweating, drinking men.

'I'm Timoti Pou,' he said.

In a corner of the wharfies' pub Sinatra told Timoti that he believed Pumpkin had not committed suicide but had been shot in the Parliament Buildings when he'd attacked the Prime Minister.

'It was your dad's hunting rifle,' said Sinatra.

Timoti was shocked into a taut, sprung, sobriety.

He followed Sinatra in horrified silence to the quiet of the White Daisy milk bar where the Greek proprietor was wiping the tables and clearing the salt cellars and the sugar bowls away.

'Two cups of tea,' said Sinatra.

'Eightpence. Closing soon,' said the Greek.

Sinatra told Timoti what Pumpkin had planned. 'I didn't believe he'd really go ahead of course, but he had the gun in that sack,' and Timoti remembered Pumpkin sleeping on the floor of his room at the hostel, cuddling the sack as if for security and he gave a kind of strangled, disbelieving sound.

'I put it under my bed,' said Sinatra, 'I thought I might be able to get him a job on the wharves cooking, he seemed a bit – lost. Of course, I didn't think he'd go through with it. I checked it, there were no bullets in it, that's why I didn't worry at first, when he'd gone.'

Timoti stared at Sinatra. 'I think my father always taught him to keep the bullets separate.'

'Something about you fellas' land and the Prime Minister,' finished Sinatra.

'Jesus,' said Timoti, beginning to make sense of it at last. 'But this is ridiculous. People don't just *kill* people in this city.'

'Pumpkin seemed to think he'd be back in time for tea,' said Sinatra wryly. 'It didn't occur to him they might shoot back. He told me he was only going to hit him in the arm, to teach him a lesson. Seems like he did exactly what he set out to do. Then one of the Prime Minister's hoons seems to have shot him back, and pretended it was suicide.'

Timoti looked at Sinatra in incomprehension. 'I can't believe this.'

'Your little brother was trying to impress you, *e hoa*.'

'Impress me?' Timoti wiped his arm across his face.

'He wanted you to notice him. He did it for you.'

Timoti, haggard suddenly, looked at Sinatra, not wanting to believe any of what he was hearing. 'But they wouldn't have *killed* him.'

'Oh, yes they would,' said Sinatra. 'Where've you been living? I've lived in the city all my life, in the back streets. It's not like the front streets. It's like cowboy city, in the back streets. If you're a lawyer you'll find out. Specially if you're a Maori lawyer. Luckily Pumpkin was carrying his birth certificate.'

'*What?* What for?'

Sinatra shrugged. 'Don't ask me.'

'But – but it would've been in the paper.'

'Don't you think the Prime Minister might have a say about what's in the paper?'

'I'm a lawyer. You're talking to me about *murder*, this isn't the wild west.' But he at once remembered what his boss had said: *there is a network*.

Sinatra shrugged, stood up. 'Just thought you should know, *e hoa*,' he said and he took a copy of *THE FACTS!* out of his pocket, threw it down on the table. 'I don't suppose you've seen this, they recalled most of the copies but not quite soon enough. I hear you're learning to speak our language so you'll know our proverb. **He whenua, he wahine, ka ngaro te tangata.** It's usually translated as, *for land and for women men die.* I've often thought it should be *for land and for women men kill.*

Timoti stared at the photograph of the defaced building.

FOR LAND AND FOR WOMEN MEN DESTROY.
THE PRIME MINISTER OF THIS COUNTRY
IS A MURDERER.

Sinatra saw him looking at the name of his home, *Rangimarie*, printed there, and the woman's name beside it.

'Oh well,' Sinatra said and he gave the ghost of a smile. 'People in this country don't care about land-stealing yet. But, oh boy, how they care about sex and sin. I thought I'd chuck it in. He hasn't got a chance, believe me. I've already been told he's resigning with health problems before the end of this week. Just remember, your brother loved you.' And he ambled out into the last of the evening sunshine, a fat, grey-haired Maori in a singlet.

Timoti still sat at the table, stunned.

'Closing,' said the Greek.

But Timoti seemed not to hear him. His thoughts went in a precise order. He had had time off work, for the exams: hadn't seen his boss since before Pumpkin's funeral.

If it was true, and if Pumpkin was carrying his birth certificate, the Prime Minister knew.

And if the Prime Minister knew, his lawyer knew.

And if the lawyer knew that the Prime Minister's assailant was Tumatauenga Pou from Rangimarie, then he would know how the people in Rangimarie had heard who'd taken their land.

And so, as his boss had so clearly outlined, Timoti Pou would never, ever be a partner in the big famous firm, his dream of a lifetime, joining the big world, the real world outside his people.

Timoti hit the Formica table with his brown fist and a kind of cry came from somewhere inside him, a cry that understood that he must give up the world he'd hoped for with its nice house in the suburbs and a Pakeha wife and respectability and success.

He understood that he would, after all, be a *Maori* lawyer, that he would be a lawyer for his people, not for himself; that he had to walk into the unstructured, uncharted areas, into the *messiness*, because he had no choice. It was what they had all expected, and what he had tried to avoid. This was the legacy that had been left to him by his little brother, who had loved him.

'Closing,' said the Greek.

And up at Prudence's house, hidden in the honeysuckle in the old streets behind the city, those who had been sitting university exams danced and sang with those who would never sit university exams and the brown beer bottles were hurled in exuberance into the overgrown garden at the back, Maggie saw one bottle fly up almost to the stars it seemed, before it fell into a bush of gooseberries.

'Look at that!' she cried out, drinking more, 'a brown shining star, look at that!'

She missed the 9.30 tram, and the 10 o'clock and the 10.30. She just caught the last tram of all, through the two tunnels, out to the sea. She sang aloud as she swayed down their quiet street:

> Blue smoke
> Goes drifting by
> Into a deep blue sky.
> My memories of home
> Will never die.

Her mother was up, waiting in the kitchen.

'You've been with that Maori.'

'Mum, I've been celebrating, it's the end of exams. I was at Prudence's place . . .'

'Do you think we don't worry, your father and I, you coming home at this hour, never knowing who you're with, where you are, what you're doing?' The voice, that hardly ever rose, rose at last in the kitchen.

'It was the end of exams, Prudence had a party, Timoti wasn't even there,' and she fell slightly against the kitchen table.

'You're drunk,' shouted her mother and she stepped forward and punched Maggie's arm hard, punched her again, knocking the bag out of her hand, hit her across the face. 'You're drunk and you disgust me, with that Maori, doing – things – with that Maori,' and her mother hit her again and again, and Maggie, her hands up to her face, backed against the wall, saw that her mother was out of control, shaking wildly.

'*You don't look like Elizabeth!*' Mrs Bennett screamed, 'it would be too much to bear if you looked like her, *it was your fault, you killed her!*' but even as the words came out of her mouth Maggie saw that her mother had shocked herself, that she put up her hand to her mouth, the shaking hand.

They heard the door of the bedroom down the hall open but Maggie picked up her bag and ran out the back door.

She could hear the sea but turned away from it and ran up to the tram terminus where the last tram stayed, empty and shadowy. She heard the car, but she stayed there hidden in a corner of the tram shed, heard her father's voice.

'Maggie,' he called out of the darkness. 'Maggie?'

She waited till the car turned round again, till it slowly drove down their street, down to the beach. Then she just walked and kept on walking.

She walked for miles and miles, along the empty tram lines, past little clusters of verandahed shops, past dark houses and hills.

Finally up the last hill, by the honeysuckle, she stumbled on to the quiet verandah. The old house was in darkness. She banged and banged on the door and great sobs came out of her mouth.

Not Prudence, but Bay Ropata, at last opened the door.

'*Kia ora, e hoa,*' he said, in his shirt.

'I killed my sister,' said Maggie.

FORTY-FIVE

Down at the end of the street, where sometimes stately liners appeared, where desultory suburban mothers and children played on long sunny afternoons when school was out, down by that sea Elizabeth and Margaret-Rose Bennett had been playing right at the edge of the water with buckets and spades, making sandcastles and pies. The tide was coming in and they ran in and out of the shallows. Their high, childish voices echoed along the beach. Elizabeth hummed sometimes, and the sea sparkled and danced in the sun, as if diamonds lay there.

It would seem that Margaret-Rose, a very small child, had seen something sparkling and gone to get it, gone into the sea, had walked laughing towards the shining thing, her hand out, unafraid.

Elizabeth, who was seven, suddenly saw – they assumed, for she was never able to tell her part of the story – Margaret-Rose go under, still looking for the shining treasure that seemed to move away from her. Instead of calling for her mother (the mother of two young children whose husband was away at the war, who had fallen asleep further up the beach where the sand was softer, a hat shading her face from the sun), Elizabeth dropped her bucket and spade, ran into the sea to save her sister.

She did save her sister, she pulled her up out of the water and started dragging her towards the shore.

By now the few people on the beach had seen, called out. Their mother screamed, ran towards the water. And Elizabeth, small in her little red bathing suit, trying to hold her sister out of the water, turned suddenly hearing the scream, fell very sharply against one of the rocks that was just hidden by the incoming tide. She caught her head on the side of a rock and fell into the sea with her sister.

The sun was still sparkling and dancing on the water, promising diamonds, when the ambulance arrived.

Elizabeth died in hospital later that afternoon.

So when Mr Bennett was shipped home from the war, his hand still somewhere in North Africa, he still had one daughter, which is the number he'd had when he went away marching proudly to the music; OUR BOYS CROSS THE SEA TO DEFEND THE EMPIRE, but it was a different daughter: Margaret-Rose had been born seven months after he went away but Elizabeth was dead and his wife was in a place people called the loony bin.

Mr Bennett looked for a long time at the photograph of the two little girls at a wedding eating pieces of wedding cake: the little girl with the eccentric hair nobody could flatten looking up at the bigger girl with the same brown curly hair that nobody could flatten, as they both gleefully stuffed cake into their mouths. He could see that they were gleeful.

They never talked to Margaret-Rose about exactly what had happened. Perhaps because Mrs Bennett was so ill afterwards. Neighbours knew, of course, heard the story from the few who were on the beach that day. But the story got muddled in time because Mrs Bennett never, ever spoke about it. (You didn't say to the tall, still beautiful Mrs Bennett, her face a mask, *how are you?* at the shops.)

Elizabeth Bennett, a dear little girl, had drowned. And not sure now, years later, if it was part of the same story, the neighbours warned their children to beware of the hidden rocks, hidden just underneath the water when the tide came in. The rocks went all the way out to the channel: that's why the sound of the foghorn could be heard in the night sometimes, in people's dreams.

It was Bay Ropata who told the story to Margaret-Rose.

Bay had driven the Bureau car down the street, looked in some surprise at what seemed to be a liner passing the top of a dairy, looked again, smiled. The neighbours saw a Maori go down the Bennett's path to the back door. He wore a hat.

Mr and Mrs Bennett had been sitting together at the kitchen table.

Something about Elizabeth, he said to them.

Mrs Bennett, stiff and angry, refused to answer, believed she could smell him. But Richard Bennett and Bay Ropata had shaken hands; rugby and the war gave them a conduit, some line of communication, so that Mr Bennett took the visitor into the Bennett's lounge where pink china tulips stood on a small table. And Mr Bennett, who had not gone to work this morning as they waited for their daughter to come home, told the story.

Mrs Bennett sat alone in the kitchen, the taut angry face of infinite pain turned away from the murmuring voices of the men down the hall.

Bay Ropata was silent for a long time when the story was finished. And then he said, 'We believe that children need to know about death. That's why we always take them to a *tangi*, so that they will see it when they are young and understand that death exists and is part of our lives. Maybe – maybe it would have been better for your family too.'

There was a rasping, gasping sound at the lounge door.

'*What would you know?* You don't understand about *pain*!' said Mrs Bennett. 'You primitive natives with your dancing and your ugly carvings and your superstitions, how could you *possibly* understand us?'

'Norma!' said Mr Bennett, dismayed.

'I understand about pain, Mrs Bennett,' said Bay Ropata, and he picked up his hat from beside the china tulips and moved towards her: that is, towards the door.

In her hand she had a knife, a stupid, useless kitchen knife and she seemed to push it towards them, pushing them away, pushing away further pain. The knife cut Bay Ropata softly. A few drops of his blood fell on to the pale green carpet.

'*Norma*!' cried Mr Bennett, horror on his face, moving to her quickly, easily taking the knife, guiding her to the couch. 'Norma.'

As Bay Ropata looked back he saw them sitting there. Mr Bennett was trying hopelessly, helplessly to comfort his wife with his good hand, the hook lying across his knee, quite still, shining there. Loud, gasping, terrible cries filled the neat tidy room and floated out into the street, drowning at last, after all those years, the respectability of the floral chintz and the china cabinet and the pink tulips.

Bay walked past the parked Bureau car down to the sea at the end of the street. The tide was coming in: he couldn't see the rocks that stretched right out to the channel, and the sun sparkled and danced on the water. He took off his shoes and socks clumsily, rolled up the bottoms of his trousers, then put his arm into the salt water. The neighbours seemed to see a stocky grey-haired Maori man paddling, looking for shellfish.

Richard Bennett finally joined him, his good hand in his trouser pocket, his hook hanging at his side.

'I am so very sorry,' he said. 'The doctor has come.'

'Only a scratch,' said Bay, who had tied his striped hand-kerchief over the cut. He still stood in the water, his shoes and socks neatly on the shore beside his hat. The beach was deserted except for a dog in the distance playing with drift-wood and the calm sea sighed gently, came in slowly. The two men stood there in silence. One of that city's still, shining mornings.

After a long time Richard Bennett, the man who was nearly an All Black, said with great difficulty, smoothing his hook over and over with his good hand: 'I certainly don't believe in all this – this psychology nonsense but –' he smoothed his hook. 'I think my wife – I think it is always in her mind that she might go mad again, not that she is mad of course – have to – go back to the mental hospital. They gave her EC –' he paused rather apologetically, 'I don't know if you know what that is . . .'

'I know what that is,' said Bay Ropata. 'It is given to Maoris often,' but Richard Bennett seemed not to hear.

'I think she – holds herself in, in fear I mean, and she never cries. And then – something like this happens and she can't act normally, there's too much inside her for her to act nor-mally.' He looked out and far away, past the sun sparkling on the water to the distant, soft hills. 'I fear for her, always. That is our life. You remember how blokes at the war tried not to think about what they had seen?'

'I remember,' said Bay Ropata.

'She loves Maggie, of course.'

Bay Ropata didn't speak for a moment. Then he said slowly: 'Sometimes unhappy people – throw their unhappi-ness about. Trying to get rid of it on other people perhaps, as if it will disappear that way.'

'Yes,' said the other man. Bay saw what a sad face he had as he stared at the sea.

'Maggie says you didn't know she was studying the Maori

language at university, not French.' He saw an appalled look cross Maggie's father's face for a moment, and then the look died and he seemed only sad again.

'I see,' was all he said. 'Yes of course. We should have guessed.'

Bay came out of the water, let his big brown feet dry in the sun. He said, speaking slowly again: 'I've noticed, in my work, when people are scared, they sometimes – build a cage around themselves for protection. But sometimes they lose the key and then they can't get out. And they do stupid things, and they lie, and they don't really know who they are. I think she needs to –' and he bent down to pick up his shoes as the tide came nearer to them, '– find the key to herself.'

But Mr Bennett was anxious, misunderstood, thought Bay was talking of Norma Bennett, of his wife. But Bay was talking of Margaret-Rose Bennett, his daughter.

The neighbours saw the two men walking up the sand to the street. The Maori was barefooted, wearing a hat and carrying his shoes.

'Please tell Maggie to come home.'

'I'll do the best I can.'

They reached the Bureau car.

'Will you – press charges?'

Bay Ropata looked at him in surprise.

'Don't be silly, *e hoa*,' he said.

*

'Yes,' said Maggie finally, 'I think I – remember. I think I've been remembering for a while. I –' she looked up at Bay, and her eyes were puzzled, 'I could hear her humming.'

'Of course,' said Bay, and she heard from his voice that he thought it natural.

She stared at the sweet-smelling honeysuckle flowers for a

long time. Bay waited, singing bits of his oratorio quietly. They were together, sitting on the verandah at Prudence's place up the hill behind the city; so strange to be there on a bright morning, sun shining, Prudence at work, your sister had saved you, your mother went to the loony bin, perhaps if your sister *hadn't* saved you it would have been all right. And she had hit Timoti, she was like her mother, perhaps she would go to the loony bin too.

She did not see his arm: he wore his jacket.

'Can I have one of the cars, Bay?' she said at last.

He looked again at her pale, drawn face, at the bruises on her face, at her crumpled white dress.

'Maybe you should have a sleep, *e hoa*,' he said.

'I will after.'

He did not ask her after what. 'OK,' he said, and threw her his car keys. '*Kia kaha, e hoa*,' he said, and she remembered it was the first thing he had ever said to her: *be strong*.

She had to get some money out of her bank account, to buy enough petrol.

But when she came to sign the withdrawal form at the bank she didn't know how she did her neat, small signature. She looked up in confusion at the teller who was waiting, tried to sign again. The words of one of the songs sang inside her head.

> Come on and cry me a river
> Cry me a river

'Margaret-Rose Bennett', she wrote.

The teller, a young boy, looked puzzled: she saw him comparing her signature to the one on her record. He cleared his throat, looked at Maggie's hair, at her grubby white dress.

'Just a sec,' he said.

He came back with an older man who said firmly: 'Your signature doesn't match. It's nothing like it.'

'I know,' said Maggie *come on and cry me a river*. 'I can't remember how to do it, how I usually do it. I am Margaret-Rose Bennett but I can't write it,' and she felt the tingling in her arms again and her heart beating in that uncomfortable way. The song words went round and round in her head. She would be taken to the loony bin. She would probably stay there for a year and a half.

The man looked at her carefully.

Maggie began to shake. 'I – I just can't remember my signature,' she said wildly, 'doesn't that happen to people?' Across the bank she saw a teller she knew. They'd been at the same primary school, she had read about her engagement in the paper. 'Ask Deveney Mason,' she said, 'she must know if I'm me.'

And she stood there shaking in the bank as they conferred in whispers about her. Then Deveney Mason looked at her, nodded, waved her hand slightly at Maggie.

'It appears you are Margaret-Rose Bennett,' said the older man.

'I thought so,' said Maggie. 'Thank you.'

And then she drove.

The yellow broom and the gorse flowers shone in the sun on the hills. It only took about half an hour to see the first of the farms, the lambs standing in the sunshine by their mothers who pulled at the grass. Sometimes goods trains whistled past alongside the road and the sheep ran into corners.

She drove, hating it, knowing it would take her hours and hours.

Every now and then along the miles and miles of thin road, past the tall ferns and the pongas, past the bush-covered hills, she would pass an old two-storey wooden hotel with verandahs, like the one she'd stayed in with Timoti, before she hit him. She passed stores advertising a fizzy drink in big letters: LEMON AND PAEROA and petrol pumps and crossroads. She passed little towns, groups of state houses, *I wonder if they do pepper-potting in the country or is it only in the cities that groups of Maoris living together make too much noise?* Horses dreamed in paddocks in the sunshine.

Sometimes she passed slow lumbering trucks full of sheep in layers making huge clouds of dust on the country roads, she heard loud bleats of distress and the sound of the straining engine as the driver changed gears, and there was a heavy pungent smell. Fifty million sheep, two million people, they were always telling them that.

She could have stopped; she should have stopped. She could have sat in the sun and had a TIP-TOP ice-cream or a scone or an apple. The country dairies sold these things next to the local eggs and the pumpkins from the farms. But she could only think of getting there, otherwise she would be taken away in a van to a loony bin, just like her mother.

She was going to Grace.

Grace understood crying rivers. She remembered the night she had slept in the same bed as Grace and how her warm, gently snoring presence had stopped Maggie panicking about ghosts and memories. Grace might want a daughter, Grace might want another child, Grace wept and cut her hair for her children, *maybe Grace will want me, or understand.*

She had not been to sleep since before the last day's exams, she drove in a dream sometimes wondering how she remembered to drive, and whether she would crash and if she did would it matter, *so this is how Pumpkin felt.*

It took her seven hours, no wonder she was shaking as she arrived finally at the crossroads where a bulldozer container was parked. She turned at last down the unpaved road past the manuka and the macracarpa trees and the dusty blackberry bushes, drove at last towards the yellow hall. The manuka and fern tent with the tarpaulin roof was gone and the hall seemed closed and aloof.

Very slowly now she drove towards the group of houses; to the neat house, with the patchwork blankets.

At the side of the hill the torn earth shone.

But Grace wasn't home.

Grace had been driven by her eldest son Paatu to the hospital in the nearest town to be with her daughter-in-law, Noelene, who had just given birth to a baby girl.

'We'll call her Ngaio,' said Paatu, drinking out of a brown bottle of DB to celebrate, 'your first *mokopuna*, your first grandchild, come on Mum, it'll make you feel better.' And Grace had smiled and nodded and wept, and gone to the hospital.

The small square box-like house was empty and so was the house next door.

Maggie peered through the window of Grace's house. A tap dripped in the empty kitchen and through the window she could see the pink and yellow and green patchwork blankets that lay neatly across the fireside chairs.

But Grace wasn't home.

She wandered down the dusty road in the sunshine, indecisive, incongruous. She had thought Grace would always be home. Auntie Rose was in her garden at the back of her little house, but she was getting more deaf than she admitted, had not heard the car. She was tending her lettuces and her tomatoes and her carrots, watching over them, and spraying Derris Dust on the cabbages to keep the white butterflies away. Auntie Rose would have made Maggie a cup of tea, and given her a big piece of fruit cake, if she had known she was there. But it was mothers, not aunties, that Maggie was looking for.

She stopped beside the wooden church, drifted across the mown grass, stood between the graves.

NGAIO POU

Aged 17 years

Moe mai e hine i to moenga roa

And next to this the turned, raised earth of Pumpkin's new grave with fresh flowers lying on the top.

The sun shone warm in the silent churchyard.

She stumbled as she crossed the road. She edged past the closed yellow doors of the hall and clambered up the hill towards the decayed carved roof she could see in the distance, falling sometimes in the long grass. Now she could hear the sea. As she approached the ruined meeting house, the building that had so haunted her dreams, she heard all the cicadas singing in the manuka trees and a bell bird, and somewhere bees buzzing lazily, all the summer sounds of those islands.

Some Maori children stared up at the white figure on the hill as they trudged from the school bus down the road to their homes. Their voices called to each other down the empty road where shadows lengthened; their schoolbags dragged in the dust.

She stopped at the shabby verandah: she heard the sea below. *Cry me a river*, went the voice in her head.

She peered into the darkness, past the carved, broken, sideways face; then taking a deep, shaking breath she stepped inside.

It was the same shape as the one she'd seen in the museum: the big carved centre pole, the sloping roof. The woven panels of reeds and flax threads were torn like in her dreams, like Grace had told her. They hung there like ragged, brown lace. Other carved, broken faces stared.

She stood there for a moment quite motionless, as if she was in her dream; waiting to see if she would receive some kind of message, if something would be solved. If Elizabeth would come.

Cry me a river, went the voice in her head again and again but no other message came as she stood there, no ghosts. She was a trespasser in the gloom, like a ghost herself. It smelt musty and damp and she shivered. Grace had told her it had once been the centre of her life. Did Grace still come here? What must it feel like if the centre of your life is falling to pieces?

Does it feel like this? Will I have to go to a loony bin?

She stood for a long time, insubstantial, still waiting for something as it began to get dark. The sound of the cicadas suddenly, oddly, changed to the sound of crickets, a higher, sweeter sound. She turned her head, looked out into the dusk. In the fading day the clouds on the horizon were so sharply edged with light as the sun went down that it looked as if their outlines had been drawn in black ink. Down past the ferns and the pohutukawa trees the darkening sea shone. A last seagull cried round past the headland.

Grace wasn't home, and up here no ghosts drifted, no **kehua** from behind the torn panels of the old house and the broken carvings. No memories. This was not her memory place. Rangimarie couldn't solve her, she was not from Rangimarie.

At last she moved and knocked an empty beer bottle near the verandah with her foot. The sound startled her: she was standing in her dreams and there was an *empty beer bottle*? Maggie laughed her odd laugh, the sound pierced the quiet air and the bottle rolled away into a mass of spiders' webs in a dark corner.

She took a long green stone pendant from the pocket of her white dress and dropped it into the dead grass inside the meeting house and then she came out onto the hill.

When she looked back for the last time she saw only a broken-down building in the dusk. It was nothing.

She drove the long road back to the city, back through the country towns, down the darkness.

In that darkness she passed the paper bus, going north. She did not know it was the paper bus, Bay Ropata's favorite mode of transport for sending Maoris home. She did not know that Timoti sat at the back of the paper bus with all the newspapers and the mail, unable to sleep, his head in his hands. He too was going home. He would stop the bulldozers. He would use Pumpkin's death to stop the bulldozers because that was the only choice he had. Pumpkin had taken the other choices from him.

But Maggie did not know these things.

It was long past midnight when she parked the dusty Bureau car beside the green so that it would be there for Bay in the morning, beside the pohutukawa trees that pushed their roots under the city.

It was many years before she completely understood why she then walked, through the dark, quiet streets in the middle of the night, to the police station.

A policeman sat at the reception desk reading *THE FACTS!* and from a wireless somewhere a woman sang a love song.

'Is Manu Taihape on duty?' It was like a whisper.

The policeman looked at her hard, gave her a very knowing smile.

'Yeah, he is as it happens, he's just gone to make me a cup of tea.'

Manu came whistling through the green-painted government door in his policeman's uniform, was so surprised to see Maggie he almost dropped one of the cups he was carrying.

'*Kia ora, e Makareti,*' he said, smiling his sunshine smile but looking at her carefully at the same time.

Because she hadn't looked in a mirror she didn't know what she looked like, why they stared at her. She had not slept for two nights: no sleep and long driving had formed black soft triangles under her eyes and her hair, like her grandmother's, like Elizabeth's, had never looked so wild. Her white dress was creased and dirty and there were bruises on her face and another on her arm.

'Are you in some sort of – what's the matter, *e hoa*?' said Manu.

Maggie had not spoken to anybody since the bank had questioned who she was. She stared at Manu silently. He misunderstood perhaps, or understood. He moved forward and sat her on the bench and gave her his cup of tea. She looked at it for a moment and then drank it in big gulps. She tasted the sugar, glad of it, remembered how Maoris always seemed to have lots of sugar in their tea.

'I'll take you home, *e hoa*,' Manu said and he pulled his policeman's jacket from the back of the door. The other policeman winked at them.

They drove the old route, through the two tunnels, past the tram terminus, down to the end of the street that led to the sea. She didn't look at the house she lived in. Where the road ended Manu bumped the police car slowly along past the cutty grass right up to the sandhills where they used to park. He turned off the lights and the motor.

'I could be parked here quite legally, looking for burglars,' he said and she could feel his grin in the darkness.

She had not been here since she had found out what happened to Elizabeth.

You could hear the sea, and the wind.

Of the past, or the invisible they can tell nothing, Dr Johnson had said.

'Do you really believe in ghosts?' she finally said abruptly.

Manu looked at her in surprise, and laughed, both at the same time.

'That's a hard case question to ask a Maori at two o'clock in the morning,' he said. And then, he said, 'Look at that cutty grass in the wind, dancing like shadows.'

'But do you?'

''Course.' But she heard in his voice that he didn't really want to answer her.

'Do you think – they might be memories?'

'Ghosts? *Kehua*?'

'Yes.'

His brown hands rested on the steering wheel.

'I dunno, they might be,' he said. 'If they could be – sort of memories of the future, as well as the past. Or other people's memories.' He stared out. 'But don't talk about it. I don't like talking about it.'

'But I have to talk to *someone*. Please Manu, *please* let me talk to you. There's such unhappiness in my house and I'm muddled up about who I am.' But she took it further than she had thought: 'Learning Maori has muddled up who I am. I –' she paused, embarrassed, not wanting to offend him and then plunged on. 'I know ghosts aren't real but I started seeing things, and dreaming, and sometimes they weren't things to do with me, they just seemed to jump into my mind. I want to be myself, I don't want to be muddled up with these funny Maori things that aren't part of me, I'm not a Maori. I don't want to dream and see things and believe in ghosts like you people do. I want to be *myself*.' And then, her voice filled with longing to make sense of her life, she added: 'But I don't know who it is.'

Finally she said: 'They might take me to the loony bin.'

And Manu Taihape laughed.

He laughed the way he always laughed, the way he had

been laughing since he was a child, since he got strapped at school for speaking Maori, since his grandfather took his belt to him in the evenings for speaking English; laughed like all the lost and the lonely and the violent and the dispossessed.

'That's how lots of Maoris feel all the time, *e hoa*,' he said finally, yet there was still laughter in his voice. 'Having to be Pakehas, *don't you know that?* Don't you know yet that's what's wrong with us? We get muddled up with all these funny Pakeha things that aren't part of us really, and we dream about them too and get carted off to loony bins. You've just tried it the other way round.'

'But that's quite different.'

'Is it? The only thing that's different, *e hoa* –' and she heard the laughter go out of his voice, 'is that it isn't compulsory for you.' And then he said: 'Of course you won't be able to *un*-learn, you can't escape. Any more than we can. It's part of you now.'

'But –' Maggie stared at him, at his profile staring now at the sea. 'Well – well, you all *have* to be Pakehas, well – that's how the world is.'

He did not answer her.

'Isn't it?' she insisted. 'That's how the world is. This is the nineteen-fifties, not the olden days. You can't go backwards. You have to be Pakehas like us.'

'*Engari me whai i to matou huarahi ano pea.*' Manu said the words stubbornly. *Maybe we should take our own road.*

Maggie had never, ever heard anyone say that; even Bay hadn't said that: that there might be another way, instead of the white people's way. She looked at Manu, disconcerted. He stared at the sea, his face blank of all expression, that look she recognised.

They sat there in silence for a long time.

The sea pounded and sighed in the darkness, Elizabeth's sea.

'I had a sister, Manu,' Maggie said at last. 'Her name was Elizabeth and she drowned here only I didn't realise till today what happened. She was saving me.'

Manu's voice sounded puzzled. 'I didn't know you had a sister. I thought you were a lonely child.' She thought he must mean 'only child'.

'It was – fifteen years ago. She was seven and she fell on those rocks out there, she had a red bathing suit,' and finally the words poured out of her in relief and release, 'and – and I have been starting to remember, I saw her at Rangimarie, and in my dreams, and once I heard her humming, you know, like a dream but I knew it was her, we were playing on the beach that day and I *remember*, I could hear her humming when I walked into the sea, I thought there were diamonds shining on the water, I went to get them, she came and saved me. But then she fell. That was my sister that was Elizabeth.' Her breath went in and out in little gasps, and then finally she said, 'My mother blamed me. That's why she hit me. I didn't know.'

The sea pounded and sighed.

'Elizabeth,' said Manu finally. And then he put the name into Maori the way he would: **Irihapeti**. And then he added after a moment, because it was natural to him, '*Ma te Atua ia hei manaaki*,' *God watch over her*. Gently, like a blessing.

They heard the wind.

And in the night by the sea, in the long grass that danced like dark shadows on the sand, who is to say for sure that a small ghost, or a memory, might not have drifted like smoke say, just for a moment. As if she had been released at last.

Margaret-Rose Bennett turned into Manu Taihape's arms and for the first time in her life wept for the loss of her only sister who had saved her and had left her.

As she wept and wept Manu held her and stroked her hair,

undoing the pins, smoothing her hair, stroking her over and over again, the way he used to. With warm, gentle hands, over and over.

As if he was her mother.

All this was a long time ago, and there are not so many left to remember.

There was an explosion, as Bay Ropata foretold. A wild explosion over language and culture and, above all, over land. But Bay died: he did not live to see it all. He died aged sixty, of a heart attack.

Sinatra lost his role as the King of the City when he died of a heart attack. He was thirty-eight.

Manu Taihape, who was nicknamed by his mates 'The Laughing Policeman', died of a heart attack, aged forty.

Hui Windsor, who had a wooden leg from the war, died of a heart attack, aged fifty-two.

Tane Thompson, who had so wanted to become a geologist and study his history, died of a heart attack. He was forty-four.

Grace Pou, Timoti's mother, died of a heart attack only a year after her youngest son committed suicide in the city. She was fifty.

Rangi Cox, smoking like Humphrey Bogart till he died, died of cancer, aged forty.

Hori Smith, named after the British Royal family, died of a heart attack, aged fifty.

Roimata, the telephone operator, died of a heart attack, aged thirty-three.

Isobel Arapeta died of cancer two months after Timoti and Maggie and Kara Rikihana passed their exams in Maori: she was forty-four. She had hidden her illness from her pupils, wanting them to pass the exams and to carry on her teaching.

Richard Bennett, Maggie's father, died of cancer, aged sixty-one.

Margaret-Rose Bennett became a teacher after all, who told the children something of their history, gave gold stars for the best drawings. Who taught the older children lines from Coleridge's poetry:

> In Xanadu did Kubla Khan,
> A stately pleasure dome decree:
> Where Alph, the sacred river, ran
> Through caverns measureless to man
> Down to a sunless sea

because they all so loved the singing sounds; but also made them aware of their own poetry, the poetry written by their own writers, poetry that could sing also.

She taught her pupils to correctly pronounce the Maori place-names which (even that far south) they were surrounded by.

And she said to her students who were going on to university: it is wonderful to read the English writers of the past, they are part of our past too. But one mustn't take all that they said as necessarily true. Dr Samuel Johnson, for instance. He was erudite and witty and compiled the first dictionary. But he was nevertheless inexperienced in some matters of the world and did not understand everything.

She had an illegitimate part-Maori child, a daughter. It was scandalous at the time down those suburban streets. She was sent away to the southern island to a cruel, cold Unmarried Mothers' Home outside the southernmost city in the country; to the south where long ago Gallipoli Gordon's Maori ancestors had been destroyed by measles. But when the time came for her to give up the baby for adoption and go back home (the adoption taking slightly longer than usual, the baby being – as the Matron so elegantly put it – a 'half caste'), Maggie and her daughter simply, one evening after tea, disappeared.

For three years, the baby next to an electric heater in a room at the back, she worked in a dairy in that southernmost city, selling TIP-TOP ice-cream and big loaves of white bread and milk and chocolate fish.

Then she trained as a teacher.

She and her daughter, both at school, lived together in that city in the south for many years, by a colder, wilder sea where sand was the colour of iron and snow came.

But she never forgot her place, the place you carry around with you, in your heart. She told her daughter how the top half of stately liners appeared above the roofs of the houses, glided past the dairy chimney; how scruffy tugs would appear between the houses, passing the lupin bushes; and of the beautiful heavy fragrance of the daphne in the air when spring came.

'Mum, you must've been a soppy girl,' Elizabeth used to say, giggling. Her smile went from one ear to the other, huge and charming, like sunshine. Like her father's smile.

And Elizabeth heard about the Bureau and those innocent, far-off days.

And she heard about her aunt after whom she was named, who drowned; and about her grandfather who was nearly an All Black. And about her grandmother who was always waiting for another, different girl.

Of Elizabeth's father, Maggie spoke very little: she could not be drawn on the subject. She did not say that she had not known, at first, which of her two loves was the father. But one day Elizabeth had smiled like sunshine, that wide, wide smile, and Maggie understood. Once she said: 'He saved my life. He listened to me.'

The daughter was fair, had the blonde hair of her grandmother, but the broader, flatter features of her father and the dark brown eyes. She was very beautiful, people stared at her in the street. Her mother taught her the Maori language as best as she was able: they spoke it casually at home for there was almost no one else to speak it with, in that cold, southern city.

*And, always, her mother sang to her. By the time she was twelve
Elizabeth knew all the words of those far-off fifties' songs that her
mother used to sing. And the songs in Maori, those old Victorian
ballads, whistled by the whalers.*

*When the daughter got older she saw on television a long, slow,
Maori land march, led to the Parliament Buildings by an old
woman. She read in the newspaper of Maori protesters in their thou-
sands, protesting about the loss of their land. She began not to
forgive her mother, Maggie, for tainting her Maori blood. She stared
at her with that blank stare that her mother knew so well. When she
was eighteen and in her second year at university she ran away
from home, travelled north, to find her people.*

Timoti Pou and Kara Rikihana became leaders of their race.

*Kara Rikihana never married but he did, after all, fulfil his oblig-
ation to Isobel Arapeta: in the wild explosion of his culture he taught
the Maori language to many people.*

*Timoti Pou married the elegant Glory Ngahuia Brown, who had
been the most beautiful girl in the Bureau, who chose, after all, to
marry Timoti Pou rather than stand for Parliament. Timoti Pou
became a well-known Maori lawyer who tenaciously worked on
Maori cases; in particular grievances concerned with land. His old
boss, the famous lawyer from Stonewall, Appleyard and White,
sometimes saw his old protegé on television, shook his head rue
fully. Finally he lost a case to Timoti Pou. The old lawyer put out his
hand in the courtroom afterwards but Timoti stared at him, walked
away. The lawyer was suddenly chilled by the look in the clear, blue
eyes.*

*Timoti Pou was knighted before he was fifty: for services to the
Maori people. He and Glory had two daughters – Timoti never
quite recovered from his disappointment at not having a son. Both
daughters became doctors, the famous Pou girls. The girls were
both fluent Maori speakers and they fought, both of them, with
their parents over the old Maori adage that said women must not*

speak on the meeting place, on the **marae**. *They were forbidden to marry Pakehas.*

Prudence McKenzie became a teacher also. Up at the university, much loved by the students for her understanding, and her parties, she lectured in psychology. She was an Only Adult, she never married, but they understood she had once loved somebody deeply, who had died.

Emily Evans astonished (and yet not) that her father's premiership so quickly seemed to count for nothing; that he was replaced so soon and so silently by another colleague (so that a man who had seemed to be so powerful became nothing but a footnote in history), married a businessman in London, hosted dinner parties and brightly pushed old pain away. She never got her fishing lodge at Rangimarie.

New Maori government departments, run by Maoris, were opened. And, finally, the Bureau was closed.

In that city, the top half of stately liners still occasionally passed the red and green corrugated-iron roofs at the end of the street, though jet trails now wrote across the sky. The wind blew, as it always had, and still on fine summer days the sea danced and sparkled, as if diamonds lay there.

Down at the end of the street an old, old lady had taken to walking on the beach when the tide was out, had taken to staring at the rocks that could be seen at low tide; stared too at the place where she had so inadvertently slept (face out of the sun under a hat, turned away from the sea) so many years ago. Understanding bleakly at last, after her husband had died who had so lovingly protected her from herself, that it was not just one daughter she had lost. But two.

And then finally one night Margaret-Rose Bennett's daughter, tall and proud, both dark and fair, who had been christened Elizabeth but *who called herself **Irihapeti**, went on a trolley bus through the two tunnels to the terminus and walked down the road that led to the sea. She breathed in at once the scent of the daphne bush that her mother had always talked about. It caught at her throat suddenly, constricted her chest in an odd way that she didn't understand and she stood stock still for a moment, hearing the sea as her mother had told.*

Then she opened the wooden gate and walked down the path of the house of her grandmother.

Who, for so long, had been waiting for her.

MUMMY'S LEGS

Kate Bingham

One day Catherine – a natural blonde – finds a hair in the shower. It is black, forty-two centimetres long and kinked into peculiar curls as though it had been badly ironed. She sellotapes it to a sheet of typing paper, slots it into an envelope and hides it at the bottom of her underwear drawer. Later, when her ten-year-old daughter lets herself in after school, the house appears to be empty.

Moving between the cherry-lined avenues of South Kensington and an old farmhouse in the Yorkshire Dales, *Mummy's Legs* is a haunting, evocative tale of life in the topsy-turvy adult world as seen through a young girl's eyes. A poignant tale of childhood, it is also a bitter-sweet story of a young girl's attempt to fix her mother's broken heart.

AFFINITY

Sarah Waters

'Now you know why you are drawn to me – why your flesh comes creeping to mine, and what it comes for. Let it creep.'

From the dark heart of a Victorian prison, disgraced spiritualist Selina Dawes weaves an enigmatic spell. Is she a fraud, or a prodigy? Can Margaret Prior trust her? Or is Margaret herself a hysteric, an addict – or a visionary with powers of her own? By the time it all begins to matter, you'll find yourself desperately wanting to believe in magic too.

'Spooky, spellbinding, exquisitely written . . . I do believe Waters is on the way to becoming a major literary star' *Val Hennessy*

'Indeed, this is such a brilliant writer that her readers would believe anything she told them' *A. N. Wilson, Daily Mail*

IN SEARCH OF AN IMPOTENT MAN

Gaby Hauptmann

BMW-DRIVING ÜBER-BABE – CARMEN LEGG – HAS A PROBLEM SOME WOMEN CAN ONLY DREAM OF: MEN, MEN AND MORE MEN.

Career girl, home-owner and flame-haired thirty-something temptress, she's exhausted with their unwelcome attentions and constant demands. What she needs, Carmen decides, is a man with higher things on his mind. So she places a rather unusual advertisement . . .

Various men respond: some exotic, some rich, some funny, some a little strange, some positively dangerous. And then a latter-day Prince Charming turns up. Funny, thoughtful, charismatic – he's everything she's looking for – except for one thing . . .

'This book is dynamite'
Telegraph

LYING IN BED

Polly Samson

Do you cover up or reveal it all; seek revenge or just reassurance; let the truth be naked as the day or cloaked in a night-time story?

The men and women of Polly Samson's debut fiction all have stories to tell, pasts to forget, futures to forge. Manipulative or meek, used or using, all are aware of the power of truth, deception and little white lies to get what they want or sometimes what they deserve. Some are concerned with the economies of speech, those little 'kindnesses' which protect our loved ones but really ourselves; some investigate the warped logic which adults serve out to children to keep them 'innocent'; all are concerned with the beds we make and the lies we tell in them . . .

'Polly Sampson is no minor talent . . . prose that makes you miss your bus stop'
Guardian

Now you can order superb titles directly from Virago

☐	Mummy's Legs	Kate Bingham	£6.99
☐	Affinity	Sarah Waters	£6.99
☐	In Search of an Impotent Man	Gaby Hauptmann	£5.99
☐	Lying in Bed	Polly Samson	£6.99

Please allow for postage and packing: **Free UK delivery.**
Europe; add 25% of retail price; Rest of World; 45% of retail price.

To order any of the above or any other Virago titles, please call our credit card orderline or fill in this coupon and send/fax it to:

Virago, 250 Western Avenue, London, W3 6XZ, UK.
Fax 020 8324 5678   Telephone 020 8324 5516

☐ I enclose a UK bank cheque made payable to Virago for £ ....

☐ Please charge £.............. to my Access, Visa, Delta, Switch Card No.

☐☐☐☐☐☐☐☐☐☐☐☐☐☐☐☐☐☐☐

Expiry Date ☐☐☐☐   Switch Issue No. ☐☐

NAME (Block letters please) ....

ADDRESS ....

....

....

Postcode ....Telephone ....

Signature ....

Please allow 28 days for delivery within the UK. Offer subject to price and availability.

Please do not send any further mailings from companies carefully selected by Virago ☐